Happy Days and Wonder Years

Happy Days and Wonder Years

The Fifties and the Sixties in Contemporary Cultural Politics

Daniel Marcus

Rutgers University Press
New Brunswick, New Jersey, and London

LIBRARY OF CONGRESS CATALOGING-IN-PUBLICATION DATA

Marcus, Daniel, 1958–
    Happy days and wonder years : the fifties and the sixties in contemporary cultural
politics / Daniel Marcus.
        p.   cm.
    Includes bibliographical references and index.
    ISBN 0–8135–3390–2 (hardcover : alk. paper)—ISBN 0–8135–3391–0 (pbk. :
alk. paper)
    1. United States—Politics and government—1945–1989.   2. United States—
Politics and government—1989–   3. Politics and culture—United States.
4. Conservatism—United States.   5. Popular culture—United States—History—
20th century.   6. United States—Civilization—1945–   7. Nineteen fifties.
8. Nineteen sixties.   I. Title.
    E839.5.M37   2004
    306'.0973'09045—dc22   2003020097

British Cataloging-in-Publication information for this book is available
from the British Library.

Manufactured in the United States of America

Contents

ACKNOWLEDGMENTS

THIS PROJECT HAD its start while I was a student in the Media and Cultural Studies program within the Department of Communication Arts at the University of Wisconsin–Madison. I thank all of the students and faculty who contributed to the inspiring atmosphere in Vilas Hall that propelled the beginnings of this book. I particularly thank John Fiske and Michele Hilmes, who served as principal readers. I also thank Jane Collins and Lew Friedland for their helpful responses. My greatest thanks go to Julie D'Acci, who in her roles as teacher and dissertation advisor was unfailingly supportive and insightful.

The book benefited greatly from the suggestions of Sousan Arafeh, Michael Kackman, Derek Kompare, and Donald Meckiffe. I have also learned much about the areas I address from conversations over the years with Jon Glazer, Travis Koplow, Marc Noland, David Tetzlaff, and Jennifer Wang. Laura Stein helped me in a crucial way to get started. Mobina Hashmi provided advice, encouragement, and generous research assistance during a critical phase. My thanks go to all of them.

I also thank my colleagues in the Department of Communication at Wayne State University, particularly Jackie Byars, Mary Garrett, Craig Allen Smith, and William Trapani, for their intellectual exchange and professional support. I am grateful for financial support from the University of Wisconsin–Madison, for a dissertation fellowship early on, and from the Wayne State University Center for the Humanities, which helped in the final stage of the project. WSU's Gary Cendrowski and Michael Merriweather contributed technical support. The staff at the Vanderbilt Television News Archive offered an invaluable opportunity to view relevant tapes of news coverage of politics and cultural issues. I also thank Leslie Mitchner, Brendan O'Malley, the manuscript reviewers, and the staff at Rutgers University Press for their helpful suggestions and efforts in getting the book published. Elizabeth Gilbert copyedited the manuscript with superb attention.

I have presented portions of the work at the Console-ing Passions Conference (Montreal, 1997), the Mid-America American Studies Conference (Iowa City, 1998), the Society for Cinema and Media Studies Conference

(Minneapolis, 2003), Bowling Green State University, DePaul University, State College of New York at Fredonia, and the University of Texas at Austin. I thank the many audience members and fellow panelists who provided valuable responses to my presentations.

This work is dedicated to my mother and late father, and to my brother and sister.

Happy Days and Wonder Years

Introduction

ON JULY 23, 1999, a small plane piloted by John F. Kennedy, Jr., disappeared off the coast of Martha's Vineyard in Massachusetts. For the next several days the nation was treated to a media spectacle of the first order. The major broadcast networks interrupted their regular schedules of programming to cover the search effort for hours on end. The cable news networks offered twenty-four-hour daily coverage. Television specials were quickly assembled that told the story of Kennedy's life—his birth immediately following his father's election to the presidency in 1960; his years in the White House and famous salute to his father's casket; his reemergence as a celebrity lawyer and journalist. Television coverage also included the public response to Kennedy's disappearance and death—the vigil and shrine constructed outside his New York City apartment; reporters' speculation about whether he would have run for political office; noted historians' analyses of the role of the Kennedy family in the nation's history. The following week, news magazines and tabloids alike featured Kennedy on their covers.

The extent to which the display was actually representative of a profound regard for John F. Kennedy, Jr., among the public is impossible to gauge. In contemporary America, it is often useless to try to distinguish outpourings of deeply held public emotion from ephemeral responses to media coverage that is expertly designed to provoke senses of familiarity, sorrow, and catharsis at the death of a celebrity. Both the media attention and the public response attest, however, to the discursive power of politically minded nostalgia. The Kennedy presidency and family saga continued to generate strong affective response in the late 1990s, forty years after John Kennedy's assassination. Many Americans seemed ready to measure their hopes for the nation by the possibility of a symbolic return to an era that most citizens could not remember in any direct, personal way.

This book examines the debate over the American past that has pervaded popular culture and national politics since the 1970s. For much of that decade, nostalgia pervaded popular culture; since the election of Ronald Reagan to the presidency in 1980, various political figures, parties, and movements have drawn upon this nostalgia to generate usable narratives of post–World War II national life. They have relied upon representations of the country's cultural and political past to provide historically rooted justifications for their own present-day politics.

In post–World War II America, popular culture and political discourse have, in fact, become interlaced—working together to shape collective understandings of the national experience. This book argues that the marshaling of themes and symbols from the repository of popular culture emerged in the early 1980s as a primary way for political agents to shape (and reshape) public memories according to their own needs. This emergence complements a more traditional use of explicitly political iconography (such as the images of former presidents) in the fashioning of the American past. The book asserts that a key factor in the shaping of these politically charged public memories has been the debate about the significance of the 1950s and 1960s for contemporary political and social life in the United States.[1]

The 1950s and 1960s have had such a powerful hold on the public imagination because they are so easily viewed in dichotomous ways. The 1950s are depicted as an era of American global dominance, personal security, and economic prosperity, but also as a time of stultifying social convention, racism, and widespread denial of national problems. The 1960s, conversely, are seen by their critics as a time marked by social unrest and chaos, the trauma of the Vietnam War, and the failure of Great Society programs, and by their defenders as a time of energetic idealism, personal liberation, and vibrant popular culture. The decades' continued iconic power is strengthened by their concurrence with the childhood and youth of the Baby Boom generation, and with the twin emergences and ascendancies of television and rock and roll.

Greil Marcus has written that in the 1950s Americans "exchanged real life for an idea of normal life," and that this normative fantasy is what survives in the nation's idea of the Fifties.[2] Because the Fifties always operated at an imaginary level, their norms have been able to maintain a hold on America's fantasy life, to be resuscitated in conservative discourse and popular culture. The children of the 1950s, meanwhile—the Baby Boom generation—have held a special place in the nation's idea of its future, as Lawrence Grossberg has maintained.[3] The generation that could redeem the sacrifices of World War II would be seen eventually as rejecting the Fifties vision of normal life in favor of political rebellion and social experimentation in the 1960s, challenging the nation's orientation toward a rewarding future. The political and cultural fallout of such challenges would come to obsess both adherents to and opponents of Sixties social movements and the counterculture for decades, and provide cogent ways to understand trajectories of personal lives, social groups, political parties, and national history.

The postwar era of American life has been represented through a wide range of forms, from family stories to popular films and television series. The meanings of the Fifties and the Sixties, however, do not circulate in the media only in long narrative formats, such as television comedies, film dramas, and major political pronouncements. Indeed, the cultural power of social definitions and representations may be shown by the offhand reference, the demonstrated assumption of a common set of understandings. Advertisements, newscasts, comedy routines, and other prevalent forms of communication in television all provide reminders of what constitutes group, public, and national memories. Madison Avenue campaigns and routinized television production practices contribute to the density of the representations of the past, a density that helps to define the common historical sense of the nation.

The proliferation of this cultural shorthand diffuses historical understandings and group memories throughout society. The wide variety of sources regarding the 1950s and 1960s contributes to the sense of continued relevance of times that continually recede further into the past. Although a number of cultural trends have derived from these decades, and a few highly visible political figures have issued major statements centered on these historical understandings, most of the discussion of the 1950s and 1960s comes from smaller efforts—the single film, the op-ed newspaper article, the song lyric that emerges from the larger social conversation. In particular, the pervasive references to these decades in popular culture has promoted the use of nostalgic themes in politics. The heterogeneity of sources about the Fifties and the Sixties strengthened the legitimacy of political discourse in the 1980s and 1990s that based its claims on definitions of national experience in the previous generation. Popular culture has confirmed the validity of nostalgic themes in politics; the political emphasis on nostalgia during the Reagan administration in turn inspired filmmakers, television producers, and writers to revisit the recent past in their work, to assert their own visions of the past.

These treatments of the past create linkages between different facets of the decades under discussion, to create a sense of a unified whole, an encompassing treatment of national experience. The broader definitions of the Fifties and the Sixties become webs of meaning that advance the interests of various social and political groups. Political conservatives treat the 1950s as a time of stable family structures centered on the heterosexual nuclear family, which they believe gives their contemporary family and sexual policy preferences historical sanction; fans of the Grateful Dead often associate their musical preference with steadfast loyalty to Sixties countercultural values of communality, antimaterialism, and social experimentation. These types of social forces engage in a continual process of definition and redefinition, by linking their own memories to wider concepts and representations. As they lay claim to powerful political symbols, social allegiances, and cultural legacies, they invite other groups to share the same sense of the previous decades of American experience. The past's relation to the present is daunting in its complexity; the combining of particular elements into coherent chains of meaning allows people to locate their society in history, and themselves within that society.[4]

To understand how memory functions in this social interplay, we need to distinguish its various levels.[5] In the terminology of this book, "personal memory" belongs to an individual, who mixes images and meanings derived from direct experience with individualized consumption of mediated information. Personal memories combine with institutionalized discourse to create "group memory," which circulates within a social group to convey senses of shared experience and identity.

Diverse groups vie for public attention and acceptance; the ability of a group to establish its memory as a widely held "public memory" is a key act of social power. By establishing its memory as relevant to the wider polity, a group succeeds in placing its interests on the national agenda. The construction of public memories provides opportunities for the creation of shared allegiances and understandings, although always subject to competing memories from other groups.

Public memories that are adopted by central institutions of memory, such as the federal government and the educational system, receive official sanction as "national memory." A group's insistence on holding memories in contradiction to national memory weakens the group's speaking position and may define the group as existing outside the bounds of social consensus.

When media offer quick-changing views of the past, citizens' historical senses are challenged. For those without direct experience of the events depicted, personal and group experience may fade as a source of stable identification, replaced by momentary identifications based on media representations of the past. Theorists of postmodernity such as Fredric Jameson and David Harvey see this prevalence of unstable, media-driven identifications as central to a crisis in historical understanding, the decline of participation in progressive movements for social change in the postmodern era, and the discursive power of conservative nostalgia that attempts to recover lost stability.[6]

Yet the ubiquity of television in particular offers a continuity of access to historical material, and a consistency to the act of cultural consumption itself. In a geographically mobile society marked by technological and social change, television's screen has been an icon of familiarity, a stable location through which discontinuous, fragmented, and variable representations of American experience have passed. Indeed, much of the sense of continuity that television offers is based on the act of visual consumption, on viewers' ability to locate themselves in history through their own past experience of viewership.[7] Television becomes the locale of memory, as personal memory, public memory, and media representation interweave. This encompassing locale allows for the mix of the factual and the fictional, the elision between politics and entertainment, and the easy movement between the various forms of celebrity that are hallmarks of contemporary American life.

Even as media imagery's diversity and its lack of memory-laden ideological coherence contribute to a sense of historical discontinuity, the television apparatus itself offers a stability to ameliorate the dislocational effects of its content. This consistency in the viewing process seems to promise that a sense of historical coherence may yet be achieved through an understanding of the content provided by the televisual apparatus. Postmodern society has not done away with the desire for continuity, for the ability of people to locate themselves in a narrative of the nation, for a sense that such a narrative indeed exists. The fragmentation of the postmodern experience may make such a desire even stronger. The effort made by conservatives to imbue their movement with a historical sense, no matter how close to myth it slides, attests to the power of historical coherence—as does the public attention to the panoply of cultural responses to the conservative effort to determine the proper American past.

Sources and Organization

Entertainment and political spheres become mutually reinforcing in their emphases on the importance of the past, even when they produce divergent meanings and interpretations. To explore contemporary nostalgia, I analyze American popular culture, including television entertainment programs, films, and popular music from the 1970s through the 1990s. I similarly examine a wide range of political and public affairs communications, including press accounts of the Reagan, Bush, and Clinton elections and administrations, political speeches and commercials, television interview programs, nightly news reports, television documentaries, scholarly monographs, and popular histories.

My emphasis on the figure of the president and presidential elections stems from a number of considerations. Modern broadcasting technology has brought endless images of the president into the intimate setting of the home, displacing or subordinating other sites of knowledge and ways of understanding the complex actions of the state. The figure of the president becomes a symbol for the democratic polity and its ability to cope with world events.[8] Most Americans tend to pay more attention to national politics during election cycles; it is during this period that the play of images and rhetoric reaches its most prolific levels, as candidates offer competing (if sometimes similar) ways of understanding the nation and its relation to voters. Finally, during much of the historical period I cover, Ronald Reagan loomed as a discursively dominant force. The figure of Reagan, and other political figures' relations to him, is crucial to the dynamics of nostalgia and representation in the 1980s and 1990s.

Although I attend to a range of sources in the public affairs media, I emphasize the reporting in outlets such as the *New York Times*, the *Washington Post, Time* magazine, and the major television networks. In recent decades, these organizations have set the agenda and determined the tone for most of the other reporting in the United States; by attending to their patterns of coverage, I can trace the discursive inclusions and exclusions that set the terms for much of the public debate on political issues. The dominance of these outlets as agenda-setters has declined rapidly in recent years, with the rise of the Internet and cable television; during most of the time period covered here, however, they remained central mediators of political discourse.

The book is divided into seven chapters. Although the nation's attention continuously moved between popular culture and the political realm, I have at times separated the cultural from the political, to better analyze developments within each realm. The first chapter analyzes the Fifties cultural revival during the 1970s, which gained wide popularity and found expression in music, films, and television. The revival inspired accounts that largely represented the experiences of white, middle-class youth. In the nostalgia of the 1970s, the 1950s became defined as a time of innocence, security, and a vibrant adolescent culture. Many of the accounts of the time, however, also defined it as inevitably yielding to a movement into adult experience and trauma, a movement associated in public discussion with the 1960s.

The second chapter looks at conservative political nostalgia during the early 1980s. Conservatives constructed a narrative of national greatness, decline, and renewal based on a dichotomous view of the 1950s and 1960s. They associated the 1950s with stable family structures, free-market mechanisms, and American dominance in international affairs. They characterized the social movements of the 1960s as responsible for the destruction of traditional and natural hierarchies, an unwarranted increase in government intervention in the economy, and the devaluing of patriotism. Conservatives sought to consolidate a new electoral majority and to legitimate major changes in government policy in the guise of respect for tradition.

The third chapter emphasizes the importance of Ronald Reagan as an avatar of conservative nostalgia, and looks at the sources and effects of his cultural appeal. Reagan embodied the nostalgic ideal of contemporary Republicanism, which argued for the reassertion of older values after an extended period of dislocating social change and challenges to American economic and military dominance. He solidified definitions of the 1950s as a high point of domestic social stability and militant anticommunism. Reagan established control of national political discourse through his use of mythic images of American experience, meeting little resistance from his political opponents in putting forward his vision of history.

In chapter four, I turn to the cultural productions of the 1980s that debated the meanings of the Fifties and Sixties in American life, producing a much more diverse range of responses than seen in the Reagan-dominated political sphere. Like the 1970s, the 1980s saw a number of nostalgic revivals of previously popular performers and styles, though none achieved the widespread popularity and long life of the original Fifties revival. Cultural producers, however, created a myriad of representations of historical events that served, at times, as the major challenge to the nostalgic discourse of conservatism. Films and television programs offered depictions of 1960s experience that celebrated and questioned American involvement in Vietnam, revisited the civil rights movement, and traced the changes in Baby Boomer lifestyles from the 1960s to the 1980s. In addition, with the solidification of Baby Boomers as prime adult consumers, nostalgia for 1960s childhoods became a new element in advertising and other cultural appeals.

The fifth chapter examines the decline of conservative momentum at the end of Reagan's term in office, the resurgence of nostalgia for the political idealism of the Sixties, and George H. W. Bush's successful linkage of Michael Dukakis to notions of liberal intellectual elitism and opposition to patriotism, brought forward from the struggles of the 1960s. As doubts grew about the results of Reaganism, veterans of Sixties-identified political and social movements tried to reclaim the legacy of their earlier involvements, and the country experienced continued nostalgia for the public lives of John and Robert Kennedy, which served as criticism of both Reagan and current-day Democrats. Meanwhile conservatives, hoping to keep the Reagan coalition together, wielded a cultural critique of Sixties liberalism, which contributed to Bush's victory over Dukakis in the 1988 presidential election. As various factions moved to stake out positions in the post-Reagan political environment, the Fifties and Sixties continued to act as touchstones to signify a broad array of attitudes toward social change, race and gender relations, and middle-class values and concerns.

Chapter six traces Bill Clinton's use of iconic figures from the nation's political and cultural past in the presidential campaign of 1992. Clinton used his fandom for Elvis Presley and John Kennedy to signify his allegiance to cultural Americana and to argue for the need for active government intervention in the economy. His campaign reinflected the Fifties and Sixties with articulations that countered the Republican narrative of postwar national experience by harking back to an early 1960s of national optimism and cultural vibrancy. The Bush campaign proved itself incapable of responding persuasively to Clinton's incursion into the discursive territory that had been dominated by Republicans for over a decade.

Finally, chapter seven examines Clinton's loss of imagistic coherence with the decline of his associations with Elvis and JFK. In this vacuum, Republicans reasserted their narrative of decline and renewal, as Newt Gingrich,

Rush Limbaugh, and other voices of the right led a new repudiation of liberalism. The appeal of conservative nostalgia, however, remained limited in the political sphere, even as its themes seemed pervasive in social conversation. Popular culture's use of the past, meanwhile, reached new levels, from the reissuing of old music on CDs to the rise of cable television channels centered on old programs. From the *Beatles Anthology* to Nick at Nite and TV Land to *Forrest Gump*, the 1990s seemed immersed in references to previous eras. Nostalgia has remained both a favorite frame of conservative political understanding and a pervasive presence in the realm of entertainment.

This book, while in the tradition of cultural studies in approach and much of its content, ventures into the realm of explicitly political communication to elucidate the links between the cultural and the political. Cultural studies, as practiced in the United States, has asserted the importance of cultural spheres and everyday life in understanding political meanings and ideologies; its practitioners have also traced such meanings and ideologies within the spheres of cultural practice itself. Rarely, however, have cultural studies scholars in the United States followed the example of British writers such as Stuart Hall in thoroughly examining political rhetoric, policy proposals, and attendant journalistic coverage.[9] In this work I show that the explicitly political sphere, however remote it may sometimes seem to a politically disenchanted American electorate, is a necessary subject to mine in the study of popular culture and everyday life, and concurrently to show the productivity of cultural studies approaches in the study of American politics. It is through the mutual reinforcement, contestation, and redefinition of the Fifties and the Sixties in both culture and politics that these decades' ideas, images, and associations have held significant power in American society for a generation.

CHAPTER 1

The Fifties in the 1970s

REPRESENTATIONS IN A CULTURAL REVIVAL

THE MEANINGS OF THE 1950s and 1960s have been contested in American politics since the advent of Ronald Reagan to national political power in 1980. Reagan called for a rejection of the legacies of the social and cultural movements of the 1960s and a return to practices and values said to have been disrupted by these movements. Conservatives looked to the 1950s as an era of stable social relations, domestic prosperity, limited government, and American economic and military leadership. They associated the 1960s with social chaos, a turn against patriotism, and wasteful government spending. Liberals were slow to respond to these conservative articulations, but those further on the left attacked the 1950s as socially constrictive, racist, and paranoid in the widespread embrace of McCarthyism. They defended the insurgent social movements of the 1960s as liberating, and many of the government programs of the Kennedy and Johnson administrations as necessary and humane.

Before the 1950s became a touchstone for conservative politics during the Reagan era, they came to be defined for the public through film, television, music, and their attendant journalistic coverage. This chapter traces the revival of 1950s cultural tropes within popular culture of the 1970s. The Fifties cultural revival in this decade provided definitions of the period as a reified past. Those old enough to have lived through the 1950s could assert their personal and group memories of the era, presenting them as valuable for public consideration. The "Fifties" emerged as a knowable series of cultural and social elements that could be taken up in ensuing social and political debate regarding the impact of the 1960s on American society.

The cultural reemergence of 1950s forms, put forward by their producers and media critics as a revival, was an acknowledgment that by the end of the 1960s, the Eisenhower era seemed historically distant to most Americans, to be considered only as nostalgia. Through a process of inclusion and exclusion of cultural and social phenomena, the 1950s were appropriated during the revival, and certain aspects of the decade's culture were recirculated as a self-conscious dredging up of the past. A limited array of cultural markers was invoked to stand in for the national experience in the 1950s, primarily markers of the social culture of childhood and adolescence. In the 1970s, the Fifties began to count above all as a time of youth, innocence, and security that presaged a movement into adulthood, which became associated in public discourse with the social trauma of the 1960s.

The Reemergence of the Fifties in Youth Culture

The 1960s had seen a number of very public changes in youth culture, centered on sexual practice, drug usage, left-wing politics, musical taste, and physical appearance. Increased sexual promiscuity by young singles was prompted by the introduction of the pill method of birth control in the early 1960s; the media presented Sixties-style sex, dubbed the Sexual Revolution, as distinctly different from what had been practiced before. Marijuana, hallucinogens, and other illicit drugs began to proliferate among white, middle-class youth in the mid-1960s. Students began to gain a reputation for political activism through participation in the civil rights movement and in protests against the Vietnam War, particularly at high-profile universities like Columbia University, the University of Michigan, and the University of California at Berkeley. Rock musicians began to be seen as generational spokespersons, linked to the other changes in youth culture through their own behavior and public statements. Countercultural styles in fashion and physical appearance were presented as explicit challenges to previous conventions and styles, as with the popularity of long hair on men and the taking up of signs of poverty (blue jeans, peasant dresses) among affluent youth.

Although these hallmarks of the counterculture were not embraced by all young people in the 1960s by any means, the breadth of change along several axes of lifestyle and identity and the visibility of youth enclaves in Berkeley, the Haight-Ashbury in San Francisco, and the East Village in New York City (among others) created a sense of widespread change. This sense of a serious shift from 1950s perspectives was abetted by the famous traumas in public life in 1960s America: the assassinations of John Kennedy, Robert Kennedy, Martin Luther King, Jr., and other public figures, civil and racial unrest in many American cities throughout the middle and end of the decade, and the long, increasingly unpopular war in Vietnam.

As the nation coped with these shifts and changes, a number of cultural fads based on previous decades of American life rose to prominence.[1] The film *Thoroughly Modern Millie* (1967), for instance, was accompanied by a small flapper craze that circulated in magazines and the fashion world, to be repeated with the release of *The Great Gatsby*, starring Robert Redford and Mia Farrow, in 1974. Film stars of the 1930s and 1940s, such as the Marx Brothers, Humphrey Bogart, and Bette Davis, also provoked renewed attention in the late 1960s, as revival houses and college campuses began to rescreen their work. By 1971 *Time* magazine could proclaim, "Without question, the most popular pastime of the year is looking back."[2]

The most widespread and long-lasting cultural nostalgia, however, was associated with the 1950s, and began in earnest in 1969. It first emerged within the counterculture's dominant cultural form, rock and roll. This nod to the Fifties was the first significant trend to look back self-consciously at the roots of rock. Within conventional rock historiography, rock and roll was created in the 1950s by melding black rhythm and blues and white country music. The first flowering of the music withered at the end of the decade, when an extraordinary number of its leading performers stopped appearing in public—within little more than a year, Elvis Presley, Chuck Berry, Jerry Lee Lewis, Little Richard, Buddy Holly, and Richie Valens were lost to the scene through the draft, sexual scandal, religious conversion, or death. The Beatles and other 1960s groups recorded their own popular versions of Fifties rock and roll songs in their first years of stardom, but the British Invasion of 1964, the advent of Bob Dylan and folk-rock, and the decline of the Fifties stars created a distinct sense of discontinuity for many American rock fans. The advent of psychedelia, blues-based improvisation, and other musical experimentation in the late 1960s reinforced the sense of difference from Fifties rock and roll, paralleling the sense of distance from the 1950s that was circulating in countercultural politics and social practices.

Rolling Stone, the best-known American rock magazine, published a series of articles in 1968, for instance, that explored Fifties rock and roll in musical terms as the foundation for contemporary music, but made no mention of the music's or the 1950s' sociological import at all. There were no attempts to augment the appraisal of the music's artistic merits with descriptions of the social context of its origins, perhaps because that social context seemed quite remote to countercultural readers.[3] By late 1969, however, the *Rolling Stone* approach to Fifties music had changed to an exploration of the wider meanings of the music's appeal, an attempt to trace the earlier era through its music. Articles made note of the revival in popularity of the music, and moved from trying to educate and remind readers of the nearly forgotten music's values to now relating Fifties rock and roll's current popularity to its historical origins.[4]

The revival took several forms within rock. Elvis Presley returned to live performance with a widely reported stint in Las Vegas. Guitar virtuosos such as Jeff Beck and Johnny Winter, who occupied roles in late-1960s rock that had no real forebears in 1950s pop, began including cover versions of old hits on their albums; fifteen of the top 100 hits in 1969 were remakes. The Beatles released "Get Back," an ode to the simplicity of earlier rock forms amid the baroque stylings of psychedelia. The band connected reversion to Fifties-style rock and roll with the burgeoning environmental movement, with publicity proclaiming that the recording was "The Beatles as nature intended. . . . There's no electronic watchamacallit," feigning technological illiteracy to move away from the contemporary complexities of industrial society.[5] Radio stations began adopting "oldies" formats, eschewing the free-form, album-oriented rock radio of the late 1960s for a tightly programmed replication of the old Top Forty.[6]

Bands arose to half-seriously replicate performance styles, social practices, and songs of the earlier era. Sha Na Na, the first and most successful of these groups, formed in early 1969, and quickly gained popularity in New York City. Its theatrical stage show presented physicalized, urban, working-class boys as the embodiment of rock and roll culture. Band members told *Rolling Stone* that they appealed to college-age audiences because they presented a vision of teen life that fans had believed would be their own future while growing up in the 1950s, only to see their actual adolescence take place in the more traumatic and serious 1960s.[7] This ascription of the social domain and style of hoods (in 1950s slang) or greasers (as they came to be known in the 1970s) as the emblematic experience of 1950s youth came to be a common trope in later media discussions of the era.

The members of Sha Na Na did not conform, however, to their pose as "juvenile delinquents from Queens," supposedly reestablishing their cultural authority after having been banished to the margins of youth culture for a decade. The band was actually formed by Columbia University students, many of whom were classically trained, and they first performed for Ivy League audiences. Band members linked their success to a disillusionment with radical politics a year after massive student unrest at Columbia, which had featured takeovers of university buildings by protesters against the Vietnam War and the school's real estate battles with a neighboring African-American community. In an atmosphere of "futility in people's political involvement," as band members put it, Sha Na Na offered comforting reversion to songs full of puppy love and nonsense lyrics. "We're playing happy music and we get happy audiences," concluded the band.

Media explanations of the revival touched on themes of nostalgia, rebellion, apathy, and sexuality. Countercultural commentators differed in their interpretations of the resurgence of Fifties rock. The highly politicized *Ramparts* magazine, in an article on Chuck Berry, equated the Fifties rock and roll sensibility with sensuality, speed, rebellion, and African-American culture, crediting it with opening new cultural worlds to white teenagers. In this view, rock and roll disrupted a crushing conformity of the time and led the way into the Sixties revolt against a wide variety of social norms. Late-Sixties interest in rock's roots is thereby consistent with social rebellion current at the time. Rock and roll had become the opening wedge in a generation's movement against an inaccessible government, a stultifying academic environment, sexual repression, and other constraining social practices.[8]

Richard Goldstein, a pioneer in American rock criticism then writing in the *New York Times* and *Vogue*, had a more mixed reaction. Goldstein notes Elvis's attempts to reconnect to youth culture (critics from the leftist alternative press were invited to his Las Vegas comeback) and locates Presley's contemporary relevance in his borrowings from black culture and his pioneering open sexuality. Goldstein, however, sees Presley's comeback mainly as an attempt to reconnect with previous fans, whom Goldstein identifies as having become suburbanites approaching middle age, bypassed by the cultural convulsions of the Sixties. Presley is still a populist hero, but to the Silent Majority invoked by Richard Nixon rather than to a bunch of surly, rebellious teenagers. Time has passed both Elvis and his fans by, making his sexuality seem innocent and even traditional in the wake of the post-Fifties Sexual Revolution.[9]

Goldstein distinguishes between a tradition maintained by cultural continuity (as with Elvis) and nostalgia that emerges from a cultural rupture. Sha Na Na's nostalgia implies a yearning for escape from a corrupted present, a leap back over the schism that divides the Sixties from the Fifties, a schism that Goldstein, as a leftist, identifies with social progress. Goldstein, like many other writers, identifies the emergence of rock and roll as a beneficent rupture in American society, a decisive intervention of honest sexuality and black culture into the white middle-class mainstream; this intervention presaged the large-scale social changes of the Sixties. To Goldstein, Fifties rock and roll as performed by Sha Na Na rejected the consequences of its original eruption.[10]

Goldstein's positioning of Elvis Presley and Sha Na Na on opposite poles in the production of nostalgia illustrates the dynamics of continuity and rupture that sociologist Fred Davis identifies as a crucial mode in the "yearning for yesterday."[11] Presley had become representative of a cultural continuity from the 1950s into the 1960s on the basis of his allegiance to his southern and working-class roots and his limited stylistic variations. His initial popularity, however, was based on the break with the past he represented to a generation of American youth; the shared sense of distinctiveness that the youth of the 1950s enjoyed led to a generational identity ripe for later nostalgic recuperation—even by those who were younger than the original cohort of rock and roll fans. As Davis states, nostalgia's ability to highlight continuities of social identity and a sense of a shared past can be particularly important when private practices have undergone significant change. In the midst of the Sexual Revolution and the burgeoning feminist movement, for instance, the stress of changed gender relations could be assuaged by a reemergence of memories of adolescent dating rituals of the Fifties for the first rock and roll generation, and an ascription of pronounced innocence to the earlier era.[12]

Despite Goldstein's criticisms, Sha Na Na at least admitted to the rupture that occurred within American society during the 1960s, because its audiences came from contemporary rock fandom. The band's acknowledgment of cultural distance from the 1950s showed in the comic, semi-parodic tone of its stage show—which it even performed at Woodstock, the ultimate gathering of the hippie counterculture that would come to be seen in later years as the opposite of the greaser culture represented by Sha Na Na.

For some older Elvis fans and other groups, the Fifties remained a touchstone in an attempt to deny meaning and significance to the countercultural and left-wing influences of the 1960s. In a more critical vein, ABC News saw Elvis in his comeback as frozen in time, violating the "wild and spontaneous" spirit of the music he helped to forge. The network reported that the youth counterculture was fleeing the show business values of Las Vegas, even as Elvis was embracing them.[13] The political, social, and cultural upheavals of the Sixties had set America on a new course, and attempts to continue in the tradition of the Fifties were doomed to irrelevancy.

To those who were willing to see the Fifties as nostalgia rather than as a way to stave off the present, however, the rock and roll revival could be a means of tempering the divisions of the Sixties. In 1969 rock promoter Richard Nader put on the first of his "1950's Rock and Roll Revival" concerts, which would ultimately play in more than seventy cities over the next decade. Nader assembled oldies acts like Bill Haley and the Comets, Chuck Berry, the Platters, and the Coasters to perform short sets of their best-known hits at Madison Square Garden, and added Sha Na Na to the bill as well. The media reported that the crowd was an unusual mixture of teenagers and those who were teenagers in the 1950s, a combination rarely seen at other rock shows. The Revivals became particularly popular in New York, where the *New York Times* reported a 1970 concert was "filled with an audience of every imaginable hair length and clothing style, drug freaks pressed against Westchester Young Republicans collaberating [*sic*] to remember all the lyrics to 'Mr. Earl' or some such."[14] Nader's concerts reassembled the rock generation through an appeal to cultural forms that predated the Sixties' explicit challenge to the terms of American postwar consensus. Into the late 1970s, the shows continued to attract teenagers and the generation of their parents. To the *Times*, Fifties music reminded audiences of the era before generational revolt led to schisms based on age, taking them back to "the days when the worst thing a kid could do was wreck a car or buy a loud record player," rather than, presumably, outrage parents with radical politics, sexual license, and drug use.[15]

This reversion to relative innocence was credited with the successful comeback tour of "Buffalo" Bob Smith, one of the stars of 1950s children's culture as host of *The Howdy Doody Show*. Smith played at more than fifty college campuses in the early 1970s, inviting his audiences to relive their earliest television memories. His appeal, according to both Smith and reporters profiling him, was the opportunity he provided his fans to momentarily forget the war, the military draft, demonstrations, and drugs—the social phenomena said to pervade collegiate life at the time. Reporters made note that Smith had been booked at campuses ranging from the University of California at Berkeley to the United States Military Academy at West Point—the polar opposites of youth experience since Berkeley's left-wing Free Speech Movement of 1964. *TV Guide* trumpeted that Howdy Doody united "protesters and jocks, cheerleaders and grinds."[16] Generational unity could be reforged on the basis of an unpoliticized, homogeneous experience of 1950s television and a willful forgetting of the divisive events of the 1960s.[17]

Many countercultural commentators, however, depicted the loss of innocence as inevitable, a necessary step for a generation that allowed it to confront the adult world, face up to social problems, and create the myriad changes in culture, politics, and social behavior that constituted the Sixties for its participants. In the counterculture press covering the revival, the Fifties are presented as a comforting but evanescent fantasy world, one that masked the urgent need for social change. In this view, the move from innocence to experience, however traumatic, created a healthy rebelliousness and openness to new ways of living and represented a defeat of racial, sexual, and cultural repression and hypocrisy.

THE FIFTIES REVIVAL GOES MAINSTREAM

The Fifties revival expanded in the 1970s, existing primarily as the consumption of entertainment with Fifties themes and the attendant reporting on cultural fads by mainstream media. Such reporting had a tendency toward glib hyperbole, and it would be easy to overestimate the importance of the Fifties for 1970s culture if guided solely by press reports. The Fifties theme coexisted with numerous other social phenomena, fads, and cultural strains, some of which assuredly involved Americans in more profound participation than did the Fifties revival. Although retrospective accounts of the era at times depict Americans of the mid-1970s as immersed in Fifties-inspired music, fashion, and behavior on a daily basis, there were, for example, only scattered manifestations of the taste for nostalgia in my own white, suburban, middle-class, teenage milieu—one of the social contexts said to be most affected by the revival.[18]

Active subcultures based on vintage cars and early rock and roll record collecting did exist, often peopled by men in their thirties and forties harking back to their own adolescence, but the large-scale consumption of Fifties-themed products does not necessarily indicate that for most fans, the revival became an organizing principle of their perspectives, behaviors, or identities.

Perhaps only the fandom generated by Elvis Presley, which was less a revival than a continuation of practices from the 1950s and 1960s, qualified as a strongly affective cultural keystone on a truly mass scale.[19] Still, the revival put into circulation a set of markings and meanings by which the Fifties came to be publicly defined, and a set of experiences and memories that was validated as the basis for the relevancy of the recent past.

A general nostalgia craze spread throughout the country in the early 1970s, and the Fifties only slowly emerged as the longest-lasting motif in the turn backward. The interest in nostalgia took many forms: old radio shows from the 1930s and 1940s were recirculated, magazines were published reprinting articles from the same period, and tourism to historic sites increased significantly. Films such as *What's Up, Doc* (1972) and *Chinatown* (1974) paid tribute to the old film genres of screwball comedy and the hard-boiled detective mystery, respectively. Both the graphic design and the copy content of advertising evoked earlier decades of twentieth-century American life.[20]

National television news programs paid scant attention to the nostalgia movement, in accordance with their emphasis on hard news reportage. ABC News, which of the three major networks had the least amount of prestige invested in the hallowed traditions of its news department, devoted relatively more airtime to the discussion of cultural issues. An ABC News report in 1971 explained the appeal of nostalgia as a yearning for the simplicities of life in the 1940s, before the Sexual Revolution and the Vietnam War—"when holding hands was a big thing" and when the country was unified by a "war everyone thought should be won." The recirculating of motion pictures from the Studio Era evoked a "simple, uncrowded, uncomplicated little community known as Hollywood," a small town of the filmic mind to which America could return.[21]

CBS television commentator Eric Sevareid warned against idealizing the past, arguing that the decades of the 1930s and 1940s, in particular, were neither so idyllic nor so unsophisticated as current interpretations would have it. Speaking in the midst of the economic recession of 1974, he noted that the major distinction between the eras was a matter of belief—Americans used to believe in a future, whereas today's society had lost its sense of historical continuity, causation, and hopefulness. The connections between past, present, and future had been cut. This disjunction allowed the past to be used as an ornamental illusion, to comfort a nation torn by economic crisis and social upheaval.[22]

Mainstream mass-market magazines were predictably behind the alternative press in reporting on a trend originating in youth culture, even though attendance at revival concerts was cross-generational. *Newsweek* and *Life* devoted cover stories to the emergence of Fifties nostalgia in 1972, and other magazines carried personal testimonials on Fifties teenage life the same year.[23] By then the popularity of Fifties culture had been evinced by the popularity of the musical comedy *Grease*, which was beginning the longest theatrical run in Broadway history up to that time; by a resurgence in interest in the careers of Marilyn Monroe and Marlon Brando; and by the continued touring of revival acts, including Chuck Berry, who scored a million-selling hit in 1972 with the smarmy adolescent sex joke, "My Ding-a-Ling."

Reportage on the Fifties portrayed the decade through a set of cultural markers, signifiers of the decade's legacy to the culture of the 1970s. In representing 1950s experiences, the media inevitably narrowed its meanings—even as reporters dredged up forgotten or half-remembered fads, political events, and celebrities, they excluded others from reentering social memory as definitional elements of the Fifties. Representation, the act of bringing the past into the present, is based inevitably on a reductionary forgetting during the processes of selection, interpretation, and presentation.[24] No one can fully recreate the past; representation becomes the process by which social actors provide definitions and markers of what is worth remembering, often based, as theorists of social memory state, on present-day needs and desires. A limited set of group memories are invoked and made available to the wider public, in the context of the current social climate. In the press reporting on the Fifties cultural revival, these markers centered on youth culture and involved music, film, fashion, and sexual practices, and, to a lesser extent, race relations, politics, and television. Early rock and roll was deemed the dominant music of the era, ranging from Little Richard (noted with approval) to Pat Boone (noted with mild reproach, even by those writers who confessed to earlier fandom). Marilyn Monroe (who graced a 1972 *Newsweek* cover), Marlon Brando (in his *Wild One* biker persona), and James Dean were featured as idiomatic Fifties film stars. (Brando had reemerged from relative obscurity with the huge success of *The Godfather* in 1972.) Fashions of the era were identified as blue jeans and black leather jackets, chinos and crew cuts, white socks and pedal pushers—the social uniforms of Fifties adolescence.[25]

This litany was presented largely without historical context, with little sense of chronology or history. Rock and roll was linked to adolescent rebelliousness, but the popularity of other cultural styles and celebrities was presented as a natural fact, with no tracing of causative relations, except the occasional mention of marketing efforts by pop culture industries. As Michael Schudson states, in modern journalism, celebrities become living monuments to their own popularity, and are presented as cultural archetypes rather than linked to specific historical events.[26] Brando and Dean represented Rebellious Youth; Monroe became the Doomed Sex Symbol.[27] The reporting on style attested to the demographic and cultural power of the generation of 1950s teenagers, who had become prime adult consumers by the 1970s. Nostalgia can be used to validate past selves by the invocation of old popular styles and the distinctive shared experiences that create identity formation. This nostalgically renewed identity can hold particular appeal for its transcendence of social divisions that have become recognized in the intervening years, among a group now riven with fragmentation and conflict.[28] Nostalgia reconvened the pre- and early Baby Boomers into a socially recognizable formation through the power of mediated group memory.

By celebrating the staying power of rock and roll and Fifties celebrity culture, the press reports positioned the teenagers of that period as culturally triumphant; even outdated styles were useful in generating a feeling of community and shared remembrance. For 1950s teenagers who did not participate in the dramatic public events of the 1960s, the reinvocation of the Fifties could reestablish their generational history as vibrant, unified, and relevant to 1970s America. For younger readers, the Fifties offered a vision of generational unity and distinctive cultural practice without the controversial, divisive elements of the Sixties counterculture, which was already fading by the early 1970s.

The insolence of Marlon Brando and James Dean gave the Fifties a veneer of hipness to compete with the culturally vibrant Sixties, while Brando's working-class, hypermasculine persona offered a contrast to the middle-class, somewhat feminized counterculture. As feminism began to challenge male prerogatives, the Fifties Brando presented a compelling figure as a rebel who was also insistently male. Marilyn Monroe's image, meanwhile, could attest to the glory of an outmoded hyperfeminine style, while her troubled history served as a critique of the style's constrictions.

Press reports did not completely ignore negative aspects of 1950s experience, but moved to contain them. Articles stressed the decade's strong sexual repression and double standard, and then located them wholly within the back seat of adolescent dating. Adult cultural and social practices were restricted to mentions of racism and the burgeoning movement against it, and to quick mentions of the Cold War, Dwight Eisenhower, Richard Nixon, and Joseph McCarthy. Curiously, television did not figure large in portrayals of the decade; in many personal testimonials of Fifties adolescence, television's only importance was as a purveyor of rock and roll on *American Bandstand* and the *Ed Sullivan Show*. Television figured more significantly in some memoirs of early childhood in the 1950s, as the domestic television set was within easier cultural reach for young children than was rock and roll.[29]

Newsweek, Life, and other magazines' attempt to explain the popularity of Fifties nostalgia emphasized the relative innocence of the period, compared with a 1960s characterized by the Vietnam War, assassinations of political leaders, and drug use among the young. Because, however, the writers describe the era as one with social and political problems of its own—racism, constrained gender roles, and McCarthyism—the loss of innocence seems initially caused not so much by the introduction of evil into an idyllic American society, as by a new awareness by the Baby Boomer generation of the existence of social trauma in the 1960s. In this view, the political turmoil and social oppression of the 1950s existed in a hazy adult world that acquiesced to injustice, a world far removed from the immediate concerns of teenagers and children of the time, who were now configured as the readership of nostalgia reportage in the 1970s.

A twenty-nine-year-old nostalgia fan states in the 1972 *Newsweek* cover story on the 1950s, "There were plenty of problems in the world but nobody cared. All we worried about were cars, records, and who broke up with whom."[30] This initial quote in the story functions to define whose experience in the 1950s counts—those whose youth and socioeconomic status at the time precluded serious consideration of social woes. The Fifties to be mined as nostalgia were an experience of white, middle-class teenagers. Their retrospective sense of personal innocence of the larger world in the 1950s becomes conflated ultimately with a sense that the nation as a whole lost its social innocence in the 1960s. As John Nerone states, group memories must compete and coexist with other groups' senses of the past; in the quest for social power, each group tries to universalize its particular group memories, to have these memories act as the archive of the past for the society as a whole.[31] Other individuals and groups may have had memories at variance from the accounts circulating in *Newsweek* and other media outlets, but it was these media accounts that gained public recognition and achieved discursive dominance. The 1950s and 1960s became defined publicly through this narrative of innocence, trauma, maturity, and nostalgia.

Both the moderately conservative *Time* and the liberal Catholic *Commonweal* agree that the 1950s were a nightmare—but as *Commonweal* stated, one in which the social and political status quo seemed so fixed and comfortable that those who lived through it did not know they should have been miserable.[32] Only the cultural phenomenon of rock and roll and the insolent performances of Brando and Dean pointed to other possibilities of life, possibilities realized in the 1960s. In the mainstream press, only in the realm of sexual relations did the passage from the Fifties to the Seventies, from innocence to experience, seem clearly figured to be progress.

Once more, the focus was on adolescent experience—writers never mention the possibilities and problems of sexual life for adults. Rather, sexuality in the Fifties became defined by teenage dating practices, characterized as creating perpetual frustration for boys and a vicious double standard for girls. The tone of the articles ranged from bemusement, easily come by through the distance that adulthood and the Sexual Revolution had created between then and now, to rage, particularly from feminist writers. Women writers, published in upper-middlebrow magazines such as *The Atlantic* and mass-market women's magazines such as *Redbook*, tied the constraints of the "good-girl" role to the boy-centeredness of female teenage life at the time and to the meager opportunities for careers and social roles beyond matrimony and motherhood. Articles by "bad girls" did not make it into print in the mainstream press, nor did autobiographical accounts by self-proclaimed hoods.

The greater freedom of the Sexual Revolution was consistently portrayed as the defeat of repression and hypocrisy. Yet for many, that earlier innocence could now be a source of retrospective enjoyment, because of its very remoteness and because it was free of the complexities that more open sexuality had brought. To *Newsweek*, Fifties nostalgia existed in part because "in those days 'swinging' meant the Hula-Hoop, not wife-swapping."[33] The advertisements for the low-budget, Fifties-themed film *The Lords of Flatbush* (1974) stated, "It was 1958, when making love meant 'making out,'" and asked its presumably adult audience, "When was the last time someone gave you a hickey?" (The film itself did not portray the time as so sexually innocent: one of the lead characters, played by Sylvester Stallone, unhappily marries his girlfriend when she tells him she is pregnant. To get an audience into the theaters, however, the distributors chose to play on notions of Fifties innocence.)[34]

To *Time* and others, the opening up of life's possibilities in the 1960s had been accompanied by a sense of perpetual social acrimony that the 1950s seemed to be mercifully without. This acrimony was associated in part with the demands of new social movements, such as feminism. During the public, explicit challenge to traditional gender roles presented by the feminist movement in the 1970s, memories of earlier, clearly defined gender arrangements became points of comparison by which to understand social change, to judge what had been gained or lost. As opposed to more recent conservative rhetoric, however, the mainstream press in the early 1970s did not lay total responsibility for the upheavals of the 1960s on left-wing social movements and the counterculture.

The quality of family life in the Fifties has become a staple of conservative rhetoric since the 1980s, but most articles on the revival in the 1970s paid little attention to the issue. In keeping with the appreciation of early rock and roll as a healthy social and cultural rupture in a deadening time, some writers configured family life as oppressive, and the burgeoning, separate teenage sphere as a site of liberation. A *Redbook* contributor recalls her adolescence in small-town Indiana, where only *American Bandstand* threatened the cross-generational homogeneity: "It was the only TV program I watched regularly. . . . The more adventurous among us would copy the dances, but none of us copied the way the dancers dressed. . . . Only 'bad' girls dressed like that. . . . [M]ost of us . . . dressed like ladies—*old* ladies. Or else like little girls. This made our mothers more comfortable (in fact, our mothers dressed like that too)."[35] The rupture between generations augured by rock and roll was celebrated in the 1970s accounts as teenagers' need to acknowledge their own sexuality and their openness to myriad sources of culture, posed against an older generation's closed-mindedness.

The potent combination of rock and roll and television became a focal point in memories of the forging of generational identity. "In 1956, my aunt told me how foolish I was to sit screaming with joy at the spectacle of that vulgar singer on TV," Maureen Orth recounts in *Newsweek*, on her first sighting of Elvis Presley. "It was then I knew that she and I lived in different worlds, and it was then that kids' bedroom doors slammed all over America. Boys wore greasy ducktail haircuts and tried to imitate Elvis's moves in front of their mirror. Girls gave up collecting charms for their bracelets for the forbidden charms of his 45-rpm records. Our parents hated Elvis and that was all right with us. From Elvis on, rock was rebellious."[36] The 1950s marked the rise of a distinct cultural world for teenagers, which encompassed fashion, film, and especially music. Rock and roll fandom became particularly useful in the rebellion against social constraints on bodily expression, constraints that fell particularly hard on girls.[37] American society increasingly became perceived, by both adults and teenagers, as bifurcated along generational lines, and rock and roll was the first, most pervasive, expressive manifestation of the schism, the first teenage salvo against a repressive and culturally obsolescent adult world.

A magazine with a decidedly different take on the 1950s was *Ebony*, the leading national African-American periodical. *Ebony* did no reporting on the general nostalgia boom, although it did create a "Whatever Happened To" column in 1971, which featured entertainers, political figures, and athletes. The magazine, however, regularly published lengthy articles on African-American history, covering all periods of American life. In *Ebony*'s articles and editorials, the 1950s achieve prominence as the beginning of the modern civil rights movement and its energizing effect on the black community. The magazine refuses nostalgia for the general era of the 1950s, when the aims of the movement had only begun to achieve victories over racism, but asserts the need to memorialize its key political moments: the Supreme Court decision against segregated schools in *Brown v. Board of Education*, the desegregation of Little Rock schools, and the Montgomery bus boycott sparked by Rosa Parks and led by Martin Luther King, Jr.[38]

Rather than separating the 1950s and the 1960s into distinct and opposing periods, *Ebony* asserts the links between the two decades, defining the 1960s as the culmination of political activity begun years earlier. For *Ebony*, the primary historical rupture appears not between a distant 1950s and a 1960s that produced the contemporary historical moment, but between those two decades and a 1970s that has witnessed the dissolution of the energies of the movement and the withdrawal of government support for its aims. The death of Martin Luther King, Jr., in 1968 haunts the magazine throughout the 1970s, as evidenced by the recurrent invocation of his name and the publication of articles about his surviving family.[39] The magazine also evinces nostalgia for the presidency of Lyndon Johnson, whose responsibility for American involvement in the Vietnam War had made him a virtual pariah in other public affairs journalism of the time, but whose support for civil rights legislation is repeatedly celebrated by *Ebony*.[40]

Nostalgia for the politics of earlier decades surfaced elsewhere during the 1970s, but it was never connected to an organized political movement in a highly visible or sustained way. In the wake of Watergate, Richard Nixon's deceptions were contrasted to the supposedly plain speaking and forthright style of Harry Truman, who was featured in the stage play and film *Give 'Em Hell, Harry!* (1975). Most political manifestations of nostalgia, however, remained fleeting and amorphous, as the nation's politics were dominated by the unprecedented problems of the Vietnam War, Watergate, and the energy crisis.

THE FIFTIES ON 1970s SCREENS

The Fifties revival reached its apotheosis when it moved from the rock music scene into the realms of film and television, with their wider demographic appeal. *American Graffiti* was released in August 1973—just a few months after the American withdrawal from Vietnam and immediately after the first congressional hearings on Watergate.[41] The film opened to critical acclaim and popular success, and intensified discussion of the Fifties in the press. The story revolves around the activities of small-town teenagers on the last night of summer in 1962, which as many reviewers commented, places the action before the assassination of John Kennedy, the full-scale American military involvement in Vietnam, and the increase in drug use by American youth. The film positions itself, then, at the end of the Fifties era, and makes the association clearer by relying on Fifties rock songs for its soundtrack.

American Graffiti was widely hailed as a commentary on social and personal innocence, on the simpler problems confronting teenagers at the time. The film was applauded as providing both enjoyable comedy and a recognition of the passing of such innocence. As *Senior Scholastic*, a magazine aimed at teenagers, stated in its review: "There is a brooding sadness. We are reminded that '62 was the end of a time that will never come again—a time when life seemed predictable and safe."[42] To the *New York Times*, the film shows the last moments of a restrictive but comforting social stasis, before the 1960s onslaught of cataclysm and disintegration, "a journey across centuries."[43]

Esquire linked the very innocence depicted in the film to the problems

1. Hanging out at Mel's Drive-In, Ron Howard and Cindy Williams begin their roles as Fifties icons with *American Graffiti*. Universal.

that the nation had faced since then—it was an innocence dangerous in its ignorance, leading to the quagmires of Vietnam and Watergate.[44] Much less common was the type of reaction provided by Pauline Kael in the left-leaning *New Yorker*—that the film falsely represents the experience of the era by concentrating on the lives of white, middle-class, teenage boys. Memories of the era were not so innocent for others—"not for women, not for blacks or Orientals or Puerto Ricans, not for homosexuals, not for the poor."[45] In this regard, *American Graffiti* continues the simplification, the radical limiting of perspective and subject matter that constituted public discourse regarding the 1950s.[46]

In the wake of Watergate, other themes of Fifties life began to be explored, particularly the McCarthy blacklist, which was portrayed in the television docudrama *Fear on Trial* (1975) and the theatrical film *The Front* (1976). The depictions of McCarthyism offered the opportunity to investigate Richard Nixon's political origins and the beginnings of the national security state, after revelations of presidential and CIA abuses of governmental power had dominated the political life of the nation for several years. In addition, the television series *M*A*S*H*, based on the 1970 film (and earlier novel), had been depicting the Korean War since 1972, yet it rarely was mentioned in discussions of the Fifties, so strong were the associations of the period with sock hops, Elvis Presley, and saddle shoes. The widespread understanding of *M*A*S*H* as a metaphor for the American experience in Vietnam, abetted by the series' tendency toward anachronism, further limited its relevancy to public memories of the Fifties.[47]

Happy Days

The tendency to center depictions of the era around teenage life was reinforced by the success of the television series *Happy Days*, which premiered in
January 1974.[48] The show recirculates the familiar markings of what had come
to be known as the Fifties. The early episodes open with Bill Haley and the
Comets' "Rock Around the Clock" (the first nationwide rock and roll hit by
a white musical act), and plots depict white, middle-class boys' efforts to score
with girls. In its most prominent seasons, the series revolves around the soda
shop and suburban living room, and shows young men's attempts to respond
to challenges to their emerging sense of masculinity. Given prime-time television's economic need to reach diverse audiences, the show displays a greater
diversity in the age of its characters than did previous representations of the
Fifties in American music and film—in *American Graffiti*, adults are largely
absent. The result in *Happy Days* is to depict a distinct teenage-boy culture,
but to ensconce that culture within secure family relations. The two major
authority figures on the show are Arthur Fonzarelli, the cool greaser otherwise known as "the Fonz," and Mr. Cunningham, the benign family patriarch, representing the two poles of experience around which the action
revolves. Richie Cunningham, the supposed lead, sometimes also displays
wisdom and a talent for leadership, but the female regulars on the show are
never solicited for serious advice and make their desires known only by their
occasional mild mocking of the main, male leads.

The social changes triggered by rock and roll had left a legacy of continued conflict into the 1970s, with the teenagers of the 1950s increasingly now
on the other, older side of the generational divide. While they celebrated the
endurance of their own cultural victories, such as rock and roll, they also
faced a new crop of troublesome teenagers. A *New York Times* writer, high
school class of 1956, credited the appeal of *Happy Days* to its depiction of the
essential harmlessness of 1950s family conflict among the white middle class:
"In the fifties, before our children became strangers, drugs were class-
conscious and color-coded: they stayed out of white suburbs. . . . Drain the
oil out of these kids' hair and they'll be normalized, ready to embark on the
paper route of life."[49] Rock and roll and sex (particularly for boys, the central
figures in *Happy Days*) do not preclude close family relations or a stable, prosperous future, but the mid-1960s addition of drug usage poses a continuing
threat to middle-class family life in the 1970s.

The very success of the youth of the 1950s and 1960s against the strictures
of the postwar family, and their own new positions as parents themselves, has
reconfigured the family as an institution worth preserving in the 1970s. At the
same time, the problems of 1950s families from the teenage point of view (the
only view represented in the press) seem small compared to contemporary

problems, as they are defined by 1970s parents. The series gave parents an opportunity to share a depiction of their younger years with their own children, explain the circumstances of their own youth, pass on their cultural legacy, and teach their children family-oriented lessons of behavior as conveyed by the teenage characters amid the trappings of a distinctive youth subculture. *Happy Days* presages the revaluation of Fifties family life that would mark conservative rhetoric in ensuing decades.

Happy Days is able to call upon mediated memories of earlier times to reinforce its nonthreatening tone. Situation comedies of the 1950s such as *Father Knows Best*, *Leave It to Beaver*, and *The Adventures of Ozzie and Harriet* had already provided a whitewashed history of the era to be passed down to 1970s audiences. Although *Happy Days* characters occasionally refer to the distance between their own "real" experiences and the representations of family life that pervaded these programs, the series also places itself within the older shows' generic traditions. The revival of these programs through syndication during the 1960s made the Fifties sitcom world easily available for cultural appreciation by 1970s audiences. Their easygoing tone was smoothly referenced by *Happy Days*, which could even seem lively by comparison, through the greater presence of rock and roll and sexual innuendo than had been allowed in 1950s television.

Television and Nostalgia

The central importance of *Happy Days'* television family during the later stages of the Fifties revival made the original 1950s family sitcoms newly relevant as a basis of knowledge about the earlier era. If, by the 1970s, what turned out to be important about the 1950s was youth culture's placement within a middle-class family structure, then previous depictions, as in the 1950s family sitcoms, became more valuable as seemingly accurate representations of the era. Lynn Spigel has documented the usefulness of old television series as historical archives, even for viewers too young to have lived through the era they depict.[50] Older products of popular culture can provide easily comprehensible archetypes and social conventions by which to define an era, and also can embody past hopes of those who lived through the era but now struggle with contemporary frustrations and disappointments.[51] In the economic doldrums of the mid-1970s, after the bitter denouements of Vietnam and Watergate, the 1950s family comedy tellingly depicted a time of economic prosperity, political quiescence, and social stability. Whereas repeats of Fifties shows in the 1960s had often been disparaged by audiences and critics as frustrating evidence of television's failed promise to create live, fresh programming, by the 1970s these shows were lauded for bringing a nostalgic hue to television, beckoning backward to the Good Old Days.[52] The historical distance the nation had traveled in the intervening years made the placidity of these shows all the more appealing to those challenged by and weary of the turmoil they identified with the new social movements, which were nowhere to be seen in 1950s situation comedy. The live television dramas that had garnered great attention in the earlier era, and which at times had starkly depicted social conflict, were not often repeated in the 1970s, and no series in the 1970s took them as an aesthetic or political touchstone.

Nostalgia originally referred to memories of a specific home, a geographic location that could not be left without danger of emotional or physical collapse. In a society marked by geographic mobility, nostalgia has shifted in its meaning to connote a sense of loss regarding the past, beyond the appeal of just one location. This past can be remembered as a collection of intensely personal memories, but more often also contains elements of group or public memories, representations and notions circulating in broader social circles. Personal memories are also often made up of remembrances of individual circumstances during encounters with broader social experiences, through the media and social discourse. This occurs most famously with traumatic public events, as when people recall where they were when they heard that John Kennedy had been shot, or how they watched the *Challenger* explosion on television.

Memories of more quotidian circumstances can also revolve around media productions and immediate circumstances of reception, however, as shown by Lynn Spigel and Henry Jenkins in a study of fans of the 1960s *Batman* television series.[53] Memories of earlier television fandom provide the sense of locationality that was provided formerly by ties to a specific geographic place; the television screen has replaced or, perhaps more commonly, become conflated with the home and hometown of the past. Richard Terdiman notes that the ability to use memory to locate oneself socially becomes attenuated in societies removed from the stable spatial relations of the rural past—in mobile urban and suburban environments, the perceptual cues to remembrance of previous experience disappear.[54] Mediated images and their apparatuses can provide such cues, and consequent senses of social as well as spatial location. Fandom becomes a marker of social positioning, and the context of television watching signifies more broadly lived circumstances. As media productions come to form integral parts of the experienced past, they function as sources of identity and points by which to negotiate changes in such identity. The historical authority of old programs, and of new programs that evoke their antecedents, is bolstered by their location at the intersection of personal, group, public, and national memory, by their provision of individual and shared experiences of the historical record.

This appeal is subject to both demographic and generic constraints. The particular sense of trajectory from the 1950s to the 1970s carried by Baby Boomers and others gave special relevance to 1950s programming and to the sitcom format that could evade the most problematic aspects of contemporary social experience. Other genres did not fare so well as vehicles of popular nostalgia. Television networks attempted to mimic dramatic film hits situated in earlier eras, but with much less success. *City of Angels*, for example, moved the *Chinatown* milieu to a weekly series in 1976, but paled in comparison with its more remote predecessors in film noir and 1940s detective films and was quickly canceled.[55] Television had difficulty handling the generic gravity of film classics, but could succeed much more easily in living up to its own comic traditions. As a quotidian apparatus, television's delve into the past seemed most appropriate when it depicted the everyday experience that constituted the sitcom domain Its reach into lost experience was eased by its tendency to conflate the past with contemporary living, through the anachronism of its characters in physical styles, speech, and social behavior.

The Success of Happy Days

ABC promoted *Happy Days* as showing "the relatively carefree life and life styles of young people in those bygone, happy, innocent days."[56] After the critical appreciation of *American Graffiti*'s emotionally complex take on a superseded teenage world, *Happy Days*' thoroughly whitewashed version was savaged by reviewers. The *New York Times* compared it to "store-bought mayonnaise" and called it "dishonest."[57] A comedy series on the vapidity of the Fifties could have worked as satire, *TV Guide* opined, but the show was not that pointed.[58] As Ron Howard, the star of both *American Graffiti* and *Happy Days*, pointed out, " 'Graffiti' is about the end of an era, *Happy Days* is about the middle of an era."[59] The film works by its acknowledgment that the Fifties are doomed to extinction; the series, in keeping with the chronologically static narratives of 1970s television, highlights the social stasis for which the Fifties became notorious in retrospect.

Despite its critical drubbing, the series marked the first successful countertrend in television comedy to overturn the dominance of socially relevant, CBS-style comedies introduced in the early 1970s, such as *All in the Family*, *The Mary Tyler Moore Show*, and *Maude*. *Happy Days* functioned as an escapist lark compared with the politicized, heavily conflictual stories offered by Norman Lear and other producers. If Lear's shows dealt with the aftershock of the Sixties in portraying new gender and race relations, continued social resentments, and the family as a site of perpetual social conflict, *Happy Days* could propel its audience backward to a time before such disruptions had imposed themselves on the national public sphere. It served as the link between earlier ABC faux-counterculture shows such as *The Partridge Family* and *The Brady Bunch*, and later ABC blockbusters *Laverne and Shirley* and *Three's Company*, which dominated late-1970s sitcom programming.

Happy Days portrays a society operating with a much greater degree of consensus than early-1970s America enjoyed; this representation in turn became accepted as the consensus view of the 1950s. The show could ignore 1970s social conflict without seeming to actively repress or exclude voices of discontent, since those voices were retrospectively considered silent in the era it depicted. Indeed, the show's occasional movements toward a social message, as when the Fonz stops a white, racist jury member from convicting a black man wrongly charged with a crime, seem to prove there was little need for social disruption by aggrieved groups to ensure that they would receive fair treatment. With the Fonz in charge, the Sixties seem unnecessary. Individuals and groups may have positioned themselves with or against this view of social harmony in the 1950s, but all had to contend with the understanding of this view as a consensus among others, and as the dominant representation publicly circulated relating to the pre-Sixties era. The assumed consensus took on significant importance in later decades, when conservatives attempted to put forward their vision of 1950s society as a model for America's future.

Happy Days' depoliticized focus on dating practices lends a condescending tone to the comedy's depictions of innocence.[60] *American Graffiti* had depicted a sexual innocence that was part of a more widespread social innocence, a depiction open to critical readings and deeper understandings of the era. *Happy Days* limits the folly of the Fifties to its heroes' sexual inexperience and romantic incompetence, creating a triple movement toward comforting its audience—younger viewers could empathize and be reassured that their own immaturity was not unusual; older viewers could take comfort in their own superior knowingness; and all fans could wallow in the placidity with which the series depicted family relations and, indeed, all other social relations as well. The Fifties are thus constructed as preliberatory but nonthreatening; the only change needed is provided by the inevitable onset of adulthood, perhaps abetted implicitly by the Sexual Revolution of the Sixties and by a very mild feminism that is displayed by the teenager Joanie Cunningham and other female characters in the series' later years.

The placidity of the social milieu is kept from tipping into total boredom by the specificity of the cultural markings of the show. The soda shop, fashions, and music create a sense of a unified and active teenage culture that contrasted with a growing sense of diffusion and pointlessness among American youth in the 1970s, after the countercultural dynamism of the 1960s had disappeared. In the dog days of the mid-1970s, *Happy Days* could appeal to young viewers by presenting teenage culture with a vivacity that masked the insipid nature of its social relations. Indeed, the insipidity was part of the appeal; viewers could embrace the perceived cultural vitality of the Fifties without portrayals of political conflict intruding heavily on their enjoyment.

Happy Days could also attract middle-aged viewers by highlighting the comedy of their own youth and by appealing to their now-superior knowledge, which in the reasonable world of the series could actually count for something.

Referring to an early episode in which the teenaged Richie Cunningham gets drunk for the first time, a *New York Times* critic writes, "How much better that Richie should get drunk and that his father should with a chuckle contemplate the inevitable hangover, than that Richie should be found in his bed OD'd on smack."[61] The very innocuousness of the series is credited with its success—which, after the introduction of its spin-off *Laverne and Shirley* in 1976, was monumental. The televisual equivalent of comfort food, the two series were the first ratings sensation since the socially conscious *All in the Family* premiered in 1971. Indeed, ABC programming chief Fred Silverman, who had overseen *All in the Family* and its spin-offs in his previous role as CBS's head programmer, scheduled *Happy Days* in direct competition with Norman Lear's cantankerous liberal *Maude*. *Happy Days* and *Laverne and Shirley* became the two highest-rated programs on American television in the mid- and late 1970s.

Laverne and Shirley

Laverne and Shirley was set in a more working-class environment than *Happy Days* and was the primary Fifties-inspired production that highlighted female experience.[62] The two lead characters are older than the usual teenage crowd that dominated representations of the decade, and they are most redolent of the Fifties in their reprisal of the figure of the female clown, which Lucille Ball and others had popularized. The series producer, Garry Marshall, made the comparison explicit: "No one else on TV is doing early Lucy. Laverne's the kind of gal who could knock the stuffings out of Mary Richards . . . [and] mop up the floor with Barbara Walters."[63] ABC advertising for the series premiere promised that the two heroines were "spunky" and "sassy," in their "uproarious" new show. The first episode pitted them against upper-class snobs, highlighting their subversive potential.[64]

Laverne and Shirley's toughness and willingness to flout social convention could be viewed as either working class, feminist, or both. Their contrast to the more decorous, middle-class, liberal feminism of 1970s icons Mary Tyler Moore and Barbara Walters thus could be enjoyed from a multiplicity of viewing positions. Although Shirley's obsession with getting married and the lack of a consistently strong feminist perspective may have precluded radical feminists from a strong identification with the series, reading positions from mildly feminist to antifeminist could be sustained, and the show could also find popularity among working-class viewers and older fans of Lucille Ball and other female comedians. Women's magazines supported the show in particular because it portrayed a friendship between two female leads during an era in which prime-time television showed few such friendships and Hollywood film was dominated by male buddy-buddy plots.[65]

The characteristic Marshall (and ABC) blandness, however, kept the show from evoking strong social conflict or giving voice to the silent specter of

Fifties revival imagery, the bad girl. As actress Penny Marshall explained, "We [she and co-star Cindy Williams] started the girls out tougher, but we keep having to pull back. . . . I thought we were going to have our hair in rollers and wear black scarves to cover our hickeys. But they don't think people want to see two toughies in their living room every week, so they mellowed us out and made us kind of blah."[66] Garry Marshall originally had introduced the characters into *Happy Days* to spice up the bland representations of women in the series. "We had trouble getting laughs with sweet, squeaky bobby-soxers," the producer stated.[67] Indeed, in the *Happy Days* episode that introduced the pair, they are depicted as physically violent and sexually aggressive. "These girls don't know the word 'no,' " claims the Fonz, and Shirley comes on to the underage Richie. When they get their own show, however, Shirley is transformed into a prude, and Laverne is generally reduced to talk rather than action. Their aggressiveness is channeled into a disdain for elitism, a class resentment that rarely is given a gendered inflection in the series.

The Rise of the Greaser

The same desire to introduce tougher, more working-class characters had led to the increased focus on the character of the Fonz on *Happy Days*, which was accompanied by the same corresponding pressure to fit the character into middle-class norms. The producers and Henry Winkler, who played the Fonz, had to fight with the network repeatedly to dress the character in a black leather jacket and boots, the apparel of Fifties hoods.[68] Marshall and Winkler also, however, made sure that the Fonz eschewed violence, befriended the well-behaved, middle-class boys on the show, and soon moved into the suburban Cunningham home. By the final years of the series, the Fonz was teaching the high school shop class, before becoming a school administrator.[69]

The massive popularity of the Fonz and his designation as the coolest youthful character on prime-time television completed a process of cultural redefinition that had begun with Sha Na Na—that the prototypical figure of youth culture in the Fifties was the urban, male, white, working-class greaser. The counterculture of the 1960s had traced its lineage back in part to the Beats of the 1950s, but this connection became increasingly obscured in the 1970s and was superseded by mainstream interest in the greasers.[70] The Beats had established their influence on the 1960s, particularly on the hippie movement, by their emphasis on nonconformist self-expression, interest in Eastern religion and philosophy, drug use, and ties to such seminal countercultural figures as Bob Dylan and Ken Kesey. Beats such as Allen Ginsberg were active in late-1960s cultural and political events, although Jack Kerouac turned his back on the counterculture. The popularity of folkish singer-songwriters such as Joni Mitchell and James Taylor in the early 1970s pointed back to the Beats by

2. *Happy Days'*s teenage boy culture returns to the family fold, cool but wholesome.
ABC/Paramount Television.

way of the figure of Bob Dylan, but with the decline of the hippies, the Beats
lost much of their cultural resonance for 1970s America.[71]

The replacement of the Beat with the greaser as the emblematic 1950s
rebel and arbiter of hip repositioned cultural authority in a number of ways.
The Beats had been configured as largely middle-class, left-wing, intellectual,
and centered in New York City and San Francisco (although these conceptions were not wholly accurate). They were tied to black culture through their
fandom of jazz, use of black idiom, and separation from dominant social institutions; Norman Mailer's famous essay defining the Beat phenomenon had
been entitled "The White Negro." The homosexuality of several major Beats
was also a touchstone in public imaginations.

The 1960s counterculture was also marked publicly by some of these
characteristics, while the greaser culture as discussed in the 1970s contained
few parallels, beyond being perceived as an urban scene. The greaser liked cars
and girls and rock and roll, was working class, usually a non-Jewish "white
ethnic," in the language of the time (such as Italian American, as with the
Fonz, and Stallone's starring role in *The Lords of Flatbush*) and decidedly unin-
tellectual and apolitical. The greaser's life was a physicalized one, in keeping
with conceptions of working-class life as being centered on manual labor,

industrial machinery, and simple pleasures.[72] The greaser may have listened to black rock and roll, but did not emulate black social attitudes or behavior. Almost the only commonality between the greaser and the Beat as avatars of the Fifties was their gender—the Fifties continued to be conceptualized as a predominantly male experience. The masculinity of the greaser, however, was counterposed to the social chaos and freewheeling expression of the counter-culture in the Sixties. The guiding concept for the Fonz was the need to act "cool," which was the display of male self-possession and control over emo-tions, through which he could face down other males' physical challenges and entice interest, and even worship, from women.

In the popular historiography of *Happy Days* and 1970s journalism, the greaser, rather than the Beat, became the true progenitor of postwar Ameri-can youth culture, as it stood in the 1970s. Why was the greaser embraced and the Beat forgotten? Youth culture of the 1970s had moved away from the pol-itics and open social deviance of the 1960s counterculture. In daily practice it was largely segregated racially, although there was crossover in terms of fan-dom for specific performers and cultural productions. Rock and roll remained the most dynamic cultural form and attracted intense and widespread interest. The greaser's linkage to energetic rock was a major advantage the figure enjoyed over the Beat in seeming to contain relevance for the mid-1970s, after the initial surge in folkish singer-songwriters had dissipated. In the Do Your Own Thing culture of the 1970s, the greaser's distinctive subcultural sta-tus could be enjoyed without defensiveness by a wide range of audiences, while the Beat's self-marginalization was linked to the Sixties counterculture's aggressive challenge to more conventional social practices. Finally, the paucity of positive representations of Beat culture in mainstream media during the 1950s prevented these images from surviving into the 1970s mainstream. The rather silly, if endearing, character of Maynard G. Krebs was perhaps the most visible representation of Beat in the history of network television (having appeared on *The Many Loves of Dobie Gillis* from 1959 to 1963), but in the 1970s, he was no match for the Fonz.

By embracing the greaser as ancestor, fans could simultaneously indulge in nostalgia and feel reassurance about the present. While the Beats challenged the postwar period with their pointed nonconformity to prevalent social mores, the greaser could be seen as more firmly belonging within an era of American political, military, and economic dominance and stability, all of which had been damaged by the time of the Fonz's debut in 1974. The Water-gate scandal and the Vietnam War had lowered public confidence in the via-bility of major American institutions. The country was in the midst of an economic recession, brought on in part by an oil embargo by other oil-producing nations; the American economy was seen as vulnerable to the vagaries of international politics for the first time since World War II. Inflation and unemployment coincided in a manner confounding the Keynesian economics that had guided government policy for two generations. The greaser's working-class status, sense of authenticity, and "street smarts" could remind blue-collar fans of the importance of their contribution to culture during an era of increased economic insecurity, the beginning of employers' offensives against unions, and journalistic practices that generally ignored working-class concerns. The 1950s car culture could hold appeal as a sign of a simpler time, when Americans did not have to worry about the price of gasoline or the effects of pollution. (That the practices considered innocent in the 1950s contributed directly to the problems of the 1970s was apparently easy enough not to consider.) The public recognition that those who went to fight in Vietnam were primarily from the working class implicitly conjoined the image of the greaser and the Vietnam veteran. By configuring the greaser as a politically innocent, stand-up guy, the nation could reclaim a sense of nobility for its tarnished troops and hold out hope for their reclamation as emotionally stable, hardy survivors of tough times.[73]

To middle-class fans, the greaser could be enjoyed as the upholder of pleasures sacrificed to adulthood and, paradoxically, as a marker of upward social mobility. The specificity of Fifties cultural expression provided a sense of history for recent decades in American life, conducive to notions of linear progress. If the youth of yesterday were primarily working-class guys who never went beyond high school in education or attitude, then their disappearance as a visible subculture marked the continued viability of the American Dream of generational advancement. The social dominance of the 1970s middle class demonstrated that personal development, economic growth, and educational opportunities had prevailed despite the social cataclysms of the 1960s and the political failures of the following decade. The Fonz indicated what the nation had lost since the 1950s, but also what it had gained.

By the late 1970s the greaser was beginning to lose his cultural specificity, and thereby his particular historical relevance. Sha Na Na began a syndicated television series, but they mixed their Fifties routines with renditions of Broadway show tunes (and even the light opera of Gilbert and Sullivan).[74] Their concert audiences became increasingly pre-teen, far removed from the rock audiences who could appreciate their performances as simultaneous parodies and tributes. Rather than enjoying firsthand knowledge of the Fifties and its music, Sha Na Na's remaining fans were children of the Fifties revival itself, their interest created by the Fonz.[75]

Similarly *Grease* had started in 1972 as a nostalgic parody of Fifties greasers and good girls, and played to a noticeably younger (meaning theatergoers in their twenties and thirties) and more working-class audience on Broadway than other musicals.[76] The 1978 film of the musical, however, conflated Fifties culture with the 1970s disco fad, by starring John Travolta, fresh from *Saturday*

3. *Grease* moves to the suburbs. Courtesy of Paramount Pictures/Wisconsin Center for Film and Theater Research.

Night Fever, and featuring a new disco title song written by Barry Gibb of the Bee Gees.[77] The film moved the action from an urban setting to the suburbs of Southern California, and retained little of the parodic knowingness of the play. It did retain, however, a rare presentation of a bad girl, sympathetically played by Stockard Channing, as a precursor to feminism.

The Buddy Holly Story (1978) inspired a reawakening of interest in the singer's music, which had not received much attention during the height of the Fifties revival, perhaps because Holly did not fit into the prevalent greaser, rockabilly, and African-American strains highlighted in rock and roll nostalgia.[78] Cover versions of Holly songs yielded hits for Linda Ronstadt and other

late-1970s performers. The film also was the first of an intermittently produced series of films on Fifties rock heroes, particularly ones who came to
tragic ends. John Carpenter's television biopic *Elvis* (1979) was well received,
and Hollywood eventually followed with films on Richie Valens (*La Bamba,*
1987) and Jerry Lee Lewis (*Great Balls of Fire,* 1989).

CONCLUSION

By the late 1970s the revival of the Fifties had lost its cultural energy.
Happy Days and *Laverne and Shirley* continued on for a few more years, but
their sense of freshness and cultural power diminished. Fifties-themed productions have enjoyed momentary, isolated success in the intervening years
(the Stray Cats in the early 1980s, reunion shows of 1950s series such as *Leave
It to Beaver,* and continued interest in the lives of Marilyn Monroe and James
Dean), but these have not been sufficient to create another large-scale revival.
The Fifties has taken its place as a source of material for the ever-churning
maw of popular culture, but as cultural productions from more recent decades
have become defined as objects of nostalgia, 1950s entertainment has lost
much of its special resonance as the repository of the past.

Rather, the resuscitation of Fifties themes has occurred since 1980 primarily in the realm of electoral politics and discussions of public policy. The
definitions of the 1950s put forward by conservatives do not bear exact correspondence to the meanings of the era that circulated in the 1970s—indeed,
conservatives embrace the rigid gender roles that were identified as the worst
aspects of Fifties experience by many commentators in the 1970s. Conservatives have also largely ignored the argument that the youth music of the 1950s
should be seen as a precursor to the social trends of the Sixties. Conservative
discourse, however, has borrowed the same narrowness of retrospective vision
that marked 1970s depictions of the Eisenhower era. Conservative articulations have continued the emphasis on the centrality, stability, and beneficence
of family life that *Happy Days* brought forward. Political nostalgia has also
played on the notions of Fifties personal and social innocence that circulated
even among some countercultural participants in the Sixties-based social
movements that conservatives oppose.

In these ways, the Fifties cultural boom in the 1970s, which first emerged
out of Sixties youth counterculture, set the stage for a conservative attack on
the social policies and movements of the 1960s. The ascription of personal and
social innocence, with its accompanying sense of personal security and
national superiority, is reasserted in conservative discourse as desirable,
achievable, and sustainable, rather than as essentially illusory and as fleeting as
childhood. The Fifties cultural revival in the 1970s was in the spirit of a visit
to the past, but the political revival of the Fifties in succeeding decades would
have us return to that era to stay.

CHAPTER 2

The Conservative Uses of Nostalgia

THE FIFTIES REVIVAL in the 1970s put into social circulation a set of cultural markers and concepts that came to define the decade of the 1950s in public discourse. In the creation of such definitions, implicit and explicit comparisons between the 1950s and the 1960s were commonplace. The Fifties and the Sixties were reified as opposing social environments. With the election of Ronald Reagan to the presidency in 1980, the comparisons between the two decades took on a more political cast, as the Sixties and their aftermath became fodder for a new conservative rhetorical and policy offensive. In particular, the feminist movement, government social spending and regulation, and opposition to the Vietnam War were brought together to stand for how the nation had changed since the Eisenhower era. This revisiting of the Sixties came not from its celebrants but from its most vociferous critics— social conservatives, free-market advocates, and neoconservatives whose turn to the right had been precipitated by the rise of the New Left and the counterculture. These conservatives, who had varying social origins and ideological emphases, all came to associate the 1950s with stable family structures, freedom from an intrusive government, and American dominance internationally. They asserted that the Sixties derailed both the dynamic movement of American history and the (ordinarily) unchanging values of American society, leading to the economic decline and social malaise of the 1970s. They called for the renunciation of Great Society programs, the stifling of social movements associated with the Sixties, and a return to the social values and public policy of the Fifties, so as to restore the nation's economic vitality and social equilibrium. Conservatives, asserting that supporters of Sixties political and cultural movements had ventured out of the mainstream of American history, invoked conservative memories of the 1950s in the hopes of establishing an antiliberal coalition wielded together by nostalgia for a simpler time.

Legislative battles, federal rule making, religious jeremiads, and economic tomes generated by conservative think tanks all contributed to a conservative ideological offensive organized around notions of decline and renewal, of tracing an American historical trajectory that encompassed the lives of American voters. In this chronology, the post–World War II years loomed as a golden age of domestic tranquility both in individual homes and in the Republic as a whole. Economic growth was configured as a result of individual effort and laissez-faire government policy. The United States had been up to the challenges of the Cold War and economic development. In this view, the Sixties destroyed American optimism and assertiveness, and the social and economic order was damaged nearly beyond repair. This damage was caused by the disruptions of racially inflected urban violence, an unwarranted and misguided increase in federal spending to eradicate poverty, the challenge to the Cold War anticommunist consensus by the movement against the Vietnam War, and the feminist challenge to traditional gender roles. The years since the 1960s had been characterized by the dissolution of families, a descent into hedonism and irresponsibility, and a disordering of natural hierarchies and social roles. Until the election of Ronald Reagan, the United States seemed no longer able to respond to international challenges to its position.

The figure of Reagan himself evoked the Fifties, the era when he first began to appear regularly on television and that seemed to define his personal style. Reagan had long railed against many of the defining features of the Sixties, going back to his first campaign for governor of California, when he made denunciations of student protests at the University of California at Berkeley a cornerstone of his campaign.[1] He had opposed the major civil rights legislation enacted during the Johnson administration, was a staunch hawk on Vietnam, and criticized the growth of the federal government and its social welfare programs.[2] Political and social nostalgia for the seemingly simpler and triumphant decade of the 1950s became an integral part of the conservative ideological offensive that characterized the Reagan presidency. Reagan's effectiveness as a leading symbol of social and cultural nostalgia imbued the conservative political offensive with an overarching sense of a national return to an earlier age, after a period of American decline. By capturing the presidency, the ideologists of nostalgia were able to generate media accounts of the historical meanings of the 1950s and 1960s and the relevance of those meanings to many aspects of American life—far beyond the cultural fads of the 1970s. Conservatives, however, compiled only a mixed record of success in passing a legislative agenda and putting into place federal policies based on their paeans to the past.

THE 1980 ELECTION

During the 1980 campaign, historical themes emerged as only a small part of the public debate. In the televised Republican reply to Jimmy Carter's 1980 State of the Union address, Senator Bill Brock charged that time had passed liberalism by, that the Democratic party was a "party of old answers and old ideas—out of touch—but the ideas of the 1960s don't work anymore."[3] Republican candidates themselves, however, tended to take aim at the Carter administration specifically, rather than the Democratic tradition, in their attempt to unseat the incumbent. Reagan's campaign focused on laying blame for America's domestic and international troubles—high unemployment coupled with high inflation, oil shortages, and the taking of Americans as hostages in Iran—specifically on the Carter administration, and thereby did little to bring older political or social debates into public discussion. The campaign was focused on the late 1970s, as Reagan and other Republicans constructed a narrative of decline that forswore connecting the immediate past to longer-term trends, in order to emphasize Carter's failed leadership.[4]

The few instances when Reagan did invoke the conflicts of the 1960s, however, were noteworthy for enunciating themes that came to be emphasized by conservatives after his election. In August 1980 Reagan visited Philadelphia, Mississippi—the site of the 1964 murder of civil rights workers James Chaney, Andrew Goodman, and Michael Schwerner, a crime that had transfixed the country and come to symbolize segregationist violence. In his speech in Philadelphia, the candidate pledged his support for "states' rights," a key rallying cry of the segregationist movement in the 1960s.[5] A few days later, he addressed the Veterans of Foreign Wars to state that the American war in Vietnam had been a "noble cause," and blamed the government for timid prosecution of the war.[6] In October he told the National Religious Broadcasters convention that "I don't think we should have ever expelled God from the classroom," criticizing the Supreme Court 1962 decision that ended mandated prayer in public schools.[7]

These implicit attacks on three of the most salient political incursions of the Sixties—the civil rights movement, the antiwar movement, and the Warren Court's invalidation of traditional political and social practices—were in keeping with criticisms of the Sixties that were lodged by other conservatives and that became amplified after Reagan's electoral victory. The Republican right, from whence Reagan came, had seen three newly prominent groups expand its ranks in the late 1970s: social conservatives, advocates of supply-side economic theories, and neoconservatives. Social conservatives had a base in southern fundamentalism, although they tried to expand their appeal to northern antiabortion forces and traditionally Democratic white ethnic voters in the North. Religious leaders such as Jerry Falwell and Pat Robertson rose to prominence among social conservatives, but other leaders in the movement were more secular political activists, such as antifeminist Phyllis Schlafly, fundraiser Richard Viguerie, and Washington lobbyist Paul Weyrich. Supply-side pro-business advocates, led by Congressmen Jack Kemp and David Stockman, were more concerned about economic issues, pushing for major tax cuts and cuts in federal spending. Some of the supply-siders were socially conservative as well, but others tended to be more libertarian in their thinking on social issues. Finally, neoconservatives wrote on social and foreign policy; many of them had once been on the left or in the Democratic party, and had their base in New York intellectual circles.

The various tendencies within the Republican right thus differed in their origins and social and ideological significance, but they could unite in agreement that the Sixties had been disastrous for the nation. Their criticisms seemed to encompass the entire complex of politics, social trends, and cultural changes that had become associated with the Sixties and their aftermath. In keeping with these criticisms, a revalidation of the Fifties surfaced in public affairs, along with praise of other, earlier decades of American life.

THE CONSERVATIVE COMPLAINT

The conservative attacks on the Sixties reflected the interconnected yet diverse social and intellectual groupings on the right. Religious leaders and other social conservatives inveighed against the social movements of the Sixties and their legacies, as well as cultural manifestations rooted in the Sixties counterculture. Supply-side economic advocates criticized increased social spending by the federal government, identifying such spending with Lyndon Johnson's Great Society programs. Neoconservatives bemoaned the decline of an interventionist, anticommunist foreign policy, done in, they claimed, by the anti–Vietnam War movement and the capture of the Democratic party by left-wing elites. By identifying the Sixties with the loss of American domestic tranquility, economic growth, and international dominance, conservatives were able to articulate their disparate issues into a common agenda and imbue it with a sense of national renewal.

On the eve of the 1980 election, James Q. Wilson announced in the conservative journal *Commentary* that "the Reagan movement is animated in large part by a desire to contain and force back the legacy of the 60's, and many of the movement's members are hoping to make clear that those who challenge traditional values must be prepared—as most are not—to pay a high price."[8] The challengers to traditional values were most often identified by conservatives as participants in the feminist and gay liberation movements, a racialized underclass characterized as the legatees of the civil rights movement, and "secular humanists" noted for their moral relativism and disparagement of religious orthodoxy.

Feminism and Families

The movements most intensively attacked by social conservatives were those of feminism and gay liberation, in part because they had gained strength in the 1970s while the struggle for racial equality had clearly lost energy by 1980. The older, established right wing of the Republicans, as organized by William F. Buckley in the 1950s, focused primarily on economic and international issues, promoting fiscal responsibility and the Cold

War. The New Right that arose in the late 1970s distinguished itself (and was distinguished by others) by emphasizing social issues that had gained public prominence over the previous twenty years, particularly those involving gender, sexuality, and religion—the Equal Rights Amendment, abortion, gay and lesbian rights, and prayer in public schools. In so doing, these conservatives wished for a return to what they envisioned as a prefeminist, pre–Warren Court America, marked by strong family structures, moral certainties, and a nonintrusive federal government.[9]

The Fifties cultural revival had been very youth oriented, until *Happy Days* contextualized teenage-boy culture within the constraining but cozy confines of the nuclear family. Social conservatives now defined the 1950s as the high point of American family life. They assigned blame to the feminist and gay liberation movements for much of the damage to the social and familial fabric in recent years. For these conservatives, the institution of the family was the key site of social struggle, with rising divorce rates, feminist challenges to male prerogatives and responsibilities, and sexual practices outside the heterosexual marital bond all contributing to a decline in traditional values.[10] Moral Majority founder Jerry Falwell stated, "We must stand against the Equal Rights Amendment, the feminist revolution, and the homosexual revolution."[11] Indeed, New Right social conservatives first succeeded at mass mobilization in their effort to prevent passage of the Equal Rights Amendment, seen by them as stripping the family of its ability to function both as a site of male leadership and as protection for housewives economically dependent on their husbands. Although anti-ERA leader Phyllis Schlafly had a long history of anticommunist activism on the far right of the Republican party, it was her new emphasis on addressing social issues and attacking feminism that propelled her into national prominence.[12]

In their attacks on feminism, conservatives argued that fundamental and natural differences in gender roles had existed throughout human history but were now elided by feminist assertions of autonomy and careerism. As seen by the right, feminist deviations from inherent, structured gender differences were in keeping with Sixties assaults on traditional social structures and hierarchies that had been crucial to the maintenance of the social order. A hierarchically organized society had been ordained by God, and encouraged personal restraint and disciplined productivity. In his jeremiad *Listen, America!* Falwell calls for the strengthening of hierarchies between men and women, parents and children, and teachers and students—all of which had been attacked in the generation gap of the Sixties or its aftermath.[13] These hierarchies depended upon clearly defined social roles and identities, consigning the values of strength, leadership, and aggression to men, and nurturance, care for others, and obedience to women. Since these differences were justified as created by God, Falwell inscribed them into the highest orders of Creation, sermonizing that "Christ wasn't effeminate. . . . The man who lived on this earth was a man with muscles. . . . Christ was a he-man!"[14]

By treating these distinctions as part of a timeless tradition, social conservatives could naturalize the structured gender roles they championed. By asserting that the timeless tradition had been disrupted only by the advent of the Sixties, they could efface the varying social trends that had affected gender roles throughout American history. The nuclear family as presented in the family sitcoms of the 1950s took on documentary value to illustrate the stable realities of American life before the disruptions of Sixties social movements. Even Allan Carlson, one of the more historically minded social conservatives, traced the changes in public attitudes toward the family through sitcom life: "*Father Knows Best, Leave It to Beaver,* and *I Love Lucy* gave way to *One Day at a Time, Three's Company,* and *Miss Winslow and Son.*" Television series had become easily accessible resources with which to represent the decline of the nuclear family, and the rise of "nontraditional" family forms and single life.[15]

Conservatives asserted a stark distinction between public and private spheres, a distinction that had been targeted for attack by many of the Sixties social movements and epitomized by the feminist claim that "the personal is political."[16] Religious conservatives saw the public world of commerce as based on the hard, impersonal competition of free-market capitalism, which was meant to be balanced by love and selflessness provided by the institution of the family. The family was the private sanctuary of care and religiosity needed by individuals who faced a broader social and economic world marked by harsh isolation and irreligious hedonism. New Right conservatives were hesitant to criticize capitalist institutions directly, except for the occasional boycotts of cultural producers and distributors who created sexual or anti-Christian entertainment. Rather, these critics sought to preserve the family as a haven from what were seen as the necessary difficulties of the economy, as well as to use the family as a training ground for the self-discipline and respect for authority considered essential prerequisites to worldly success and righteous behavior. The feminist assertion of careerism among women threatened to unbalance the delicate equation of public and private by weakening the ability and desire of women to sustain mothering and family life.[17]

Heritage Foundation spokesperson Connaught Marshner complained that the women's movement had created "a new image of women: a drab, macho feminism of hard-faced and hard-hearted women."[18] Career-minded women, shaped to fit the needs of the business world, threatened to poison the private family sphere with inappropriate values. In addition, feminist women were seen as having developed an antimale cantankerousness, as shown in public, political battles against sexism, and as having brought this attitude into the realm of the family, an institution meant to unite individuals and provide private respite from public struggles. Female autonomy thus threatened the moral upbringing of children and the male self-confidence and aggression needed to thrive in a competitive economy.

Men, who were presumed to be more suited naturally to the business world and to be hungry for domestic peace, did not hold the same sort of threat when positioned within the family, especially when balanced by properly feminine women. Conversely, men might have been seen by some New Right women as simply incorrigible; Rebecca Klatch notes in her study of New Right women that conservative housewives considered it their responsibility to provide warmth and care in family life, and worried that career women lacked the requisite unselfishness needed to maintain this feminine role. As Klatch states, "the underlying fear expressed in this critique is the fear of a total masculinization of the world."[19] Thus New Right antifeminism could hold appeal to women who believed themselves properly subordinate to men and to those suspicious of "masculine" values and behavior.

The worrisome intrusion of public values into the private family sphere took several forms beyond female careerism and insubordination. The continuing importance of rock music, drugs, and sexualized mass media entertainment in youth culture led social conservatives to worry that children were being bombarded by antitraditional values held over from the Sixties counterculture and its rejection of discipline, obedience, and self-restraint.[20] The federal government was also identified as a threat, first by its banning of organized school prayer, then by its curricular suggestions to local school boards (on subjects such as sex education), attempts to mandate busing for school integration, and legalization of abortion.

The threat of the government to family life went beyond specific issues, however, and seemed in large part to stem from the government's apparent capture by secular humanists who scoffed at traditional religious values. Religious conservatives had urged the Carter administration to sponsor a conference on ways to strengthen the idea of the traditional family, and expected the born-again Carter to be sympathetic. Under pressure from feminists, the administration transformed the meeting into one supportive of nontraditional family forms. Conservatives felt betrayed, charging that the federal government had been covertly taken over by Sixties-style social radicals.[21]

In the conservative policy journal *The Public Interest*, Allan Carlson enunciated the attack on federal policies regarding families in the name of traditional, pre-Sixties values.[22] Carlson identifies the years from 1946 to 1960 as a halcyon period for the nuclear family, accompanied by rapid gains in prosperity. Unlike other commentators, Carlson does not take for granted the naturalness of the nuclear family; rather, he argues that, while desirable, the nuclear form needs support from the government to thrive. Carlson concedes that the nuclear family as a haven of healthy relationships was never predominant in American society, but considers it as an important normative standard that gained strength through institutional support in the post–World War II era. The nuclear family had come increasingly into crisis, however, starting in the 1960s, with a growing divorce rate, drug use among the young, and confusion regarding gender roles. Carlson blames the therapeutic state for family instability, as family counselors and social workers within Great Society programs led the way toward toleration of other relational forms of domestic life. With the federal government's withdrawal of necessary support, the nuclear norm withered in the face of the Sexual Revolution, leftist attacks on traditional social forms, the feminist movement, media cynicism, and the increasing antitraditionalism of the liberal Protestant churches.

Race, Civil Rights, and Social Programs

The first major social movement of the 1960s had been the civil rights struggle. Conservatives of the Reagan era rarely criticized the civil rights movement directly, although some had opposed it in the past. The ethos of equal opportunity and desegregation that had marked the movement at its height in the early and mid-1960s had attained hegemonic status in American politics, though white supremacist logic could still undergird appeals to white populations.

Falwell's history was a common one—as a minister in Virginia during the conflicts over segregation, he had sermonized against political activism by African-American religious leaders such as Martin Luther King, Jr., had led an all-white church and founded an all-white school, and had spoken of "the alleged discrimination against Negroes in the South."[23] By 1980, however, he described King as "noble" and claimed inspiration from King and other ministers on the left for his own entrance into political activism, which had gone against a decades-long fundamentalist Christian aversion to such worldliness.[24] Falwell claimed to support equal opportunity policies while opposing affirmative action, and to reject racial bigotry while lacing his sermons with phrases such as "welfare chiselers," "urban rioters," and "crime in the streets," whose meanings would not be lost on his Lynchburg, Virginia, congregation.[25] Along with the nontraditionalist White House Conference on Families, the Carter administration had earned the enmity of the Christian right for its lack of sympathy for Christian institutions that had segregationist roots. The secular nature of the federal government was particularly felt as a threat when the Internal Revenue Service began questioning white, southern religious schools' tax-exempt status in the late 1970s, pursuant to laws denying such status to racially segregated organizations. (Christian right educators saw such laws as products of the 1960s, as indeed they were—but they had remained largely unenforced during the Nixon and Ford presidencies.)[26]

Conservative activists and writers began to couch racial appeals in terms of traditional values, which were said to be lost within a black underclass abetted by a government shot through with liberal, secular humanist perspectives. The continuing poverty among African Americans, they charged, was the result of the Great Society programs started by Lyndon Johnson in the mid-1960s, which had rewarded indolence, nontraditional family structures, and parasitism. Feminism and the Sexual Revolution also contributed to poverty by their destruction of the nuclear family, defined as the only viable economic and spiritual framework for individual achievement. This articulation of feminism, the decline of traditional values, and federal efforts to end poverty was brought into public discussion most forcefully by George Gilder.[27]

In little-noticed books published in the 1970s, Gilder had charged that feminism had destroyed men's chances for responsible maturity by weakening marital pressures on men to become hard-working providers for wives and children.[28] After the Reagan election, Gilder published *Wealth and Poverty*, which quickly gained prominence as a quasi-official pronouncement on the moral dimension of supply-side Reaganomics.[29] (David Stockman, appointed budget director by Reagan, had advised Gilder in the writing of the book, and promoted it around the White House.)[30] From the outset, Gilder asserts that the antipoverty programs initiated by the Johnson administration had all foundered by encouraging financial dependency on government and abetting the dissolution of families.

For Gilder, poverty persists because the current generation of poor people is "refusing to work hard."[31] By reducing benefits for the poor, the government will force welfare recipients to straighten up and lead more moral lives, resisting the desires that lead them to drugs, crime, and family breakups. "All of these social problems are ultimately erotic," Gilder stated in the 1970s, and in *Wealth and Poverty*, he offers a solution: "The only dependable route from poverty is always work, family, and faith."[32] He dismisses the reasons offered by liberals to explain poverty—racial discrimination, lack of educational opportunities, the loss of blue-collar jobs in the declining industrial economy of the 1970s—as irrelevant; only a traditional family structure provides the proper impetus for men to work, and once instilled, the drive to be a provider ultimately can conquer any obstacle. He refuses to address the efficacy of large-scale social spending and government policies in the building of the American economy; policies such as the GI Bill, western and suburban development, and government-mandated doubling of industrial capacity during World War II are rhetorically effaced by hypothetical stories of individual drift or determination. By dismissing structural inequalities and long-term macroeconomic trends, Gilder removes the rationale for government intervention into the "private" economy, and relocates meaningful economic activity to the individual family unit, the hard-working striver, and the creative entrepreneur.

Other conservative economic manifestos of the time, such as Jude Wanniski's *The Way the World Works*, William Simon's *A Time for Truth*, Milton Friedman and Rose Friedman's *Freedom to Choose* (also a Public Broadcasting System miniseries), and Charles Murray's *Losing Ground*, all shared Gilder's rejection of federal social spending and his call for a return to policies that predated Johnson's presidency, if not Franklin Roosevelt's.[33] Roosevelt's New Deal had inaugurated the idea in the United States that responsibility for the functioning of the economy ultimately lies with the federal government, following the principles set down after World War I by John Maynard Keynes. Although this claim continued to be debated over the decades, the 1960s had seen Keynes's followers seemingly achieve final victory in asserting the government's right (and need) to offer leadership on financial matters. At the beginning of the 1970s Richard Nixon had proclaimed, "Now I am a Keynesian," marking a bipartisan consensus on the efficacy of deficit spending and other New Deal hallmarks.[34] Only the sector of the far right that was libertarian in its economics remained unconvinced; its political leader was Ronald Reagan.[35]

From the position of consensus Keynesianism, it was a small step to the justification of government regulation of specific economic sectors and the intensification of benefit programs. The Kennedy administration had expanded Social Security and unemployment insurance—two popular features of the New Deal—and had instituted Medicare along similar lines. The Johnson administration had continued the expansion of eligibility for such universal programs, and had also introduced or expanded more directly means-based programs such as Food Stamps, Aid for Dependent Children (AFDC), Women, Infants, and Children nutritional support (WIC), Medicaid, and public housing assistance. (Means-based programs are those whose benefits are targeted toward recipients with specific income levels—usually the poor and near-poor exclusively.) The Nixon administration, under pressure from a Democratic Congress, had also signed off on continuing universal and means-based programs, and had increased their benefit levels and expanded their eligibility bases.[36] Now, in the early 1980s, conservatives took issue with the ideological basis for New Deal–type intervention by the government and, particularly, with the post-1964 move toward direct payments and assistance to the non-aged poor.

Conservative writers focused on social trends and government policies that they attributed to Lyndon Johnson's Great Society and War on Poverty efforts in the mid-1960s. They mixed rhetorics of moral opprobrium, compassion, and theoretical certitude into their analyses of poverty, government spending, and social phenomena. They castigated the poor, whom they often configured as African American, drug dependent, irresponsible in childbearing and parenting, and devoid of a sense of responsibility for their behavior.

Writers placed ultimate responsibility for underclass pathology, however, on white, liberal elites in control of government programs, think tanks, and media outlets, who excused such behavior and rewarded it financially. Conservatives could escape from charges of beating up on the (racially specific) poor by saving their heaviest criticism for white bureaucrats; they showed their compassion for the poor by charging liberals with the infliction of continued poverty on the underclass through failed government policies.

According to this argument, liberals from the New Deal onward had lost sight of the power of the market to create prosperity. The social conservatives tended to separate the world of commerce from the private world of the family, but supply-siders configured the market as sharing the private sphere of individual action with the family, to separate the economic system from the public sphere of government they wished to curtail. Further, conservatives charged that the attack on traditional virtues in the 1960s had led liberal social policy to wander from the eternal verities of human (or at least American) behavior, from the hard-headed producer values of self-restraint, sacrifice, and hard work that resulted in wealth. By stressing the importance of moral character in the creation of personal success, conservatives linked the corporate manager with the blue-collar worker, each assumed to share the values of hard work and autonomy of character. They also shared, in this view, a burden imposed by liberal bureaucrats, who attacked producer values and the efficiencies of the market in the name of the poor.

Keynesianism had fallen into crisis in the simultaneous inflation and high unemployment of the 1970s, and conservatives now took the opportunity to rail against its emphases on government action, borrowing money, and macroeconomic measures that obscured individual economic pursuits. They charged that liberals' deviation from the values of free enterprise, thrift, and American individualism had come at the expense of the poor they had purported to help, as well as those just above the poor on the economic and social ladder.

The 1960s had been a decade of solid economic growth in the United States. The conservative writers gave credit to Kennedy for a sizable tax cut in 1962 (though some preferred to laud Republicans in Congress for forcing Kennedy's hand), which they argued was responsible for the surge in economic activity, and some claimed to have learned from Kennedy's success in their own calls for large tax cuts in the 1980s. Their criticism of Kennedy-era initiatives such as Medicare and expanded Social Security was muted in the face of the continuing popularity of these programs. Their main attacks targeted the means-based programs started by Johnson and the increasing share of the federal budget that social spending took in the 1970s. They argued against the effectiveness of these programs with the claim that poverty had been reduced by the effects of the overall growth in the economy from the mid-1940s to the late 1960s, but then the poverty rate had begun to stagnate just when benefit increases rose to new levels.

These arguments met with objections from supporters of the programs. As in most arguments concerning the economy, different sets of statistics were employed by the two sides to prove their cases. Supporters of the programs claimed, for instance, that the poverty rate had continued to fall throughout most of the 1970s, though at a slower rate than during the high-growth 1960s. Liberals treated all government benefits as income in determining the number of people falling into income categories defined as impoverished; conservatives tended to be more restrictive in what they defined as poor people's income, resulting in higher numbers of people defined as poor.[37]

When it suited their arguments, economic conservatives collapsed virtually all domestic spending programs under the rubric of Johnson's Great Society campaign, which had been characterized by urban renewal, neighborhood development efforts, the creation of the domestic VISTA corps modeled on the Peace Corps, and increased financial assistance to the poor. They castigated the urban programs as corrupt boondoggles run for the benefit of a centralized Washington bureaucracy, although Johnson's original program emphasized community-run efforts.[38] A favorite rhetorical device was to divide the amount of social spending by the federal government in the 1970s by the number of poor Americans, yielding a high per capita total. Because poverty had not been eradicated, the writers argued or implied that the money must have been wasted by liberal bureaucrats, pilfered by scam artists, or spent unwisely by the lawful recipients. In such calculations, they effaced the difference between antipoverty programs such as AFDC and Food Stamps and universal programs such as Social Security and Medicare.[39] The latter took up by far the largest part of federal social spending, and only a portion of their totals went to the poor. Thus the increased aging of the population and federal benefits for senior citizens in the 1970s became numerical fodder to exaggerate the fiscal impact and profligacy of 1960s social policies toward the poor. In terms of 1980s federal budgets, programs specific to Johnson's Great Society were fairly small, but conservatives were successful in creating the impression that vast sums had been squandered with no positive result.

Some differences existed among the popular economic writers, and these are reflected in their slightly varying judgments on twentieth-century American history. All of them, however, share the narrative of liberal overreaching, economic decline, and national loss of moral compass since the mid-1960s. George Gilder puts great emphasis on the feminist challenge to the family and focuses on economic declines in the 1970s, although he also criticizes Johnson administration social policy. Jude Wanniski, the foremost popularizer of supply-side economics from his position at the *Wall Street Journal*, makes tax cuts and free markets central to his program, and goes back to tariff policy in the 1920s and New Deal taxation practices to trace American economic decline; he identifies 1966 as the year the economy went into a final spin, as the impact of Kennedy's 1962 tax cut was destroyed by new increases in taxes and spending on the Vietnam War.[40] Milton Friedman, who had been preaching free market doctrine for decades, also targets both the New Deal foundations and the Great Society reforms for attack, whereas Irving Kristol, a neoconservative apostate from the left, supports federal spending on the poor within politically palatable universal programs and thus celebrates the economic legacy of Kennedy's policies in the early 1960s, while disagreeing with targeted programs specifically for the poor, which expanded under Johnson.[41]

In linking economic status to moral behavior, criticizing the impact of federal policies on individuals and families in the private sphere, and leaning for evidence on anecdotes of a racial underclass, the free-marketers and supply-siders constructed a rhetorical field they could also share with the social and religious right, their allies in the Reagan movement. Their common rejection of the legacies of the Sixties, whether in regard to economic policies, social movements, or cultural trends, helped to cement the alliance by offering a clear chronology by which adversaries could be located, victories and defeats tallied, and turning points identified. Reagan also made the unifying links explicit, as in a nationally broadcast commercial during the 1982 elections, when he blamed "big spenders" for both causing inflation and ending prayer in public schools. This identification of Great Society economic programs with Warren Court antitraditionalist edicts served to define the Sixties as a wholesale, multifaceted attack on the national polity.[42]

By linking white liberals with a black underclass, the economic writers could re-create a dynamic common during the white southern resistance to the civil rights movement, when white southerners resented the interference by white northerners who used the powers of the federal government to end segregation. In this parallel move, supply-siders and free-market advocates could turn white resentment of welfare benefits for African Americans into an assault on antibusiness liberals. Although the writers all refrain from criticism of the desegregation movement, and some identify racism as a central problem of pre-1965 American life, they rearticulate forbidden racial resentment by whites into a status resentment against liberal defenders of the welfare state, the policy critics' adversaries in Washington political circles and academia.[43]

The ability to link supply-side and free-market ideologies to a moralistic nostalgia for previous eras of economic growth and white supremacy was a key to cementing the Reagan coalition. The ensuing conversion to Reaganomics of a significant portion of the northern white working and lower-middle class had been foreshadowed by the move of southern working-class whites away from Democratic economic policies during the civil rights era. Before the 1960s, southern, working-class whites had generally been the third most liberal facet of the New Deal coalition on economic issues, after African Americans and Jews.[44] Southern white resentment of the Kennedy and Johnson administrations' support for civil rights began to be reflected in increasingly conservative economic positions, although such movement was not entirely consistent or complete by 1980. Northern blue-collar whites had lagged in their abandonment of Democratic economics, with a breach not evident until the late 1970s.[45] Conservatives linked their attacks on social spending and their support for tax cuts for the wealthy to an earlier era of economic growth, less turbulent gender and racial relations, and simple moral truths. The Reaganomic proselytizers brought the cultural nostalgia generated in the 1970s into the policy debates about federal budget categories, Department of Health and Human Services regulations, and the structure of tax brackets.

Vietnam and the Cold War

The final social movement of the Sixties that came under attack by conservatives was the campaign for American withdrawal from Vietnam. This attack was spearheaded by Reagan himself, along with neoconservatives who hailed the 1950s as a period of anticommunist certitude and who called for a return to Cold War assertiveness in pursuing American interests abroad. Many of the neoconservatives had battled Stalinism as members of Trotskyist, socialist, and democratic left organizations starting back in the 1930s, and they continued their distrust of Soviet leadership after abandoning most of their left-wing positions in the 1960s and 1970s.[46]

After a general absence of public discussion of the war following the withdrawal of American troops in 1973 and the victory of Hanoi-led forces in 1975, the Vietnam War began to be revisited culturally in the late 1970s, with popular, high-profile films such as *The Deer Hunter* and *Coming Home* detailing the plight of American veterans of the conflict.[47] In the political and journalistic spheres, conservatives once again initiated a reconsideration of a crucial issue of the 1960s. Conservatives linked American defeat in Vietnam to liberal control of the federal government and the unruly Sixties counterculture. They warned that antimilitarism by liberals had continued throughout the 1970s, leading to a weakened posture toward the Soviet Union. The defeat in Southeast Asia heralded a decline in American power internationally, which was dramatically demonstrated by the oil crises of the 1970s and the taking of American hostages by forces associated with the Ayatollah Khomeini in Iran. Conservatives urged the United States to regain its military toughness to counter the Soviet Union and other hostile forces, and cautioned that the dovishness of liberal elites continued to betray American interests in world affairs.[48]

Although many commentators on the right made mention of the Vietnam debacle, neoconservatives such as *Commentary* editor Norman Podhoretz produced the most elaborate arguments regarding Vietnam's impact, in concert with Republican politicians, particularly Reagan himself. In a number of books and articles in the late 1970s and early 1980s, Podhoretz bemoans the influence of the antiwar left in insidiously spreading a dovish defeatism throughout the nation in the face of a continuing threat by the Soviet Union.[49] He hopes to revive a strong bipartisan anticommunism that had been forged in the late 1940s, which he credits with providing a sense of purpose to the nation, a surge of social energy, and a prosperous economy, culminating in John Kennedy's adventurous, idealistic belligerence. Podhoretz blames the Vietnam experience for the move away from the Kennedy policy of rolling back Soviet power. Richard Nixon's policy of détente and containment, whereby American troops could avoid combat by the use of proxy wars to stymie new Soviet offenses, while the Soviet Union was allowed to achieve military parity, is portrayed as an understandable but unfortunate retreat. Even this partial retreat is not secure, however, in the face of Soviet aims to achieve military dominance, abetted by American liberals' and leftists' anti-Americanism and sympathy for indigenous, pro-Soviet communist movements around the world.

Podhoretz, who had been part of the antiwar left in the 1960s, argues that American troops should not have been sent to Vietnam at all, because the cost to the United States was too great in waging an unwinnable war. He insists, however, that American motives were "born of noble ideals and impulses," and that the debacle should not deter aggressive pursuit of democratic interests in the future.[50] He identifies a contemporary "culture of appeasement" as a legacy of the Vietnam experience, akin to that of the British facing Hitler in the 1930s. The new American culture of appeasement is led by liberal policy elites, academic and cultural intellectuals, and homosexuals, united in their contempt for middle-class Americans and ready to allow the Soviet Union to dominate the globe.[51]

Many conservatives charged that the war had been fought "with one arm behind our back," echoing Gen. William Westmoreland's complaint that civilian politicians had limited the ability of military commanders in the field to wage war.[52] Ronald Reagan had begun making this claim as early as 1974, while campaigning against George McGovern's reelection to the Senate, seemingly placing blame for the debacle on doves like McGovern who had urged the government to withdraw.[53] Questioned intently by reporter Elizabeth Drew on the subject during the 1980 presidential campaign, both Reagan and fellow hawk George H. W. Bush conceded that American troop involvement in the war was a mistake from the start, because the war was unwinnable, which would make the Westmoreland charge moot if not wrongheaded.[54] On the stump, however, Reagan sketched narratives of brave, patriotic troops betrayed by the liberals who sent them to fight in the first place.[55]

The emphasis on the tragic results of a "limited" war seemed to point toward the (usually unspecified) liberal-imposed limitations on military strategy themselves as the cause for the tragedy. By focusing on the "noble impulses" of American militarism (as enunciated by Podhoretz) and on the courageous qualities of individual soldiers, Reagan could sidestep questions on the wisdom of the war that could have buttressed dovish positions, without stating exactly what more he would have done to win it. A public that had come to largely oppose the war and was still highly leery of American ground troops fighting in other countries was not likely to welcome an attempt to rhetorically reenact Vietnam combat strategy, especially one that promoted an even deeper commitment of resources toward the war. Reagan's insistence on the righteousness of the effort, however, moved to absolve the nation of guilt over the destruction in Vietnam and the American troops' haunting experiences during the war, and yet also to conflate the Johnson and Kennedy administration liberals, who had unwisely (if "nobly") started the war, with the campus protesters who had opposed it. This pairing of civilian officials and Sixties radicals was then put into opposition to the mainstream American "boys" and families who had to face the consequences of the war.[56] Reagan's criticism of both Vietnam policy and the protesters who opposed the war evoked a nostalgia for a past America that won its wars and displayed political and social unity while doing so, particularly, implicitly, in World War II. In order to gain support for a renewed Cold War against the totalitarian foe of the postwar era, the Soviet Union, Reagan hoped to harness nostalgia for the successful fight against the totalitarianism of Germany and Japan in the 1940s.

POLITICAL NOSTALGIA IN ACTION: THE REALM OF PUBLIC POLICY

Once Ronald Reagan took office, his administration took steps to put conservative nostalgia into action within economic, social, and foreign policies. The focus of the administration was on its economic package, which combined increases in military spending, cuts in domestic social welfare programs, and tax decreases. The financial and military restructurings took precedence over the social issues pressed by the New Right. The Reagan administration enjoyed significant political capital in its first months, generated by Reagan's electoral victory, the concomitant takeover of the Senate by Republicans, a cowed Democratic party, and Reagan's survival of the attempt on his life in March 1981 by John Hinckley.[57] Yet even with such strengths, the administration had to be aware that polls showed most Reagan voters had chosen him mainly as an alternative to Carter, and that the public disagreed with the new president on many points.[58] Issues such as abortion and prayer in public schools were seen by the administration as too divisive, likely to face significant opposition in Congress, and fundamentally unchangeable without amending the Constitution. Reagan and his associates preferred to spend their political capital on changing federal budget priorities and taxation policies.[59] As Trent Lott, then a leader of the Republicans in the House of Representatives, said, "It's economics, strictly economics. We're not talking about abortion or busing, we're talking about budget controls, spending cuts, and tax rate cuts."[60]

Reagan domestic aide Martin Anderson, a major contributor to the administration's policies on social spending, claimed that the proposed budget for the 1982 fiscal year, the first to be created by the Republicans, did not constitute a rollback to spending levels or priorities of earlier eras.[61] Reagan's agenda was not to cut social welfare spending, he argued, but merely to control its continued growth. Anderson also saw Reagan's budget as targeting the upper end of the social welfare scale, to reduce government benefits to affluent citizens in the 1982 budget. Budget director David Stockman was particularly adamant on cutting budget items for the middle class and wealthy, to escape charges of unfairness in cutting benefits to the poor as well—although both Reagan and Congress restored most of Stockman's suggested cuts to the middle and upper classes.[62] Critics of the administration countered Anderson's analysis by pointing to Republican plans to make absolute cuts in spending on the poor in later years of the budget process, to allow benefits to stagnate and thus be effectively reduced by inflation, and to mainly cut means-tested programs that served lower income levels.[63]

The administration's proposals, if accepted completely, would have drastically reduced the federal role in combating poverty through direct spending programs. Reagan and Stockman effectively sought to repeal the post–New Deal reforms that had garnered conservative criticism. The two prongs of their strategy were a plan called the "New Federalism" and a budget proposal that eliminated or reduced specific Great Society programs. The New Federalism, in keeping with Reagan's "states' rights" philosophy, would have put total administrative responsibility for two major programs for the poor and near-poor, AFDC and Food Stamps, onto state governments, in exchange for federal compensation for some state spending responsibilities.[64] Historically, the federal government had been more responsive to the demands of minorities than were many state governments, and critics contended that at a time when poverty was associated by many voters with racial and ethnic minorities, state governments would revert to even lower funding levels of poverty programs. Many governors were wary of taking more responsibility for politically unpopular welfare spending; they suggested instead that states take over federal programs for education and transportation, which enjoyed much more widespread voter approval. The stalemate resulted in no great changes in either direction, although federal financial support for some state-administered social programs did decline. Increases in state-level social spending made up for some but not all of the federal cuts.[65]

Other legacies of the Great Society were slated to be dropped altogether, or severely cut back. These included the Job Corps, Head Start, WIC nutrition programs, immunization programs, VISTA, the Legal Services Corporation, and the Community Services Administration.[66] Conservatives charged that these programs, created in the 1960s, were failed attempts at "social engineering," and that the proper treatment of the poor consisted rather in demonstrating that the eternal values of personal initiative and hard work were the only paths out of poverty.[67] The administration also suggested cutting Social Security disability benefits, Social Security pensions for those retiring in years to come, and unemployment compensation, thereby rolling back some of the expansion of "universal" programs that had occurred in the 1960s and early 1970s.[68]

Congress balked at some of these cuts, and positively screamed in bipartisan unison at the idea of cutting either Social Security retirement payments or joblessness benefits that were helping middle-class industrial workers weather the high unemployment levels of the time.[69] Democrats were able to salvage the budgets for the more demonstrably successful Great Society programs, such as Head Start and WIC; agencies such as the Legal Services Corporation were significantly cut back but survived.[70] In general, the administration cuts targeted benefits for the working poor more than for the most desperately impoverished; congressional Democrats worked to ensure that the lowest income levels received continued protection. The result was annual spending reductions of between 27 and 35 billion dollars, mainly from the means-tested programs that benefited the upper ranks of the poor and those marginally better off. Means-tested programs had accounted for 18 percent of federal spending but absorbed 40 percent of the budget cuts.[71]

The neoconservative Nathan Glazer identified the economic package as the final confirmation of the New Deal's presence in America's political economy, in that even Reagan and his associates left most of its structures standing: "The Reagan administration thus represented the complete acceptance of the New Deal welfare state—but not of the Great Society state, or at least not of all of it. Reagan was neither the Goldwater of 1964, nor the Reagan of earlier campaigns, and his victory was that of a conservatism that accepted the major lineaments of the welfare state."[72] Glazer understates the severity of the cuts that the administration had planned for later years if it had met with complete initial success in 1981—there were some in the administration who would have preferred rolling back important aspects of the New Deal as well.[73] Politically, then, it proved possible to attack the Great Society programs of the mid-1960s but not the New Deal and New Frontier programs of earlier times. The country largely accepted a return to Eisenhower and Kennedy spending principles, but was not ready to embrace the economic practices of Calvin Coolidge. Reagan had captured a significant part of the New Deal coalition, but he had not managed, or made a great effort, to destroy Franklin Roosevelt's limited social welfare programs. Rather, he succeeded in cutting back programs associated with the federal response to the civil rights and antipoverty movements of the 1960s.

The budget for the 1982 fiscal year, along with the supply-side restructuring of the tax code, became the economic foundation for the entire Reagan presidency. The administration never succeeded in passing other momentous changes in budget priorities. The 1981–82 recession, accompanied by Reagan's lowered public approval ratings, weakened his position with Congress, which restored many of the cuts targeting middle-class benefits in 1982. It also restored some of the taxes that had been cut in 1981.[74] (Some of those tax cuts had actually originated with congressional Democrats trying to outdo the administration in showing their support for business interests.)[75] Democratic victory in the Senate elections of 1986 deepened the stalemate that prevented great changes in any direction; the stasis continued to the end of the Reagan presidency and throughout George Bush's term in office. Remnants of the Great Society remained in the form of direct payments to the very poor, Medicaid health coverage, Head Start educational programs, and Food Stamps and nutrition programs. These allocations, however, did not enjoy the political legitimacy that kept pre-1965 universal programs such as Social Security, Medicare, and unemployment compensation from ongoing political attack.

Reagan personnel policies also lurched toward pre-1965 norms. After the Carter administration had elevated women and members of racial minorities to decision-making positions in new numbers, Reagan hired few women or people of color at the subcabinet level.[76] Layoffs of federal employees due to budget cuts hit these groups of workers particularly hard. Women administrators were laid off at 150 percent the rate of men in similar positions; minority workers at all levels were laid off at a 50 percent greater rate than nonminorities. The number of women and minorities named to federal judgeships fell drastically.[77]

In specific instances, the administration was prepared to hire individuals whose opposition to the social movements of the 1960s was particularly egregious. M. E. Bradford, a longtime segregationist whose writings on the Confederacy continued to defend the concept of states' rights to the point of seeming to condone slavery, was suggested to head the National Endowment for the Humanities. His name had been put forward by social conservatives, and he was the leading candidate for the NEH post until neoconservatives objected and alerted the administration, Congress, and the press that Bradford had written nasty things about Abraham Lincoln. In this internecine fight between those on the right with leftist roots against those with segregationist roots, the New York intellectuals prevailed over the southern right. Bradford was dropped from consideration, and the administration named William Bennett to the position. Bennett, who had published in the neoconservative bastion *Commentary*, had supported the civil rights movement as a college professor in the South in the 1960s.[78] He went on to become a major voice calling for moral renewal in America, based on old-fashioned virtues.

Reagan's nostalgia for pre-Vietnam certainty and the projection of American force around the globe emerged in a significantly increased military budget and the appointment of neoconservatives such as Elliott Abrams and Jeanne Kirkpatrick to visible positions within the foreign policy hierarchy. The CIA, under the direction of William Casey, rehired many agents previously purged following agency scandals that had emerged in the mid-1970s. The administration, however, faced a world different in key respects from that of the post–World War II era. The United States was no longer economically dominant, and the administration had little success in dealing with trade issues. Reagan continued to pursue good relations with China, a nation that had been anathema during earlier periods of the Cold War. The American public still suffered from the "Vietnam psychosis" (in the words of Senator Brock during his 1980 State of the Union rebuttal) that restricted administration ability to send American troops into major battle.[79] Eventually, limited numbers of troops were sent to Lebanon and Grenada with wildly different results, but the administration had to resort to the proxy-war option in combating Marxists in Nicaragua, El Salvador, and Guatemala, in the face of continuing public concern over American policy in Central America. The Lebanon debacle and ensuing Iran-Contra scandal (discussed in chapter five) showed the limitations of American ability to influence events internationally.

Ronald Reagan had made charges that the United States had fallen behind the Soviet militarily into a keystone of his 1980 campaign. The administration commenced a drastic arms buildup immediately upon taking office, redolent of the arms race of the 1950s and 1960s, before the United States and Soviet Union had begun negotiating staged increases in weapons in the SALT talks of the late 1960s and 1970s. Certain figures in the administration, such as civilian defense official Richard Perle and nuclear expert Edward Teller, hoped to regain 1950s-style military superiority over the Soviet Union and urged a consistently confrontational stance; others, such as Secretary of State George Shultz and arms negotiator Paul Nitze, maneuvered for military parity, arms agreements, and an essentially Nixon-style détente.[80] The rise of Mikhail Gorbachev and Soviet perestroika during Reagan's second term strengthened the hands of the relative moderates, and by the end of Reagan's presidency, the old Cold War paradigms were manifestly obsolescent, except, apparently, during the semiannual creation of the Pentagon budget.

Whereas economic and military policy proposals with nostalgic appeal were implemented during the legislative process and in executive-branch decision making, social policies such as abortion, school prayer, and support for prefeminist, heterosexual family norms received far less attention from the administration in its early days. The religious right and its secular allies urged the administration to take the initiative on social issues, but with Reagan and his associates focusing on passage of the economic package, it was left to a handful of Republican senators and representatives, such as Orrin Hatch and Jesse Helms, to introduce legislation to enact the New Right agenda. The Republican Senate held a number of hearings on New Right issues, allowing leaders of the movement to gain public and political attention, but little of their agenda passed into law. On issues such as abortion and school prayer, federal law had been shaped by Supreme Court rulings and could only be changed by recourse to constitutional amendments, whose passage presented insurmountable obstacles. The right did succeed at the margins of such issues, as in narrowing the availability of abortion and guaranteeing student religious groups access to public school facilities.[81]

Its main legislative effort, however, was the Family Protection Act (FPA), a multifaceted bill put together by Paul Weyrich and the right-wing think tank the Heritage Foundation, and introduced in the Senate by Reagan friend Paul Laxalt. The Family Protection Act was meant to stop federal attacks on traditional values, and included tax breaks for those families in which wives did not work outside the home, invalidation of federal laws against domestic abuse, restrictions on teaching about homosexuality in public schools, dismantling of Title 10 gender equity efforts in education, and stronger laws against pornography. Tighter restrictions on the availability of food stamps were thrown in to the FPA for good measure. The Moral Majority, the chief lobbying group for the measure and inexperienced in legislative matters, arranged for portions of the bill to be considered by five different Senate committees, a tactical error that virtually guaranteed its defeat before reaching the Senate floor.[82]

Many New Right proposals were stymied through legislative maneuver by Democrats and socially liberal and moderate northern Republicans, who managed to block bills before members had to make potentially embarrassing votes against old-fashioned values; others were filibustered into oblivion. The powerful business lobbies that were intent on passing Reagan's economic proposals ignored the social issue legislation, and the New Right showed its regional and ideological limitations in failing to commandeer majorities, even when framing its bills as defenses of the normative American family against liberal overreaching.[83]

The religious leaders hoped to create tuition tax credits that would benefit private schools, an initiative that had enjoyed some popularity in Congress in the late 1970s without ever becoming law. A bill to create the credits was reintroduced in 1982, only to find Congress reluctant to add to the massive tax cuts it had passed the previous year—an example of the precedence pro-business issues enjoyed in the capital and their attendant consequences for other items on the conservative agenda.[84]

The New Right, with all its rhetorical bluster and fund-raising abilities, was unable to dominate the administration's domestic policies. The effort to end IRS challenges to segregated schools was initially approved by Reagan, at the urging of Ed Meese, who had the closest ties to the New Right among Reagan's top aides. The move was condemned harshly in the press, however, as redolent of Jim Crow discrimination, and Reagan quickly reversed his position.[85] Meese was consistently outmaneuvered by other Reagan aides, particularly the more pragmatic James Baker, White House chief of staff, and Michael Deaver, Reagan's image consultant, both of whom recognized the contentiousness that major changes in abortion rights and the separation of church and state could cause.[86] Nancy Reagan, protective of her husband's popularity above all, also counseled caution in tackling controversial issues.[87] The New Right rank and file were needed as troops in Republican electoral campaigns, and the top leaders of the party hoped that occasional supportive remarks by Reagan would suffice to inspire the faithful, without much actual legislative progress. Secular right leaders such as Paul Weyrich and Richard Viguerie quickly showed dissatisfaction with such tactics, but religious leaders like Falwell and Pat Robertson remained active in their support for the Reagan presidency.[88]

The most lasting moves to enact the New Right agenda were the appointments of socially conservative judges to the federal judiciary, which received little public attention until the pro-choice majority on the Supreme Court became threatened during the subsequent Bush administration. Civil rights law enforcement also suffered, with an initial 9 percent cut in its budget at the federal level; the Justice Department reduced litigation on discrimination in employment, housing, and education, although Reagan took pains to deny it in public speeches.[89] The right also served as a brake on many legislative and executive-branch proposals that might have lent support to their adversaries. They rooted out supporters of feminist agendas in the federal bureaucracy, affected federal policy on educational curricula, and protested (but did not eliminate) federal response to the AIDS crisis that had begun to claim the lives of thousands of gay men and others.[90] The intensification of criminal penalties for drug possession and sales resulted in the incarceration of thousands of people, particularly members of racial minorities.[91]

The efficacy and limitations of conservative political nostalgia during the early 1980s are shown by the changes in public policy during Reagan's first term. The attempt to roll back the Great Society programs of the mid- and late 1960s met with partial but significant success, but the basic New Deal programs as developed through the early 1960s remained intact. Specific executive-branch policies followed New Right principles, but a Congress still partially controlled by Democrats (and Republicans with socially liberal constituencies) proved resistant to major legislative overhauls along New Right lines. Reagan's judicial appointments offered a better opportunity to counteract the social liberalism that had been pushed by the Warren Court and other federal judges in the generation after World War II.

Reagan evoked the early period of the Cold War in his rhetoric, but mixed adventurous and confrontational militarism with a recognition of the limits of American power characteristic of the Nixon presidency. Like Nixon, Reagan's term in office was also marked by a deviousness to circumvent such limits in the face of liberal opposition, as shown in the Iran–Contra scandal. In the areas of social relations, little legislation was passed, but Reagan's reaffirmation of prefeminist and anticountercultural values had an impact on the era's social tenor.

CONCLUSION

Parlaying the cultural nostalgia for the Fifties that had circulated in the 1970s into the basis for a political offensive in the 1980s, conservatives constructed a narrative of recent American history in which the Fifties and Sixties were counterposed. For conservatives, the Fifties represented social and family stability, free enterprise, and military strength, while the Sixties represented social and family chaos, excessive and injurious government spending, and attacks on nationalist values. They reactivated appeals that had been dormant in public discussion, using memories of struggles for states' rights and against the antiwar left to bolster their coalition. Once in power, the Reagan administration used the appeal of nostalgia to enact the conservative agenda of reduced social spending, resurgent militarism, and social conformity.

When conservative appeals to earlier times were in concert with business interests' priorities, they resulted in significant, public changes in economic policy. In other areas of policy, however, activity that escaped the public eye, such as foreign intrigue and the revamping of the federal judiciary, was more successful in actually enacting the nostalgic agenda than was open struggle in the political sphere. The right enjoyed some legislative, regulatory, legal, and international victories; it was also effective in influencing social trends of the time. It did so, primarily, through the figure of Ronald Reagan.

As discussed in the next chapter, Reagan was ultimately the grand organizing principle of the conservative movement in the 1980s. His personification of an era of American economic and military dominance and assumed social homogeneity, and his enunciation of traditional values and beliefs, communicated the political and social nostalgia that underlay the conservative call for changes along many axes of American life. By his domination of the political discourse, he placed the Republican senses of recent American history at the center of public affairs. Politicians, activists, and other public figures in the political sphere came to position themselves (or be positioned by others) in relation to this conservative historiography of American glory, decline, and renewal. Reagan's evocation of the pre-Sixties past united disparate elements in the conservative coalition. He constituted the public presentation of the movement's themes with more effectiveness than any other contributor to conservative discourse in the 1980s.

CHAPTER 3

Nostalgia Embodied

RONALD REAGAN AS ICON

RONALD REAGAN'S CAPTURE of the presidency in 1980 enabled him to articulate and embody the political nostalgia of the conservative movement that coalesced around him. The preponderance of the attention given to the presidency in American politics and media, abetted by astute media management on the part of Reagan's political team, guaranteed Reagan the central role in the conservative ideological offensive. Although Reagan's actions enjoyed only piecemeal and intermittent support from the majority of the electorate, his ability to control the field of political discourse imbued the conservative movement with his personality, concerns, and image. The president's ideological image was able to make the disparate elements of conservative thinking cohere into a seemingly unified whole. The political stances of his administration were legitimated by his public qualities.[1] Beyond his specific attempts to enact laws and policies redolent of the past, Reagan's influence was felt on the general political and social mood of the nation, through the nostalgia–laden aspects of his public figure.

Reagan's persona evoked the post–World War II period of American international ascendancy, domestic social stability, and militant anticommunism. He embodied older values after an extended period of dislocating social change and challenges to American hegemony. His appeal created the potential for new alliances in the American electoral system, for the creation of a Republican majority to displace the Democratic, New Deal–based coalition that had been intermittently dominant in the postwar era. He played upon notions of the 1950s and 1960s, among other decades, to consolidate this new majority, and to legitimate major changes in federal policies in the guise of respect for tradition. His recitation of iconic themes of American history was dependent on ideas that had been passed down largely through film, television, and other cultural productions. For a period in the mid-1980s, Reagan's project seemed on the way to long-term success; it benefited particularly from an absence of effective counternarratives by the Democratic political opposition. Ultimately Reagan's political nostalgia and attempt to create a permanent Republican majority failed, but left a strong legacy in American politics in the years following his retirement.

REAGAN'S PERSONA AND THE LOOK BACKWARD

Not so long ago, we emerged from a world war. Turning homeward at last, we built a grand prosperity and hopes, from our own success and plenty, to help others less fortunate. Our peace was a tense and bitter one, but in those days, the center seemed to hold. Then came the hard years—riots, assassinations, domestic strife over the Vietnam War, and in the last four years, drift and disaster in Washington. . . . For the first time in our memory, many Americans are asking, "Does history still have a place for America, for her people, for her great ideals?"

—Ronald Reagan, national paid political broadcast, election eve, 1980

The conservative narrative of American glory, decline, and potential revival had its most persuasive spokesperson in Ronald Reagan. Reagan was seen by supporters as embodying, or at least performing, the virtues of the pre-Sixties past, to which the United States should return. Reagan himself used themes from the narrative of national rise and fall throughout his presidential campaigns and administration, situating himself as the protector and promoter of the glories of the American past against those who refused to acknowledge or appreciate them. Reagan's politics were meant to appeal to those sectors of the electorate who saw the Sixties and their aftermath as a direct challenge to their social positions and identities or, at least, as unsettling and traumatic for the nation as a whole. Reagan promised a refashioning of America's course, in accordance with its pre-Sixties direction as it became defined by the conservative movement.

The 1950s were put forward as the stopping point of American historical progress, and functioned in conservative rhetoric as the repository of the accumulated virtues and values of the past. Reagan effectively combined nostalgia for the Fifties with evocations of previous eras as well. His personal embodiment of the past created a cultural logic that acknowledged earlier developments in American experience while locating their ultimate meaning in the Fifties, as the teleological culmination of American domestic prosperity and international dominance.

Several aspects of Reagan's image tied him to meanings of the past. He played upon his small-town roots and rags-to-riches story, and told many stories of days gone by in the Midwest and Hollywood. Older members of the electorate were familiar with Reagan in several public guises, from movie actor to commercial pitchman. He linked himself to previous presidents in his rhetoric, and used imagistic visions of the American past to buttress his points, most of which were based on the political conservativism of a generation earlier. In his public demeanor, professions of conservative personal values, and cultural tastes, Reagan embodied a belief in and yearning for a nation undisturbed by the social controversies and political traumas of post-1963 America.

Reagan's persona and politics were noted for their nostalgic tinges by the time he entered the White House. Commentators during his previous campaigns had emphasized Reagan's tendency to describe the American past in celebratory, Disneyesque tones, going so far as to compare his speeches to those made by the animatronic robots found in Disneyland's and Disneyworld's Hall of Presidents.[2] After his election, *Time* magazine featured Reagan as its Man of the Year with the headline, "Out of the Past, Fresh Choices for the Future." The article describes Reagan's small-town "Main Street, U.S.A." childhood, traces his rise to fame and fortune as an actor in the 1940s and 1950s, and asserts that "intellectually, emotionally, Reagan lives in the past. That is where the broad vision comes from; the past is his future." The magazine expresses doubts that the country will follow this vision, but, in keeping with the usual media attempts to offer support to incoming administrations, also states that "after several years of *The Deer Hunter* and *All the President's Men*, perhaps *The Ronald Reagan Story* is just what the country ordered." After the twin traumas of Vietnam and Watergate, Reagan's evocation of prewar, small-town America, and of family-oriented Hollywood productions of the past, could offer comfort to the ailing nation.[3]

Reagan rhetorically linked himself with several eras of American life through the figures of previous American presidents. He praised Calvin Coolidge as the role model for his own presidency, and returned Coolidge's portrait to a place of honor in the White House. Coolidge gained Reagan's praise for his opposition to an activist federal government, support for tax cuts that spurred economic activity in the 1920s, and parsimony toward the federal budget.[4] (Coolidge himself had been seen as a nostalgic figure during his presidency, recalling the staunch morals and financial hard-headedness of New England Puritans, although this linkage was surely lost on most of the Reagan electorate.)[5]

Shortly after Reagan's election, the conservative columnists Rowland Evans and Robert Novak heralded the "Reagan Revolution" for its goal: "to return the republic to the status quo of an earlier day. . . . In foreign and national security policy, that earlier day might be fixed at 1955," signifying a return to the staunch anticommunism of the early Cold War and America's unchallenged position at the top of the noncommunist world.[6] In such a scenario, Evans and Novak continued, "there would be no flinching from confrontation with the Soviets. The nation would seek to resume a firm, unwavering leadership of the West."[7] In domestic policy, they announced the marker point as 1925—the height of the Coolidge administration, before the onslaught of New Deal government regulation of business activity.[8] Of course, that regulation was prompted by the onset of the Depression, which for many older voters was still associated with the Republican economic policies that had preceded it. During the 1982 recession, ABC News noted Reagan's admiration for Coolidge and compared the 1920s and the 1980s; the Republicans were hoping for another boom, but would it be followed by another bust?[9]

Others also saw a possible link between Reagan and the Eisenhower administration, which began enjoying revisionist praise from historians and pundits after decades of relative inattention compared with the presidencies of Roosevelt, Truman, and Kennedy. A slew of books on the Eisenhower presidency were published in the wake of Reagan's election. Some reviewers offered the hope that the new Republican in power would follow in Eisenhower's footsteps, with the former president now hailed as an active yet calming influence on his times, and surprisingly moderate in his politics.[10] Republicans sought to minimize the significance of Reagan's heavy reliance on aides by noting Eisenhower's own hands-off management style.[11]

Reagan rarely mentioned Eisenhower, however, perhaps in part because they came from opposite factions that had been wrestling for control of the GOP for thirty-five years. The president that Reagan referred to most frequently, in fact, was Franklin Roosevelt; Reagan cited FDR as his first political hero. This citation might have seemed curious coming from an inveterate critic of the government programs that had originated in the New Deal, but Reagan explained his support for Roosevelt by claiming that New Deal spending programs were emergency measures Roosevelt enacted specifically to deal with the Depression, and that Roosevelt never foresaw them as permanent parts of the American economy.[12] Indeed, Reagan invoked Roosevelt in his attacks on government spending, quoting FDR on the need for government efficiency and budget reductions during his 1980 speech accepting the nomination at the Republican convention. (The quoted remarks had come from the 1932 presidential campaign, before Roosevelt's election; he reversed himself on many economic issues soon after he was elected.)

Reagan's praise for Roosevelt was an attempt to woo voters who were traditionally Democratic, to make them comfortable with the idea of voting for a right-wing Republican; he also invoked Roosevelt's wartime leadership to show the wisdom of being steadfast and strong in the face of a totalitarian foe.[13] Reagan's continuing support for FDR, however, may also be seen as a vestige of Reagan's own past as a New Deal Democratic liberal. Although he rejected the Democratic path in later years, he never brought himself to reject his first political hero, and tried rather to separate his personal reverence for Roosevelt from political support for New Deal programs.

In addition to invoking specific presidents, Reagan often used anecdotes from the past to illustrate his points, particularly to pay tribute to the qualities of the American character. These tales were usually apocryphal or taken from scenes of old Hollywood dramas. In his rhetoric, Reagan borrowed the appeals to optimism and national strength that Hollywood had emphasized during the 1930s and 1940s, in the midst of the Depression and World War II.[14] Even when not based on specific films, Reagan's stories shared the individualist tilt of classical Hollywood narratives, effacing the importance of organized political action, economic forces, and social movements throughout the nation's history.[15] Reagan credited the ending of segregation in the American military, for example, to the heroic example set by a black soldier at Pearl Harbor, which supposedly resulted in the immediate end of segregation. In actuality, President Truman ordered military desegregation in 1948, following notable racial unrest in the military during the war, and after a lobbying effort by civil rights organizations.[16]

Reagan's past was highly imagistic, approaching myth rather than history, featuring static tableaux meant to illustrate enduring qualities of the nation rather than to provide causal explanations for historical change. The use of mythic scenes in his speeches increased with the ascension of Peggy Noonan as a key ghostwriter of the president's commemorative addresses. In his second inaugural address, Reagan invoked presidents such as Washington and Lincoln, as well as anonymous individuals, in attesting to the nation's greatness in meeting its challenges: "A general falls to his knees in the hard snow of Valley Forge; a lonely President paces the darkened halls and ponders his struggle to preserve the Union; . . . a settler pushes west and sings a song." As Benjamin Barber and Garry Wills point out, these allusions play like a sequence of film shots, and are notable for their individualism. Reagan hails the general and not the army, the introspection of Abraham Lincoln rather than his radical extension of the power of the federal government over the states, and the single settler who would likely have perished if not part of a larger wagon train. Reagan's tableaux articulated nationalism as unchanging American individualism, represented by a narrow strata of leading men.[17] The Reagan team ably appropriated important elements of what Lauren Berlant has called the National Symbolic, the images, themes, events, and places that are the rough material of national identity.[18] For Americans, motion pictures and television have long been key sources of such material, and Reagan's invocation of such scenes imbued American identity in accord with the values of the conservative movement. His narrative of rise, fall, and resurgence arranged the elements of the National Symbolic into a comprehensible explanation of recent history, after nationalist readings of the American past had come under increasing question.

Reagan's own past corresponded to common views of the progression of American history through the decades of the mid-twentieth century. J. Hoberman wrote that Reagan's prepolitical career was an amalgam of images: "Good Joe, Patriot, Cowboy, and Corporate Logo."[19] The Good Joe was the hopeful, staunch friend of Depression-era films, whose optimism and dedication were then called upon during the 1940s war years to defend his country. Reagan's image as a Westerner coalesced during the ascendancy of cowboy narratives in Hollywood in the postwar years, as the conquering of the continent reasserted itself as the central American myth. Reagan had acted in a number of 1950s Westerns, and had his biggest television audience as host and occasional star of the western anthology series *Death Valley Days*. Finally, Reagan became a public spokesman for General Electric, one of the most visible American corporations, during the Eisenhower years of bureaucratization, the spread of consumer goods, and the revaluation of corporate culture. Reagan's show business persona and career traced an arc of American experience that iconically buttressed his political call for a return to values and policies of earlier eras.

Although Reagan's image was composed of several facets of his life and film career, the cultural logic of his movement through the decades, from small-town boy to corporate symbol, allowed him to seem essentially as unchanging as the national values he celebrated. Nancy Reagan asserted that he had not changed at all since she had met him in the early 1950s.[20] His conservatism had emerged in that decade, and remained essentially unchanged as well. Reagan's politics first came to wide public attention in 1964, when he made a speech in support of Barry Goldwater's presidential bid, an address broadcast nationally. This speech was, in fact, The Speech, as Reagan and his associates called it, created when Reagan had toured the country in the 1950s promoting General Electric. The Speech departed from other conservative rhetoric of the 1950s in not specifically attacking the New Deal (General Electric was a major federal contractor), but it was strongly anticommunist (both GE and Reagan had fought communists in unions), pro-business, and generally antigovernment. The Speech castigated government as the adversary of the common citizen, a bothersome and inefficient stifler of private initiative and freedom, and worst of all, the enforcer of taxation.[21]

By 1964 Reagan had already given The Speech hundreds of times at employee dinners and civic functions, first arranged by GE and later booked by Reagan himself. Reagan continued using The Speech as his rhetorical keystone throughout his political career; he adapted it to specific issues and locales, but it remained recognizably familiar to reporters who covered Reagan over the course of three decades.[22] Reagan's evocation of the American past, and particularly of the 1950s, coalesced around a personal and political persona that had gone unchanged for thirty years.

Just as Reagan had completed his own ideological and stylistic development in the 1950s, so he argued that the United States needed to return to the policies and values of that era as a touchstone for the future. The Fifties could be seen to hold all of the positive values of the American past, just as the 1950s constituted the final stopping point of Reagan's personal development. The Reagan persona acted in accordance with conservative historiography, which asserted that traditional American values and social structures had remained unchallenged domestically until the 1960s. Given the nation's fondness for the notion of progress, the decade of the 1950s thus enjoyed discursive resonance as the (last) high point of American society.

Reagan performed the role of exemplar of pre-1960s America. In so doing, his public persona benefited from association with iconic figures from the Fifties, particularly the suburban dad and the tough anticommunist. Reagan's soft-voiced but stern pronouncements recalled paternal authority figures such as Robert Young in *Father Knows Best*, as did his earnestness and easygoing sense of humor. Nancy Reagan's public adoration of her husband, mimicking the moves of deferential 1950s family sitcom wives, buttressed his image as domestic patriarch. In response, critics delighted in speculating on the First Lady's degree of power and manipulation behind the scenes, as if to puncture the Fifties traditionalist veneer that the couple presented.

With his linkage to the Hollywood-mediated cowboy, his own fondness for western apparel, horseback riding, and wood chopping, his anticommunism and World War II stories, Reagan mimicked the majestic persona of John Wayne, whose cowboy-soldier-anticommunist persona made him the biggest film star of the 1950s.[23] As Richard Schickel notes, Wayne was heavily identified with two nation-defining experiences, the settlement of the West and the victory in World War II. Wayne's stature grew to mythic proportions as he became a folk-heroic figure of cultural authority. To Schickel, writing during the tumult of the late 1960s, Wayne was already a nostalgic figure, reminding his fans of "a time when right was right, wrong was wrong, and the differences between them could be set right by the simplest means."[24] In a 1979 tribute to his friend, Reagan lauded Wayne for his "enduring strength" and as the symbol for "the force of the American will to do what is right in the world"; he quoted Elizabeth Taylor as saying that Wayne "gave the whole world the image of what an American should be." In the new era of international challenges to American power, questioning of social and national identities, and relativist ethics, Wayne was an icon of earlier certitudes. Reagan also celebrated Wayne for his antigovernment politics and straightforward moral teaching.[25] Five years later, the memory of the Duke was enlisted to return the favor: at the 1984 Republican convention, clips of Wayne's movies introduced the party's film in praise of Reagan.

Reagan's penchant for blaming communists for virtually all international problems and challenges to American hegemony was the strongest and most direct evocation of the 1950s in his rhetoric. Reagan dubbed the Soviet Union "the evil empire" early in his administration, and regularly blamed protests against his nuclear arms buildup and Central American policies on communist-front organizations.[26] Verbal attacks on the Soviet Union resonated in the wake of the Soviet invasion of Afghanistan, and the press responded with new "exposés" of Soviet malfeasance and malevolence, as in a *Newsweek* cover story on KGB activities in the United States that read like the *Reader's Digest* in prime 1950s Red Scare mode.[27] Domestic McCarthyism in the 1980s, however, never really took hold, although congressional conservatives tried to revive the infamous House Un-American Activities Committee, a major vehicle for Red-baiting from the 1930s to the 1960s. Rather, Republicans were able to strengthen their association with patriotic and nationalist themes, while liberals and Democrats remained on the defensive regarding their patriotism and support for the United States against foreign challenges.

The militancy of Reagan's anticommunism added a punchy masculinity to his evocation of 1950s middle-class life, while his calm gregariousness humanized the extremes of his Cold War politics. His persona was approachable without being dull. While his touch with the glamorous Hollywood life and his hold on political power provided an authoritative star persona, Reagan's own appreciation for old Hollywood forms and tales of the American past invited voters to identify with his position of insider-as-fan. Reagan seemed to believe his own myth spinning, and thereby dramatized a stubborn mythic belief in America that had been shredded for others by the events of the 1960s and 1970s. Reagan offered a past that was stable, comforting, and complimentary—which, for his supporters, seemed more important than whether it was true or not. The press regularly reported Reagan's historical gaffes during the 1980 campaign and early in his presidency, but the public responded largely with indifference.[28] Reagan's audiences were protective of Reagan's faulty memory to protect themselves from the unsettling antagonisms of the recent American past.[29]

As students of memory have found, recollections of the past take shape out of current needs and pressures. Nostalgia thrives when the stability of personal identity is challenged by rapid social change, discontinuity, and dislocation.[30] As the United States lost its dominance over global events, saw the decline of its industrial center and traditional family forms, and experienced continual if disorganized social contestation in the aftermath of Sixties political movements, nostalgia for pre-Sixties America reasserted the desire for certitude and stability. Reagan offered a return to a simple belief in the nation's prospects, a belief that voters retrospectively identified with the 1950s and earlier eras. Frances FitzGerald, in her study of grade-school history textbooks, found that texts from the 1950s were particularly seamless in their presentation of the American past, celebrating a perfect, never-changing nation that was the special child of destiny.[31] Reagan's recitation of these themes invited voters to return to a position of credulity and belief akin to the childhood roles of 1950s grade-schoolers and 1930s–1940s fans of Hollywood productions.

THE FIFTIES AND THE SIXTIES

The sense of the 1950s that Reagan evoked was, of course, a narrow one—no figure or movement could comprehensively represent an entire decade of life for a complex society in the modern world, nor was that conservatism's goal. Reagan's selection of elements of Fifties life was meant to reassert conservative norms of social life, government policy, and international action. These elements, moreover, were constructed as the unchanging truths of the American character and the ambitions and goals of the American people. The middle-class suburban lifestyle, heterosexual nuclear family, and technocratic-corporate culture were taken as norms that were disrupted only by the crises of the Sixties. These elements of 1950s life were not only an incomplete quantum of American experience in the 1950s, they also can be considered as somewhat aberrational themselves. The emphasis on marriage and childbearing that arose in the postwar years actually served to reverse many of the demographic trends of the first half of the century.[32]

The 1950s saw a lowering of the divorce rate, the average age of newlyweds, the average age of first-time parents, and women's educational levels relative to men's. The average number of children in a family rose, as did the dominance of large corporations in the economy relative to the self-employed, small businesses, and the farm sector. The percentage of people living in metropolitan suburbs rose dramatically; church membership also increased significantly. The Baby Boom era's emphasis on the primacy of private, domestic family life, with tens of millions of Americans ensconced in single-family suburban homes, working in offices or large factories and going to church regularly, was not a continuation of traditional American practices, but a newly dominant norm that still described only a minority of Americans' lives. Rather than being an aberration from a previously unchanging norm, the Sixties' challenge to Fifties social forms and ensuing reversal of 1950s demographics in regard to marriage, divorce, and childbearing actually reconstituted trends from earlier in the century. The Sixties emphasis on political involvement, youth culture, and sexual ferment echoed both the Progressive Era's social and political reform movements and the 1920s' embrace of jazz and changes in sexual mores.[33]

Reagan and other critics of Democratic social programs identified the increasing deviance from Fifties family forms and middle-class values as the result of increased government spending in the 1960s and 1970s.[34] The 1950s family thus became a symbol of the self-reliance that conservatives called for in rejecting government intervention in the economy. Yet as Stephanie Coontz points out, the 1950s suburban middle class "was far more dependent on government handouts than any so-called 'underclass' in recent U.S. history." The GI Bill of Rights, government dispensation of wartime assets to private corporations, federal support for technical research, Federal Housing Administration and Veterans Administration loans and guarantees, highway funds, and school and university construction all contributed to the creation of the postwar white middle class.[35]

Conservatives naturalized and privatized this postwar transformation, crediting the personal ambition, initiative, and discipline of the white middle class and the wealth-producing activities of the corporate economy. David Stockman explained the decline of the urban center of the Michigan congressional district he represented in the 1970s as evidence of the failure of Great Society spending: "When you have powerful underlying demographic and economic forces at work, federal intervention efforts designed to reverse the tide turn out to have . . . no impact whatever."[36] The "demographic and economic forces" he credits with the decline of the urban center, on closer inspection, included federal grants to exurban towns and businesses, loans for sewer construction, and highway construction that had subsidized suburban and exurban life for two generations. Disparaging the effectiveness of government spending programs, conservatives related tales of individual initiative and heroic entrepreneurship as the ways to financial success in America. This rhetoric flattered middle-class voters with credit for their own upward mobility, praising them for their supposed self-sufficiency and individual agency.

The Republican celebration of Fifties family norms could resonate with 1980s voters through a combination of personal memories, media representations, and the absence of a strong alternative vision of domestic life. The Fifties could take on the hue of a Golden Age for those who retrospectively enjoyed the simplicities of childhood, augmented by the continuing memory of hackneyed but comforting shows such as *Father Knows Best* and *Leave It to Beaver*, which continued to circulate in reruns into the 1970s. *Happy Days'* great popularity continued the circulation of this vision of Fifties domestic stability and security. Many Americans understood that the stereotypical family of the Fifties no longer held sway, but since no positive image of the contemporary family had risen to replace it, the changes since the 1950s in domestic arrangements continued to be viewed by Reagan supporters as aberrant, chaotic departures from a once-cherished norm.[37] In the absence of strong belief in the alternatives to the values defined by conservatives and dramatized in cultural artifacts, the Fifties could evoke a retrospective sense of social cohesion and belonging.

Conservative calls for a return to Fifties family dynamics were accompanied by an effort to resuscitate older entertainment values as well. The festivities for the first Reagan inauguration were centered on Frank Sinatra and other old-time show business celebrities—Ethel Merman, Charlton Heston—

and Republicans applauded the return of old-fashioned glitz and glamour to the capital, after the more austere style of the Carter White House. The master of ceremonies role was assumed by actor Efrem Zimbalist, Jr., who had been best-known for two television roles—a hip 1950s detective on 77 *Sunset Strip* and a prime defender of the social order against 1960s mayhem on *The FBI*—before lapsing into obscurity in the 1970s. The inauguration featured the return to the limelight of figures from the 1950s and early 1960s after their displacement by youth culture and New Hollywood figures.[38] At the time, *Harper's* magazine editor Lewis Lapham summed up the celebration's mood as "Sinatra yes, Dylan no," an embrace of wealth and upper-class optimism as a revolt against Sixties moralism and bohemian revelry. To Lapham, Reagan meant to "reenact the pageant of the 1960s" with a conservative twist and to mimic "the vigor of President Kennedy's New Frontier" with its conflation of glamour, politics, combativeness, and celebrity (with JFK buddy Sinatra in tow).[39]

Reagan himself, of course, was an entertainer from another era, another Efrem Zimbalist, Jr., if he had not run for governor of California in 1966. His pre-Sixties persona had survived into the 1980s, and proved more useful in the political sphere than it would have in the entertainment world.[40] Indeed, most of Hollywood's attempts to follow the Republicans' cultural lead fell flat; the television networks trotted out several old tough-guy stars, such as Robert Stack and Mike Connors, to star in law-and-order series in the wake of Reagan's victory, but none of the shows caught on.

At the beginning of his career in governance, Reagan's pre-Sixties image was useful politically as a directly anti-Sixties statement. After Goldwater's defeat in 1964, Reagan had moderated the antigovernment rhetoric in his speeches and stressed the possibilities of a positive restoration of older political values. Reagan opposed the flurry of civil rights legislation ending segregation and ensuring voting rights for southern blacks, as he would later oppose fair housing laws meant to end segregation in housing.[41] He also implied that Martin Luther King, Jr., had been responsible for his own death, by weakening the rule of law through his civil disobedience campaign in the segregated South.[42] Reagan supplanted Goldwater and, later, George Wallace as the favorite politician of the southern right; his calmer demeanor created a broader appeal, particularly to women, than either of the former had enjoyed. Reagan criticized racism to northern audiences in the 1960s, but never addressed the issue in the South, or criticized Wallace; rather, he invoked his antifederalism to reiterate his support for "states' rights," rallying support from southern segregationists and post-1960s antisegregationists alike.[43]

He centered his 1966 gubernatorial campaign on quashing the student unrest at the University of California at Berkeley. Berkeley had catalyzed the student protest movement with its Free Speech campaign in 1964, and had remained one of the most politically turbulent campuses in the country. California had also experienced the Watts uprising in 1965, one of the most violent civil disturbances among a string of urban riots in the mid-1960s. Reagan promised a crackdown on political unrest, drug and sexual experimentation, and public outrageousness, a pledge that appealed to suburban, middle-aged whites.[44] "A small minority of beatniks, radicals, and filthy speech advocates have brought such shame [to Berkeley]," charged Reagan in a typical 1966 campaign speech, ". . . the campus has become a rallying point for Communists and a center of sexual misconduct."[45] When he became governor, Reagan began his close association with future White House aide and attorney general Ed Meese; Meese had caught Reagan's eye through his work as chief prosecutor of Berkeley protesters in Alameda County.[46] Reagan had already been attacking liberalism for ten years, starting at a time of docile students in universities and quiet activism in minority communities; by 1966, he could define his antiliberalism as a rejection of the social tumult of the Sixties.

Reagan and other conservatives hoped to capitalize on public memories of the Sixties as a time of national trauma, social contestation, and violence. Reagan benefited from the absence of strong public memories, particularly outside California, of his own role in the divisive issues of the time. Reagan's policies as governor regarding the state budget and taxation were occasionally mentioned in media treatments of his candidacy and presidency as relevant to the dominant political initiatives in Washington during his term in office. Reagan's actions in quelling campus unrest, however, went virtually unmentioned in the nonleftist press of the 1980s. Reagan had sent state and National Guard troops repeatedly onto the Berkeley campus, most dramatically during a controversy over the continuation of the improvised People's Park, which had resulted in the killing of a protester and a mass of injuries for both protesters and troops.[47] The actual events of the Sixties protest movements were sufficiently remote by 1980, with its very different political mood, that Reagan's participation in the People's Park incident, one of the most controversial acts by a governor in the 1960s, was essentially lost to contemporary political discussion.

Rather, Reagan's Fifties-based persona helped him avoid the negative associations his involvement in Sixties controversies could have engendered. Although he was a chief ideologue of the far right during the 1960s, he escaped responsibility for the era's divisiveness, even as his political movement continued to rail against the conflictual nature of the decade's public events. Since Reagan clearly wished the Sixties had never happened, he was not held responsible for the violent backlash against it that he had helped to lead. In public memory, the extremism of the 1960s traversed an arc from the right wing to the left wing of American politics over the course of the decade. The segregationist right was largely held responsible for the clashes of the early

1960s; the Black Power movement and the antiwar left were largely deemed the disruptive forces of the late 1960s. Because Reagan only gained political power in 1967, his conservative contribution to the decade's divisiveness went unremarked in the 1980s.

By the time of his inauguration as president, his conservatism could be taken as a fundamental reaction against the Sixties and post-Sixties social movements, rather than against the more politically popular programs of the New Deal and presidencies of Roosevelt, Truman, and Kennedy. In 1960 Reagan described Kennedy's program as basically communist; by 1980 he was invoking Kennedy in order to appeal to old-time Democratic voters disillusioned with post-1965 liberalism.[48]

THE PAST AND THE FUTURE

Reagan and other conservatives stressed that they did not want to revel in nostalgia simply for its own sake, but that the past contained valuable lessons for the future. Reagan campaign aides worried that their candidate would seem too dated and trapped in his small-town vision to an electorate who lived in cities and suburbs, many of whom had no personal memory of the Depression, World War II, or even of the 1950s themselves.[49] Reagan always stressed his optimism for the future, and accused Democrats of giving up on America. In his acceptance speech at the Republican convention in 1980, he stated that Democrats "say that the United States has had its day in the sun, that our nation has passed its zenith. . . . that the future will be one of sacrifice and few opportunities. My fellow citizens, I utterly reject that view. . . . We need a rebirth of the American tradition of leadership at every level of government and in private life as well."[50] The embrace of "tradition" could thus be characterized as a "rebirth" that would lead to new opportunities for the future. Only by going backward could the nation move forward. His campaign material intoned, "Let's Make America Great Again" and "Renew America's Strength with Great American Values."[51] The appeal to tradition could be applied even to radical changes in course; Reagan's proposals for major federal policy changes could be cloaked in the rhetoric of enduring American values and past practices.[52]

Traditional conservatism had stressed exactly the sacrifices and communitarian ethos that Reagan rejected in his celebration of supply-side simplicities and radical individualism. As an individualist conservative, Reagan embraced the far-reaching changes that contemporary capitalism had produced, changes that in the transition from an industrial to a postindustrial economy were particularly wrenching in the 1970s and early 1980s. Reagan's policies were meant to assist businesses in the process of constant modernization, which contributed to the social upheaval his nostalgic image tried to assuage.[53] Notions of tradition can give the sanction of social continuity and precedent to movements for change, providing historical cover, as it were, for disruptive events and initiatives.[54]

Reagan's words promised change; his style promised continuity.[55] In his rejection of New Deal, New Frontier, and Great Society programs, Reagan was suggesting a major change in the government's relation to the citizenry, and changes in the relative status of the wealthy, the middle class, and the poor. Yet his rhetorical style evoked Franklin Roosevelt and Frank Capra in his can-do optimism in American values and positing of American consensus.[56] By placing radical change in a stylistic frame of familiarity, Republicans hoped to legitimate their redirection of policy, particularly regarding the economy.

Reagan often charged that his Washington-based opponents were out of touch with the American people, and that his proposals stemmed from time-tested virtues, common sense, and previously dominant social practices. Many of his policy initiatives actually originated in Washington-based think tanks like the Heritage Foundation and the American Enterprise Institute, produced by the conservative counterparts to the liberal intellectuals he excoriated for being out of touch with down-home American experience.[57] Further, his major financial initiative, the supply-side tax cuts and budget reductions of 1981, had originated with the promotion of the idea by one economist, Arthur Laffer, and a lone editorial writer for the *Wall Street Journal*, Jude Wanniski. Reagan's economic policies had never been subject to any sort of test, time-based or otherwise, before becoming the operative basis of the American economy.[58]

The Nostalgic Sources of Reagan's Appeal

Various segments of the electorate responded to Reagan's paeans to the past. Conservative nostalgia touched on social, economic, and political issues, each containing strong reference to the Fifties/Sixties split. Reagan's appeal as a strong leader, distinct from specific issues, also contained a nostalgic element. Reagan's popularity has often been overstated, and there were other sources of his appeal beyond that of nostalgia, but his historiographic efforts provided a powerful overarching theme to his presidency. The nostalgic theme contributed to the ideological coherence for which Reaganism was known, which indeed seemed to make a label such as "Reaganism" appropriate. Reagan's coalition formed itself in part by how its members defined themselves in regard to the events of the Sixties.

Such a definition depended on an understanding of "the Sixties" as a concept. Only if the Sixties were recognized as a fairly stable set of trends, images, and events could the conservative movement define itself against its effects and consequences in American life. The Sixties had gained such a coherence, inflected differently by varying social groups, long before the election of

Ronald Reagan. As noted by commentators in the late 1960s and early 1970s, its meaning was based in large part on the stark contrasts which seemed to distinguish the period from the Fifties, and by the dramatic events of the decade—assassinations, civil disobedience, war, and rapid, major changes in social styles and entertainment forms. The passing of the large Baby Boom generation through major, seemingly distinct periods of life—childhood, adolescence, young adulthood—contributed to the sense of drastic change that permeated both the 1960s themselves and the derivative, more formless 1970s. By the early 1980s it was easy for Americans to mark political and social perspectives by relating them to the definitions of the Sixties that survived.

The continued relevance of the Sixties could be seen soon after Reagan's election by the public response to John Lennon's murder. As a leading emblem of Sixties culture and social life, Lennon had continued to represent its values even during his retreat into private life in the mid-1970s. His violent death just as he was returning to public performance evoked a tremendous sense of loss, particularly on the heels of Reagan's victory. Some conservatives feebly tried to claim Lennon as one of their own, but beyond tributes to his musical talent, he was celebrated and mourned generally for his role in the development of youth culture, pacifism, and his social nonconformity—hardly conservative themes.[59] For many countercultural sympathizers, Lennon's death, just after Reagan's election, registered as the final end of Sixties utopianism that had lingered through the 1970s. Hard times were ahead for those whose identities had remained rooted in the accomplishments of Sixties social movements and rebellious youth culture.

For conservatives whose identities were formed *against* these movements, Reagan's election appeared as a long-awaited validation of their opposition to the Sixties' influence on contemporary America. Eliott Abrams, a second-generation neoconservative who became a key policymaker on Latin America in Reagan's State Department, always had felt at odds with his generation's politics, starting when he combated the Students for a Democratic Society's antiwar campaign during the 1960s. He resented the attention that Lennon's death received: "John Lennon was not that important a figure in our times. . . . Because Lennon was perceived as a left-wing figure politically, anti-establishment, a man of social conscience with concern for the poor . . . he's being made into a great figure."[60] Conservatives saw Reagan's election as a chance to reclaim the culture from the drugs, sex, and rock-and-roll deviations of the Sixties.

The conservative attempt to erase the Sixties can be seen in the praise of Barry Goldwater that accompanied Reagan's ascension. Although Goldwater had enjoyed a long career in the Senate, his 1964 campaign for president had remained a prime example of political fiasco, both for its ideological extremism and for its magnitude of defeat. Yet despite its status as disaster, Goldwater's bid proved useful to the Republican right; many of the New Right activists who organized support for Reagan had first met in the Goldwater campaign, and Reagan initially achieved political celebrity by his nationally televised use of The Speech in favor of Goldwater. After Reagan's victory, Goldwater was acclaimed by Republicans as an elder statesman of the party, a prophet finally honored for his prescient campaign against Democratic policies of the 1960s (and before).[61] At a *National Review* banquet to celebrate the 1980 electoral results, George Will commented, "It took approximately sixteen years to count the vote in the 1964 election, and Goldwater won."[62] Reagan's victory opened the door for the conservatives of the GOP to rewrite the 1960s.

The ability of the Reagan movement to move the country beyond the effects of the Sixties was symbolically illustrated by Reagan's survival of an assassination attempt by John Hinckley shortly after taking office. After a string of national bad luck, it seemed, Reagan showed the wherewithal to escape yet another potential disaster. His image of tough-guy strength was enhanced, and the humorous aplomb he displayed immediately after the shooting (telling the doctors treating him that he hoped they were all Republicans, for example) evoked the calm, secure presence of the suburban sitcom dad. After starting his presidency with historically low approval ratings for a new chief executive, Reagan saw his political popularity surge upward in the wake of the attempt on his life, providing the momentum to pass his major legislative initiatives on the budget and taxation. Indeed, Reagan's survival of the shooting was the most popular act of his first term—his popularity peaked in April and May 1981.[63] Although the nation was to endure another recession soon thereafter, and foreign policy debacles such as the military and diplomatic defeat in Lebanon blemished his administration's record, Reagan's survival of Hinckley's attack began a series of confidence-building events that made Reagan's pledge of national revival seem plausible to many Americans.

Lawrence Grossberg points to the special status of the Baby Boom generation as key to understanding the conservative cultural and political assault on the Sixties. At its beginnings, the Baby Boom was seen as the culmination of national progress, the manifestation of the prosperity, safety, and optimism Americans had secured for themselves and their futures after the sacrifices of the Depression and World War II. Many of the early Boomers, however, turned out to be a rebellious lot, spurning the advantages their parents had worked to provide them and attacking the rules by which their parents had lived.[64] The political activism and counterculture of the Sixties were seen by their opponents as attacking the keystones of American life—God, family, the military, material prosperity, and education—in favor of Eastern religions and atheism, the Sexual Revolution and feminism, antiwar protests and draft dodging, hippie antimaterialism, and campus disruptions and dropping out.[65] While many Boomers led lives quite like those of their parents, those who did rebel enjoyed huge media visibility and public attention. Given the particular association of the generation as a whole with the ultimate fulfillment of America's promise, their political, social, and cultural rebellion effectively questioned the values and direction of the entire society.

The conservative cultural project in the 1980s, Grossberg argues, was to disarticulate Baby Boom practices from national senses of purpose and identity. Conservatives hoped to replace what they saw as a hedonist, immoral, youth-oriented culture with a revaluation of nuclear families that would constrain rebellious youth and feminist impulses. By proposing their own negative memories of the Sixties as the basis for a newly coherent national consensus, conservatives could remove the New Left and countercultural challenges to ideas of national progress and greatness and look forward to a new, late- and post-Boomer generation that seemed increasingly to reflect certain conservative values—materialistic ambition, belief in military power, and support for business prerogatives, among others. Reagan repeatedly professed his belief in the new generation of young Americans; whereas John Kennedy had made an appeal to the younger generation on the basis of its public responsibilities to the nation, Reagan largely celebrated his own youthful followers for their pursuit of personal financial success and other privatized activities.

Conservatives who wanted to devalue notions of public spending and deflect appeals to the public good by racial and gender activists saw the push to privatism in 1950s America as the preferred model for contemporary society. After the collective ethos of the New Deal and World War II, Americans had been urged by media and business elites to find personal satisfaction in the private consumption of consumer goods, family activities, and individual ambition in the postwar era.[66] Even the response to the ultimate public issue of nuclear war was channeled into the building of family bomb shelters—private consumption underground to double the rise of suburbia above it.[67] The 1960s emerged as an era of refound public activity, as many Baby Boomers and marginalized groups sought to find personal fulfillment and liberation in social activism and cultural experimentation on a mass scale. The self-proclamation of the rebellious factions of the younger generation as the Woodstock Nation in 1969—after its largest public gathering to date, during which personal privacy was all but impossible—pointed to the emphasis on collectivity in Sixties culture.

The public movements of the Sixties created new demands on government, academic, and business elites, and inspired the proliferation of new interest groups, such as environmentalists, in the 1970s. Although the demands of social groups were always contested on a case-by-case basis, by the mid-1970s elites were discussing the necessity of squelching these demands en masse. After defeat in Vietnam and amid continuing stagflation, the Trilateral

Commission published *The Crisis of Democracy*, an influential treatise in elite circles.[68] The book argued that contemporary democracies were overloaded by new demands from citizens, and it called for a reduction in democratic activism by the new social movements in order to preserve business profit margins and military strength. The conservative attempts to roll back the Sixties sought to reprivatize social concerns, to once more identify the family and privatized production and consumption as the proper spheres of individuals' attention. By defining the Sixties political movements and attendant counter-culture as violent, unruly, and destructive, conservatives could limit public and governmental attention provided to the movements' legatees in the 1980s.

Conservatives often asserted that their own entrance into civic activism had been forced on them by the excesses of the government and liberal groups, and that they asked no more from government than to be left alone. A New Right minister told the attendees of a Heritage Foundation meeting, "We're not here to get into politics. We're here to turn the clock back to 1954 in this country."[69] Insofar as they allowed for parallels between their own activism and that of the Sixties, conservatives claimed inspiration from the early civil rights movement, which was not identified with the cultural excesses or violence of the later 1960s.[70] After the defeat of the Equal Rights Amendment (ERA), the nonelectoral movement that attracted the most conservative activism was the fight against abortion. Ironically, the goals of the movement amounted to transforming a private medical decision regarding a pregnancy into a public one that warranted governmental interference, in the prohibition of abortion. The right-to-life movement thus followed in the steps of the Sixties movements that many of its participants excoriated, in its emphasis on turning what could be considered private actions into public controversies. The antiabortion movement, with its rhetoric of basic human rights and reliance on disruptive civil disobedience, sought the high moral position formerly held by those in the fight against racial segregation and discrimination.

In a book that called for the overturning of the Supreme Court decision in *Roe v. Wade*, Reagan asserted the similarity between such a reversal and the *Brown v. Board of Education* case that overturned school segregation.[71] He gave the fight for greater governmental control over reproduction an antigovern-ment slant, however, by defining it as a fight against federal fiat, since it was the Supreme Court that had imposed the legalization of abortion over state laws in *Roe v. Wade*. Despite the opinion polls that showed the majority of Americans supportive of the continuing legality of abortion, Reagan thus labeled legalization a case of misplaced judicial activism, the type of judicial overreaching that conservatives had opposed in the Warren Court years. Judi-cial activism was associated with the Sixties social movements and counter-cultural permissiveness, and was prime evidence for conservatives of the capture of the federal government by "special interest" groups. As the anti-abortion movement began to rely more heavily on extralegal methods of stopping abortion, conservatives in government both compared antiabortion activists to the fighters against racial discrimination and associated a pro-choice stand with Sixties liberal social programs and hedonism.

The generative dynamic between political leaders and their followers is a complex one, as political actors attempt to enunciate themes that will resonate with their supporters and potential converts. It is difficult to determine to what degree the conservative narrative of American history produced support by specific groups for the conservative agenda, and how much the rhetoric of Reaganism simply reflected back the conceptions of those who were already its supporters. By the 1980 election, the conservative historiographic themes were just beginning to emerge in a coherent way, but Reagan's appeal already had a generational cast. Reagan's biggest margins over Carter came from voters who had come of political age in the 1950s and early 1960s—voters who had been acculturated during the postwar era, only to see those who followed them agewise disrupt the vision of American dominance and righteousness.[72] Meanwhile, voters aged eighteen to thirty in 1980—the heart of the Baby Boom, who came of age in the Sixties and its aftermath—split their votes between Carter and Reagan, the only age constituency not solidly for Reagan. Fifty-four percent of this age group identified with the Democrats, as opposed to 35 percent identifying with the Republicans, despite the unpopular Carter at the top of the Democratic ticket.[73] Republican identification remained low for this generational cohort throughout Reagan's term in office, even during his dominating presence in the 1984 election campaign.[74] The conservative renunciation of the Sixties continued to reflect and exploit the sharp divide between those who identified with the Fifties and those who identified with the Sixties.[75]

Such a divide can be seen by the varied estimations of the relative importance of the feminist movement to women of different ages. Younger women were more likely than older women to consider the women's movement to be of prime historical importance.[76] The life choices of women in their forties and fifties in 1980 had already been made by the time the women's movement rose to public consciousness in the late 1960s, and thus many saw the movement as irrelevant or threatening. The more conservative among them saw feminism as a disruptive force that threatened their own identities as homemakers; nonworking women gave Reagan a majority of their votes in 1980. Younger women were more likely to register the changes in women's social status as directly relevant to their own life choices; younger and working women split their votes evenly.[77]

The cogency of the conservative historiography should be best understood as organizing an inchoate set of elements of Reagan's appeal into a coherent historical narrative. Reagan's 1980 campaign offered a clear renunciation of the demands of the Sixties social movements, without putting his version of postwar history at the center of his drive for the presidency. Thus his repudiation of the Sixties could attract certain groups of voters whose relationship to the Fifties and the Sixties may not have been fully articulated in a political sense. The ensuing conservative narrative of dominance, decline, and imminent resurgence, as expressed throughout his first term, worked to anchor Reagan's appeal in the seeming certitudes of history, tradition, and lived experience.

Each age group, of course, contains its own schisms, cleavages, and competing social groups. Conservative attacks on the Sixties resonated with those groups challenged by the new social movements for civil rights and feminism, no matter what their age. White men, white southerners, and nonworking women all gave Reagan their support; African Americans and younger working women supported Carter. Although Carter managed to win a slim majority of union voters, Reagan's ability to attract Democratic, low-, and middle-income white men—who came to be known as "Reagan Democrats"—was seen in the political world as a backlash against the "special interest" groups that had emerged in the Sixties. While Republicans made inroads on constituencies that had remained nominally Democratic in the 1970s, they became positively dominant among southern whites, the first of the New Deal supporters to abandon the Democrats during the schisms of the 1960s. By the 1984 election, Reagan enjoyed a 44 percent lead over Democratic candidate Walter Mondale among these voters, and in only one 1984 southern election for the Senate did a Democrat attract more than 35 percent of the white vote.[78] Republicans held a 20 percent advantage in party identification among white southerners.[79]

The anti-ERA and antiabortion movements provided a focus for an antifeminist backlash that challenged feminism's claims to speak for all women. Reagan and other conservatives also questioned the right of civil rights leaders to speak for black Americans, in an attempt to attack affirmative action and antipoverty programs without being seen as openly racist.[80] Reagan's antifederalism and others' criticism of "welfare bureaucrats" attracted whites resentful of African-American claims on government. The recurrent emphasis in conservative discourse on crime and social pathology was racially coded to refer to black Americans, although the majority of the poor (and the majority of criminals) were white. As Herman Gray argues, the depiction of the poor (read as black) as immoral, irresponsible, and menacing worked to strip the civil rights movement of its old position of moral authority; traditional-family advocates and conservative religious leaders sought to replace the movement as the providers of a moral framework with which to understand poverty and the social positioning of African Americans.[81]

Race has always been an important component of social identity in America. With the widespread changes in race relations in the 1960s, race has become even more crucial as a fulcrum of political identity, with the defection of white southerners from the Democratic party being its most visible manifestation.[82] Northern working-class whites have also used race to gauge the commitment of the political parties to their interests.[83] By asserting that Sixties antipoverty efforts both failed to benefit the poor and were responsible for national economic decline, Reagan and other conservatives began to separate white votes from lower-class and African-American concerns more forcefully than at any time since the New Deal began.

The 1960s were widely understood as the crucial turning point in the struggle against racial discrimination. For conservatives, the success of the civil rights movement in overturning Jim Crow laws and practices should have allowed the racialized concerns of African Americans to drop from the national agenda—conservatives declared victory over white racism and suggested retreat and withdrawal from the field of post-1965 initiatives. Civil rights supporters, while invoking the moral authority of Martin Luther King, Jr., and other activists of the earlier period, struggled to loosen the identity of their movement from such close association with the 1960s, asserting that America's racial problems had deep historical roots (in the continuing impact of slavery) and contemporary relevance (in the continuing discrimination and racism of the 1980s). The 1960s became a usable touchstone for conservatives to deflect these claims, by pointing to the widespread positive changes in law that the movement produced, and concurrently to the supposed failures of the Great Society and the War on Poverty.

Charles Murray displayed this conservative logic in *Losing Ground*, one of the key texts that attacked Great Society programs in the 1980s. Murray opened his book with a comparison of the years 1950, 1968, and 1981 in American life. He depicted 1950 America as imbued with the spirit of free enterprise but blind to racial injustice and poverty. By 1968 racial justice had prevailed, yet the country was coming apart from controversies over race and Vietnam. As Ronald Reagan took office in 1981, the nation was in even worse shape, with a declining economy that hit the poor particularly hard. Murray, who later coauthored *The Bell Curve* with its assertions of black biological inferiority, blamed federal policies that offered initiative-sapping benefits to the working-age poor for the existence of a despairing underclass. The dramatic differences between the 1950s and 1960s in American racial dynamics became an argument for the cessation of governmental action to ensure equality.[84]

In the late 1970s a plurality of Americans believed that Sixties antipoverty programs had had no strong positive or negative effect on the nation, while 30 percent thought they had been beneficial. With another decline in the economy and the rise of conservative attacks on the programs near the end of the decade, there was a slight shift toward believing such programs actually made the economy and the plight of the poor worse.[85] Governmental generosity to the poor was associated with good economic times; with the financial disruptions and continued rise in crime in the 1970s and early 1980s, such generosity was increasingly seen as naive and as a threat to the middle class.[86] Conservative discourse was not able to delegitimate universal spending programs such as Social Security and Medicare, but other domestic governmental spending lost its cogency in providing Keynesian and humanitarian benefits.

Instead, government spending was increasingly depicted as a drag on the economy and an unfair tax burden on the middle class. Reaction to the taxation burden first gained political momentum with the 1978 passage of Proposition 13 in California, which reduced property taxes and decimated state and local funding.[87] Sixties-inspired social planners were decried as ineffectual and insufficiently concerned with the anxious financial situation of the middle class. In the wake of double-digit inflation and unemployment, Sixties idealism had no place in the new, cold realities of life in the 1980s.

Yet Reagan himself, while evidently turning a cold shoulder to the poor, evinced optimism for the economy as a whole on the basis of the revelations of supply-side theory. With the end of energy price shocks and the recovery of the major economic indicators near the close of Reagan's first term, conservatives occupied the new position of economic optimists and attacked liberals as sour pessimists suffering from a depressing preoccupation with those left behind in the Reaganomic recovery. The poor had been transformed from the final project in a national teleology of Keynesian economic progress into an undeserving, uncomfortable reminder of the limitations of social policy.

Conservatives did not forsake a sense of national destiny, however—they insisted on its importance in regaining a sense of American strength and self-confidence. Whereas liberals in the 1960s had defined the nation's goal through the fight for racial equality and the War on Poverty, 1980s conservatives found it instead in the renewal of Cold War animosity toward the Soviet Union, and called for another national crusade to contest communist plans for world domination. In the wake of the Soviet invasion of Afghanistan, Cold War attitudes seemed contemporary as well as reminiscent of the Fifties. However, to gain public support for drastic increases in military spending and a more belligerent international stance, Reagan and his supporters had to overcome public hesitation over foreign military adventures. The administration had to face the lingering trauma of Vietnam.

Campaign pollster Richard Wirthlin told Reagan that his comment that the Vietnam War had been a "noble crusade" was the candidate's biggest gaffe during his 1980 run for the presidency, the one statement that caused his support to drop among the electorate.[88] Although the Baby Boomer generation had been split during the war between supporters and opponents of American involvement, the war was almost unanimously unpopular by the late 1970s. The conflict was abhorred by all age groups for the American lives lost, the national divisions it created, and for what seemed its sheer meaninglessness, given its physical and emotional toll on the country. World War II and the Vietnam War stood in stark contrast to each other—the first accorded honor as a victorious crusade that attested to national unity, beneficence, and strength, the second detested as a losing debacle that challenged those same notions.[89] Yet the negative consensus on the war did not prevent it from remaining divisive, as debate continued as to who should be held accountable for the defeat and what the national attitude toward the war's veterans should be.

The controversy over the design of the Vietnam Veterans Memorial illustrated these divisions. Hawks saw the memorial as a rebuttal to doves and the aspersions they had cast on American troops in charging that the war was criminal. Doves hoped the memorial would constitute an expression of national regret and loss. The memorial was the site of intense disagreement and lobbying during its planning process, and continued to be a site of competing memories at completion. Conservative critics, who saw the memorial, with its black walls sunken into the earth, as a stark modernist criticism of the war, successfully lobbied to add a statue at the site depicting three bedraggled GIs in a pose of mutual support.[90]

The image of American conduct in the war shifted in the 1970s from My Lai to the POWs—from atrocities against the Vietnamese to victimization by communist torturers, as in the highly popular film *The Deer Hunter*.[91] The idea spread that GIs were still in Southeast Asia, missing in action, held captive by communists, and abandoned by their own government.[92] Conservatives revamped the image of Vietnam veterans as noble victims of communist aggressors, weak-willed liberals, and treasonous protesters. The protest movement was depicted as the opposite of the boys who had gone to fight—cowardly, antipatriotic, and elitist, obscuring the participation of veterans in the movement.[93] This opposition was best illustrated by the apocryphal story of protesters spitting on troops as they returned to the American soil, which became a favorite line of conservatives—repeated by everyone from Rambo to George H. W. Bush.

To place blame on Sixties liberals and radicals was not, however, enough to revalidate the Vietnam War in public memory or dispel public disillusionment with the use of American troops abroad. The war continued to be extremely unpopular throughout the 1980s, and Americans remained leery of committing troops to conflicts in Central America and elsewhere. Reagan offered a rhetoric of closure regarding the war, in an attempt to move beyond its implicit challenge to a renewed militarism. The president asserted that critics of the Cold War and governmental authority in international affairs had only a narrow following and that their attitudes had been superseded by a return to older values, just as the vets had supposedly returned from battle with their faith in America intact.[94] Reagan paid scant attention to the Vietnam Veterans Memorial when it was constructed, but found it acceptable to preside over the unveiling of the statue of the three soldiers near the monument in 1984. Although Reagan asserted that the United States had entered the war to help ensure freedom for the South Vietnamese, the war's ultimate meaning seemed to be nothing other than to dramatize the American soldiers' love of country.

Reagan often referred to American troops as sons, implicitly addressing the older, World War II generation of parents who could truly appreciate sacrifice of life for the country.[95] This mode of address constructed the public counterpart to an intimate family circle which held no place for those who protested. (In reality the parental generation during Vietnam supported the war considerably less than younger white males, who were the most enthusiastic hawks of the time. In general, young adults during the war were more passionately for or against the war than their parents' generation.)[96] Reagan's paternal rhetoric fit his stance as a father figure, to whom both the pre- and the post-Baby Boom generations could look for confirmation of America's strength and self-confidence.

Reagan aides delighted in the success with which he assumed the role. Press aide David Gergen credited Reagan's popularity during the 1984 reelection campaign with this dimension of his appeal, which did not extend to other GOP candidates so thoroughly: "Reagan has become a father figure—he transcends the party."[97] Peggy Noonan made note of it in seeing the crowd reaction to Reagan during the campaign: "See how they love Daddy?"[98] The men's movement associated with *Iron John* author Robert Bly was beginning, with a newfound emphasis on re-creating filial ties with fathers real and vicarious. Reagan filled the role in the political realm, as in his symbolic welcome home to veterans whose return from battle had not been publicly celebrated at the time.

Reagan was seen as true to masculine values of strength, consistency, and executive competence, as exuding the toughness the nation needed to face up to the Soviet Union and that men needed to face up to the challenges of feminism. Reagan's political victories on the budget and taxation contributed to the impression that he was a strong leader; after the floundering of the Carter presidency, Reagan was once more making the presidency the dominant institution of American government. This restoration of power in an individual (however actually dependent on his staff he may have been) made identification with his agenda attractive to those citizens who felt that their own social positions had been challenged and besieged in recent years. As David Gergen explained, "The whole theory going in was, if we go to the country and just try to sell conservatism straight up, it's not going to work. You don't have that kind of base in the country to do that. . . . The point was, if Reagan can be successful, and show that he is effective, people would come to believe in Reagan. And as they believe in Reagan, they would eventually come to agree with him on issues, and see him as sensible, and eventually his philosophy would have a lot more impact."[99] Reagan functioned as the site of identification for voters who may not have embraced the Republican agenda wholeheartedly, but who found his display of power comforting. Reagan's militarism and sense of his own agency bore easy comparison with the cultural heroes of childhood. As even a twenty-eight-year-old Democrat stated in 1984, "He's a man who, when he says something, sticks to his guns. It's a John Wayne type of thing, you know, the Cavalry."[100] Indeed, nearly two-thirds of 1984 Reagan voters identified his leadership, personality, and effectiveness in the White House as the main reasons for their support, rather than specific issues or policy successes.[101]

Reagan was a true master of ceremonies. With the creation of nationalist spectacles ranging from the invasion of Grenada to the 1984 Olympics to the reopening of the renovated Statue of Liberty, Reagan rehabilitated nationalism after a generation of revisionist criticism of American motives, values, and domestic and international relations. The Sixties had produced a stream of historical works that challenged academic and political orthodoxy regarding the

4. Reagan at the Air Force Academy in 1984, performing one of his favorite presidential duties—saluting. Courtesy of Ronald Reagan Library.

American role in the Cold War, the nation's racial history, and the morality of previous presidents and other public officials. Reagan's embrace of a pre-Sixties historical vision of American greatness and uniqueness answered the Sixties generation of critics with televised public celebration, often sponsored by private corporations willing to foot the bill. The economic privatization and commercialization of public historical memory linked Republican antigovernment moves to popular culture and support for business prerogatives; critics whose historical vision was lacking both financial sponsorship and access to the main television networks were further marginalized.[102]

The spectacles were in part another effort to gather support for a post-post-Vietnam militarism; soon after the intervention in Grenada, Reagan proclaimed, "Our days of weakness are over. Our military forces are back on their feet and standing tall."[103] Coming immediately on the heels of the defeat of American forces and policies in Lebanon, the Grenada campaign functioned as a show of patriotism (retrieved American students kissed the ground upon their return to the United States) and a display of American power. American policymakers may have hoped the Grenada operation and other military actions would create a new image of American might for other governments, but the intervention also took its place in the stream of nationalist spectacles for domestic reception. The spectacles had a forced quality to them, an urgency in their celebration of nationalist values that belied the anxiety that had been plaguing the nation about its place in a post-Vietnam, post-OPEC world. The invasion of a tiny country such as Grenada hardly proved the return of American military prowess; capturing the most medals in an Olympics boycotted by many of the strongest national delegations of athletes hardly showed the superiority of the American social body. Yet each produced loud manifestations of patriotic sentiment and reinforced notions of Reagan's leadership. If the Vietnam intervention and its prolongation were to show the rest of the world that the United States remained dominant, then the spectacles of nationalist Reaganism were meant to convince Americans themselves that their country had regained its place at the top, led by a strong paternal presence.[104]

The Campaign of 1984

The 1984 Reagan reelection campaign was the most protracted of the patriotic spectacles that sought to allay national insecurity and reinstill an optimistic sense of national destiny. Of all the spectacles, the reelection campaign was the one most focused on Reagan and the use of his personal public image to convey meaning. By embodying national faith and optimism, Reagan sought both to show the national capability for renewal and to place himself and his policies above criticism. White House aide Richard Darman set the tone in a memo to the campaign planners: "Paint Reagan as the personification of all that is right

5. The 1984 Republican presidential campaign, an apotheosis of patriotic spectacle. Courtesy of Ronald Reagan Library.

with, or heroized by, America. Leave Mondale in a position where an attack on Reagan is tantamount to an attack on America's idealized image of itself—where a vote against Reagan is, in some subliminal sense, a vote against a mythic 'AMERICA.'"[105] The campaign tried to force Democratic nominee Walter Mondale, who had spent his political career in the broad liberal-to-moderate mainstream of the northern wing of the Democratic party, into a position akin to that of the radical revisionist historians—nay-sayers at the celebration of national greatness.[106] Conversely, by attacking Reagan, Mondale seemed to attest to the marginalization of the broad swath of liberalism he represented, to delegitimate all of American liberalism in the act of rejecting Reagan. The conservative movement's project to establish a commanding position was thus crucially based on the personal qualities of Reagan and the nostalgia he evoked for the days of American dominance and stability.

Reagan's masculine qualities were placed into sharp relief in the 1984 campaign by the contrasting style of the Democratic nominee. Mondale's lack of televisual charisma came off as weakness (and boring to boot), and he aligned himself with a feminist agenda by his selection of a woman for his running mate. Whereas younger voters in the 1970s were notably more liberal than their elders, Reagan carried young voters by 58 to 41 percent in his 1984 reelection campaign.[107] After decades in which younger voters identified primarily with the Democrats, by the mid-1980s party identification for this demographic group was evenly split between the two major parties.[108]

Reagan's restorationist themes were repeated throughout the campaign. His media team designed advertisements meant to produce feelings of patriotism rather than to address thought on any specific issues. "The ads work," stated his media coordinator, Doug Watts. "I mean they produce results—faith and confidence."[109] The Republicans raided the storehouse of props in the National Symbolic, effectively leaving Democrats little to work with that could connect them to positive American traditions or memories. Reagan's convention film and consequent television advertisements extolled him for "rebuilding the American dream," while shots of the Statue of Liberty renovation flashed on the screen. His cowboy image was emphasized; he was shown on horseback and chopping wood.[110] Peggy Noonan, whose Irish Catholic family had a Democratic background and whose first political hero was John Kennedy, wrote speeches for Reagan associating him with the New Deal–Cold War past of the Democratic party. Reagan visited the site of a 1960 Kennedy campaign stop in Connecticut and made reference to Kennedy's campaign, using the tones of Noonan's youthful enthusiasm: "Even though it was the fall [at the time of Kennedy's visit], it seemed like springtime, those days. . . . I see our country today and I think it is springtime for America once again."[111] In his attempt to woo traditionally Democratic voters, Reagan borrowed the memories of another generation, the generation whose idealism was sparked by Kennedy's New Frontier; Reagan offered another display of faith in American destiny, now rearticulating the optimism featured in the New Frontier to coalesce a Republican majority.[112]

Because Reagan's past was mythic, he could easily make claims on the historical roots of his political opposition. Such cooptations were abetted by the sense that the nation had undergone drastic changes since the days of Roosevelt, Truman, and Kennedy; the degree of change weakened the exclusivity of current Democrats' claims to the legacy of those previous Democratic presidents. By dismissing the period between Kennedy's assassination and his own election as a temporary aberration, an unforeseen wintertime of the national soul, Reagan could invoke an American past of unchanging values, and thus could offer platitudinous links to historical themes divorced from a well-developed sense of cause and effect. The past and present melded into an undifferentiated testament to American goodness and superiority, which voters needed only to accept to ensure a future just as vaguely pleasing. The narrative of decline and restoration in the postwar world was needed to explain the obvious travails of recent national experience, but once publicly understood, it could be superseded by an ahistorical tribute to American values that traversed time without change. Four years into the Reagan presidency, the restorationist theme could shift from an urgent plea for the reversal of recent change to an acclamation of the reversal's accomplishment.

Reagan's campaign advertisements depicted a smiling America of July 4th celebrations, family get-togethers, and small-town life. In this sense, by the middle years of his presidency, Reagan fostered, as Sidney Blumenthal writes, "nostalgia for the present. Our current happy days are depicted through a gauzy lens. Reagan persuades us that thinking about the present is an act of remembrance. He erases time. . . . No past, no present, no future—we have only an enduring sense of place."[113] Politically, senses of place have been key-stones of nationalist movements, which define the national people by their ties to the permanence of the land. Senses of time achieve importance insofar as time is conceived of as a shared history, which is often conveyed mythically to illustrate national values and character. To introduce into the shared historical consciousness events that contradict or challenge the national character can be seen as rejecting the people's history. To turn one's back on the people's history is to turn against the nation. If a social group holds memories at variance to the national memories circulating at a specific time, it risks being defined as outside the mythic constructs of the nation. Reagan's double nostalgia, for the pre-Sixties past and the Eighties present, worked to link together the Sixties disrupters of the nation and the 1980s opponents of Reaganism, defined jointly as twin traitors to the American Dream.

The Response of the Democrats

The response by Democrats and other figures on the left to the Reagan ideological offensive was muted, particularly regarding the conservative historiography that buttressed Reagan's appeal. Although liberal journals of opinion made note of Reagan's historical errors and Disneyish view of the American past, few political figures tried to counter the attack on the Sixties that served as a linchpin to the Republican coalition. Democrats seemed shell-shocked in the face of the 1980 election, were prone to exaggerating Reagan's popularity, and abetted the restructuring of tax policy as much as they tried to lessen the changes in the federal budget.[114] Opposition to Reagan tended to be couched in piecemeal, programmatic terms, as Democrats used their leverage in the House of Representatives and state governments to maneuver around the political landscape, rather than take on Reagan directly in the rhetorical field he had mastered. This inability to project a historical vision, to link the past with the future in meaningful ways, continued to plague Democrats into the 1984 presidential election.

During the Democratic primaries, John Glenn, Gary Hart, and Jesse Jackson made attempts to link themselves to positive aspects of the Sixties, with mixed results. Glenn tried to trade on his association with New Frontier daring-do and his personal friendship with John Kennedy. His media adviser,

Scott Miller, counted on nostalgia for the optimism of the Kennedy era to provide support among a disparate electorate: "We can all agree that this man, in America's shining moment, was the ideal. That's common ground. . . . This guy can be our face to the world as he was in 1962. He can be America."[115] Simple reversion to 1962 was not sufficient for Democratic voters, however, as Glenn seemed to evade the intervening twenty years of American experience rather than to explain them. Democratic voters resentful of Reagan's claim to personally embody America chose not to opt for another celebrity-turned-politician.

Gary Hart also played on links to Kennedy by claiming the fallen president as his original inspiration to go into public service and by trying to evoke him stylistically. Hart surprised many voters and pundits with his strong showing in the primaries, but was unable to shake off accusations of glibness and opportunism. His personal evocation of Kennedy's style created skepticism that he was inauthentic and hollow, a candidate suitable only for 1980s yuppies. His limited success, however, did demonstrate that the New Frontier could serve as a touchstone for Democratic candidates in their efforts to locate themselves historically.[116]

Jesse Jackson, despite his troubled relations with much of the civil rights leadership over two decades, clearly referenced the Sixties movement in his public persona. To skeptical white minds, however, his association with the separatist Nation of Islam also linked him to the more controversial Malcolm X and the militant Black Power movement of the late 1960s.[117] Jackson's identification with African-American politics and cultural expression was both his strength and his limitation, and in the 1984 campaign he never succeeded in transcending his ties to the historically specific movements for racial justice of the Sixties.

The failure of Walter Mondale's challengers prevented the Democratic response to Reagan from functioning effectively on the fields of history and memory. Mondale continued the practice of appealing to discrete interest groups on specific issues, without making his appeals cohere through a compelling historical narrative. Mondale located himself in history through identification with the traditions of the New Deal; while Americans supported New Deal programs that continued to provide them benefits, the Roosevelt era was increasingly remote from the historical experience of most voters, and Mondale seemed historically obsolescent.[118]

Reagan's Unstable Popularity

The lack of a coherent, sustained response by Reagan opponents was all the more striking because of the president's potential weaknesses. Retrospectively the 1980s have been seen as an era in thrall to Reagan's persona, but his presidency was not a particularly popular one for much of his term in office.

After the brief surge in support brought forth by the assassination attempt, Reagan's popularity levels plunged in the face of the recurrence of economic recession in the middle of 1981. Broad sectors of the population were hurt by the financial downturn and the reduction in government domestic spending programs; the renewed militarism of American foreign policy also attracted criticism, especially from the large movement against nuclear weapons. Democrats did well in the 1982 congressional elections; in January 1983, Reagan's approval rating stood at 35 percent, historically very low.[119]

Reagan benefited from a number of factors in maintaining the chimera of broad popularity. First, he always managed to retain the support of the American right, so that his support levels never dropped below one-third of the electorate. A vocal, active body of supporters conveyed a sense of momentum for conservative policies. Second, in the window of opportunity provided by his shooting, Reagan was able to pass the central pieces of his economic agenda, which set new terms for further debate. Third, Reagan performed publicly as if he were popular; after the anxious last years of the Carter presidency, Reagan acted as if he enjoyed being in the White House and had secured the widespread support of the American people. Members of the press often took their cue in assessing his popularity from this performance of popularity, and thus reinforced the sense that Reagan dominated the political landscape.[120]

Finally, Reagan aides made much of the fact that Reagan's personal popularity rankings were higher than the approval ratings for his policies, arguing that Americans liked the man as president even when they disagreed with his policies. This led Democrats and other critics to identify specific policy stands as Reagan's area of vulnerability and base their opposition around specific, piecemeal issues rather than broader senses of values and history. In fact, American presidents' personal popularity rankings are virtually always higher than their performance approval ratings; Reagan's high numbers in that area were more important in the way they were interpreted by the press and the opposition than as indicators of broad popular support.[121]

As general economic indicators began to improve in 1983 and 1984, Reagan did enjoy an upsurge in popularity, which continued until the Iran-Contra scandal did serious political damage to his administration. This popularity was manifest across many of the cleavages in American society, including divisions based on age, gender, region, and class. The attention paid to Washington politics during the 1984 election year gave Reagan's popularity levels in that year a greater discursive weight than had been given his unpopularity two years earlier. The 1984 election and attendant nationalist spectacles were thus the apotheosis of Reaganism, a relatively brief period that loomed larger and longer in retrospect. The conservative political offensive had been outlining the themes of the administration for a number of years, and this persistent discussion also seemed to give Reagan's role in American society greater heft. Reaganism did indeed dominate the political landscape of the 1980s, but not because Reagan and his policies were consistently popular. Rather, Reagan's message coincided with certain long-held views of American values and greatness, and their reinvigoration achieved a rhetorical dominance beyond the day-to-day positioning of political actors and movements. The absence of a persuasive, active counterpart to Reagan's historiography allowed this dominance to continue unchallenged for many years.

Large sectors of the electorate were inconsistent in their support for Reagan, or consistent in their opposition, yet their opinions and political movements lacked an overarching coherence, and they achieved only isolated victories against the Republican campaign. Oppositional political movements rarely produced historical narratives as encompassing and compelling as Reagan's, and hence found their public support to be uneven and their aims lacking in historical reach. Their very opposition to Reagan served to socially and politically marginalize them, to function as acts of self-differentiation from the broad trajectory of American greatness and goodness that Reagan sketched. The group memories of anti-Reagan sectors of the polity were left largely unarticulated in the political sphere, although they may have remained vibrant to individuals. Conservatives assertively tried to transform their group senses of the past into public knowledge, while liberals and leftists were consistently on the defensive, offering neither compelling stories nor uplifting homilies for use by the wider public in defining the nation's history or future.

Organized politics and official political discourse were in thrall to Reagan, but many Americans remained more circumspect. It was in the field of popular culture that any dynamic sense of opposition to the conservative historiography persisted. The ongoing search for historical narratives that could credibly explain recent American experience found expression in a range of cultural forms. In films, television shows, music, and other cultural arenas, the meanings of the American past continued to be debated and contested; the displays of nostalgia and memory proved more varied in the cultural sphere than were the manifestations that proclaimed the conservative dominance in politics. In the 1980s, popular culture repeatedly called upon notions of recent American experience to provide dramatic (and comic) tension, relevance, and depth to its material, and to respond to the historical storytelling of the conservative movement.

CHAPTER 4

Popular Culture and the Response to Conservative Nostalgia

EVEN AS THE REPUBLICAN VIEW of the American past dominated the political realm in the 1980s, popular culture produced myriad representations of historical events and eras that, at times, challenged the nostalgic discourse of conservatism. In particular, films, television programs, musical acts, and other cultural products responded to the Reagan era by exploring the meanings of the Sixties for America in the 1980s. Some of the biggest hits of the decade contained examinations of the Vietnam War, the historical experiences of the Baby Boom generation, and the social and cultural changes that marked the post–World War II era. Other productions, while not representing the past directly, implicitly evoked the relation between past and present and contributed to the widespread cultural discussion that followed Reaganism's use of the past in political discourse. Given the failure of the Democrats to put forward their own vision of the past effectively, the realm of popular culture constituted the strongest response to conservative attempts to define the Fifties and the Sixties. Films, television series, songs, and novels kept alive alternative sets of memories and historical understandings, preventing conservatives from monopolizing social and national memories of the recent past.

MEMORIES, MEDIA, AND THE PAST

Representations circulated by the media were not, of course, the only images of the past remembered by many Americans. For those alive in the 1950s and/or the 1960s, media imagery mixed with personal memories to form the subject material for personal historical interpretation. How do such interactions work? Why do people remember, and what forms do political, social, and personal memories take? What roles do age, social identity, and contemporary context play in maintaining and revising memory? Memory theorists and researchers are increasingly exploring these questions, and some tentative answers have emerged, relevant to contemporary nostalgia and the discourses of the past that circulated in American media and politics during the 1980s and 1990s.

Memory researchers argue as to the predominant forms of recall and meaning production regarding the past, but most assert the importance of isolated moments and images, and of figures who condense and dramatize meaning.[1] People tend not to remember long narratives, but memories themselves gain importance through their placement within the specific narrative of the rememberer's life.[2] In addition, people tend to learn more deeply from their personal experiences than from their exposure to media images.[3] To synthesize these separate findings, we may say that events and historical narratives become condensed through memory into isolated but emblematic images and representative figures, and are understood in the context of the life of the memory holder. The greater personal experience the memory holder has had with the event remembered, the richer the memory will be. Hence participants in Sixties political and cultural movements, for instance, will have more complicated and profound memories of events associated with the movements than those who did not participate. Active remembering, however, is dependent on catalysts of remembrance and a belief in the continued relevance of the memory.[4] Both catalysts of remembrance and signs of relevance may emerge either from one's personal circumstances or from the greater social context in which one lives.

Most people are socialized politically during their late adolescence, when they adopt partisan and policy preferences that tend to be long-lasting. Even as memory of a specific event or situation decays, attitudes based on the memory may persist.[5] Groups whose social and political identities are based on events from decades ago may have vague memories of the events but hold on to the consequent formations of identity. Group and public memory tend to further dissociate remembrance from linear sequencing of time, as memories from many sources converge; individual elements are conflated, reorganized, excluded, or newly emphasized.[6] The memories that persist may mostly be a selection of seemingly isolated images, interpretations, and meaningful figures, which find coherence within the context of the individual narrative of personal life, and through group identity.

Because entertainment narratives primarily focus on the appeal of their stars, celebrity figures and the characters they play are particularly useful as touchstones of mediated memory. Because star personas are often multifaceted, celebrities evoke a multiplicity of values that can be taken up by competing groups. The easy ability to isolate celebrities of the past from their context in the entertainment industry, by means of film clips and records of peripheral public appearances, creates an iconicity that reduces their connection to a specific time. As S. Paige Baty notes in her study of Marilyn Monroe's continued appeal, this reduction in historical specificity can imbue celebrities' persona with contemporary relevance, if they express values that remain at issue in social life.[7] Conversely, a particularly coherent star persona that changes little over time, such as John Wayne's, gains in iconic power by its claim to historical stability.

Information about political events tends to be learned through the media, rather than through direct experience; explicitly political memories are thus prone to bear the mark of simplicity and decontextualization common to media memories (abetted by the lack of complexity and context often found in media treatments of politics themselves).[8] Some particularly dramatic events, whether lived directly or learned about through the media, may be vividly recalled by all holders of the memory—the classic example being the assassination of John F. Kennedy.

Media representations can evoke nostalgia for an era before one's own life, a previous Golden Age available to those who have come after through media consumption and stylistic revival. For those too young to have direct experience of a social phenomenon or its immediate portrayal in the media, later understandings can still contribute to identity formation, in which newcomers from the following generation share a memory of a particular social group. Such sharing helps group members to locate themselves in history, just as taking up a specific historical legacy allows them to share a group identity with others. The Grateful Dead inspired a new generation of fans in the 1980s and 1990s, many of whom saw their fandom as an act of allegiance to the values of Sixties social and cultural movements; "Deadheads" refused to let Sixties principles wither in the face of Reaganism.[9] Similarly, for those who actually lived through the period, celebrity figures and other imagery can serve as representations of a younger self's potential that has yet to be realized, or a freedom that has been compromised to the complexities of adulthood.[10]

The public nature of politics for many youths in the 1960s led to their participation in dramatic events, as well as the opportunity to witness such events through the media. The attachment of these young people to identity-defining memories may be expected to be relatively strong, and the parade of Sixties images in the media during the 1980s served as continual catalysts to memories that reinstilled the importance of their group identities formed during their youth. Thus, for instance, civil rights activists in the early 1960s continued to value civil rights and to identify with the left (albeit with some changes in attitude) in the 1980s.[11]

Many people who came of political age in the 1960s, of course, never got involved in activism or sympathized with the New Left. Political differences within an age cohort always exist; what those of similar age share, at least in part, is a recognition of an agenda, a definition of what issues and social problems are crucial to political identity (subject to other axes of social difference). A generation is marked not by its similar responses to its historical and social context but by a shared recognition of what constitutes this context.[12] The civil rights movement, the Vietnam War, and the social experimentation of the counterculture provided a framework of understanding for both liberals and conservatives, for hawks and doves, for those who defended the Sixties legacy and those who opposed it. The continued media definition of these issues and movements as part of a coherent historical period both reflected and reiterated the notion that the 1960s were a crucial period of American life, an era that remains a relevant touchstone in the formation of political and social identity.

THE AMERICAN PAST IN THE 1980s

Like the 1970s, the 1980s saw a number of nostalgic revivals of previously popular styles and performers. None, however, achieved the widespread popularity and long life of the Fifties revival in the 1970s; each stylistic re-creation tended to be limited to a specific medium, rather than spreading across music, film, and television as the Fifties revival had done. Still, the revivals contributed to the range of representations that helped to constitute public memory of the 1950s and 1960s. In particular, styles and themes of the 1960s became subject to widespread revival for the first time. Many of the references to the past, however, took form not as nostalgic revivals of cultural styles, but as explorations of the meanings of American history. Such productions depicted and evoked the dramatic events of the 1960s and explored the felt distance between that decade and the America of the 1980s.

The Sixties in Film and Television

While nods to the past intermingled with more contemporary styles in the 1980s popular music scene, it was in film and television that the meanings of the Sixties were most explicitly discussed in the context of the conservative recitation of Fifties virtues and Sixties failings. Films and television programs served as repositories of memories, images, and interpretations of the 1960s that often countered the conservative attack and expressed a more multivalent take on the recent past. High-profile films played on generational memories and provoked controversy regarding their political leanings, historical accuracy, and relation to legacies of the Sixties. Many other television entertainment programs, docudramas, and news reports added to the national conversation on the meanings of recent American historical experience and its relevance to contemporary concerns. Some of these works were initiated by cultural producers whose social and political identities had been formed during the era they were now documenting. Their productions functioned as a response to Reagan's attack on the Sixties at a time when the Democratic party failed to effectively challenge Reagan's rhetorical dominance and his vision of American history.

The historically minded films of the 1980s treated several aspects of the 1960s—the Vietnam War, the civil rights movement, the contrasts between the 1960s and 1980s for Baby Boomers. The subjects largely corresponded to the historical experience of the early Boomers, repeating the litany of events that had come to represent the Sixties in public memory. Like the Fifties cultural revival in the 1970s, the Sixties films of the 1980s highlighted the experience of youth. Some of the films, however, emphasized the reaction of older Americans to the social and political challenges associated with Sixties youth movements. Whereas the older Fifties revival had represented largely private experience (however shared within a generation), the 1960s' association with public events and experiences led to stories representing a significant diversity of experiences and a broader range of characters.

Vietnam in American Film and Television

Hollywood filmmaking went through three phases regarding Vietnam from the late 1970s to the late 1980s.[13] These phases roughly follow a path from depictions of the war as brutal and insane, and criticism of American intentions within it, to support for the nobility of doubly victimized American troops as described in conservative rhetoric, to a condemnation of the war as a waste and destroyer of the American spirit.

In the late 1970s the first wave of Vietnam dramas, such as *Coming Home* (1978), *Who'll Stop the Rain* (1978), and *Apocalypse Now* (1979), were upscale productions that questioned U.S. involvement in the war.[14] The films aim for historical complexity and feature many performers well known for their leftist politics, including Jane Fonda, Jon Voight, Marlon Brando, and Martin Sheen. The films portray the costs of the war to both Americans and Vietnamese, and generally correspond to the disillusionment with the war that marked the late 1970s. Their tone is often one of absurdity and brutality, similar to some of the well-known literature inspired by the war, such as Robert Stone's *Dog Soldiers* (brought to screen as *Who'll Stop the Rain*), Tim O'Brien's *Going After Cacciato*, and, most compellingly, Michael Herr's *Dispatches*, which depicted the war as a charnel house of meaningless violence and sacrifice, without coherent direction or honest leadership.[15] (Herr worked on the screenplay of *Apocalypse Now* and, later, *Full Metal Jacket*.) Many of the films focus on events stateside in tracing the long-term effects of the war on American society, and depict the psychological and physical toll on those involved in the war.

The depictions of the war in the first phase offer little comfort to viewers. *Friendly Fire* and *A Rumor of War* were two television films based on nonfiction accounts that provide only the sense that the nation must confront the tragedy directly to glean whatever knowledge can be gained in the process. *Friendly Fire* portrayed the efforts of a midwestern couple to discover how their son died in the war, and the government's obfuscation regarding the human error that had resulted in his death. *A Rumor of War* depicted an atrocity against Vietnamese civilians by American troops as a predictable aspect of a conflict whose meaning and purpose had become incomprehensible to the soldiers immersed within it. The two films aimed to leave viewers sadder but wiser about the realities of war in general and American involvement in Vietnam in particular.[16]

Conservatives sought to replace these downbeat educations in war's destruction with a new set of lessons—the need for American strength in the world and the nobility and guiltlessness of those willing to fight for the nation. The second phase accompanied Ronald Reagan's revaluation of America's intentions and role in the war, and was inspired by the persistent claims that American soldiers remained imprisoned in Southeast Asia. *Uncommon Valor* (1983), *Missing in Action* and its sequel (1984 and 1985), and, most spectacularly, *Rambo: First Blood Part II* (1985) replay the war through contemporary missions to free the remaining POWs, allowing the heroes to kill great numbers of Vietnamese and castigating Washington policymakers for their timid prosecution of the war and abandonment of GIs and veterans since the American defeat.[17] Whereas the first, stateside, Rambo film, *First Blood* (1982), presented an antiauthoritarian, populist pro-veteran stance that could be read as coming from the right or the left, its sequel and the other POW-MIA dramas function in accordance with the conservative criticism of the left as betrayers of the nation.[18] The Vietnam veteran (and returned POW) had often been portrayed in television dramas of the 1970s as psychotic and flashback-prone, and in the films of the late 1970s as emotionally fragile and socially disoriented. In the mid-1980s, the veteran is transformed into the isolated but avenging angel of a reborn American patriotism, assertiveness, and toughness, in keeping with Republican calls for national greatness, militarism, and individualism.

Rambo takes his place in the pantheon of Reaganite heroes, a powerful figure of the recovery of American military might, individual physical prowess,

6. The revenge of the hypermasculine Vietnam vet in *Rambo: First Blood Part II*. Tri-Star.

and purity of intent. His hypermasculinity coincides with the conservative movement's attempt to revalue male strength in family relations and its reaction against the achievements of feminism. Rambo, though seemingly self-sufficient in his physicality, is actually dependent emotionally on his old commander, Colonel Trautman. Trautman is a father figure who attempts to reconcile Rambo to the greater society, just as Ronald Reagan offered fatherly public tributes to Vietnam veterans who felt estranged from the nation that sent them to war. In the POW-MIA films, as in Republican rhetoric, fathers and sons recombine to reassert American international strength and warrior values, after the Sixties' generational divide and feminism's gendered antagonisms had challenged patriarchal authority.[19]

After a decade and more of public disillusionment with the war, the POW-MIA theme of the films deftly represents the national feeling of victimization and loss of agency that had continued in regard to international affairs. *Rambo* star Sylvester Stallone disclaimed any political message in the film beyond love of country and gratitude toward war veterans, but by narrowing the war to the scenario of rescuing POWs within a strict Cold War frame, his film effaces the experience of the Vietnamese people during the war and America's impact on the region.[20] Displays of firepower replace attempts at historical complexity. The straining emotional response, through highly stylized brutality, makes *Rambo* in particular of a piece with the contemporaneous public spectacles of Reaganism. It shares the quality of a willed return to a state of pre-Vietnam American innocence, despite John Rambo's cynical take on established authority.[21] Many Americans seemed grateful for the chance to see the nation as innocent victim—"Rambomania" spread across the country, led by Reagan's endorsement of the film.[22] The excessive nature of *Rambo*, however, left it open to refutation by a new movement toward realism that pervaded the final wave of 1980s Vietnam films.[23]

This final phase started with *Platoon*, which functioned as a realist debunking of Stallone's fantastic adventures.[24] The films of the third phase replace revenge fantasies with ground-level depictions of the war and its effects on the Americans fighting it. Patricia Aufderheide points out that the initial, darker third-wave films came from the margins of the film production scene, rather than from the major studios.[25] Smaller producers who were more prone to making downbeat, critical stories had emerged in the 1980s, sustained by the emergent VCR market; the larger studios entered into similar productions only after *Platoon*'s great commercial success.[26]

In press accounts of *Platoon*'s impact, many veterans praised the film's verisimilitude; others pointed out flaws in its supposed realism. Most reviewers concentrated on the film's depiction of the peculiar horrors of the Vietnam experience, while conservatives criticized the film for concentrating on the terror of war to the exclusion of its greater historical context.[27] Liberals had

7. GIs abuse civilians and torch a village in Oliver Stone's *Platoon*. Orion.

scorned *Rambo* for its historical simplicities, but defenders of the war now pointed to the tragic aftermath of the conflict throughout Indochina to show the need to go beyond a grunt's-eye view of the war. Recent immigrants from Vietnam interviewed in Los Angeles, however, gave the film credit for dramatizing the problematic interactions between American GIs and Vietnamese villagers, which in the film nearly lead to a massacre.[28]

Films of the third wave tend to portray the later stages of the war, after American idealism and the wisdom of intervention had already become questioned both domestically and by troops in the field. The troops' preoccupation is survival, rather than a belief in the purported goals of the war. As with the POW-MIA films, few trustworthy authority figures are depicted; the GIs are cynical about officers and operate in disorienting circumstances. As with the late 1970s dramas, Vietnam veterans stateside tend to be emotionally fragile, attempting to pull together the fragments of their lives sundered by their wartime experience.

The emotional toll of soldiers also is a persistent theme in 1980s literary efforts on the war, as veterans began publishing in greater numbers. A number of veterans' books were realist, detailed examinations of day-to-day experience that served as precursors to *Platoon*. John Del Vecchio's *The 13th Valley* looks at a large military campaign through the experiences of an infantry platoon; the courage and expertise of the unit's members are unable to prevent eventual psychic breakdown and death. Robert Lee Mason's memoir *Chickenhawk* details the bravery and terror of helicopter pilots, and Stephen Wright's *Meditations in Green* traces the disillusionment of one enlisted man. Hawks and doves might read these stories with different emphases, but all of the books

sought to immerse readers in soldiers' day-to-day experiences and their emotional consequences, to bring personal memories into the public arena. Other
novelists also addressed themes of veterans' difficulties in emotional reintegra-
tion and adaptation stateside, as in Bobbie Ann Mason's *In Country*, which
traces the devastating effects of the war on a group of veterans while holding
out hope that family and public acknowledgment of the war's trauma can lead
to personal and national healing.[29]

The films of the third wave offer a wider range of experiences within
Vietnam for their stories. The popular *Good Morning, Vietnam* (1987) gives audiences the opportunity to experience GI life in Vietnam vicariously through the
story of a radio disk jockey, thereby largely avoiding the dynamic of violence
and guilt that was common to depictions of infantry activity. The film also
allows for a speech by a Viet Cong bomber in which he emotionally states the
case against U.S. intervention.[30] In *BAT 21*, Gene Hackman portrays a member
of a bombing squadron who survives being shot down. Rather than becoming
the subject of a standard POW story, Hackman's character avoids capture, but by
operating at ground level he is confronted with the violence and destruction of
the war that had previously seemed remote to him; by the time he reaches
safety, he has forsworn further involvement in the conflict.[31] The Vietnam films
of the late 1980s staked out claims regarding the war that often ran counter to
the Republican efforts to revalidate the American military involvement in
Southeast Asia; senseless loss, American hubris, and the loss of national ideals
remained themes that circulated widely despite the renewed militarism, anticommunism, and pronounced nationalism of the Reagan administration.

Television news divisions had covered the war extensively during the
years of American troop involvement, but after the fall of Saigon, Vietnam
quickly disappeared as a subject of special reports and documentaries. In the
early 1980s the major networks returned to the topic with a number of
reports, often detailing the fate of veterans of the war and the war's role as a
destroyer of national confidence and consensus.[32] PBS produced a multipart
history of the conflict that carefully modulated its position on the intentions
of the warring parties and the ultimate meanings and lessons of the war.[33] It
was only after the success of *Platoon* and other realist films that networks put
forward fiction series that treated aspects of the Vietnam experience for Americans—HBO's irregularly scheduled *Vietnam War Story*, CBS's *Tour of Duty*,
and ABC's *China Beach*.

Tour of Duty, like *Platoon*, features the misadventures of a group of
infantry soldiers.[34] The series format provides ample time for a wide range of
opinions about the war to be voiced, by the characters themselves and
through the narratives that the producers choose to tell. In addition, the
action starts in 1967, as disillusionment with the war is growing but has not
become universal. Viewers can hear the "one hand tied behind our back" the-

sis juxtaposed with stories depicting the futility of the "strategic hamlet" concept. The status of the skeptics and critics of the war is enhanced by the retrospective nature of the series—audiences in the late 1980s know the unsuccessful outcome of the war for American forces, so that optimists among the soldiers (usually officers) look particularly foolish. The series is noteworthy in its intermittent efforts at giving voice to the rival forces—one episode is told from the point of view of the Viet Cong, and the Viet Cong and North Vietnamese forces are usually depicted as professional and capable of nobility.

China Beach, created by *Rumor of War* screenwriter John Sacret Young, focuses on medical personnel, particularly nurses, who treat the physical and emotional injuries of American troops and must cope with their own sense of horror and frustration.[35] The series creates a heretofore unexplored position of identification for viewers—that of American women serving in Vietnam—which allows viewers to experience the pathos and drama of the war while retaining a sense of noble intent and helpfulness. The series' emphasis on the wounds that Vietnam inflicted onto the bodies and souls of Americans corresponds with the reflective tone of many of the productions of this period.

Sasha Torres takes *China Beach*'s theme to be the importance and difficulties of memory in dealing with trauma, trauma that makes straightforward depiction and remembrance problematic. These dynamics of memory are depicted by the series by the use of extended flashbacks initiated by characters' contemplations. These ruminations are portrayed as important for both individual healing among the characters, and for the nation as a whole.[36] *Tour of Duty* also revisits the war to enrich understandings of its failure, to assert that the war entailed complications beyond the schematic views of hawks and doves.[37] In both series, a return to the events of the war is necessary for the nation to achieve an understanding that has eluded Americans for a generation.

The series' ambivalences and assertive polysemy can be seen as in keeping with network financial imperatives to attract viewers from many different perspectives. At a time when conservatives' arguments regarding the war were going virtually unchallenged in the political sphere, however, the programs' multivalent approaches effectively challenged the simplicities of political rhetoric, particularly the penchant for scapegoating the left for losing the war. Although neither show attained great popularity, each managed to stay on the air for a number of seasons, and *China Beach* enjoyed a noteworthy run on Lifetime in repeat syndication. (*Tour of Duty* continued to be run intermittently on TNT, particularly on Memorial Day.)

Television also dealt more obliquely with the war's meanings through several action series that featured Vietnam veterans as major characters. *Magnum, P.I.*, *Simon & Simon*, and *The A-Team* portrayed veterans' efforts to reintegrate into American society, with varying degrees of success, after the trauma of serving in Indochina. Thomas Magnum and his combat colleagues fight crime in Hawaii while enjoying marginal but comfortable lifestyles; members of the A-Team roam the world as antiauthoritarian do-gooders, relying on the ingenuity and camaraderie they developed in Vietnam to sustain their precarious mission. The series' enshrinement of veterans' experiences as haunting but noble paralleled Reagan rhetoric; the parallels were reinforced off-screen by the conservative political activism of *Magnum*'s Tom Selleck and *Simon*'s Gerald McRaney. McRaney went on to play a career military officer in the sitcom *Major Dad*.[38]

The Civil Rights Movement

The other great national dilemma of the Sixties, as understood in retrospect, was the civil rights movement. The first major representation of the movement on 1980s screens was the television documentary production *Eyes on the Prize*, which offered a detailed and dramatic recitation of the efforts against southern segregation in the early 1960s, narrated by SNCC veteran Julian Bond.[39] The series benefited from the extensive coverage by television news cameras that the movement enjoyed in the 1960s, and was able to include both classic moments—Martin Luther King, Jr.'s speeches, the fire hoses and German shepherds used to disrupt protests in Birmingham, Alabama—and more obscure footage. The program's detailed and personalized presentation of the period asserted the continued relevance of the struggle for civil rights and celebrated the accomplishments of several rights organizations, at a time when conservatives sought to consign civil rights concerns to history and regularly attacked the established civil rights leadership. The series was successful enough on public broadcasting to spawn a sequel, which dealt with the Black Power movement, the death of King, and the dispersal of energies in the movement.

Hollywood responded with *Mississippi Burning*, a popular if controversial film that depicts the search for the killers of three civil rights workers in Philadelphia, Mississippi (the town in which presidential candidate Ronald Reagan came to praise "states' rights" in 1980).[40] The film dramatically depicts the violence against African Americans under segregation, but reserves the most heroic roles in the events to white FBI agents, which spawned criticism by African-American and other commentators.[41] By making a white southerner (played, again, by Gene Hackman) the ultimate hero, the film offers the South, and by extension all of white America, hope for redemption. The film leaves open the question of the extent to which the nation has indeed been redeemed in the years since. The authorial expectation of audience sympathy for the movement points to a belief that the nation has moved forward in the struggle for equal rights and fair treatment of minorities, as conservatives argue; the decision to see the events of the case through white eyes (and FBI eyes at that) offered evidence to the film's critics that white ethnocentrism

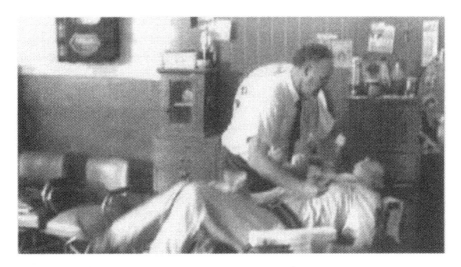

8. White American divided, but coming around: FBI agent Gene Hackman confronts a racist police officer in *Mississippi Burning*. Orion.

continued to dominate representations of American society. Director Alan Parker's claim that the film needed white leads to be commercially viable seemed to buttress black activists' claim that the integrationist movement's goal of full inclusion in American society remained unfulfilled.[42]

The popularity of *Mississippi Burning* inspired a number of other films about the South in the 1960s; films such as *Shag* (1989) and *Heart of Dixie* (1989) featured young people caught between rebellion and social convention, and did not fare well at the box office. Another little-seen film, *The Long Walk Home*, tells the story of the Montgomery bus boycott, generally credited as the first major protest of the civil rights era, through the experiences of a white middle-class housewife (Sissy Spacek) and her African-American housekeeper (Whoopi Goldberg).[43] The film thus seeks to represent two racial perspectives, and also identifies the movement with the later move toward feminism, in that Spacek's character defies her racist husband to show sisterly support for her employee. A similar narrative strategy of dramatizing the early days of the movement through the experiences of a white family and a black housekeeper was featured on *I'll Fly Away*, a critically acclaimed series that never gained much popularity during its run on NBC. The use of a female black/white pairing to explore southern racial dynamics was repeated ten years later in Lifetime's longer-running series *Any Day Now*.[44]

One filmmaker who repeatedly mined the 1960s for material was Oliver Stone, who rose to prominence with the success of *Platoon*. Over the next several years, Stone addressed key figures and events in the recent history of the nation with his films *Wall Street* (financial corruption in the Reaganomic

1980s), *Born on the Fourth of July* (also about Vietnam, focusing on its aftermath for a devastated, disabled vet), *JFK* (about the assassination and its investigation), *The Doors* (the counterculture), *Nixon*, and *Heaven and Earth* (returning to Vietnam, focusing on a Vietnamese woman and an American GI). In Stone's historiography, the murder of a progressive and reform-minded JFK by a right-wing conspiracy led to the soul- and body-destroying debacle in Vietnam, the desperate search for meaning among the young (with its attendant bids for transcendence and self-destructive hedonism), and the rise to power of Nixon.

Stone's films warn of a betrayal of the nation's best instincts by defenders of privilege and militarism, a betrayal that began in the 1960s and finds its apotheosis in a contemporary America coming apart at the seams (as in his films *Talk Radio* and *Natural Born Killers*.) Some of Stone's most popular films, such as *Platoon* and *Wall Street*, revolve around a young man's search for a father figure, but the role models featured often symbolize America's worst instincts rather than its best. The films inspired heated discussion in the press and academic circles on the gender and racial politics in Stone's work, and on the importance of historical accuracy in treating controversial themes. The films' high profiles demonstrated the continued commercial viability and discursive weight of explorations of the 1960s within popular culture.[45]

Yuppie Angst and Nostalgic Reversion

In addition to revisiting the public events of the 1960s, films and television programs also traced the distance between the values and expectations of the period and the purported realities of Baby Boomer life in the 1980s. In dramas and comedies of regret, nostalgia, and bewilderment, the 1960s were represented as a time of youthful idealism, extravagant if vague expectations, and exciting cultural progress. These energies were shown to be fading by the 1980s, replaced by a baleful, hard-won maturity.

The first film to explicitly explore this dynamic was John Sayles's *The Return of the Secaucus 7*, which announced the arrival of the new independent American cinema in 1981.[46] Manifestly low-budget and from a discernedly left-wing perspective, the film dramatized the disillusionment and modest hopes of Sixties activists facing uncertain futures at the dawn of the Reagan era. The film's themes and structure were echoed two years later in *The Big Chill*, a major-studio release produced by former 1960s media activist Michael Shamberg.[47] In *The Big Chill*, the past political activities of seven friends who reunite for a friend's funeral remain vague, but their occupational changes are carefully drawn to be emblematic of the shift from public-mindedness to private materialism—a public defender has become a real estate lawyer, an inner-city teacher has turned to celebrity journalism, a psychologist has descended to drug dependence and dealing. Their deceased friend was never able to

9. The comfortable but compromised achievers of *The Big Chill*. Courtesy of Columbia Pictures/Wisconsin Center for Film and Theater Research.

accommodate the turning away from Sixties values, and had become a lost soul before killing himself.

The group expresses regret at the diminution of their dreams and the clouding of their original, unifying purposes. The happiest of the survivors, however, is also the most conservative, a small businessman prospering in the Reagan era and impatient with Sixties political and social nostalgia (while steadfastly refusing to allow new additions to his Sixties record collection). The film was alternately hailed as an authentic voice of the historical experience of the Baby Boom generation and criticized as a whiny, half-hearted yuppie (before the label was popularized) tract.[48] It helped to solidify the notion that the Sixties generation had become sell-outs, and that those wanting to live according to Sixties ideals had faded into social and cultural obsolescence.

The Big Chill's combination of Boomer upward mobility and nostalgic regret was brought to television by *thirtysomething*, which inspired a similarly mixed critical response.[49] The central couple in the series' circle of middle-class friends and relatives are Michael and Hope, who continually evaluate and compare their present domesticated, corporate lives with their earlier artistic and feminist ambitions. The paths not taken are represented by Melissa, a single woman and photographer, who is beset by neuroses about her romantic and work life, and Gary, a politically rebellious but immature academic. The series' most famous episode mimics the old *Dick Van Dyke Show*, as Michael tries to make sense of his life by measuring it against the domestic ideal represented by the model 1960s television family. The series' dramatic development shows Michael and Hope growing into acceptance of their roles within a traditional, middle-class nuclear family, even as Michael is first tempted by, but ultimately becomes disillusioned with, cut-throat corporate politics. In perhaps the only strong protest seen on American entertainment programming against government policy during the Persian Gulf War, he quits his job in advertising in a fit of residual dovish disgust at the rampant jingoism around him.

Novelists also visited the emotional distance between the Sixties and the present day, but, not having to cater to advertisers, often concentrated on social groups beyond yuppies. Much of Ann Beattie's early fiction sets characters in the hangover of the Sixties, stumbling through life after the utopian hopes of their youth have faded; Beattie takes up this theme in the mid-1970s and moves away from it by the late 1980s, as the Sixties recede further in memory and history. Thomas Pynchon, however, centers his 1990 novel *Vineland* on the betrayal and failure of Sixties hopes at both the personal and the national levels, leaving characters adrift in an era of soulless commercialism and government repression of countercultural impulses. The popular film and television depictions of the Sixties legacy feature privileged professionals muddling through with varying degrees of acceptance to present social circumstances; the works of Sayles, Beattie, and Pynchon offer tragicomic visions of quirky outsiders bewildered by the seeming return to social dominance of pre-Sixties mundanity. Sometimes obstinate in their self-marginalization, they hold on to a sense of the Sixties that prevents them from sinking into a complacency they see growing around them, leaving them without the compensatory sense of security that is a central promise of Fifties political nostalgia.[50]

One television series enjoyed huge popularity by comically mining the contrasts between Sixties values and contemporary conservatism. *Family Ties* split the warring impulses between the Sixties and the Reagan Eighties generationally, as two liberal parents contend with their Reagan-loving teenage son, in a reversal of the generational dynamic of *All in the Family* and other post-Sixties productions.[51] In *Family Ties*, it is Sixties-based attitudes of anti-materialism, social concern for the disadvantaged, and open-mindedness toward others that are imbued with an aura of steady maturity, through the portrayal of the family's upper-middle-class parents, an architect and a public television programmer. The series' comic energy, however, stems from Michael J. Fox's portrayal of their son Alex as a greedy, know-it-all Reagan youth; as impetuous and immature as Alex is, he seemingly has time and determination on his side in his battle against the mild Sixties homilies of his parents. Perhaps that is why Ronald Reagan claimed it as his favorite show on television.[52]

Fox branched out from television to film stardom with *Back to the Future*, one of the 1980s' biggest hits.[53] The film's time-travel narrative offers a playful contrast between the 1950s and 1980s, but it did not spark a widespread revival of Fifties styles. Indeed, the film's 1950s youth culture is portrayed as deficient in the saving graces of the 1980s—Fox's character has to import rock and roll and technological playthings into the 1950s during his journey through time. The film does share the wistfulness of nostalgia in its enactment of a desire to rewind history, to return to a point in the past so as to live the intervening years over again. Yet the 1950s it depicts are hardly idyllic, and the positive, adult authority extolled by social conservatives is absent from the decade, except for the outcast Doc Brown. The film plays off the debate about the nation's past to create a comic tension of similarity and difference between the decades; the power of its Fifties surroundings comes from the active discussion beyond the world of the film regarding the past, while the film's narrative thrust is based on the desire to not remain stuck in the previous era.

The films *The Flamingo Kid* (1984) and *Dirty Dancing* (1987) revisited the early 1960s, the years *American Graffiti* had defined as the last innocent period before the onslaughts of the later part of the decade. *The Flamingo Kid*, directed by *Happy Days* mogul Garry Marshall, keeps a light-hearted tone throughout, but *Dirty Dancing* offers hints of what is to come, as the heroine of its coming-of-age story becomes more aware of the civil rights movement and other social concerns just as she awakens to her sexuality. If childhood memories of an apolitical 1950s had contributed to the era's definition as an innocent age in the 1970s Fifties revival, then *Dirty Dancing* depicts a Sixties concern for social justice as another sign of innocent youth rebelling against uncaring adults. Once taken up, Sixties activism can function as an entry into adulthood and a maturity more enlightened than that of the previous generation's.[54]

Every age is someone's Golden Age of childhood innocence. As late and post-Boomers reached adulthood and gained access to media production in the 1980s, the 1960s began to be reconfigured by those whose associations with the period were at variance with the usual identification of the late 1960s as an era of social chaos, political divisiveness, and widespread violence. *The Wonder Years*, created by producers born in the late 1950s, depicted the adolescent travails of its hero with a tone of rueful but appreciative nostalgia.[55] The series does not ignore the public events of the time—the premiere episode takes place in the wake of Robert Kennedy's assassination and features a major character learning of her brother's death in Vietnam. The focus of the series, however, is on a fundamentally innocent exploration of teenage sexuality and romance, friendship, and personal ethics, taking place in a suburban environment so often identified with 1950s sitcoms like *Leave It to Beaver*.

The prime authority figure, however, is not the family's father, as in Fifties family comedies. Rather, the adult voice of the young hero serves as an

ever-hovering narrator to explicate the meanings of his younger self's experiences. The vantage point of the present allows him to rewrite the 1960s from
the perspective of a younger cohort of the Baby Boom generation, to define
the era as a source of worthwhile personal values and familial coping skills.
The success of *The Wonder Years* shows that the work of a younger group of
cultural producers can provide complications to popular meanings of an era.
The series provides a much more positive and somewhat less tendentious portrayal of the late 1960s than found in previous political or cultural discourse.

Playing on generational memories and images of the Sixties was not a
guaranteed route to commercial success; the South-in-the-'60s films that followed *Mississippi Burning* failed at the box office, and the low-budget, har-
rowing Vietnam drama *84 Charlie MoPic* (directed by war veteran Patrick
Duncan, who had previously worked on HBO's *Vietnam War Story*) never
found a significant audience. The most fully elaborated on-screen treatment of
the relation between the Fifties, the Sixties, and the contemporary era may
have been *Almost Grown*, a drama that aired on CBS in 1988–89. Produced by
David Chase, who went on to create *The Sopranos*, *Almost Grown* travels between
the early 1960s, the late 1960s, and the 1980s to trace a couple's courtship,
marriage, and divorce. Along the way, the series touches on Fifties dating
practices, Sixties campus and national politics, and Eighties grapplings with
adult responsibilities, family breakups, and changing gender and sexual identities. Scheduled in CBS's slot for high-toned, women-friendly drama against
ABC's *Monday Night Football*, *Almost Grown* lasted only half a season.[56]

OLD MUSIC IN THE NEW DECADE

Fifties motifs maintained a lower level of popularity and visibility in the
Reagan era than they had enjoyed in the 1970s, despite the conservative
paeans to the 1950s in political discourse. Music had been the medium that
had introduced the first Fifties revival, but musical echoes of the Fifties took
shape only intermittently in the 1980s. The Fifties-themed rock band the
Stray Cats renewed interest among rock audiences in rockabilly in the early
1980s, and various Fifties rock and roll performers continued to perform.
Wynton Marsalis ushered in an era of neoclassicism in jazz, basing his music
on song structures and styles from the 1930s, 1940s, and 1950s. Several rock
singers, including Linda Ronstadt and Carly Simon, looked back to music of
their parents' generation to record albums of torch songs from the 1950s;
Ronstadt enlisted Nelson Riddle, who had been Frank Sinatra's prime musical arranger in the 1950s, to collaborate on her albums *What's New* (1983) and
Lush Life (1984), which enjoyed significant popularity. Taken as a whole, these
musical efforts offered a more multiplicitous view of Fifties culture than the
1970s revival had presented, but they generally were enjoyed as individual
productions rather than considered part of a nostalgic movement. In the frag-

mented 1980s musical market, each foray into the Fifties attracted fans on its own terms, but never coalesced into anything larger.[57]

Music based on 1960s rock and soul was much more prevalent, through the recycling of styles, reunion of bands, and continued commercial vitality of performers from the period. By the mid-1980s, album-oriented rock (AOR) radio stations had joined the traditional "oldies" stations in basing their programming on older records; AOR stations concentrated on the mid-1960s to the mid-1970s for their playlists, featuring artists such as the Beatles, the Rolling Stones, Jimi Hendrix, and Led Zeppelin. The stations created a sense of continuity for guitar-based rock that encompassed the period between the introduction of the Beatles to the end of the later Baby Boomers' adolescence. The music of this period eventually came to be labeled "classic rock," and demarcated the time when the Baby Boom generation could enjoy the sense of occupying the leading edge of contemporary culture through its fandom for new forms of rock.

Although the sense of a close connection between 1960s rock and the political and social tumult of the era may have dwindled as the music was recycled into "classic rock" formats, the residual associations between the music, the counterculture, and 1960s youth politics could still be enjoyed by those who wished to see the Sixties as a positive resource for contemporary society. Conservative critics of the Sixties certainly saw the connections as alive and influential—Jerry Falwell rails against the Rolling Stones and the Who in his book *Listen, America!* and Allan Bloom identifies Mick Jagger as the prime role model for the relativistic, mindless hedonism he sees as the dominant danger for American society, a legacy of the Sixties.[58] After rock had lost much of its political edge, it retained a legacy of rebelliousness, which had been employed by its earlier fans against the constraints of family life. In the conservative project to revalue the family, the lingering resonances of rock's initial subversiveness had to be attacked. Ironically, the conservative attacks on rock imbued the music's performers with an aura of continued significance that many of them otherwise would have found hard to sustain—in the 1980s, only by the work of his self-proclaimed enemies could Mick Jagger seem to be a threat to the social order.

The sense of classicism and generational influence associated with Sixties pop was also manifest in the increasing use of rock and soul as background music in public forums. Restaurants replaced Muzak with Motown for mood music; television sports programs began using rock arrangements in their opening, closing, and incidental music. Rock and soul's new ubiquity attested to the music's lasting value amid cultural change, validating the Baby Boomers' embrace of music despised by many of their parents. The cultural importance of 1960s rock was confirmed by the continuing nostalgia for the Beatles and by the highly visible reunions of bands from the 1960s. Simon and

Garfunkel reunited for a Central Park concert in 1981 that attracted hundreds of thousands; members of the Temptations joined forces with the popular contemporary band Hall and Oates to hit the concert trail again. The most culturally resonant reunion may have been the comeback of the Grateful Dead, the avatars of the hippie experience. The Dead had broken up at the start of the 1980s; by the late 1980s, they had reconvened some of their audience and added younger acolytes, with concert tours that ritualistically reenacted the communitarian ideals of the counterculture and a coterie of "Deadhead" fans and merchants trailing the band across the country.[59]

Two other performers from the 1960s, Cher and Tina Turner, also enjoyed renewed popularity in the 1980s. Both came to be symbols of female independence after they separated from their husbands to pursue solo careers. Cher had started her transformation from Sixties symbol of puppy love in the 1970s; after recurrent career setbacks, she reemerged as a film star still capable of garnering the occasional hit record on her own in the 1980s. Tina Turner had escaped an abusive marriage to Ike Turner and, after years of relative obscurity, returned to stardom with "What's Love Got to Do With It?" Her image combined her previous earthy sexuality with a new maturity and survivor's wisdom. The career of each singer traced the evolution of female identity from subservience to autonomy during the feminist period; they were reminders that feminism had wrought changes in the legacies of Sixties youth culture, just as it had in other areas of American society.[60]

More than any other performer in the 1980s, Bruce Springsteen constructed a historically minded cultural and social agenda through the evocation of past musical styles. Springsteen enjoyed widespread popularity in his persona as the voice of the white working class, perplexed by contemporary economic problems and sustained by memories of youth. His use of older musical styles, commingled with contemporary arrangements, argued for the continued relevance of old values from a period of American ascendancy and optimism among the working class. Springsteen updated the greaser image with an explicitly populist political stance; this updating was in part achieved, paradoxically, by introducing Depression-era folk themes into his musical mix. Springsteen thus alternated styles based on the greasers' Fifties rock and rhythm and blues with the musical roots of the Sixties counterculture's protest folk-rock, as if Elvis had begun singing Bob Dylan songs.[61]

This combination of Fifties rock and Thirties-Sixties folk made Springsteen's music accessible to a wide range of political positions; his darkly critical anthem of Vietnam veteran alienation "Born in the USA" was taken up as a manifesto of jingoistic pride during the orgy of defensive patriotism in 1984, accompanying the Olympics and Reagan's reelection. Reagan's campaign aides, wanting to reach white working-class voters through conservative populist themes, tried to enlist Springsteen in their efforts, apparently ignorant that the singer's songs pointed to the failure of Reaganomics to benefit his core audience. After Springsteen rebuffed his aides' overtures, Reagan persisted in his claim that Springsteen's music was allied to the nation's return to basic values and patriotism under Republican leadership.[62]

Even in post-punk and rap—the forms of 1980s pop music that made the biggest claims toward experimentation and innovation—the Sixties influence was heavily felt. Bands emerging out of the punk movement explored the archives of mid-1960s garage rock, with its punk-like emphases on simplicity and energy. The most prominent of these bands was the Replacements, who lent the punk aesthetic to their performances of music from the 1950s to the 1970s, blurring generic boundaries within rock to distill its legacy down to adolescent angst and proudly stupid, sybaritic excess. As punk gave way to a more diverse alternative music scene, a number of minirevivals based on past musical artists and styles quickly succeeded each other. Generic coding of new bands by reference to old styles eventually became rampant, if not obsessive, as "The New Psychedelia" yielded to REM's "folk-rock" in enjoying critical attention. Each succeeding cycle, however, seemed to diminish in significance, as the novelty of revival wore off. In rap, the predominant practice of sampling—the mixing of musical passages from old records behind new vocals—led to the redistribution of 1960s productions in soundbite portions. The work of James Brown, Led Zeppelin, and other performers became elements of radical stylistic pastiche that accompanied social commentary from young African Americans, often protesting the racial conditions of Reagan America. The renewal of interest in Brown's pioneering and assertive funk of the 1960s particularly connected contemporary black music to the era of Black Pride and Power.

CULTURAL SHORTHAND

Rap exemplified the increasingly cut-and-paste aesthetic of a burgeoning digital culture. The rise of sampling intensified the trend toward the use of quick references to the past as an efficient method of communicating cultural meanings. The meanings of the Fifties and the Sixties do not circulate in the media only in detailed, coherent narratives, nor do they contribute to the formation of public memories exclusively in such form. The cultural power of social definitions and representations comes as much through the use of short snippets that encapsulate meanings and concepts in iconic form. Cultural and political actors invite viewers and listeners to participate in the transformation of personal and group experiences into public and national memory by the quick offhand reference, the demonstrated assumption of a common set of knowledges, understandings, and opinions. Long-form television and film productions contribute to this cultural shorthand as well, as figures such as Rambo attain iconic status and become subject to wide social discussion.

Newscast narrations, comedy routines, and other short forms reinforce and redirect the meanings of longer narratives and create senses of direction and vitality for public memories, validating the concerns expressed by such memories as important to the polity. The most prevalent short cultural form, of course, is the commercial advertisement.

Advertisements, in either print or television, can refer to the past both stylistically and through their explicit content. The ephemeral quality of the quickly changing modes of advertising aesthetics makes it difficult for a particular style to achieve anything more than transitory prominence. Reference points in ads, however, construct a litany of what the advertising industry considers culturally comprehensible to its demographic targets, within the immediacy of an ad. In the 1980s advertisers made use of images of the Fifties and Sixties in a number of ways to achieve such comprehensibility.

One common strategy was to depict nostalgic scenes of an earlier period to evoke feelings of childhood security and joy, which could be regained through the product advertised. General Motors thus used Fifties imagery in its advertisements in the mid-1980s to depict the desire Americans had in the earlier time for the distinctive styles of Detroit cars.[63] The ads evoked nostalgia both for the childhood days of the company's targeted customers and for an era of American industrial supremacy and imagination. The ads promised that by buying GM cars in the 1980s, customers could share in the sanctioned desires of a more innocent time and in the recovery of American pride and prosperity.

Because those consumers whose childhoods encompassed the 1960s were gradually coming to dominate the prime consumerist caste (defined as between eighteen and forty-nine years of age), scenes and styles evoking the 1960s became fodder for advertisers. By associating products with styles once cherished but that also had gone through a period of relative obsolescence, merchandisers introduced kitsch as a primary element of 1980s consumption. Kitsch offered assertive simplicities to sophisticated consumers, taking them back to the days before their taste became educated. Reversion to childhood tastes offered consumers the opportunity to inversely display their cultural knowingness by feigning innocence—a strategy in keeping with the willed move back to the joys of Reaganite political innocence (which is not to say that all kitsch-lovers were Reagan supporters). Nostalgic cultural artifacts and styles evoked a potent combination of cultural sophistication and political innocence, providing the moral latitude for uninhibited spending by those prospering in the Reagan boom.

The advertisers' use of nostalgia did not play only into the Reagan social agenda, however. By imbuing the 1960s with a nostalgic hue, advertisers and consumers blurred the distinction between the 1950s and 1960s that conservatives had sought to amplify. The two decades began to meld together into an idyllic past that had produced cultural classics, whether in automobiles, music, television, or household items (sometimes conveyed through the use of black-and-white film stock in the ads). The advertisements of the earlier periods could themselves be invoked, as when Coca-Cola repeated its "I'd Like to Teach the World to Sing" campaign at the ad's twentieth anniversary in 1991. In its own time, the original spot connected Coke's appeal to youth with the folk music scene and its pacifist, internationalist overtones.[64] With the Cold War over in 1991, Coke could claim its long-term commitment to international harmony (under American direction) through the ad's re-creation. Here the innocence of the Sixties recalls the counterculture in its flower-power mode—clearly not in keeping with the conservative agenda.

During the George H. W. Bush administration, two contradictory advertising strategies appeared with nostalgic inflections. The first celebrated the virtues of what Republicans had come to call "family values," epitomized by *Good Housekeeping*'s "New Traditionalist" campaign.[65] Aimed at a generational cohort now taking on parental responsibilities, the campaign was not so distinctly antifeminist as Connaught Marshner's New Right manifesto from which it took its name. Its celebration of domesticity, however, implicitly criticized the attacks on the nuclear family associated with the counterculture and the feminist movement.

The other strategy celebrated not the newfound authority based on parenting, but the antiauthority strains of the New Left and the counterculture, now steered toward materialist spending. For example, a 1992 Isuzu advertisement depicts the development of rebellious 1960s tots into today's adventurous adults, who retain their Sixties distrust of established authority.[66] This antiauthoritarian streak aligns them with Isuzu, presumably both because of the stylings of the company's vehicles and because of its upstart status in the auto industry. The antiauthority gambit became unsurprisingly ubiquitous in advertising aimed at pre-adult boys in the 1990s, in Madison Avenue's attempt to reach the supposedly alienated Generation X. Advertisers often used the same strategy, however, to reach consumers in their forties and fifties, playing on purported group memories of youthful experimentation and rebellion. This approach was easily communicated through the use of late-1960s styles—psychedelic music, hippie apparel, long and unkempt hair—as powerful, if also silly, signs of freedom and adventure. Adults of the 1990s had dropped the appurtenances of youth, but could reconcile their early desires with the wisdom and responsibilities of age by the purchase of the proffered product.

The music television networks MTV and VH1 premiered in 1981 and 1985, respectively, and shared many stylistic elements with advertising (many video directors came from the advertising industry). The radical pastiche of the music video viewing experience emerged out of a dynamic of familiarity and difference, which made the cultural past into a prime resource by which to register meaning quickly—videos had to gain attention through stylistic differentiation, but attain comprehensibility in their short time spans. Video-makers adopted the styles of previous decades in their productions by using sets that made specific references to older television texts or by replicating the look of 1960s film stock. The most famous, perhaps, of music video's referencing of the past was Madonna's play on Marilyn Monroe's image in "Material Girl," which used Fifties images of femininity in the (perhaps ironic) service of Eighties greed.

News programs also featured the clichéd signs of older images to quickly communicate the passage of time and the disparity between past and contemporary experience. The tight schedules and routinized practices of television news gathering make the use of stock footage a regular component of reporting. Thus when ABC News in the 1980s mentioned the Sixties counterculture in its stories, such mentions were almost invariably accompanied by quick shots from Woodstock of young people cavorting in the mud, perhaps discarding various parts of their clothing or stumbling through a drug-induced haze. Sixties phenomena that could be represented by visually compelling imagery were included in quick retellings of history, while less visually accessible or interesting experiences found little room on television broadcasts. The Sixties increasingly came to be represented by some of its most extreme and dramatic moments, sustaining the argument that stark contrasts existed between the 1950s, the 1960s, and the contemporary period.

News reports in the 1980s occasionally kept track of generational changes, using the youth experience of the counterculture as a touchstone for comparison. The theme of the passing of the Sixties was invoked when short hair on men became popular in the early 1980s, when various Woodstock anniversaries were celebrated, and when yuppies become the focus of media attention.[67] Reporters took cultural experimentation, political rebellion, and social licentiousness to be the hallmarks of the Sixties generation in its youth, now superseded by careerism and privatism. Correspondents argued that the short-sighted rebels of yesteryear had become the sellouts of today. Echoing conservative critiques, they blamed the hedonism of the Sixties for drug dependencies, personal loneliness, and sexually transmitted diseases in the 1980s.[68]

The most positive reports on the 1960s covered the achievements of the civil rights movement and nostalgia for the Kennedys; beyond these, nothing of value seems to have lasted. At their least critical, reporters adopted an elegaic tone to note the passing of utopian dreams, as in this commemoration of Woodstock by ABC in 1984: "The 1960s: the youth of America were in open rebellion against the affluent society of their parents. . . . The counterculture of the Sixties left its mark but it really was a fairy tale. Like all fairy tales, [it] had to come to an end. Woodstock came to pass, but not to stay."[69] Events like Woodstock remained as symbols of another age, a measure of the distance the nation had traveled since the 1960s. This was so for both attackers and defenders of the Sixties, and while 1980s television reports on the Sixties tended to be critical, the striking, if narrow, visuals accompanying many of the reports may have communicated another story. The 1984 ABC story was accompanied by a shot of dancers at Woodstock silhouetted against a large, setting sun, expressing a fluid ecstasy in their movements that offered a seismic contrast to the rest of the nightly program's mundane news reports. For some viewers, that vision of communal, transcendent harmony may have meant more than the ascription of obsolescence that the narration imposed upon the hallmarks of the Sixties.

The films, television, books, and music of the 1980s contained patterns of exclusions, absences, and reductions regarding the experiences of the nation during the 1960s. Yet they also preserved a more complex range of representations of the era in the face of conservative assaults on the Sixties. The popularity of many of the recyclings and representations of 1960s culture showed the limits of the Republican rhetoric in the attempt to dominate national memory. Cultural presentations involving the war in Vietnam, the civil rights movement, the youth counterculture, rock and roll, and other phenomena of the era offered a variety of visions of America, and circulated memories and historical understandings counter to the discursive dominance achieved by conservatives in the political realm.

MEDIA AS INSTITUTIONS OF MEMORY

For those whose personal experiences have not involved public participation in the defining events of an era, however, a sense of historical continuity can be threatened by the very media through which the notion of Sixties relevance is maintained. Michael Schudson emphasizes the importance of "institutions of collective memory" in keeping specific memories within public view.[70] Government, the educational system, social groups, political movements, and the media are among the keepers of memory, which enable specific perspectives based on group memory to make claims to national attention. The very name of the New Right think tank the Heritage Foundation (founded in 1973) attests to the importance conservatives placed in reinvigorating pre-Sixties memories and visions of American life. On the left, groups such as the NAACP and other civil rights organizations attempted to keep positive memories of Sixties social movements circulating, as with their campaign for a national holiday to commemorate Martin Luther King, Jr.'s birthday.[71] Efforts such as the Vietnam Veterans Memorial in Washington, D.C., inspired battles by various groups to have their group memories taken up nationally and institutionalized within the national memorial.[72]

None of these institutions, however, enjoys the ubiquity of popular culture's distribution of entertainment and information through television, film, radio, and musical recordings. Organizations such as the Heritage Foundation and the NAACP are organized around motivating, ideological principles, and their invocation and use of memory serve to preserve the historical continuity of their respective causes. Mass media, however, are not so organized, and most media outlets' presentation of the past tends to be more fragmented, diverse, and changeable than memories asserted by social interest groups. The economics and organizational structures of television, in particular, favor constant recycling of older material, which juxtaposes a mélange of styles from different production periods.[73] This trend has accelerated with the rise of cable networks, coincident to the conservative ideological offensive of the Reagan era. One channel that made use of the new 1980s structure of television in explicit furtherance of a political cause, however, was Pat Robertson's Family Channel, founded in 1988. The channel surrounded its religious and political commentary with reruns of entertainment series from the 1950s and 1960s, offering visions of the past that correlated closely with the aims of Robertson's political movement. Robertson's campaign for a return to Fifties truths was reinforced by the channel's ability to situate its viewers within Fifties culture, to call up visible cues to nostalgic memories of televisual enjoyment, and to link the imagined world of Fifties America to contemporary news reports and political pronouncements.

For those citizens whose social and public identities have not been forged in the crucible of direct experience of the events or eras depicted, personal and group experience may fade as a source of stable identification, replaced by momentary identifications based on shifting media representations of the past. Theorists of postmodernity such as Fredric Jameson and David Harvey see unstable, media-driven identifications as central to a crisis in historical understanding, which has crippled progressive movements for social change based on historically based class and other group identities. In the postmodern era, the power of conservative nostalgia comes from its promise to recover lost stability.[74]

Yet if the content of popular culture undergoes constant change, the ubiquity of television in particular offers significant access to historically minded material, and a consistency to the act of consumption itself. In a geographically mobile society, television's screen has become an icon of familiarity, a stable location through which discontinuous, fragmented, and variable representations of American experience have passed. Indeed, much of the sense of historical continuity that television offers is based on the act of visual consumption, on viewers' ability to locate themselves in history through their own accumulated experience of viewership.[75] Television becomes the site of memory, as personal memory, public memory, and media representation interweave.

As critics of postmodern media insist, this encompassing locale flattens the meaning of what passes through it, creating the mix of the factual and the fictional, the conflation of politics and entertainment, and the easy movement between various forms of celebrity that are hallmarks of contemporary American life. Even as electronic media's lack of memory-laden ideological coherence contributes to a sense of historical discontinuity, the television apparatus itself offers a stability to ameliorate the dislocational effects of its content. This offer of stability and locationality in the viewing process seems to promise that a sense of historical coherence may yet be achieved. Postmodern society has not done away with the desire for continuity, for the ability of people to locate themselves in a narrative of the nation, for a sense that such a narrative indeed exists. The fragmentation and discontinuity of postmodern experience may make such a desire even stronger. The effort made by conservatives to imbue their movement with a historical sense, no matter how close to myth it slides, attests to the power of the idea of historical coherence—as does the public attention to the panoply of cultural responses to the conservative effort, the inculcation of alternative and opposing definitions and understandings of the American past.

CONCLUSION

The politics of nostalgia and history were played out in the 1980s within a mixture of individual memory of personal experience, media consumption, group memories preserved and asserted by institutions, wider historical senses among generations, cultural revivals and recyclings, political pronouncements from partisans in government, fictional narratives from participants in events of the past, news reports within the routinized practices of corporate media, and feelings of continuity and discontinuity produced by viewer interaction with television. The conservative ideological offensive had offered a compellingly simple view of the American past, one that could be summarized as a decline, fall, and renewal of American spirit, values, and power. This narrative covered the years since World War II and featured an easy periodization based on the stark contrasts between the Fifties and the Sixties. In the political realm, opponents of Reaganism were largely unable or unwilling to challenge the conservative narrative on its own historico-mythic terrain. It was left to popular culture to serve as a repository of differing senses of the past, and to at times complicate and resist this conservative narrative, particularly regarding the decade of the 1960s.

These complications came from a variety of sources—continuing fandom for Sixties rock, criticism of American involvement in Vietnam, revisitation to the triumphs of the civil rights movement, and a new ascription of innocence to the Sixties by a younger generation of media producers. These phenomena contributed to a discourse that invoked Sixties political or cultural movements as positive national resources. Popular culture served as a repository of memories, images, and interpretations that conservatives wished to write out of the national narrative, even as media representations also identified the 1960s with a rather narrow, if spectacular, range of experience. Many of the social divisions, cultural differences, and political antagonisms passed down from the earlier decades persisted in the wake of the conservative historiographic movement, which had sought to return to a social consensus it asserted had existed in the pre-Sixties era. As discussed in the next chapter, the waning of conservative political momentum in the later days of the Reagan administration further endangered the success of the nostalgia project, as voices from the left gained new attention in putting forward their version of the Sixties in the political domain. Despite the conservative efforts, the meanings of the American past remained unresolved in the complex interactions between memory, culture, politics, and nation.

CHAPTER 5

Contests and Contestations

THE SIXTIES LEGACY DURING
THE DECLINE OF REAGAN

IN THE LATE 1980s the conservative movement experienced an extraordinary sequence of scandals and mishaps that threatened its strong position in American politics. Public disgrace touched the fundamentalist religious community, Wall Street traders, the savings and loan industry, and the military and foreign policy apparatus of the Reagan administration. Despite several years of economic growth, disparities in financial conditions between classes and races took on new visibility with the advent of mass homelessness. The last years of Ronald Reagan's second term saw a public questioning of the political, economic, and social direction of the nation, and of Reagan's legacy to the future. As doubts grew about the results of Reaganism, voices on the left found a new hearing, particularly regarding the relation between the past and the present. Veterans of Sixties political and social movements tried to reclaim the legacy of their earlier involvements, and to assert their relevance in combating what they saw as Reagan's pernicious influence. The country also experienced continued nostalgia for the public lives of John and Robert Kennedy, which served as criticism of both Republicans and Democrats in the current day. Meanwhile, conservatives hoping to keep the Reagan coalition together wielded a cultural critique of Sixties liberalism in the political arena, with decisive results in the 1988 presidential election. As political factions scrambled to stake out positions in the new post-Reagan environment, the Fifties and the Sixties continued to help form the vocabulary, images, and ideas that drove American politics in the 1980s.

THE DECLINE OF REAGANISM

The conservative ideological offensive in the 1980s was built upon a number of social movements, ideological causes, and political and economic claims.[1] Reagan and his associates asserted a new militarism in foreign policy, with particular emphasis on opposing the Soviet Union and on combating terrorism associated with Islamic fundamentalists and other American adversaries in the Middle East. Republicans placed their faith in the private market for economic growth, arguing that tax and spending policies should channel funds to the business class, who they claimed were responsible for American competitiveness internationally and a prosperous economy domestically. Conservatives relied upon the newly active fundamentalist Christian community for campaign workers during elections and for funding of various traditionalist social causes, and to set a tone of cultural and social retrenchment after the supposed excesses of the Sixties.

During Reagan's second term, each of these foundations of contemporary conservatism came under attack through a succession of scandals and mishaps. After enjoying extraordinary popularity in the middle of the decade, Reagan's presidency once again drew mixed reactions from a majority of the public. Reagan's image as a strong leader, conservatives' image as prudent economic stewards, and the Christian Right's image as upholder of traditional moral values became increasingly suspect. In addition, a number of other issues—continued international challenges to American dominance economically, record budget deficits, highly visible levels of homelessness in many cities, and the rise of AIDS and charges of government inaction in fighting the disease—elicited concern that Reagan's claims of bringing the nation back to greatness were ephemeral and misguided. Conservatives lost their ideological momentum, and new political space opened for attacks on Reagan and his legacy.

The most damaging scandal to Reagan's reputation was that of Iran-Contra, the selling of weapons secretly to Iran and the channeling of sale proceeds to Nicaraguans seeking to overthrow the Sandinista government.[2] While Oliver North became a conservative folk hero during the scandal, Reagan's image as a strong president was tarnished by revelations of deceit, ignorance, and incompetence in acceding to demands by Iranian officials who were working in concert with kidnappers of American hostages in Lebanon. Reagan's image as the "teflon President" who deflected all criticism was met by the media image of Iran's Ayatollah Khomeini, who had been demonized for years in American discourse; Reagan's secret dealings with the government of such an adversary contradicted the president's public role as defender of American values and purveyor of American strength against terroristic foes from alien cultures. Reagan's power and popularity had been closely tied to his performance of optimistic, determined leadership as president; the visible concern and panic that spread throughout the administration as the scandal was made public reduced the possibilities for potential supporters to identify with his performative strengths as chief executive. Conservatism no longer seemed so steadfast and triumphant.

The Wall Street crash of October 1987 also raised doubts about Reagan's stewardship of the economy. Although the crash did not trigger a recession, the idea of endless growth and the go-getter entrepreneurial discourse of conservative polemics began to falter in the face of huge monetary losses on paper. Leftist warnings about the speculatory tendencies of Reaganomic growth began to gain credibility (especially after widespread corruption and losses in the savings-and-loan industry were revealed immediately after the 1988 elections). Revelations of insider trading and other illegal transactions involving Wall Street titans Michael Milken, Ivan Boesky, and the brokerage firm Drexel Burnham Lambert fed worries that the benefits of Reaganomic financial activity mainly benefited small groups of corrupt corporate elites, while middle-class incomes stagnated and homelessness spread among the poor. As American trade deficits remained at high levels, anxieties about American economic competitiveness continued to be articulated in the media and elsewhere.[3]

Scandals involving illicit sexual activities and financial corruption among leading televangelists, such as Jim and Tammy Bakker and Jimmy Swaggart, damaged the Christian Right's claims to constitute a moral vanguard in American society.[4] Conservative assertions of the rebirth of luxury and glamour in the Reagan ascendancy were buffeted by additional scandals involving hotel owner Leona Helmsley and the first family of the Philippines, Ferdinand and Imelda Marcos, who had served as embodiments of glamourous authoritarianism and materialistic excess during the 1980s.[5] With the Marcoses deposed and trying to avoid the legal reach of Filipino authorities, Iran-Contra prosecutions in the offing, and Helmsley, Milken, Boesky, Jim Bakker, and Swaggart in jail, the corridors of power in the Reagan Eighties seemed to be leading increasingly to the prison-cell door.

After Democratic gains in Congress in the 1986 elections (including the retaking of the Senate), Reagan's domestic agenda stagnated. Even Reagan administration successes augured the end of Reagan's influence. The successful rapprochement with the Soviet Union, instigated by Mikhail Gorbachev's policy of perestroika, made Reagan's previous antipathy to communism seem obsolescent and reduced the power of anticommunism to keep the conservative coalition together. Whereas Reagan had enjoyed popularity among two-thirds of Americans in polls in the fall of 1986, his support plunged by 20 percentage points in the wake of Iran-Contra and barely improved for another year.[6] More than half of poll respondents stated the United States was "on the wrong track," and wanted the next president to take the nation in a new direction.[7] The ideological momentum of Reaganism seemed spent. In 1988 a *Newsweek* cover declared "The 80's Are Over," identifying the decade particularly with Reagan, the greedy excesses of the rich, and the Cold War.[8] With the winding down of Reagan's presidency came a reappraisal of domestic priorities and the nation's future role in world affairs.

NOSTALGIA FOR THE KENNEDYS

The disillusionment with Reaganism coincided with renewed interest in the political legacies of John and Robert Kennedy. A yearning for the presidency of John Kennedy had been a feature of American politics for a generation; during the 1980s, its persistence represented an inchoate rejection of the attacks on the Sixties that were circulating at the time. Nostalgia for the Kennedys functioned in part as a critique of the recent conservative dominance; the Kennedys represented another path to American greatness, one that the nation had forsaken or lost from view. The complexity of their political legacies, however, made the memory of John and Robert Kennedy appeal to many different political factions and identities: Democratic activists and white liberals, to be sure, but also Cold Warriors, Catholics, blue-collar voters, and African Americans. In the late 1980s it was particularly a renewed interest in the lost promise of Robert Kennedy that took shape as a cogent attack on the results of Reaganism.

The Retrospective Popularity of John Kennedy

The image of John Kennedy underwent secular canonization immediately upon his death, starting with the blanket television coverage of the four-day period of national mourning after his assassination and continuing with an outpouring of magazine articles, books, and television specials commemorating his life and death within the first years afterward.[9] His personal qualities were the initial focus of commemorations; his attributions were said to include wit, a sense of irony, irreverence, a cosmopolitan style, and a belief in reason. Kennedy's presidency had had its share of controversies, including the Bay of Pigs debacle, the Cuban missile crisis and other run-ins with the Soviet Union, and his cautious maneuvering between segregationist Democratic politicians and the integrationist civil rights leadership. After his death, however, the theme of Kennedy's capacity for growth and improvement while in office was used by his defenders to attest to the importance of the loss suffered by the nation with his death. Jacqueline Kennedy initiated the Camelot motif of his presidency as a lost time marked by charm and grace.

Aware that some voters were too young to have anything more than inherited reverence for Franklin Roosevelt and the New Deal, Democrats attempted to secure the support of younger voters with the sanctified image of Kennedy and his appeals to youthful idealism, as in the creation of the Peace Corps.[10] The sudden, dramatic nature of his death and the continuing questions about the assassination made the loss of Kennedy seem to be a turning point for the nation, a historical event of primary importance. As criticism of the Warren Report grew, the increased sense of indeterminacy about the circumstances of Kennedy's death prolonged the assassination as a hot story among reporters.[11] The lack of closure on the issue contributed to the long life of the Kennedy legacy as a site of contestation to be fought over by various claimants.[12] As the 1960s grew more tumultuous with violent uprisings in urban slums and the prolongation of the Vietnam War, Kennedy became a symbol of an increasingly tenuous sense of American optimism and idealism, a stricken warrior whose death seemed to open the door to an era of uncertainty, strife, and discord.

The continued political prominence of Robert Kennedy held out the promise of a return to glory, with the younger brother's increasing identification with issues of race and poverty deepening the public sense of the older brother's commitments in those areas. Robert Kennedy's eventual opposition to Lyndon Johnson's Vietnam policy also lent credence to the belief that John Kennedy might have averted massive American involvement in the war, despite the latter's escalation of American participation in the early 1960s.[13] Robert Kennedy's death in 1968, soon after Martin Luther King, Jr.'s assassination, added to the sense of national chaos, and the three fallen leaders of the 1960s formed a triptych of national loss and liberal martyrdom. Robert Kennedy's political associates, as well as reporters who covered his career after JFK's death, stressed the younger Kennedy's growth in his last years, echoing commemorations of JFK.[14] The Kennedys starkly dramatized the contingent nature of the nation's political fortunes and the souring of hopes that they had inspired among liberals during the New Frontier. Their deaths continually posed the question "What might have been?" to the nation.

In the late 1960s leftist revisionist historians began offering a critique of the New Frontier that tarnished its image in several respects. The left opposed "corporate liberalism," accusing it of fomenting the Cold War and leaving economic power in the hands of a corporate elite. John Kennedy was faulted for foreign adventurism and bellicosity, which threatened world destruction during the Cuban missile crisis and culminated in the tragedy of Vietnam.[15] His commitment to equal rights for black Americans was questioned, and his other domestic programs were judged minor initiatives that did nothing to change power relations between rich and poor.[16] In this judgment, Kennedy's style had overshadowed the mediocrity of his achievements. The political isolation of the left and its decline in the 1970s limited the effectiveness of these critiques, and as the liberal wing of the Democrats assimilated certain leftist positions (particularly in foreign policy), criticism of Kennedy dimmed on the left. Edward Kennedy's position as standard-bearer of the party's liberal wing in the 1970s continued to strengthen his family's association with liberal causes. Many Democrats held out hope for an Edward Kennedy presidency, even after the scandal of Chappaquiddick.

Assaults on the Kennedy mystique gained greater attention in the post-Watergate revelations of government misdeeds in the Cold War era. John Kennedy was accused of plotting Fidel Castro's assassination and acceding to the FBI's harassment of Martin Luther King, Jr. His sexual adventurism and at least indirect connections to the Mafia were disclosed and widely discussed.[17] In the wake of Watergate, his administration could be seen as one in a line of deceitful, power-abusing presidencies, and supporters of Richard Nixon tried to exonerate Nixon by showing precedents for his actions by Democratic presidents Kennedy and Johnson.[18]

John Kennedy in the 1980s

Despite the accusations of personal and political misconduct, Kennedy's popularity remained essentially unaffected among broad swaths of the American electorate. Large segments of the American public remained steadfast in their appreciation of the fallen leader. Thomas Brown attributes the strength of this appreciation to Americans' desire to return to a time they associated with national power and optimism; their "projected fantasies of omnipotence and wish fulfillment" found an apt target in the young, seemingly virile president who had stood up to the Russians and tried to reconcile the races.[19]

Because of his early death, John Kennedy could remain a Cold Warrior to hawks and a disarmament advocate to doves, a supporter of civil rights to some and a symbol of tough white ethnicity to others. Kennedy's vaunted capacity for growth could combine with the facts of an early death to maintain the sense of personal charisma. As Slavoj Žižek notes, an ongoing but unfulfilled sense of possibility allows the power of symbols to remain undiminished; when possibility is actually realized, its power in the symbolic realm can dissipate, because reality rarely (if ever) lives up to the utopian hopes that constitute symbolic projections.[20] Perhaps even more than when Kennedy was alive, the nation's hopes for the future, as of 1963, could be retrospectively placed on his shoulders—and his death offered an explanation, of sorts, of why things had gone awry in the years since. As Lance Morrow stated in a *Time* magazine cover story twenty years after Kennedy's death, "his death enacted his legislative program and at the same time seemed to let loose monsters, to unhinge the nation in some deep way that sent it reeling down a road toward riots and war and assassinations and Watergate."[21] Kennedy here becomes the first victim of the travails of the dark side of the Sixties, troubles the nation might have avoided if JFK had survived. For both liberals and conservatives who look back to the events of the 1960s with regret, Kennedy becomes the symbol of lost national opportunity.

The visual presentation of the Kennedy years on television in the decades after his death contributed to a sense that his administration was a turning point in American history. Americans were treated to much more extensive visual reminders of the Kennedy presidency than those of his predecessors. Use of television newsfilm grew rapidly during the early 1960s, after the creation of newly portable cameras and shooting techniques specifically to capture the 1960 presidential campaign. Kennedy provided extensive access to both still photographers and television news producers, who were able to provide close-up views of Kennedy, his family, and political associates. Many of the controversial public events of his tenure were also captured on newsfilm, including civil rights protests and segregationist responses, demonstrative antics by Soviet leader Nikita Khrushchev, the Berlin crisis, events in Cuba, and, of course, the assassination itself. Kennedy's actions could thus be portrayed as bearing on the modern televisual world, while the largely black-and-white look of the visuals signaled the distance between then and now, providing nostalgic echoes of a time now passed.

Kennedy's assassination also provided a clear chronological cue for celebrations of remembrance. In 1983 a host of media outlets commemorated the twentieth anniversary of his death, which provided new opportunities for partisans to claim the Kennedy legacy and for broad, sweeping examinations of the early 1960s as a historical period. The *Washington Post*, for instance, featured an array of columnists who debated whether Kennedy was a social liberal, moderate, or conservative, and whether he would have further escalated American involvement in Vietnam.[22] Conservative George Will depicts Kennedy as an anticommunist, tax-cutting moderate, with obvious parallels to Ronald Reagan, in order to show that liberals have hijacked both Kennedy's image and the Democratic party in the years since 1963. Old-time moderate Joseph Kraft notes Kennedy's respect for his elders and gradualist approaches to thorny problems, which allowed the national "center" to hold; after Lyndon Johnson speeded up the pace of reform and the war, "the center was gone" from national life and has never been found. Meanwhile, liberal Mary McGrory paints Kennedy as idealistic, caring, and hoping for peace—in obvious contrast, in the liberal view, to the Reagan administration.

McGrory, as a Kennedy admirer during his presidency, puts forward a raw emotional tone in her piece—her title on this anniversary of his death is "You Had to Be There to Know the Pain." Kennedy's "magic" as a leader is conveyed by the power of the mourning of those left bereft by his loss; the section is accompanied by a photograph of fifth-graders showing utter shock at the news on November 22, 1963. The clean-cut children—in Texas, no less—stand in for a generation whose disorienting historical experience is traced back to the assassination. Kennedy's death, according to liberal *Post* writer Nicholas Lemann, "permanently changed the tone of the country from light to dark . . . the pivot on which the postwar age turned." In this view, the conservative call for a return to national glory has clearly not been fulfilled by President Reagan's own tenure in office.

Time, Newsweek, the *New Republic,* ABC News, the *Today Show,* and *Good Morning, America* also extensively covered the 1983 Kennedy commemorations.[23] Several commentators associate Kennedy with youth, and opine that national youth died with him—America lost its idealism in 1963, and has since faced the recurring problems of hard adulthood. Kennedy's popularity abroad is also a common theme; America's dominant status at the time was shown by the world's grief when he died. ABC's news special *JFK* features the former British ambassador to the United States stating, "Everybody liked being led by the United States at the time, they liked to have President Kennedy as the leader of the Western world. That was his major triumph."[24] Even as Reagan had asserted a more aggressive foreign policy and hailed the United States as a beacon of freedom for the world, public doubts about American standing in the world persisted. Given the Reagan administration efforts to magnify terrorist and communist threats to the United States, it is not surprising that contributors (and foreign diplomats) express nostalgia for a time when the world seemed to like America.

In a *Newsweek* survey of remembrances of Kennedy, working-class commentators—a barber, a hotel maid, and others—relate a sense of national security in the world with JFK at the helm to a sense of personal safety, since lost in everyday life; the nation's heightened crime rate since the early 1960s seems to have been triggered by the shooting in Dallas.[25] At a time when Reagan was belittling government's ability to solve problems, and seemed to ask Americans to do nothing more than to get rich, several writers also note Kennedy's call for a nationalistic idealism and belief in the institutions of civic life.[26] The Peace Corps is mentioned as the embodiment of this belief; polls continued to report that the Peace Corps—a testament to both American idealism and American superiority—remained among the most popular aspects of American foreign policy of the post–World War II era, appreciated by both liberals and conservatives.[27]

Polls throughout the 1970s and 1980s showed Kennedy to be the most retrospectively popular president in American history; a *Newsweek* poll accompanying its special section shows JFK outdistancing Franklin Roosevelt, the second most popular choice, by a three-to-one margin. Respondents associated Kennedy with a concern for working people, the effort to end racial injustice, and an active governmental role in society. He was thought to have inspired young people to political activism. Two-thirds of respondents said the nation would have spent more money to help the poor if Kennedy had lived.[28] Given that social spending increased more under Lyndon Johnson than under Kennedy, this response shows both the association of Kennedy with Sixties liberalism in general and a clear differentiation between Kennedy's legacy and the Reagan social spending cuts that were in force at the time the article was published. The *Newsweek* remembrances are largely free of the more scandalous aspects of Kennedy's private behavior while in office; his legacy in 1983 is seen in political and stylistic terms, amid continued international tensions, domestic racial strife, and another highly stylized presidency.

In 1988 the media went through another round of commemorations for the twenty-fifth anniversary of the assassination, in largely the same terms. CBS News devoted a prime-time special to a replay of its coverage from the assassination, and featured an eight-part series on its evening news show treating JFK's legacy.[29] (The two CBS news anchors in the intervening twenty-five years, Walter Cronkite and Dan Rather, had played major roles in network coverage of the shooting.) Given the strenuous effort of the Reagan administration to signal an American renewal of spirit, it is noteworthy that these and reports from other networks continue to picture an America unredeemed after the fall out of innocence in 1963. They take up the themes of Fifties innocence and Sixties trauma that were raised in the Fifties cultural revival in the 1970s, and place the turning point squarely at Dealey Plaza in Dallas, "the day twenty-five years ago that changed everything," in the words of Dan Rather.[30] CBS interviews singer Billy Joel, who states, "We were never really kids after that. Life just wasn't Mickey Mouse, rock and roll and shiny cars. It was different, everything was different after that."[31] A CBS report repeats the turning-point refrain the following evening, in a report that once more focuses on the younger generation's experience of the time. The report's visuals and background audio depict 1963 America as a land of children riding bikes, teenagers smooching on a couch, surfing, football, and pre-Beatles vocal groups singing about puppy love. The ensuing changes in American family life, international economic status, and recreational habits are succintly encapsulated by the reporter: "It was a time when Mom did the cooking, not microwaves, when there were still Studebakers but no Mazdas, when Coke was just cola." For this generation, the assassination sets off the turmoil of the 1960s, which leads to Vietnam, cynicism, and insecurity, and whose divisive aftermath continues to plague America. The sense of irretrievable loss, undiminished by Reagan's efforts, pervades CBS's report on the teenagers of 1963. The story concludes with a wistful scene of JFK on a yacht, in bright sunshine, before the show's end credits are accompanied by Lesley Gore's early-1960s anthem of teen trauma, "It's My Party," and its claim that "You would cry too, if it happened to you."[32]

The hangover has been long; even 1980s teenagers, interviewed by CBS, felt nostalgia for a president they never knew, claiming that JFK had unified the country.[33] Kennedy could embody 1960s liberalism's highest hopes and ideals without the attendant costs. His tenure in office represented civil and equal rights but not the Black Power movement, urban uprisings, or controversies over affirmative action. A white teenager states that if JFK had lived, "the race riots of the late '60s might not have happened." Kennedy seemed to care about poverty but kept domestic spending in check. He conducted an assertive foreign policy but might have avoided full involvement in the quagmire of Vietnam. NBC News reports that Kennedy represented "a vision that anything was possible if we tried hard enough. It was the zenith of what was called the American century."[34] The problems of contemporary America, by contrast, seem stubbornly resistant to Reagan's claims of a return to this greatness.

Reagan's efforts are depicted as echoes of Kennedy's, without the sanctification of martyrdom to give them lasting power. If, as the more conservative commentators assert, Kennedy's achievements were largely rhetorical and televisual, the television reports depict Kennedy's style as a genuine emanation from the man, and as having real results by inspiring people to take action. One Peace Corps volunteer says "It wasn't the glamour" of Kennedy that inspired his participation, "it was the guts."[35] An NBC reporter pointedly remarks that Kennedy "didn't need a teleprompter" to communicate with the nation, that his charm and wit were real; he put to them to use in creating the Peace Corps and the space program, and in pushing forward civil rights.[36] Reagan, in contrast, at the end of his term, and at the end of a particularly dispiriting presidential election, seems largely to have failed in putting his televisual skill to use in achieving much beyond his own electoral success.

Coverage of the Kennedys was not restricted to the news departments of the television industry. Since the 1970s, family members had been the focus of docudramas, biopics, and miniseries, depicting the public events and private dramas of their lives. The Kennedys became the catalyst for an ongoing examination of 1960s politics within the television movie genre, which included stories about JFK, RFK, Jackie, the Kennedys' conflicts with Jimmy Hoffa and J. Edgar Hoover, and the lives of Martin Luther King, Jr., and Lyndon Johnson. The Kennedy-themed programs, which usually featured very positive portrayals of their heroes, attracted good ratings for over fifteen years.[37]

Robert Kennedy Redux

After many years of his memory seeming secondary to his brother's, Robert Kennedy also enjoyed a resurgence of media interest in 1988.[38] The twentieth anniversary of his death provided opportunities for new evaluations of his legacy. These evaluations functioned as even more pointed critiques of Reagan conservatism than did the nostalgia for President Kennedy, in that Robert Kennedy was heavily identified not only with the New Frontier of the early 1960s but also with the more controversial political atmosphere of the late 1960s. Robert Kennedy became associated with challenges to the political establishment from the left—by the United Farm Workers, welfare recipients, and the antiwar movement. The differences between the Robert Kennedy of 1968 and the Ronald Reagan of the 1980s seemed vast; how was the nation to understand the change in direction for the country that the passage from Kennedy to Reagan signified?

The media reports on Robert Kennedy contain the usual debunking provisos about abuse of power during the Kennedy administration, the question of Vietnam, and the dangers of succumbing to Kennedy style. The recurrent frames of the reports, however, are much more positive, and point in admiration to Kennedy's combination of toughness and concern for the underdog, his ability to attract support from both white blue-collar workers and African Americans, and his personal growth after the death of his brother. Once more, the theme of growth allows Kennedy supporters to dismiss early misdeeds as either steps in a learning process or simply irrelevant, and to claim the potential for greatness for their hero, if he had not been stopped by assassination.[39]

For Democrats, Robert Kennedy was the last candidate who seemed able to keep the New Deal coalition together, at least in the North. For liberals, he had come to represent a last, lost chance to maintain liberal political ascendancy. His qualities as reported constitute an implied rebuke to both Democrats and Republicans in the late 1980s; liberal Democrats lack his toughness, pragmatism, and ability to unite the races, and conservative Republicans lack his concern for the poor, vision beyond materialistic values, and desire for racial justice. Revisiting the Kennedy 1968 presidential campaign serves to mark the distance between then and now, the change in political mood between a past time of social upheaval, mass political action, and public concern over power and equality and a current time of political apathy, disgust for contemporary campaigns, and widening gaps between classes and races. The invocation of the Kennedy brothers implicitly questions the legitimacy of the Reagan revolution and places Reagan himself in a position of usurper (just as Lyndon Johnson was seen as one by many in the Kennedy camp). Reagan's hold on political power had been accompanied by conservatives' claims that they were following a well-defined trajectory of American destiny, in accordance with unchanging values, interrupted only by the social upheaval and traumas of the 1960s. For anti-Reagan Kennedy supporters, the positions of the Kennedy brothers are aligned with, extend, and expand New Deal and other progressive traditions. In this view the traumas of the 1960s, specifically the assassinations of the standard-bearers of liberalism, were not the apotheosis of liberal misdirection, but rather the opportunity Reagan and other conservatives needed to dominate the political landscape.

A 1988 review of the events of 1968 in *Time* magazine concludes that if Robert Kennedy had lived, the "long historical tumble of the past 20 years" might have been avoided, and that RFK's death may have been the most important historical event of the post-World War II era.[40] The loss of Kennedy can be given this magnitude of importance only insofar as he is perceived as the only alternative to the capture of the presidency by two men vastly different from himself—first, Richard Nixon, then Ronald Reagan. If the American political journey through the 1960s, 1970s, and 1980s could have been quite different if not for a series of assassinations, the foundation of Reagan's triumph is then revealed as arbitrary, opportunistic, and laden with national tragedy, rather than as a fulfillment of national destiny.

Discussion of the Sixties was complicated by differing chronological schemas as to how to define the constitutive events and trends of the era. In this, a division between the early and late 1960s became a useful conceptual device to show support or criticism of various aspects of the decade. The celebration of the New Frontier provided an argument against the conservative attacks on the Sixties by positing the early 1960s as a time of hope, idealism, and national strength. In a manner, conservatives such as Reagan acceded to this definition of the early years of the decade by lauding John Kennedy and claiming some of his legacy. While Reagan criticized the leadership of civil rights organizations, tried to weaken the Voting Rights Act, and made racially coded appeals to whites, he and other conservatives asserted their steadfast support for equal rights laws, thereby displaying their purported respect for the civil rights movement and the leadership of Martin Luther King, Jr. Conservatives could also point to Kennedy's tough stances against the Soviet Union to justify their own military buildup.

For liberals, paying tribute to Robert Kennedy allowed some of the events and movements of the later years of the decade to be celebrated as well. Robert Kennedy was identified with the expansion of JFK domestic initiatives into Lyndon Johnson's Great Society programs, the continued efforts at integrationist racial justice which coincided with the more separatist Black Power movement, and the movement to end the war in Vietnam. These more controversial developments could be defended under the protective covering of Kennedy greatness and widespread popular appeal. By the late 1960s, the American left had developed a more wholesale critique of American power relations at home and abroad than enunciated during the Kennedy administration, and Robert Kennedy was a pioneer in the increased openness of the left wing of the Democratic party to such a critique. By invoking his legacy, now clearly abandoned by those in power in Reagan's Washington, left-leaning liberals could reassert their project of racial reconciliation, international peace, and greater equality back into the mainstream of American political discussion, away from the marginalized precincts of the Jesse Jackson campaigns and other left-wing projects.

SIXTIES ACTIVISTS TALK BACK

Kennedy nostalgia was not the only response to Reagan based on the politics of the 1960s. The late 1980s also saw a wave of efforts by veterans of Sixties social change movements to reinvoke personal and group memories of their experiences. They sought to claim national attention by answering the conservatives' criticism of the New Left and the counterculture. By placing group memories in the public arena, left-liberal writers and activists hoped to reinscribe public memories with the values of the civil rights and antiwar movements and take control of their public representation.

The major progressive incursions into the fight to define the Sixties in the realm of public affairs came in a series of publishing projects. Participants in Sixties social movements addressed the history and legacy of the era, joined by sympathetic historians and reporters. Although none of these efforts enjoyed the major popularity of conservative attacks on the Sixties such as Allan Bloom's *The Closing of the American Mind*, several did attract the attention of readers and the news media and received reviews in major publications. Todd Gitlin's *The Sixties: Years of Hope, Days of Rage*, Tom Hayden's *Reunion*, James Miller's *"Democracy Is in the Streets,"* and two biographies of Martin Luther, King, Jr., David Garrow's *Bearing the Cross* and Taylor Branch's *Parting the Waters*, achieved the most visibility.[41] These books continued the practice of separating the Sixties into two parts—an early 1960s that featured the rise of constructive social criticism and needed change in American society, and a late 1960s of violence, frustration, and vast social division.

Gitlin, Hayden, and Miller go over much of the same territory in their histories of the left in the Sixties, and their goals are similar—to delineate the lessons of the Sixties, to separate what is productive in their legacy from the mistakes all the authors admit were made. They depict the 1950s as a time of public quietude and private frustration among middle-class youth. The young arrive at college at the turn of the decade with a desire for authenticity and meaning in their lives, and find it in existential philosophy and calls for political action.

Gitlin's wide-ranging history encompasses both political movements and the rise of the youth counterculture. He credits two student organizations, the Student Nonviolent Coordinating Committee (SNCC) and Students for a Democratic Society (SDS), as the primary catalysts of progressive change during the decade, thereby providing a strongly generational cast to his analysis. SNCC organized the wave of lunch-counter protests against segregation in the South, and later helped with voting rights and other empowerment projects for southern blacks. SDS became the largest left-wing student group in the country, organizing protests against the Vietnam War, university policies, and racial injustice. Hayden's memoir details his activities as the leading voice of SDS, as a civil rights activist in coordination with SNCC, and as a leader of the antiwar movement. Miller's book is an examination of the early days of SDS and its guiding principle of "participatory democracy," an attempt to find social structures that would facilitate civic participation among groups traditionally marginalized or ignored in America. This emphasis on direct participation by local political actors was meant to reduce and bypass the hold on economic and governmental power by an entrenched technocratic and bureaucratic elite, as had been described by sociologist C. Wright Mills during the postwar era.[42] Such participation in public events could also provide the existential experience for which young activists hungered.

The authors see SNCC and SDS in the early 1960s as positioning themselves just to the left of the Democratic party, and the groups' projects as attempts to push liberals to live up to their professed principles. Gitlin, Hayden, and Miller stress that the New Left was born out of American traditions, influenced by the work of Mills and democratic theorist John Dewey as well as by American and European cultural radicals. They credit the student left and civil rights movement with initiating momentous changes in racial attitudes and laws, helping to force an end to the war in Vietnam, setting the stage for the women's, gay, and environmentalist movements, and creating heightened public consciousness that governmental and corporate power should be held up to close public scrutiny.

Although the student movement reached its greatest numerical strength in the late 1960s and the largest antiwar protests took place in 1970, Gitlin, Hayden and Miller see the New Left peak and begin to decline in 1964 and 1965, just as its critique of racial and economic power relations was beginning to enter public discussion, the major civil rights laws were being enacted, and Lyndon Johnson introduced his Great Society programs and War on Poverty. According to the three authors, at this time of seeming success for progressive forces, SDS and SNCC began to disintegrate. SNCC and other black activists began feeling betrayed by white integrationists and turned to a more separatist Black Power philosophy, thereby dampening white support for further progress in racial justice. The urban uprisings of 1965–1968 and the entrenched political power of urban elites also damaged the developing liberal and radical efforts against poverty.

SDS grew quickly in response to the American escalation in Vietnam, but to Hayden and Gitlin, who were members of the SDS "Old Guard," the newer members and leadership were politically unsophisticated and emotionally volatile. SDS disintegrated into political sectarianism and guerrilla fantasy within a few years, a decline full of dramatic episodes that each author painstakingly, if masochistically, records. The chance for an institutionalized New Left joining and influencing a broader liberal consensus to extend the gains of the early 1960s was lost, and the late 1960s were marked by increased violence, frustration, and the splintering of the movement. (Included in this splintering is the birth of the radical feminist movement, which the authors laud as a necessary correction to New Left sexism, yet still associate with the painful dissolution of the larger movement.)[43] The New Left succumbed to its own political immaturity, flawed leadership structures, naïveté regarding communist and third world political movements, and the impatience of its youthful activists.

Hayden was heavily involved in the more radical efforts by the New Left in the late 1960s, before marrying Jane Fonda and becoming a Democratic politician in the 1970s. He places greater emphasis than the other authors on the culpability of the political leadership of the nation and, more generally, on the older generation of Americans, for denying claims for racial, political, and economic justice, and for the repression directed at New Left and civil rights activists (the text of his book is periodically interrupted by FBI reports on his activities at the time, made available through the Freedom of Information Act). Although he argues that the young protesters (and himself) committed serious political missteps, he places greater responsibility for the anguish of the late 1960s on adult authorities who were old enough to know better. His own newfound political and emotional maturity in the 1980s can be seen as superior to both his own youthful behavior and the response by elites in power back in the 1960s. In his memoir, Hayden's estrangement from his parents, brought on by his father's failure to be a loving and understanding parent, is paralleled by the New Left's estrangement from American institutions, after the political establishment thwarted the protesters' efforts to improve the country they loved. Hayden metaphorically returned home in the 1970s by rejoining the liberal wing of the Democratic party and building a family of his own with Fonda. Hayden thus stakes a claim to the care and concern for family that was a hallmark of conservative rhetoric in the 1980s, and asserts the need for the same ethic of concern for those social groups still marginalized. (Hayden and Fonda divorced soon after the book was published.)

All of the authors explicitly state their aim to reclaim the spirit and gains of the first half of the 1960s as a counterweight to the Republican dominance of the 1980s. They compare the selflessness, idealism, and experimental spirit of the early New Left with what they see as the greed, selfishness, racism, sexism, and ideological rigidity of the Reagan movement. For all three authors, the relevant political and cultural events of the Sixties revolve around the actions of youthful activists in the civil rights and antiwar movements, continuing the emphasis on youth as the privileged prism by which to understand the era. The activists they depict attempted to make connections across racial, class, and generational divides through political organizing, and the histories stress the relevance of those efforts for the nation as a whole. Their focus on the political leadership of the youth movements, however, limits the breadth of their portrayals of the period.

The books' appearances in the late 1980s proclaimed a new public assertiveness by participants in Sixties movements regarding their contributions to the nation and their resentment of conservative attacks on the legacies of the Sixties. The books received generally positive responses in the media, and the authors gained status as experts on the era, occasionally interviewed by or placing articles in major publications.[44]

The volumes by Garrow and Branch received similar positive attention, and from a more ideologically diverse range of publications, continuing the notion of a national consensus on the basic civil rights issues of the early 1960s.[45] Their books were praised for documenting the nobility, courage, and righteousness of King and his colleagues in the movement against segregation. Both books portray the early 1960s as the height of the movement's activities and achievements, when the issues seem simple in retrospect. From the perspective of the 1980s, the gaining of legal rights for blacks and the ending of explicit Jim Crow policies are less problematic than addressing subtle racism and economic inequality, as King tried to do in his later years. Although Garrow warned in his epilogue against deifying King at the expense of understanding and acknowledging the movement as a whole, both books continued the focus on King as a singular figure of immense historical significance, a focus that had grown in the years since his death.[46]

Not all participants and historians of the New Left agreed with the emphases of Gitlin, Hayden, and Miller. The editors of *Social Text*, positioned in the 1980s further to the left than the three, published a volume entitled *The 60s without Apology*, in which contributors, while admitting the left's weaknesses, sought to reclaim the late 1960s as a time of substantive and far-reaching activism.[47] The writers in the anthology, and in the similar effort *Sights on the Sixties*, find that the most profound transformations in cultural and social relations occurred during this period; rather than losing its soul to a reductive sympathy for communist obscurantism, as Gitlin, Hayden, and Miller had declared, the left's actions had remained in the best traditions of native radicalism.[48]

Authors in the latter anthology, which appeared after the publication of *The Sixties* and *Reunion*, accuse Gitlin and Hayden of remaining too closely tied to the national centers of left activity, which had self-destructed in the late 1960s; the SDS Old Guard authors' narrative emphases on national structures in a decentralized movement blinded them to the diversity of localized projects around the country that remained vibrant into the 1970s. The anthologies claim a greater diversity of social experience under the mantle of Sixties social movements, including, for instance, reports on older women's opposition to the Vietnam War, soldiers' resistance to the war, and more extensive coverage of the feminist movement.[49] The anthologies, however, did not enjoy the same cultural visibility as the memoirs; their more radical stances, lack of political celebrity, and publication by university rather than mass market presses limited their access to reviews in major media outlets and accompanying publicity.

Feminist writers of the 1980s also emphasized the late 1960s as the era in which the women's movement emerged into the national spotlight, in many ways out of women's dissatisfaction with the sexism of the New Left. Writers in *Ms.*, the most popular feminist magazine, saw the Sixties as a crucial but flawed effort to open American life to participation by previously excluded social groups, and the crucible in which feminist activism was formed. Like the contributors to women's magazines in the 1970s, *Ms.* writers identified the 1950s as a time of patriarchal constraints that began to be contested during the tumult of the Sixties. *Ms.* noted Reagan's election in 1980, and the accompanying calls for a return to Fifties norms, with alarm. It began a column dedicated to reporting on the Christian Right, and Gloria Steinem analyzed the New Right agenda repeatedly in her own column. Most of *Ms.*'s attention went to the Right's attack on abortion rights, but also addressed its political organizing, the Family Protection Act and similar attempts at legislation, and its social and critical critique. *Ms.* saw the Reagan appeal to nostalgia as aimed squarely at the feminist movement and the gains it had achieved against male prerogatives that had been prevalent in the 1950s. Articles in the magazine about the New Right, and the accompanying critique of conservative nostalgia, declined in the mid-1980s, just as others on the left were beginning to address the history of the Sixties. The magazine continued to celebrate the history of the feminist movement, however, with occasional retrospective articles that linked its rise in the late 1960s to the present day. The ascension of Marcia Gillespie to the editorship in 1993 signaled a return to an explicit critique of the family values ideology of conservatives, particularly in Gillespie's own column.[50]

Meanwhile, two of the leading celebrities of the left in the late 1960s, yippies Jerry Rubin and Abbie Hoffman, resurfaced in very different circumstances. Rubin transformed himself into a paragon of yuppie careerism in New York City, confirming suspicions by some critics that the Sixties generation of protesters had become Me Decade solipsists in the 1970s and materialistic sellouts in the 1980s. Rubin's former partner Hoffman, however, retained his radical credentials and was active in environmental and Central American solidarity work before his death in 1989.

Responses from the Right

The resurgence in leftist and liberal discussion about the Sixties inspired further criticism of the era by writers on the right. Two other Sixties veterans whose work attracted notice were the two most active apostates from the Sixties left, David Horowitz and Peter Collier. Horowitz and Collier had been among the editors of the well-known New Left magazine *Ramparts* in the late 1960s and early 1970s. *Ramparts* had published the writing of many significant figures on the left (including Gitlin and Hayden) and had been closely associated with the Black Panther party. Horowitz and Collier abandoned the left after the demise of *Ramparts* and after their disillusionment with criminal activities by Panther members in the mid-1970s. After writing a series of popular biographies of American family dynasties, they declared themselves Reagan supporters in the mid-1980s and organized the Second Thoughts conference and accompanying anthology, in explicit response to the work of

Hayden, Gitlin, and Miller. Second Thoughts featured fellow participants-turned-critics of the New Left, plus leading neoconservatives and representatives of the Nicaraguan contra movement. Many of the former leftists at the Second Thoughts conference gave mixed, rather than altogether negative, reviews of the results of the movement, which raised the ire of the neoconservatives, many of whom had been apostates from the Old Left and reviled the New Left.[51]

Horowitz and Collier published two vitriolic books on the Sixties, *Destructive Generation* and Horowitz's memoir *Radical Son*.[52] In earlier criticisms of the left, they had agreed that the New Left claimed American precedents, but in these books they claim that the founders of the New Left were committed communist revolutionaries from the start, and that the entire movement constituted a Fifth Column aimed at destroying the nation.[53] The left is responsible for continuing racial animosity and the fostering of an underclass mired in social pathology, the spread of drugs and AIDS, and continued sympathy for totalitarian movements abroad. Horowitz and Collier position themselves as their generation's Whitaker Chambers, rising to warn the nation of impending doom.[54] They see the left as more powerful in the 1980s than in the 1960s, as it has effectively infiltrated the foreign policy apparatus of the Democratic party and leading media outlets and journals of opinion, in the cause of worldwide communist revolution. Horowitz and Collier fight nostalgia for the Sixties with nostalgia for the Fifties, evincing a McCarthyite disposition more strongly than most of the right in the 1980s (especially in the midst of Gorbachev's perestroika reforms in the Soviet Union), repeating the arc of political conversion undertaken by the neoconservatives of the previous generation. Horowitz and Collier succeeded in attracting conservative financial and logistical support, but their argument about the essentially criminal enterprise of the New Left and its legatees did not travel much beyond die-hard conservative circles.[55]

The absence of conservative appreciation for New Left activities was not simply because they occupied opposite poles in American politics, but also because of the internal dynamics of conservative activism. The right also had seen an upsurge in youthful political activism during the 1960s, centered on the Young Americans for Freedom, a student group founded by William F. Buckley. YAF suffered from factional division throughout the 1960s between social conservatives and libertarians. The social conservatives supported the war in Vietnam, defended the social order against militant political protest, and reviled the counterculture of their contemporaries. The libertarians tended toward a radical antigovernment stance that included opposition to the war (or at least to the draft) and repressive drug laws; many libertarians held sympathy for the counterculture's emphasis on personal freedom, the free-wheeling style of the New Left, and the left's critique of bureaucratic, corporate liberalism. After years of tension, the social conservatives purged the libertarians from YAF in 1969. Many of the social conservatives went on to become activists in the Republican party and the New Right, and attained leadership positions in the 1970s and 1980s. The libertarians tended to have more tortuous and checkered career paths and were not a significant force in leadership circles in the conservative movement in the 1980s.[56] Some of the New Left's critique of modern bureaucratic life did eventually influence political circles associated with Jack Kemp, who borrowed the Sixties term "empowerment" to describe new antipoverty efforts by conservatives.[57]

The vilification of the New Left and the counterculture in most conservative circles can be seen to have roots in the conservative movement's own bitter faction fights, and in the failure of those conservatives who appreciated aspects of 1960s youth movements to sustain their own political careers. The New Left had concentrated its criticism on Democratic party liberals, and urged new emphasis on localism, personal freedom, and opposition to bureaucratization. Conservatives in the public eye ignored these parallels to their own present-day concerns, dismissed the Sixties left as unredeemable, and attempted to link 1980s liberals to what conservatives considered the worst excesses of the Sixties.

CONSERVATIVES AND THE NEW CLASS

The neoconservatives who upbraided the former 1960s activists at the Second Thoughts conference had a long history of criticism against the New Left and the counterculture. Much of their criticism centered on the left's purported dominance in what neoconservatives deemed to be a "New Class" of well-educated, professionalized elites in public and cultural spheres. Their attacks on the denizens of Manhattan, Cambridge, and Washington aligned them with more traditional conservatives who had long attacked East Coast liberals. The joint attacks of neoconservatives and New Right activists against cultural and social liberalism aimed to isolate middle-class liberal and left reformers from cultural traditionalists below them in class standing, to consolidate a new conservative majority based on cultural, social, and foreign policy issues. By defining post-Sixties white liberalism as narrowly upper middle class and East Coast in character, conservatives also sought to renew support for business class objectives by those less affluent voters who opposed liberalism on cultural and social grounds. This strategy was invoked throughout the Reagan period, and proved decisive in maintaining conservative control of the presidency in the 1988 presidential election.

The Neoconservative Complaint

Neoconservative intellectuals' turn toward the right after a background in left and liberal movements had often been inspired by a distaste for the 1960s student left's critique of bureaucratic rationality, Cold War anticommunism, and professorial and administration prerogatives on university campuses, as well as by a reaction against antiwhite, anti-Zionist, and anti-Semitic strands within the Black Power movement. As they saw the New Left and consequent social movements begin to influence liberal Democrats, particularly in the McGovern 1972 presidential campaign, they consolidated a theory of a "New Class" of intellectual, bureaucratic, and cultural elites who were putting forward their own interests in power, disguised by a concern for the poor, defense of the welfare state, and personal liberation.[58]

In their formulation of a New Class gaining power in American society, neoconservatives echoed the arguments of more traditional conservatives who had been declaiming against the "Liberal Establishment," as named in a book of that title by Republican activist M. Stanton Evans in 1965.[59] In a conservative counterpart to C. Wright Mills's work from the left on the "Power Elite" (which had inspired SDS), Evans identified this Establishment as dominant in Washington politics, eastern media companies, and the northern Protestant churches. Though small in number, liberals were able to decisively influence the direction of public opinion through their control of institutions such as the executive branch of the federal government, the *New York Times*, major book publishers, and the film industry. Evans saw the main thrust of postwar liberalism as an attack on piety, replaced by support for moral relativism and materialism. In *The Emerging Republican Majority*, Kevin Phillips's influential 1969 treatise on changes in American politics, Phillips took up Evans's description and added a more specifically economic argument.[60] He asserted that this Establishment, which included diversified corporations run by professional managers, had displaced an old-time industrial and commercial elite as the dominant economic sector. The corporate elites in the newly liberal establishment had internalized New Deal values, stated Phillips, which led the private sector's technocrats and planners to ally with government bureaucrats against small entrepreneurs and localized family capitalists.[61] Neoconservatives in the 1970s, who tended to have been well-connected planners, academics, and journalists in the 1960s, took up the conservative critique after the New Left had attacked the "Establishment" from the opposite political direction.[62] Neoconservatives were distressed particularly by their perception that liberals had taken on New Left values in the 1970s to become antibusiness, soft on communism, and dismissive of traditional middle-class pieties. They saw the New Class of liberal elites as marked by a tendency toward abstraction, radical skepticism, cosmopolitian sophistication, and lack of reverence for social institutions; John Kennedy in the early 1960s had been praised as a harbinger of a new generational elite through his combination of such qualities, but neoconservatives in the 1970s now charged liberals with undermining American society.

Neoconservatives contrasted liberal professionals to business managers; the highly educated, postindustrial New Class was found in the public and information sectors and depended on an expanded public sector in its pursuit of class interest and political power. "The simple truth," stated Irving Kristol, "is that the professional classes of our modern bureaucratized societies are engaged in a class struggle with the business community for status and power."[63] This struggle was played out in the realm of cultural policies, environmental law, government regulation, and tax and budget priorities.

To neoconservatives, the 1960s were crucial to the development of the New Class, as the counterculture directly challenged middle-class morality and business prerogatives, the antiwar movement questioned the Cold War and American motives abroad, and federal social programs expanded, vastly increasing the power of planners and welfare state bureaucrats.[64] Neoconservatives saw the New Left and the counterculture as enjoying ratification and publicity by academic and media elites. The counterculture, stated Norman Podhoretz, was against "all middle-class values—work, ambition, discipline, monogamy, and the family."[65] This attack had now spread beyond youth culture, particularly through the feminist and gay liberation movements and the cultural relativism of the 1970s. The Heritage Foundation's Burton Pines saw the counterculture's distinguishing characteristic as its nihilism, and argued that "liberalism today is tainted by this nihilism, and much of the liberal movement has been captured by the counterculture New Left and New Politics."[66] The economic and social conflicts of the 1970s could thus be traced back to a unified New Class arising in the 1960s, although at the time, the New Left and the youth counterculture positioned themselves as opponents of modern technocratic elitism.

Other conservative commentators who rose to prominence in the 1980s joined in the attack on the New Class, according to their own emphases and policy preferences. In his attack on government spending for the poor, Charles Murray claimed that the expansion of the welfare state was due to a shift in elite opinion between 1964 and 1967 regarding the cures for poverty, a shift toward rewarding the nonworking poor that the majority of the country never supported.[67] George Gilder, in his defense of the prefeminist family, depicted the antitraditional culture of eastern academia as rife with sexual dysfunction, violence, drugs, and loneliness.[68] Art critic and *New Criterion* founder Hilton Kramer complained that social power was held exclusively by liberals and leftists with stylishly rebellious veneers, who dominated Manhattan cultural life. If pro-regulation lawyer and lobbyist Ralph Nader was the quintessential New Class power-monger in the eyes of Irving Kristol and *Wall Street Journal* opinion page editor Robert Bartley, then literature professor and *Dissent* editor Irving Howe appeared so to Kramer.[69]

The New Class Meets Conservative Populism

The populist-minded New Right also embraced theories on the rise of the New Class, and continued Kevin Phillips's contention that corporate elites should be considered part of the New Class sector, insofar as major corporations tend to be internationalist rather than nationalist in orientation, and quite ready to profit from social and cultural trends that moral traditionalists find discomfiting.[70] Sociologist Donald Warren described the attitude of what he termed Middle American Radicals, who complained that "the rich give in to the demands of the poor, and the middle income people have to pay the bill."[71] The racial identity of the poor need not be specified; it was enough to claim that the primary results of the Sixties emphasis on equality were "busing, affirmative action, hiring and enrollment quotas [and] reverse discrimination," in the words of Burton Pines.[72] Conservatives saw upper-middle-class liberals in league with poor blacks, against what they saw as mainstream Americans. Populism had often identified a male, practical, producer ethic as the central element of American society, binding the nation with a vision of classlessness, but at the expense of racial minorities as well as wealthy plutocrats.[73]

Conservative populists inherited populism's historical distrust of large, remote institutions in American society; their conservatism identified liberal control over both public and private sector behemoths as the cause for American decline. However, most conservatives defended rather than attacked the prerogatives of the business class, and deflected traditional entrepreneurial resentments against big business onto the New Class of government regulators.[74] Populists and advocates of the corporate agenda could unite by means of this deflection. New Right fund-raiser Richard Viguerie and *National Review* publisher William Rusher each identify the essential split in American politics as between the producing and nonproducing classes.[75] Whereas left-leaning populism had used the distinction rhetorically to attack owners and financiers of large capitalist enterprises, conservatives now lumped together a racialized poverty class with upper-middle-class defenders of the welfare state as the parasitical nonproducers sapping America of its strength, exploiting the hard work of both business managers and rank-and-file workers.

Conservatives identified the Great Society programs of the 1960s as the crucial weapons of the liberal assault on hard-working Americans. Former secretary of the treasury William Simon complained that "the redistribution of wealth from the productive citizen to the non-productive citizen had become the principal government activity" and targeted the 1960s as the time when "this process had roared out of control."[76] Viguerie spoke of "members of the establishment who never got their hands dirty earning a living," who had gained power through their access to the media and the political culture of Washington.[77] The governmental, information, and media sectors of the economy are distinguished from those businesses where real work is done, tied to traditional mercantile, industrial, and commercial activities. With the former sectors all expanding rapidly in the 1960s and 1970s, the tumult of the Sixties is associated with the decline in American industry and in the social power of people who work with their hands rather than with their mouths.

The Politics of Voice

Historian David Farber has identified this split between the vocal and nonvocal classes as key to understanding social resentments in contemporary America.[78] Right-wing populism may target the poor who are thought to do little work, or cosmopolitan elites who gain affluence and influence without productive labor, which is associated with industrial and agricultural production. In the 1960s Barry Goldwater and, particularly, George Wallace targeted government bureaucrats and East Coast intellectuals as liberals imposing economic burdens and immoral values onto hard-working middle Americans. Many of the issues of the 1960s were played out in the public arena, bringing social visibility to activists who acted in the name of the poor or the young. Their protests and disruptions were brought to widespread public notice by the new abilities of television networks to extensively broadcast events live or within hours of their occurrence. To populist conservatives, government and media elites of the 1960s and the student and civil rights protesters seemed like two sides of the same coin, part of one large conglomeration of those who used the media to dominate cultural and political discourse. In this view, SDS, Black Power advocates, liberal Democrats, and New York sophisticates could be linked together and contrasted to "Middle Americans," who lived their lives off-screen and without special claims to public visibility.

In the late 1960s, Richard Nixon sought support for his policies by claiming to speak for the "Silent Majority" who preferred a quiet social order to the disruptive methods of the advocates for change in the 1960s.[79] Nixon articulated the interests of blue-collar workers, middle managers, and economic elites as a shared emphasis on productive work and material prosperity, as opposed to the critiques of industrial society and materialism circulating in the counterculture. A lack of esteem for physical labor also seemed a hallmark of intellectual circles. "By the late 1960s," Farber states, "the divide . . . between those who produced and those who schmoozed would gain visceral meaning with the prime-time events all America watched."[80] This was perhaps most dramatically illustrated at the 1968 Democratic National Convention, when scruffy antiwar activists faced off against blue-collar Chicago police.

Nixon's vice president Spiro Agnew was best known for his attacks on media elites and student protesters in the name of the Silent Americans who respected law and order and went about their business without making demands on government. Agnew argued that "the student now goes to college to proclaim rather than to learn," raising "clamor and cacophony."[81] Taking aim at campus protesters and the extravagant displays of the counter-culture, he warned that "people cannot live in a state of perpetual electric shock," and "America must recognize the dangers of constant carnival."[82] In this argument, student protesters were positioned as children of the elite, spoiled by permissive child-rearing philosophies and determined to get their way by access to the media controlled by their parents. In later conservative rhetoric, all of liberalism becomes identified with this dynamic of effete, upper-middle-class whites in league with parasitical blacks, using government and media to gain and sustain their social power.[83]

Far from being ignored by the media, "Middle America" became the sub-ject of extensive news coverage after Nixon's victory in 1968.[84] Barbara Ehrenreich suggests that portraits of blue-collar reaction and racism were pro-jections by conservative upper-middle-class elites who resented attacks on their authority in the 1960s. She points to the wave of labor militancy at the end of the decade, the largest strike wave since the 1940s, and to continued support for congressional Democrats by blue-collar voters.[85] Such voters retained admiration for FDR, JFK, and RFK, but with Robert Kennedy's death, many felt alienated from the national Democratic party. The working class may have retained its economic liberalism, as Ehrenreich argues, but white blue-collar voters supported Nixon by a small margin in 1972, when the AFL-CIO refused to endorse George McGovern for president.[86] The image of average Americans as sick of "limousine liberals" had been estab-lished, and it continued over the course of the next two decades, reempha-sized by the concept of white ethnic "Reagan Democrats."

Ronald Reagan had built his political career on combined attacks on gov-ernment policymakers and student protesters, and in 1980 had effectively asked middle-class voters to join with the wealthy business class in an aban-donment of welfare state policies and the rejection of Sixties cultural values. In the wake of repeated economic downturns and the rise of foreign compe-tition in the 1970s, the producing classes (particularly in Rust Belt industries that were most beleaguered) seemed in need of help and appeared incapable of sustaining support for the poor in the face of Japanese, OPEC, and Euro-pean economic challenges. Reagan pushed a wedge into the 1960s apotheo-sis of the New Deal coalition, which had combined white industrial workers, liberal professionals, and poor blacks and whites. A new Republican realign-ment of northern and southern working-class whites, middle-class entrepre-neurs, and wealthy business elites was heralded by conservatives as the new dominant force in American politics.[87] In Reagan's 1981 inaugural address, he invokes a litany of those to be included in his alliance—"professionals, indus-trialists, shopkeepers, clerks, cabbies, and truck drivers"—a cross-class coali-tion, united in its work ethic.[88] Republicans also saw the coalition united in its rejection of liberal interests in the 1960s, defined by conservatives as cultural liberals, African Americans, and other poor nonwhites.

The Republican coalition was inherently unsteady, however, as the business wing of the party instituted rollbacks on unionism and on social spending that had benefited white ethnic workers, and large swaths of the middle classes refused to follow the New Right's social traditionalism. By the late 1980s the recurrent scandals within the bulwarks of the conservative movement and the uneven prosperity of Reaganomics put the coalition in even greater jeopardy. In the 1988 presidential election, however, George H. W. Bush was able to utilize the conservative rejection of Sixties-based liberalism yet again, to retain the White House, at least, for Republican conservatism.

THE 1988 ELECTION

In the presidential campaign of 1988, George Bush and his political consultants played upon the notions of liberalism that had emerged in the late 1960s and grown in conservative discourse during the intervening two decades. He castigated Democratic nominee Michael Dukakis as emblematic of liberalism's weaknesses—citing a lack of patriotism, softness on issues of military strength and crime, and disrespect for the traditional values of middle America as fatal flaws in the Massachusetts governor. Dukakis, as a former Harvard professor who notably lacked passion in his public presentations, was made to represent an enervated, effete liberalism that did not recognize the day-to-day concerns of voters in the producing classes. At a time of ambiguous economic signals and incomplete prosperity, Bush was able to wage his campaign around cultural and social issues relating to patriotism and crime, issues that were legacies of the political and cultural conflicts of the 1960s. He also positioned himself within the grand narrative of middle-class ascension in the post–World War II era, further strengthening his claim to defend middle-class interests and values.

The Populist Preppie

I may not be the most eloquent, but I learned early on that eloquence won't draw oil from the ground. And I may sometimes be a little awkward, but there's nothing self-conscious in my love of country. And I am a quiet man, but I hear the quiet people others don't—the ones who raise the family, pay the taxes, meet the mortgage. And I hear them and I am moved, and their concerns are mine.   —George Bush, Republican National Convention, 1988

Bush's speech at the GOP convention used the concept of voice to tie together several themes for his campaign. His "quiet people" echoes Richard Nixon's Silent Majority to describe sectors of the electorate who believe they make no special claims on government. Bush's own inarticulateness is linked to simple traits of mind, and thus to belief in life's simple truths that help people get by. This simplicity of thought is implicitly counterposed to the tendency toward sophistication, abstraction, and condescension said to mark the New Class of information-age liberals, who are too busy declaiming to the media to pay attention to those who do not enjoy access to the public arena.

Republican campaign advisers had to fashion an image of Bush that could stand on its own, outside the shadow of Reagan, for Bush to seem sufficiently strong to be elevated to the presidency. They also had to counter suspicions of Bush as belonging to the eastern elite himself, given his background as a wealthy son of a former United States senator, with strong ties to the Rockefellers and other East Coast financial titans. Such concerns seemed well-founded when *Newsweek* accompanied Bush's announcement of his candidacy with a cover story announcing Bush's need to fight the "Wimp Factor," a designation based in part on his aristocratic manners.[89] The Democratic National Convention had also highlighted Bush's wealthy background, connecting him to images of country-club Republicanism.

Republican media adviser Roger Ailes responded by remaking Bush in the image of Gary Cooper's star persona—a taciturn westerner whose inarticulate manner was a badge of sincerity and quiet inner strength. Ailes slowed down Bush's speaking rhythms and lowered his speaking register. Bush emphasized his adult life in Texas and predilection for country music and pork rinds. Just as Ronald Reagan evoked pre-Sixties culture by his association with John Wayne, Bush carved out his own claim to traditional notions of American masculinity by this agglomeration of cultural elements.[90]

Indeed, many comments by Bush during the campaign seemed to efface his family and educational background. After a barrage of criticism aimed at him by *Doonesbury* cartoonist Garry Trudeau, Bush accused his fellow Yale graduate of "coming out of the elite of the elite."[91] Perhaps true to Yalie form, Bush also took swipes at his alma mater's Ivy League rival in Cambridge; he labeled Harvard a "philosophical cult normally identified with extremely liberal causes."[92] Asserting the need for a strong defense, Bush argued that "several Bostonians don't like it, but the rest of the country will understand."[93] Conservative academics joined in the Ivy-bashing; William Bennett argued that "the Brookline-Cambridge world . . . [has] disdain for the simple and basic patriotism of most Americans . . . [that is] the crowd with which Mike Dukakis runs. . . . They don't like what most Americans think and believe."[94] In the early 1960s Cambridge had been celebrated as providing the brain trust for the New Frontier; the associations of the New Left and its legacies with the Ivy League and the Democratic party now allowed Cambridge to become rhetorical shorthand for anti-Americanism and cultural elitism.

Bush's attack on Ivy League intellectuals can be understood as borrowing from both older elite traditions and the conservative populism of the 1970s and

1980s. Bush represented a WASP business class that had dominated the Ivy League before World War II, but faced competition for educational status and social power from the more diverse entrants to elite schools after the war (students who would go on to make up the so-called New Class). Although many members of the Ivy League intellectual community aligned themselves with the business class, there were some who aligned themselves with the New Left and antiwar movement in the 1960s and took increasingly antibusiness positions in the 1970s. By criticizing Harvard, Bush could signal his own participation in the producing-class realignment heralded by Republicans since the 1960s, joining the alliance of owners and workers, from the top end of the coalition.

He effaced his elite economic status by appeals to anti-intellectual populism and the values of hard work, positioning himself in the purported mainstream of American commerce and culture, just as the interests of the business class had become increasingly equated with national economic destiny in the 1980s. Countering his opponent's stay at the Kennedy School of Government at Harvard, Bush claimed Texas was a better place to learn about the world, and that his contribution to the economy was more real—"I didn't study a monograph on the effects of economic growth, I started a business."[95] Michael Dukakis was a member of the talking class who had wrested away some of the power of traditional business elites; Bush could now claim to be a regular guy on the basis of his entrepreneurial participation in the private economy.

For voters working in older sectors of the economy, Bush offered a nostalgic vision of American economic dominance based on roll-up-your-sleeves hard work and practicality. This practicality was contrasted to the abstractions of intellectual elites. Intellectual thinking was also associated by the Bush campaign with the revisionist political criticism of the New Left, thereby linking Dukakis to opponents of American dominance by way of his intellectual pedigree. Republicans questioned Dukakis's patriotism and accused Dukakis's wife, Kitty, of burning an American flag during a 1960s antiwar protest.[96] Bush waxed nostalgic about the bipartisan consensus that he said marked American foreign policy until the death of John Kennedy and the opposition to the Vietnam War. He claimed, however, that "the liberal elite do not understand—they never understood—the common sense behind the consensus," as if American foreign policy had always been the product of average Americans outside of eastern circles of power.[97] Bush used the split in the Democratic party and liberal circles that had begun with Vietnam to suggest that eastern liberals of the pre-Vietnam era were beyond the pale politically, rather than major architects of foreign policy for decades through such eastern-associated institutions as the State Department, the Central Intelligence Agency, and the Council on Foreign Relations.

Bush's use of issues like the death penalty, prison furloughs, the Pledge of Allegiance, and a strong military were meant to appeal to the Reagan Democrats that Republicans still needed to win national elections.[98] Given the economy's meager benefits to those below the upper-middle class in income during the Reagan years, GOP strategists identified social and cultural issues as the key to retaining these middle- and working-class voters. Speechwriter Peggy Noonan also positioned Bush as a defender of the upwardly striving middle class by relating his personal history to the popular narrative of the rise of the middle class after World War II.

Defenders of the Postwar Middle Class

Now, we moved to Texas 40 years ago, 40 years ago this year. The war was over, and we wanted to get out and make it on our own. Those were exciting days. We lived in a little shotgun house, one room for the three of us. Worked in the oil business and then started my own. And in time, we had six children. Moved from the shotgun to a duplex apartment to a house and lived the dream—high-school football on Friday night, Little League, neighborhood barbecue. People don't see their experience as symbolic of an era but, of course, we were. And so was everyone else who was taking a chance and pushing into unknown territory with kids and a dog and a car.

—George Bush, Republican National Convention, 1988

Ronald Reagan was able to imagistically traverse the decades of pre-Sixties American life through his film roles and public persona. George Bush makes his own claim to emblematic status through this narrative of postwar upward mobility in the suburbs, recasting himself as a modern, domesticated pioneer. The elements he recounts encapsulate the dominant myth of middle-class independence, hard work, and family togetherness that Republicans have claimed to reinstill in the nation. Of course, for the Bush life experience to conform to this vision of autonomy and meritocratic success, key factors of his story must be excised—the $400,000 loan he received from an uncle to start his oil company, the list of business contacts he was given by his investment banker/United States senator father, and the oil depletion allowance in federal tax policy that provided huge profits to oil companies during Bush's years in the industry.[99] These excisions parallel the gaps in other conservative narratives of the private economy as the engine of American prosperity, which feature the middle class as individualistic self-creators, autonomous heroes of their own lives.

By reciting his own journey from young pioneer heading off to "unknown territory" to wealthy business owner, Bush testifies to the possibilities of the American Dream, and the success of the postwar generation in fulfilling its ambitions. Sixties protests and the counterculture challenged the deepest assumptions of this effort. Republicans' revaluation of pre-Sixties America served to reassure voters that the ambitions of the postwar adult generation were worthwhile, and that such success was accessible to a younger post-

Sixties generation as well. The Bush campaign film at the 1988 convention shows scenes of rioting and demonstrations from the 1960s and early 1970s, which yield to images of reestablished domestic tranquility from the Reagan years (including shots taken directly from Reagan's 1984 convention film, which had been called "A New Beginning").[100] The national narrative sketched is of exciting yet reassuring progress in the 1950s, disruption and chaos in the 1960s and 1970s, and reestablishment of middle-class order and security in the 1980s. Bush emerges as a celebrant of what Allen Hunter has termed "suburban pastoralism," the belief that the "suburban, middle-class family . . . was the natural unit of society, upon which the rest of the social order rested, and for which it was organized."[101] The Republicans position themselves as the key defenders of this suburban ideal, which has needed defending since the 1960s from threatening blacks, disrespectful and druggy kids, the breakdown of gender roles, and foreign challenges to American security and prosperity.

On the campaign trail, Bush claimed that the United States had been mired in an "Easy Rider" society that glorified crime and drugs, until Reagan's election turned the nation toward appreciating Dirty Harry, the Clint Eastwood law-and-order character Reagan had quoted during fights with Democrats.[102] *Easy Rider* (1969) and the original *Dirty Harry* film (1971) had actually been released within two years of each other, tracing the turn in movies from a short-lived countercultural ascendancy to appeals to the Silent Majority. The movement in taste between the two films becomes a metaphor for the realignment from Great Society permissive liberalism to conservative, disciplined producerism (of a rather vengeful sort). In keeping with the linkage of Democrats to Sixties challenges to traditional values, Bush cast aspersions on Dukakis's patriotism and emphasized his own reverence for the American flag and the Pledge of Allegiance. Even more explicitly than had Reagan, Bush seized hold of the most direct symbols of American patriotism and nationalism. His campaign worked to reinforce the association of contemporary liberals with the rejection of nationalist values by the antiwar left of the 1960s.

Bush's choice of Dan Quayle as his vice president served as a counter to the notion of a rebellious, ungrateful Baby Boomer generation. Bush proclaimed to associates that the television camera's fondness for Quayle reminded him of John Kennedy's televisual image, and he hoped that Quayle would strengthen the ticket's appeal to younger voters.[103] Quayle and his wife, Marilyn, challenged the association of the Baby Boomers with countercultural leftism, working to make the social bases of protest appear even more narrow.[104] When it was revealed that Quayle, a putative supporter of the Vietnam War, had dodged the draft and the Vietnam War by joining the Indiana National Guard, the campaign struggled to redeem his image, which was now open to charges of cowardice from old Vietnam hawks and hypocrisy from doves. The divisive events of the 1960s would not be so easy for the Boomer generation of Republican politicians to simply dismiss as a temporary interruption of national glory or as irrelevant to their own lives.[105]

Michael Dukakis made his own bid to exemplify the American Dream by highlighting his family's immigrant background and thrifty suburban lifestyle. Dukakis, however, appeared essentially befuddled in dealing with Bush's recitation of the New Class–Silent Majority themes throughout the final campaign. After establishing a significant lead over Bush by the middle of the summer of 1988, Dukakis's campaign wilted in the face of the Bush onslaught that positioned the Democrat as a post-Sixties anti-American. Dukakis tried to link himself to the Democratic trinity of Roosevelt, Truman, and Kennedy at his party's national convention, but voters were more likely to associate him with George McGovern and Walter Mondale, remembered by nonliberals as whiny, upper-middle-class losers.[106]

Campaigning in Alabama in 1984, Bush had told an all-white crowd that the Democratic party of Mondale and Tip O'Neill was not the Democratic party Alabamans remember.[107] This Republican adoption of the cause of the historically segregationist southern wing of the Democratic party against its liberal northern wing was more dramatically illustrated by the 1988 Bush campaign's use of Willie Horton as a figure of racialized menace. Horton, a rapist and murderer who committed additional crimes while furloughed out of a Massachusetts prison during Dukakis's time as governor, provided an embodied, visible example of the link Republicans claimed to exist between upper-middle-class white liberals and a black underclass.

Dukakis regained some momentum late in the campaign by embracing a more populist attitude, literally taking off his suit jacket, rolling up his sleeves, and becoming more vocal in campaign appearances. He began to address economic issues beyond the budget deficit, invoking traditional Democratic ties to blue-collar workers and criticizing country-club Republicanism. He had been urged to do so by a number of campaign aides, including David Kusnet, whose "On Your Side" theme of Democratic economic populism became the focus point of the Dukakis campaign in its last month. Kusnet went on to write a book offering Robert Kennedy as the role model for future Democratic success, and urged Democratic candidates to combine compassion for the poor with a tough loyalty to producerist middle-American interests.[108] The small upsurge for Dukakis in the last stages of the campaign probably accounted for the even split between the two candidates of the blue-collar, Reagan Democrat, and retired persons' vote. Dukakis won the support of the poor, and Bush, like Reagan before him, won support from most middle- and high-income voters.[109] Tellingly, the only major occupational categories that favored Dukakis were teachers and the unemployed.[110]

CONCLUSION

The late 1980s saw a greater diversity of voices regarding the Sixties in the public affairs sphere, which accompanied the varied representations of the period within popular culture. Participants in the progressive social movements of the time reasserted their own versions of America's recent past. The conservative movement centered around Ronald Reagan faltered in the wake of a number of scandals involving its foundational themes, an uneven prosperity, and the gradual movement of Reagan off the national stage. American politics continued to be seen in relation to the divisions and social identities created in the 1960s, but the national conversation no longer seemed so one-sided.

The 1988 presidential election was played out amid the echoes of the 1950s and 1960s still reverberating in national life. Rather than overturning the conservative narrative, however, the election served as another confirmation of the negative attitude toward the Sixties that was a cornerstone of GOP politics. The Bush campaign assembled an array of themes that harked back to Richard Nixon's Silent Majority strategy from the late 1960s, in claiming to speak for a socially and culturally conservative Middle America against a narrow strata of upper-middle-class liberals and clamorous, dangerous minorities. Republicans claimed to represent a producer-oriented alliance of corporate managers, entrepreneurs, and workers whose interests were united in a growing economy and whose values originated in a consensual vision of upward mobility, common-sense thinking, and family strength. The legatees of the Sixties were accordingly identified as nonproductive, removed from the daily concerns of most Americans, and dismissive of national values. This definition could be applied equally to liberals who had converted to New Left and countercultural principles and to a pathological black underclass.

Republican hopes for a long-term realignment in the electorate now had to depend on the strength of these associations, without the image of Ronald Reagan to inspire the pleasures of nationalist belief. Throughout the Bush administration, Reagan's successor struggled to maintain ideological momentum. The Persian Gulf War provided the only spectacle grand enough to do so, and during the war, Bush's support among voters soared. Bush's popularity subsequently shrank in the face of growing economic woes, however, and the opportunity arose once more to challenge the Republican view of national experience. In 1992 Democrats at last found, in Bill Clinton, a candidate who would engage the debate on Republicans' own terms and revalidate an alternative version of the 1950s and 1960s. In the political sphere, the Republicans' effective and nearly exclusive hold on the images and memories in the National Symbolic was about to end.

CHAPTER 6

The Reinflection of the Past

THE PRESIDENTIAL ELECTION OF 1992

THE 1992 PRESIDENTIAL CAMPAIGN occurred after twelve years of Republican rule, during which values identified with American life in the 1950s were reasserted by those in power. The ideological momentum of Reaganism, however, had stalled through a succession of scandals, increasing economic stagnation, and the replacement of the potent figure of Ronald Reagan with George H. W. Bush as president. Economic anxieties grew among many segments of the electorate, and Bill Clinton asserted his claim to economic leadership in the face of GOP attacks on his character, many of them rooted in the cultural and political clashes of the 1960s.

The Clinton campaign made use of familiar figures within popular and political culture to reinflect meanings of the 1950s and 1960s for contemporary America. In particular, the campaign invoked the legacies of both Elvis Presley and John Kennedy, to place Clinton symbolically as the inheritor of popular cultural and political legacies. Clinton answered Republican nostalgia with his own connection to an American past, to claim allegiance to familiar icons of American greatness. Clinton also combined cultural and political elements to argue for renewed government activism in addressing economic problems, and for the ability of Democrats to represent the interests of white working-class and middle-class voters. The Bush campaign proved itself incapable of responding persuasively to Clinton's incursion into the territory of the National Symbolic that had been dominated by Republicans for over a decade.

THE BUSH ADMINISTRATION

During his presidency, George Bush neither evoked nor rhetorically addressed the nostalgic conservative agenda as effectively as had Ronald Reagan. Only during the Persian Gulf War and in internal policy disputes over domestic issues did his administration rely on historical reference to American experiences in the 1960s. After a bitter 1988 campaign in which he questioned the patriotism and values of Democratic nominee Michael Dukakis and other liberal Democrats, Bush initially softened his rhetoric in his need to negotiate with the Democratically controlled Congress.[1]

The Persian Gulf War inspired public discussion of the wisdom of a major American military effort abroad, the largest since the war in Vietnam. Opponents of the war raised the possibility of another protracted quagmire, while supporters of the war took pains to differentiate the intervention from the conflict in Vietnam by reference to differences in combat terrain and policy aims. In light of standard conservative criticisms of the purported limitations imposed on the military by civilians during Vietnam, the administration also expressed its willingness to do what it would take to win. Bush explicitly responded to public fears by stating, "This will not be another Vietnam. This will not be a protracted, drawn-out war."[2] American military planners were sensitive to the possible decline in support for war aims if quick victory was not achieved. During the military action, the press was heavily censored and restricted from free movement in the area in order to prevent the kind of critical and depressing reports that had contributed to public disaffection with the war in Vietnam.[3]

After the cease-fire Bush proclaimed, "By God, we've kicked the Vietnam syndrome once and for all."[4] Supporters of the war exulted that not only had the U.S. military learned how to win wars once more, but public resistance to the idea of the nation's going to war had been overcome. Despite the media-led orgy of nationalism that accompanied the fighting, public fear of protracted war may have remained. The most popular symbols of public response to the war were the yellow ribbons used to signify the wish for a safe return by the troops. During Vietnam, the yellow ribbon had come to signify hope for the return of POWs; now, all GIs seemed hostage to the designs of the warring governments.[5] When Saddam Hussein and his regime survived the war, the results of the conflict seemed less clear-cut and less resonant of World War II, and closer to the unsettling ambiguities of other American foreign policy strategies in the decades since. Still, the largest American military campaign since Vietnam had met with approval by most Americans, and augured the increased use of limited campaigns in the future.

In domestic affairs the Bush administration largely sought to continue the Reagan agenda, just as key policymakers such as James Baker (secretary of state), Richard Darman (director of the Office of Management and the Budget), and Nicholas Brady (secretary of the treasury) had played key roles in the Reagan presidency. One faction of the Bush domestic affairs team that did favor change finally connected conservative antigovernment attitudes with those of the 1960s New Left, after years of New Left demonization by Republicans. Secretary of Housing and Urban Development Jack Kemp and White House domestic policy aide James Pinkerton put forward what they described as an "empowerment agenda," designed in part to address problems of poverty without resort to federal bureaucracies. By measures such as selling public housing to its tenants, offering tax breaks for job training, and restructuring welfare, empowerment advocates hoped to replace Great Society programs with market mechanisms and individual initiative.[6]

Designers of the plan borrowed the concept of empowerment from New Left rhetoric in the 1960s, which had criticized social stratification and unresponsive government bureaucracies. The new agenda "was closely aligned with the New Left's aim of dismantling centralized bureaucracies. What was distinctly new, however, was the fact that the 1990s version of empowerment was premised on the demonstrated bankruptcy—economic, political, and social—of the Great Society bureaucratic model," wrote one of the plan's proponents, White House aide Charles Kolb. "The 1990s version of empowerment . . . acknowledge[s] the primacy of individuals *and* market mechanisms in creating a more rational, efficient, and productive ordering of society."[7] The conservative approach to empowerment sought to harness Republicans' predilection for individualism and the market to the cause of actively fighting poverty. The Republicans did not share the emphasis of the New Left on participatory democracy, although they did make reference to community activism at times. Participatory democracy assumes a civic, public sphere of action, a conception of individuals' finding fulfillment as political actors. Republican individualism holds little place for such action or the creation of political space in the service of egalitarianism, preferring to focus on economic activity and individual agency through the market. The Republican empowerment agenda ultimately was in line with the diagnoses by Charles Murray and other critics of social welfare spending that government programs themselves were the cause of poverty. In their bid to establish new poverty policies, the empowerment proponents rarely moved beyond vague principles of decentralization and market mechanisms, and the proffering of tax cuts to both rich and poor; their proposals were shot down by more powerful figures in the administration, such as Darman and Chief of Staff John Sununu.[8]

Indeed, the administration increasingly seemed to wish to benefit politically from social division, rather than by leading another War on Poverty, however market oriented. Bush delayed passage of a new civil rights bill, claiming it supported racial quotas, and his aides planned a 1992 presidential campaign that centered on the issues of crime and quotas—Willie Horton redux.[9] Bush may have wanted a spirit of bipartisanship during his presidency, but the next presidential campaign promised to be one of accusation and social rancor, no matter who the Democratic opponent would be.

The rise of Ku Klux Klansman, Nazi, and white supremacist David Duke to prominence in Louisiana politics effectively denied the Bush campaign the use of the crime and quotas themes in 1992. The extreme consequences of the racialized logic of the 1988 campaign and contemporary Republican rhetoric regarding the underclass were made evident in Duke's victory in the Republican primary for governor in 1991. Some Republicans scurried to denounce Duke's candidacy; Bush hesitantly followed. Duke's tendency to mouth the words of other conservatives against welfare in the service of his supremacist agenda raised the specter that Bush would be seen as abetting American Nazism if he based his campaign on thinly disguised racial themes.[10]

Instead, Bush faced a candidate who offered Republicans a chance to run against aspects of the 1960s beyond the rise of welfare and the civil rights movement. The candidacy of Bill Clinton resulted in a new round of political discourse revolving around the meanings of the Fifties and Sixties for contemporary America, but one with quite different dynamics than the Bush-Dukakis campaign of 1988.

CLINTON AND THE LEGACY OF THE 1960s

In the 1992 campaign Bush returned to some of the tactics that had brought him success in 1988, attacking Clinton as the embodiment of the excesses of the 1960s that had disrupted the 1950s suburban dream, excesses to which the Democratic party remained in thrall. Bush's attacks against Dukakis, however, had been based on the Democrat's performance and policy stands in office, rather than on Dukakis's personal behavior; the Massachusetts governor's life story aligned more closely to paradigms of conservative virtue than to Sixties threats to the social order. Republican attacks in 1992 got more personal. As antiwar protester, draft dodger, drug user (however slight), and adulterer, Clinton seemed to personify the deviance of the New Left and the counterculture, violating the Fifties norm in almost every way. The Bush campaign decided to use "trust and taxes" as its theme. Clinton was not to be trusted to show mature leadership or hold patriotic values. He was a 1960s radical behind a centrist veneer, and thus was likely to raise middle-class taxes like other Democratic inheritors of the 1960s legacy.[11] Clinton needed to show the electorate that he could be trusted with the economic stewardship of the nation, and that his values placed him within the American mainstream. He did so by invoking his ties to figures from the nation's political and cultural past.[12]

At the end of the primary season Bill Clinton's national popularity ratings were quite low, although he had secured the Democratic nomination. Clinton's popularity began to rise dramatically during the summer. The electorate's search for an alternative to Bush increased as the economy staggered with no apparent response from the White House, and independent candidate H. Ross Perot's temporary removal from the race focused attention on Clinton. Clinton responded with a slew of television appearances during the preconvention period, normally a time when candidates maintain low public profiles.[13] The Democratic convention itself displayed a united and well-organized party intent on addressing issues of job creation, educational opportunities, and health care reform—areas of importance to independents and Reagan Democrats. The Republicans attempted to shift the attention of the public to sociocultural issues at their convention, but in so doing, they alienated voters who were primarily concerned about the recessionary economy or who were more socially tolerant than the far right.

Bill Clinton's image during the presidential primaries was nothing if not multidimensional. He was an ever-shifting agglomeration of adulterer, slick politician, centrist, southerner, policy wonk, yuppie, and husband of an active feminist. The shifts in Clinton's public identity were influenced by Clinton campaign efforts, his opponents' charges, news media stories, and the interpretations by viewer-voters of the entire campaign spectacle. Since the definitions of Clinton put forward were inconsistent and most voters were not greatly attentive during the primary season, Clinton's identity was still unfixed for many voters at the beginning of the summer. The production of significations entered its crucial phase.

Many of the Bush campaign's attempts to signify Clinton's threat to voters revolved around the challenges to established authority and morality that Republicans had defined as the causes of American decline in the 1960s—draft dodging, drug use, sexual license. By placing Clinton's participation in the activities of the 1960s within a discourse of accusation tied to American decline, Bush aimed to activate negative inflections of the Sixties and define any community not sharing his interpretations of the past as outside the social and political bounds of the 1990s.[14]

This theme of exclusion emerged most explicitly in the Republican questioning of Clinton's antiwar activities while in Britain and of his trip to Moscow in 1969. Accusations of treason and communism were not far below the surface of conservative attacks on Clinton's activities in the late 1960s. Only slightly less histrionically, Marilyn Quayle devoted her speech at the GOP National Convention to deriding the Clintons and others of her generation who she said had protested the Vietnam War, experimented with drugs, and generally turned their backs on middle-class values. "Not everyone joined in the Sexual Revolution or dodged the draft," Quayle stated. "Not everyone concluded that American society was so bad that it had to be radically remade by social revolution. . . . Not everyone joined the counterculture."[15] Quayle spoke for the conservative Baby Boomers who had spent decades seeing their generation heavily identified with activities they abhorred, and who felt beleaguered by challenges to the "traditional" lives they had decided to lead.[16] In this respect Marilyn and Dan Quayle functioned as the 1980s version of Julie Nixon and David Eisenhower, the straight kids who had pleased their parents in stark contrast to their disruptive, troublemaking contemporaries who had enjoyed anointment as culturally hip and socially adventurous.

The Republicans faced great difficulty, however, in affixing the identity of Sixties political and cultural radical to Bill Clinton. Clinton's policy stands were moderate, his appearance and family were clean-cut, and even his perceived slickness evoked Eighties yuppie careerism rather than Sixties otherworldly idealism. Perhaps most important, Clinton was a white southerner—an identity that evokes its own set of strong associations, most if not all of them seemingly at odds with Sixties radicalism. As a southerner, Clinton clashed imagistically with social memory of the counterculture, which had been heavily identified with Greenwich Village and Berkeley, California, with the privileged children of the East Coast and the social anarchy and innovation of the West Coast. American imaginations find it difficult to hold onto the image of an antimilitaristic, psychedelicized, left-wing white southerner. Clinton's southern roots afforded him protection against the charges of Sixties deviationism and embedded him more securely in American history in an identity that, while open to political controversy and regional suspicion, resonated with a strong sense of American tradition.

CLINTON, ELVIS, AND JFK

Clinton's southern roots, while deflecting Bush's articulation of the Clinton identity as Sixties deviant, did not guarantee that he would actually be perceived as trustworthy and genuinely understanding of the plight of the middle and working classes. Before the election, future Clinton speechwriter David Kusnet had published *Speaking American*, which argued that Democratic presidential candidates had lost the common touch and needed to reaffirm their moral and social ties to Middle America.[17] The book enjoyed influence in Democratic circles and coincided with the down-home populist bent of Clinton campaign chief James Carville. As the campaign progressed, one particular aspect of Clinton's southern identity, his association with the figure of Elvis Presley, worked to solidify Clinton's image as being in the mainstream of American life and sincerely concerned with the anxieties of white middle- and working-class voters. By equating himself with Elvis, Clinton became a figure of reconciliation and familiarity, and a representative of white working-class experience in American life during an election centered on gaining the trust of swing voters faced with economic anxiety and social dislocation. Clinton's invocation of John Kennedy also contributed to the creation of a historical narrative that positioned Clinton as the redeemer of the best hopes of the 1960s rather than as a participant in countercultural and New Left activities that were vulnerable to widespread criticism. Clinton's use of Kennedy as a role model redefined the Republican narrative of greatness and decline with a Democratic spin, locating the turning point of recent American history at the loss of a Democratic president, rather than as a result of Democratic policies.[18]

The Formation of a Metaphor

Clinton presented himself as a devoted fan and inheritor of the legacy of Elvis Presley, abetted by his slight physical resemblance to the King and similar regional accent. Clinton's appearance on the *Arsenio Hall Show* on June 3 initiated the reclamation of his image after the bruising allegations of adultery that had dominated the primary season. Clinton wore sunglasses and played "Heartbreak Hotel" with the studio band. Clinton's visual echoes of Presley and his physical enactment of cultural performance made the linkage to the King appear natural, not simply political hype. After the song, Hall began his interview by saying, "I know you're an old Elvis fan," and asked which image of Elvis Clinton had supported for inclusion on a new U.S. postal stamp, whose design had been decided by referendum. Voters had chosen a rendering of the young rockabilly Elvis of the 1950s over the older Las Vegas Elvis of the 1970s. Clinton responded, "I led a national crusade for the young Elvis. . . . I think it has to be the young Elvis. That's when he had all his energy and real raw, new, fresh power. It would have been a shame to do the old stamp."[19] For Clinton, the association worked on several levels. He was a generation younger than George Bush; he was placing his youthful energy against Bush's suspect health. Bush's second term promised more of the same of the last twelve years; Clinton valorized newness and the innovative impact Elvis had on American culture. Clinton had no foreign policy or federal experience; inexperience becomes admirable and invigorating as "raw, new, fresh power." Finally, Clinton was not merely aligning himself with the majority of voters who participated in the Postal Service referendum on the stamp and selected the young Elvis; he was placing himself in their lead, in a "national crusade" to make a notoriously insensitive Washington bureaucracy heed the voice of the people. In a nontraditional site of political discourse, Clinton could establish links with skeptical voters by demonstrating a lifelong appreciation for America's cultural past.

References to Elvis, which Clinton had used sparingly in the primaries, increased in the following months (as did the candidate's appearances in nontraditional televisual forums). The Democrats listed Elvis as "Entertainment Coordinator" at their national convention[20] and considered serenading Clinton's appearance at the convention with an Elvis tune (no metaphorically suitable song was found, and they went with Fleetwood Mac instead).[21] Albert Gore opened his speech at the convention by confessing that his dream had always been to come to "Madison Square Garden and be the warm-up act for Elvis," linking himself (a nominal native of and senator from Tennessee) to the Elvis-Clinton equation.[22] The Democrats were putting on a show, and Elvis, ubiquitous in American culture since his death, was the headliner.

Clinton continued the theme into the fall. His campaign referred to his plane as "Air Elvis."[23] Clinton appeared in a large number of nontraditional venues and provided access to gossip magazines and MTV—the media that covered Elvis covered Clinton too, and in the same way. "It's a lot more important to get five pages in *People* magazine than five minutes on 'MacNeil/ Lehrer,'" said Clinton media strategist Mandy Grunwald, who arranged a *People* cover during the convention not just for the candidate but for his wife and daughter as well.[24] "Hillary and Bill talk about tag-team parenting, their bruising run for the White House and staying in love," the *People* headline stated.[25] To further cement the association, Clinton called in to the national radio program *Rockline* to talk about Elvis with the band U2, whose 1992 stage show featured nightly, unsuccessful attempts to get George Bush to come to the telephone at the White House and speak to the band and, by extension, its large audience of fans. Clinton's *Rolling Stone* interview was illustrated with a photograph of the candidate dressed in blue jeans and a blue workshirt in front of a painting of a White House that resembled a southern plantation house. Despite his Yale and Oxford education, his feminist wife, and his avoidance of military service, Bill Clinton had become the small-town southern boy who makes good.[26]

The Meanings of Elvis

The figure of Elvis Presley in American culture is multidimensional, to say the least. Elvis's complexities are related to differences of generation, gender, region, and race within American society, but also reflects changes in Elvis's life and career through time. Clinton's use of Elvis was itself multidimensional, as, surely, was the interpretive work done by viewers of the campaign. Certain aspects of the Elvis myth possess greater cultural power than others, however, and key aspects of Elvis's identity persisted throughout the campaign. The figure of Elvis was most powerful as a symbol of youthful sexuality contained within a family structure, of class mobility and regional loyalty, and of the rise to dominance of rock and roll as a cultural form.

Elvis's impact on the culture of the 1950s was initially quite disruptive. His success announced the arrival of rock and roll as a major cultural force, as music that could appeal to the majority of white youth, and as a conscious break from and challenge to adult mainstream culture. Borrowing heavily from black cultural forms, Elvis put open sexuality into American culture as no male had since Al Jolson, and the specter of a sexualized (and biracial) teenage audience caused consternation among many adults. Yet Elvis's relation to 1950s mainstream society was nothing if not mixed. His challenge to society was contained as he went into the army, married, and replaced concerts of epic abandon (by performer and audience) with tame, shoddy movies. His love for his mother was as big a part of his legend as his stage movements and leering delivery. Elvis contained and mediated the contradictions of white country and black rhythm and blues, rural and urban, social order and chaos, duty and rebellion, the reassuring comfort of conformity and the risky excitement of deviance. Presley seemed to reconcile values and meanings often constructed as opposites in American society, and which Reagan and Bush had worked to keep apart. Elvis combined religiosity and sexuality, youthful rebellion and love of family, white culture and black culture—as well as working-classness and wealth, regional identity and national identity.

Elvis was a native son of the white working class. His rise to stardom and wealth from exceedingly humble origins validated the myth of the American Dream. Even after having amassed a fortune, however, he never forgot where he came from. He brought his father to Graceland to live with him, gave away Cadillacs on a whim, and decorated Graceland according to his own working-class tastes. In the 1960s and 1970s Elvis's fans were concentrated in the lower- and middle-middle classes and the white poor, particularly in the South. The southern working class looked to Elvis as the superstar who had stayed home, close to his fans, who did not pass them by, as much of the culture seemed to do. To "those who, all through the sixties, lived in an America that was ignored or damned by the Rolling Stones and the counterculture," writes Greil Marcus, Elvis brought "reassurance tinged with a memory of excitement and independence."[27] The fact that Elvis never varied from his original range and combination of styles—rockabilly, gospel, rhythm and blues— linked his image with enduring and steadfast values, and the powerfully and specifically American musics of blues and country. Elvis demonstrated that America's class and social system included mobility, and that such mobility need not mean betrayal. An association with Elvis made visible the possibility that the upwardly mobile Clinton could still have blue-collar interests at heart, that his sexual adventures did not prevent love of family, that he could reconcile racial gaps perceived to be widening. Elvis was particularly useful as a symbol of working-class triumph, a reminder of a time when blue-collar workers achieved their greatest levels of economic prosperity and security, in keeping with the apogee of American global dominance. Appreciation of the young Elvis correlated to nostalgia for a triumphant era for class and nation, lost to a destabilized economy and Vietnam.

To other Americans, Elvis may have become increasingly irrelevant in the 1960s and an embarrassment in the 1970s, but his death freed his image from its tether to an overweight, dazed corporeal body. Elvis could once again be a charismatic teenager coming out of nowhere to shake up the 1950s; or a devoted son who recorded numerous gospel albums; or a flashy millionaire with the common touch; or even, now, a phantom, a mystery in life and death, a leading celebrity in gossip magazines. While maintaining the loyal fandom of his core audience, Elvis could once more be taken up by other social groups who had not listened to his music or cared about him for years.

Elvis now belonged to his fans, to history, to the popular culture at large. A guest columnist for *USA Today* caught the egalitarian play of signification that surrounded Elvis, even as his figure was compared to mythic political and religious leaders: "I always object when people say that Elvis is an icon. Icons are static as Mount Rushmore, unmoving as the Vatican. But Elvis is elusive. The King may have left, but he has moved into the language, better loved, still a lively current. In dying, Elvis joined the rest of us in the supermarket parking lot, the pizza palace, bowling alley, the doughnut shop. His myth and music live in all these places. Why should his spirit be anywhere else?"[28] Elvis is configured as elusive, but placed in the terrain of the plain-living middle and working classes. He emerged out of this milieu to successfully fulfill fantastical ambitions, yet remains within reach of those stuck in the mundane surroundings of what Richard Nixon called the Silent Majority.

This egalitarianism leads to a perceived universalization of Elvis as symbol. Elvis becomes a unifying agent, big enough to contain the myriad contradictions and pleasures that lead to massive popularity, or at least renown. This unity is a legacy of a cherished myth of the Baby Boomer generation, whose large numbers fed a belief in strong generational identity, unified by television, rock and roll, and knowing where they were on November 22, 1963 (although Elvis's first fans predated the Boomers). Whether illusory or real, this feeling of generational unity was hard to shake. After spending pages excoriating Presley ("Elvis was not hip at all, Elvis was a goddam truck driver who worshiped his mother"), rock critic Lester Bangs ends an obituary bemoaning the broken cultural bonds that Elvis had forged: "We will never again agree on anything as we agreed on Elvis."[29] Elvis is seen as the unifier of a generation that the Republicans define by its schisms. To the Republicans' vision of an America unified only by the separation and subtraction of disruptive elements, the figure of Elvis answers by reconciling disruption and stability, the mixing of white and black culture, sexuality and piety, rich and poor.

Despite his wide impact on American culture and the reverence of some of his followers, Elvis had a troubled career and life, and became a bad joke to many former fans and perpetual detractors. After his death, the figure of Elvis went from being a bad joke to being an affectionate one—a testament to the liveliness, ludicrousness, and power of both American popular culture and the workings of fate. Early Elvis is a figure of awe; late Elvis is a figure of fun. Clinton's attitude evinced the common combination of fandom and skepticism; he loved Elvis but did not take him all that seriously. This allowed Clinton to appropriate the King for his own devices even as he paid tribute to him, without seeming exploitative or presumptuous. Clinton sang "Don't Be Cruel" when faced with tough questioners. When Wisconsin Democratic senatorial candidate Russ Feingold livened up his own button-down image by using Elvis in his campaign advertising, Clinton praised Feingold, saying,

"The real reason that I so deeply, deeply support him is that Elvis supports him."[30] Clinton was both a fan and a superstar-in-the-making in his own right. Presenting himself as a fan of popular culture, another boy-dreaming-of-being-Elvis, Clinton equated himself with all who followed Presley or contributed to the circulation of meanings of Elvis after his death. Clinton's bid for popularity was advanced by voters' identification with him; this identification was articulated by Clinton through his proffered identification with the fan-voters. Clinton knew the music, and he got the joke.

Clinton's identification with Elvis offered more than new articulations to be understood by big Elvis fans. Clinton's appreciative but self-aware and self-parodying relation to Elvis could be a model for voters' approach to the political scene. It was hard not to be keenly aware of Elvis's weaknesses and failures, yet die-hard fans persisted in their adoration and other rock fans respected his achievements, or at least the devotion of his fans. Contemporary politics calls for a similar double consciousness of cynicism and fandom, an awareness of show business hype and the absurdity of staking out beliefs and identities based on its ephemeral products and solipsistic performers. Yet that staking of belief and emotional investment continues. In an age of deep cynicism regarding the American political system, Clinton called for voters' belief in spite of themselves and all they knew about political power's operations. Clinton asserted that only by acting on this belief might things change, that the nation's economy and sense of itself could be revitalized by voters placing their trust in him.

Clinton's own heartfelt but self-aware commitment to Elvis could be replicated in voters' skeptical but activated commitment to his campaign. Voters' awareness of Clinton's personal foibles and inconsistent politics could coexist with vigorous support, just as fans are ironic devotees of problematic figures and forms of pop culture. His playful, knowing use of Elvis implied his acceptance of voters' cynicism toward him, but asserted a claim to their support nonetheless. By contrast, the Republicans' unironic approach to the campaign made their manipulations, when seen through by doubting voters, grounds for outright loss of trust and consequent rejection.

The Mixing of Metaphors and the Creation of Unity

Elvis's ability to be a figure of cultural breadth, to subsume contradictions and use them productively, legitimated Clinton's own multifaceted persona. Using his own seeming contradictions, Clinton positioned himself as a unifying figure. A southerner educated in the North, a small-town, fatherless boy living a yuppie life, an anti–Vietnam War protester who supported the Persian Gulf War, a white Baptist who made many appearances in black Baptist churches, Clinton offered himself as a symbol of reconciliation to a nation undergoing a crisis of fragmentation. In his acceptance speech at the Democratic convention, Clinton opined that Republicans always want to divide people into "us and them," but that the point of America is that "there is no them, there's only us."[31] Such public proclamation of his reconciling powers opened Clinton to accusations of slickness and phoniness; Clinton's inculcation of Elvis strengthened his claims to authenticity, by establishing his life-long attraction to a universalized cultural Americana. Clinton's cultural tastes rooted him to the South, and to America. He had not learned to play Elvis tunes on the saxophone overnight.

Clinton's affinity to Elvis was a metaphorical relation that positioned Clinton closer to the economically and culturally insecure swing voters of 1992. His appreciation of Elvis connoted a respect and concern for the white working class that liberal Democrats had been perceived as having abandoned. While Clinton may have fashioned specific policy positions to address the needs of this segment of the electorate, it was his cultural tastes that provided the strongest evidence of his concern, rooted in his own humble background. Voters approach candidates with a great deal of skepticism; they may consider political stands to be manipulative ploys to win their votes. A long-standing personal characteristic is more genuine; its very remoteness from the world of politics gives it greater efficacy as a symbol of values shared by a candidate and the electorate. Even as Clinton publicly highlighted his fandom during the campaign, the original sources of his affection for Elvis seemed apolitical; this affection was thus more effective as a political factor, seemingly beyond the criticism and skepticism that specific policy stands can provoke. Systems of belief, Murray Edelman states, are "more effectively evoked by a term that implies the rest of the cognitive structure without expressly calling attention to it."[32] Clinton's claims to the loyalty of the white working class were not limited to oblique cultural expressions, but his more obvious policy statements gained credibility by his linkage to Elvis and his modest white southern roots.

Clinton's duality as successful yuppie and old-time Elvis fan corresponded to the mixed message of his economic plan, which was presented as benefiting both bosses and workers. Clinton's campaign advertisements positioned him as a thoughtful, serious executive. He appeared in a suit, seated at an imposing desk, presumably looking over policy papers, while a scroll of business leaders who had endorsed him sped across the screen. Yet Clinton often appeared in shirtsleeves and without a tie in personal appearances, and the recitation of the story of his trouble-filled youth in Arkansas formed a major part of the biographical film presented to Democratic convention delegates and home viewers. By positioning Clinton stylistically in both the 1950s southern working class and the upwardly mobile 1990s executive elite, the campaign could reinforce Clinton's combination of concern for the beleaguered industrial middle class and high-tech business sense. Clinton's affection for Elvis balanced his fast-track careerism and the aura of seriousness he tried to create in challenging an older, incumbent president. The press corps referred to him among themselves as "Elvis with a calculator."[33]

Clinton's relation to Presley repositioned not only his own identity, but that of Hillary Rodham Clinton as well. She could now be not just feminist career woman, but also the upper-middle-class girl who breaks class barriers to follow her heart and settle down with the small-town southern boy (Elvis's girlfriends in his movies often enjoyed a higher class position or more stable social status). For those parts of the electorate perhaps most threatened by Rodham Clinton's established persona, this redefinition could contain her threat and place her in a new, positive light.

Clinton's linkage to Elvis brought forward memories and connections that challenged the dominant Republican perspectives, disentangling symbolic combinations crucial to GOP success and bringing together concepts and identities previously construed as disparate. Clinton's use of Elvis exploded the conservative linkages of religious belief and repressive social sanctions, of Democrats and anti-Americanism, of liberal elitism and social license. Clinton-Elvis separated white working-class concerns from racist resentments, love of family from constrained social roles, a strong sense of American identity from international militarist domination. In their stead, new webs of meaning connected an appreciation for popular culture with a realistic sense of life's difficulties during an era of economic and social dislocation. Clinton-Elvis combined urban culture with small-town values, a plan for economic growth with a belief in social inclusion, and memories of a seemingly simpler time with the rise of a new generation to political power.

Clinton and Kennedy

The King was not the only mythic figure of modern America that Clinton appropriated. Democratic candidates have traditionally invoked the legacy of John Kennedy in their campaigns, though usually in largely facile ways; as a directly political figure, JFK is in reach of even those Democrats who share few stylistic or programmatic characteristics with the late president. For Clinton, it was even easier: he was close to the age of Kennedy when the latter became president, had Ivy League credentials, and presented himself as an energizing force after a long period of Republican torpor, as Kennedy had in urging for a national revitalization after the Eisenhower administration. Clinton even had the film to prove his claim to the Kennedy mantle of leadership: his meeting as a teenager with President Kennedy at the White House premiered nationally to striking effect at the Democratic convention. (In 1960 JFK had arranged to be publicly interviewed by Franklin Delano Roosevelt, Jr., before the pivotal West Virginia primary, for his own, indirect touch with the legendary sovereign of the prior generation.[34] Indeed, in his book on the 1960 campaign Theodore White reports that a southern senator, seeing the

10. A teenaged Bill Clinton meets President Kennedy. Courtesy of Getty Images.

adulation Kennedy was receiving from teenaged girls on the campaign trail, had stated that JFK combined "the best qualities of Elvis Presley and Franklin D. Roosevelt."[35])

Clinton claimed that his original inspiration to enter public service came from Kennedy's example; the candidate modeled his plan for a national service corps after the Peace Corps and arranged to be accompanied by one of the Peace Corps' initial organizers, Harris Wofford, at his proposal's announcement. Clinton campaign buttons repeated the image of Clinton shaking hands with Kennedy, with captions that proclaimed "The Dream Lives On" and "The Torch Is Passed to a New Generation." *Time* magazine repeated the imagery, along with the latter rhetorical echo of Kennedy's inaugural speech, in its "Man of the Year" story on Clinton after the election.[36]

John Kennedy was associated with a new activist attitude toward the presidency, after the slow waning years of the Eisenhower administration. This attitude was linked to the popular programs of Social Security and Medicare as well as to the idealism of the Peace Corps and the bravura of the NASA space program. Clinton used Kennedy's legacy to argue the case for active federal intervention in addressing domestic problems, after years of Republican attacks on government programs. In addressing the concerns of financially insecure middle- and working-class voters, Clinton called his economic program "Putting People First" and argued that government concern for the population's job skills and education levels was a proper response to globalization and recession.[37] The Bush administration had shown reluctance to go beyond reliance on impersonal market mechanisms in dealing with the recession; Clinton's "Putting People First" theme demonstrated a personalized concern for the deleterious effects of economic downturns, and his invocation of Kennedy pointed to the potential for efficacious government action with the right person in the White House.

Clinton's combination of Elvis and JFK as symbolic forerunners was a potent one in the generational politics of a pop culture campaign. Elvis and JFK are two of the foremost sons of modern American bereavement; with a few other figures, such as Robert Kennedy, Martin Luther King, Jr., and Marilyn Monroe, they configure the public loss of the last four decades. Elvis and JFK have undergone the same deheroicizing process after their premature deaths—tales of sex, drugs, missing corpses, and enigmatic widows. The revelations were not exactly demystifying, however; the myths changed but grew, became tarnished but also more complex and excitingly scandalous.

Clinton combined Elvis and Kennedy to re-present the 1960s as the early 1960s, a time of idealism, hope, and effective social change. Elvis and JFK created the Sixties while standing apart from them. Elvis created the youth culture that heavily defined the Sixties, yet he was metaphorically absent from the decade, cranking out movies in Hollywood or holed up in Graceland (which was to become, after his death, the White House of popular culture). It took the Beatles to reconvene the teenaged audience into the counterculture. In public memory, JFK set the stage for the intense politicization of the decade but did not live to see its apotheosis, and thus was not implicated in the national trauma of the late 1960s. In fact, since his assassination is identified as the catalyzing moment, the event that began the slide of 1960s idealism into national tragedy, JFK is positioned as the ultimate victim of the decade's trauma, an evocative symbol of what might have been. Because Elvis and JFK are responsible symbolically for so much of the 1960s yet did not fully participate in them, they became useful touchstones for a candidate who wished to appeal to segments of the electorate with widely varying and ambivalent opinions of the decade.

Elvis and JFK provide Democratic answers to the Republicans' national chronology of 1950s normality, 1960s deviance and trauma, 1970s hangover and stagnation, and 1980s return to health and glory. Elvis explodes the narrow definition of the 1950s put forward by Reagan, creating opportunities to link the disruptive Democrats to the best of the 1950s through the history of rock and roll. Clinton crashes the GOP Fifties with Elvis, the patron saint of the white, working-class greasers who are now seen as the embodiment of hip Fifties youth culture. The Fifties sitcom family structure was amended by *American Graffiti, Happy Days,* and *Grease*—the tough but domesticated Fonz became the authoritative focal point, displacing patriarchs such as Robert Young from their positions of dominance. If America is watching 1950s repeats, Clinton-Elvis says, which would you choose—Elvis Presley or Perry Como? Clinton did not say that the American dreamworld of the Fifties resuscitated by the Republicans was a lie that needed to be challenged and superseded, as Sixties protesters had; he said the revival was incomplete, that the Republicans were leaving out the best part—rock and roll, the era's most emotionally powerful cultural legacy.

Having established himself in a superior version of the 1950s, Clinton continued his deflection of Republican criticism by redefining the 1960s. By invoking JFK, Clinton could replay the 1960s with a new happy ending. JFK is seen by the generation that came of age with his presidency as having activated America politically as Elvis did culturally. Kennedy's public persona combined a concern for the downtrodden with a masculinist toughness. No president had successfully reconciled these qualities since JFK's death, with Democrats increasingly associated with concern for the oppressed and Republicans increasingly associated with tough leadership. Clinton's inculcation of Kennedy corresponded to his effort to position himself as a tough Democrat, yet one whose recognition of life's difficulties contrasted with Bush's patrician distance from the realities of economic insecurity.

Elvis's theatrical masculinity supplied Clinton with a replacement for Kennedy's Cold War militarism, and by combining Kennedy's hard-headed idealism with Elvis's down-home roots, Clinton promised to fulfill JFK's promise without sliding into the radicalism of the late 1960s or bowing to the interests of those famous post-Sixties "special interests." Clinton informed *Rolling Stone* that a woman on the campaign trail had told him, "You've got to go in there and redeem the Sixties generation." Clinton claimed allegiance to his generation's taking up of political activism, but decried its "excesses" related to black militancy and violent opposition to the Vietnam War.[38] Taking a page from Reagan and GOP speechwriter Peggy Noonan, Clinton described the time of Kennedy's presidency as "warm and hopeful summer days" before "a lot of America's innocence died."[39] He could now honor JFK by using public service to cure the nation's domestic problems, as JFK was beginning to when cut down. Clinton met Republican efforts to define him through the events of the late 1960s by reclaiming the 1950s through Elvis and the 1960s through JFK. Clinton made claim to a positive vision of the 1960s by ending the decade around 1964.

RESPONSES

Many reporters defined the race between Clinton and Bush as a battle between generations, each man carrying the representational load for the time of his youth. Bush was said to have been formed by his World War II experience, and Clinton by his idolatry of JFK and the trauma of Vietnam. Observers asked whether the country needed the older generation to cede power to the younger in order to stay current with a fast-changing world, or conversely, did the Baby Boomers now have the maturity for leadership after their juvenile outbursts in the 1960s.[40] Each candidate seemed well made for his role, from Bush's cluelessness about supermarket check-out scanners to Clinton's squirming about marijuana.

The media responded to Clinton's invocations of Elvis and Kennedy with relish. Newspapers and magazines were full of references to Clinton as Elvis, JFK, or both; the late-night talk show comedians featured comparisons between Clinton and his two purported forebears in their opening monologues. As might be expected, the tabloids that regularly featured Elvis and JFK as conspiracy-theory and gossip fodder took to the campaign and disclosed that a still-alive or ghostly Kennedy was advising Clinton in the taking up of his cause.[41] More conventional outlets reiterated the connections as well. Elvis and JFK sell in the media industries, and journalists seemed particularly glad to liven up their daily political reports with considerations of the King. The *New York Times* reported in a headline about the "Rumors That Elvis Advises Clinton,"[42] and the conservative *Washington Times* published a lighthearted look at a future Clinton White House, replete with architectural references to Elvis and JFK. After all, Bill Clinton was "Elvis in Camelot."[43] The progressive *LA Weekly* urged its readers to "VOTE FOR ELVIS" on the cover of its election issue.[44] The press may have occasionally bemoaned that trivialities overshadowed serious issues, but they were responsible for much of the circulation of meanings in the campaign, including the mix of the political and the cultural. In the media's attempt to convey a meaningful sense of Clinton to their customers, the candidate's playful use of Elvis and respectful use of Kennedy seemed newsworthy.

Clinton and Bush

In a campaign, candidates form a dyad of meaning and countermeaning; any new articulation of one can rearticulate the other. The Republicans began to take notice of Clinton's use of Elvis during the summer, and tried to turn it against him. They failed miserably. Rather than trying to strip Clinton of his connection, the Bush campaign settled for besmirching the image of Elvis and asserting that the linkage was inappropriate for a presidential candidate. In doing so, as J. Hoberman states, "Bush elected to play the sternly befuddled dad," completing the scenario set up by Clinton's embrace of Presley.[45] At the Republican convention, Bush accused his opponent of following "Elvis economics."[46] What Bush meant by this is unclear, but could be thought to mean that Clinton's plan displayed ignorance and stupidity; that it was flashy but insubstantial, created to appeal to the lowest common denominator; or that it was profligate and foolish in the way it would spend money. All of these meanings insulted not just the King, of course, but his fans. With comments like this, Bush came off as more patrician Yankee than macho Texan, more complacent, rich snob than someone who identified with the hopes and dreams of Middle America. After all, to many voters, "Elvis economics" may not have sounded so bad—Elvis went from being very poor to being very rich.

Bush persisted in his attacks, claiming that because of Clinton's waffling on issues, his opponent had "been spotted in more places than Elvis Presley" and "The minute he has to take a stand on something, he starts wiggling."[47] The attacks did not resonate; without Lee Atwater, his southern, guitar-playing 1988 campaign manager, Bush seemed out of his element. The Republicans hired an Elvis impersonator to trail Clinton through Texas with nasty questions, but they did not get it quite right. The *Washington Post* reported that the GOP Elvis "was a grotesque caricature of Clinton's beloved idol—so plump that he barely fit into his Las Vegas-style jumpsuit, his pompadour black and greasy. He was, one could see as the buses rolled by, definitely the King in his decline."[48] Bush did not like the music, and he did not quite get the joke. Rather than showing up any discrepancies between Elvis and Clinton, which might have countered the Democrat's articulation, the Republicans merely displayed their own misconstrual of Elvis. The Republican Elvis made Clinton's Elvis just that more appealing.

Clinton jumped on the opportunity provided to him by "ol' Bush" (as he began calling the president). In Nashville, Clinton stated, "You know, Bush is always comparing me to Elvis in sort of unflattering ways. I don't think Bush would have liked Elvis very much, and that's just another thing that's wrong with him."[49] Clinton's success in asserting his affinity to Elvis left Bush the role of the unhip, old-fashioned father, stripped of authority by the raw energy of

youth. Even Peggy Noonan, when searching in print for an appropriate authority figure Bush could emulate, could only come up with Ward Cleaver.[50]

Whereas Clinton's affinity to Elvis seemed both self-parodying and natural, Bush's response seemed purely manipulative and artificial, as did the
Republicans' continual placement of Democrats as beyond the pale. Republican party chief Rich Bond put it as plainly as possible on the first day of the
GOP convention: "We are America. These other people are not America," an
articulation so bald and explicit as to lose its naturalizing potential and thus
most of its discursive power. By campaign's end, Bush was reduced to awkward, desperate rhetorical devices in his attempt to reinscribe the late Sixties
into Clinton's identity, warning voters that "This guy is crazy—way out, far
out, man."[51] In the dyadic dance of campaign articulation, Clinton-as-Elvis
repositioned Bush from authoritative military leader to out-of-it elitist, a cultural obsolescent on the losing side of cultural, and political, history. The president, stated Clinton campaign guru James Carville, "stinks of yesterday."[52]
Rock and roll's emergence and triumphant incorporation into a transformed
culture became a metaphor for the emergence of a new, Clinton-led political
formation of the 1990s.[53] Clinton would rejuvenate, but also hold true to,
American values and ambitions.

As polls began to show Clinton pulling away from Bush, the president
claimed his own identification with another figure from the post–World War
II American past, Harry Truman, who had come from behind to win the 1948
presidential election. Bush's claim was based on his own position as an incumbent president who had followed a legendary leader, faced an uncooperative
Congress, presided over mixed economic results, and suffered from a low
standing in the polls. Bush equated his own toughness as a campaigner with
Truman's reputation for plain speaking.[54] The historical remoteness of the
1948 contest between Truman and Republican challenger Thomas Dewey
allowed Bush to put forward his comparison, as most of the electorate would
not likely remember or know Truman's uncharacteristically progressive 1948
platform, which included national health care and increases in public housing.
The same remoteness to the culture of 1992, however, made Truman not
merely a nearly empty signifier but also a nearly powerless one. Bush's invocation of Truman made the president appear all the more outdated, placing him
in a pre-rock and roll world that was gone forever. In addition, any positive
stylistic attributes of Truman that still resonated had already been taken up by
independent candidate H. Ross Perot, whose appearance and voice resembled
Truman's and who was more believable than Bush in the persona of the feisty
outsider. Indeed, Perot's presence in the race also made the Bush campaign
appropriation of conservative populism more difficult, as the maverick bil-
lionaire captured that discursive terrain with his folksy yet belligerent demeanor. Perot's unrelenting emphasis on contemporary economic issues also

made Bush attempts to attack Clinton for events in the 1960s seem increasingly irrelevant and evasive.

The Final Tally

In the attempt to ascertain the effects of campaign discourse, Perot's involvement in the race makes statistical analysis of the electoral results even more problematic than usual. The poor state of the economy was usually credited as the central theme of the election, and the deciding factor in Clinton's victory. A plurality of voters trusted Clinton to improve the economic conditions that Bush had seemed powerless to solve and, perhaps worse, uninterested in even addressing.

Clinton did not substantially enlarge Mondale's or Dukakis's vote totals, while Bush's support plummeted compared with Reagan's triumph in 1984 or his own victory in 1988. Clinton kept the Democratic base, even with the presence of another candidate against the status quo. In a sense, Perot can be seen as having taken away a good portion of votes that had previously gone to the GOP, without capturing confirmed Democrats. Most exit polls stated that Perot had taken equally from the major party candidates; if Perot had not run, Clinton thus would have substantially enlarged his totals (as polls showed during Perot's summer hiatus from the campaign). Without Perot's presence, then, Clinton would have easily surpassed the performances of Mondale and Dukakis, taking away votes that had been consistently Republican in recent presidential elections.[55]

Perot seemed to take northern votes away from Clinton and southern votes away from Bush. Clinton did a little better than his Democratic predecessors in the South, particularly among born-again Christians (though Bush received an easy majority of their votes). Clinton's invocation of Elvis may or may not have helped him reach the core of Elvis's fans. More important, Bush's elitist response to Clinton's cultural references may have been damaging to the GOP. Bush did particularly poorly in the South, although the recession had hit harder in the Northeast and on the West Coast. Bush's negative comments about Elvis may have contributed to the sense that Bush was removed from the everyday experiences and attitudes of many Americans, a crucial weakness for a president in the midst of a recession.

Clinton did reach more Reagan Democrats nationally than had the Democratic candidates of the 1980s; thus it may be that Clinton's combined use of Elvis and JFK imagery enabled him to deflect charges of social radicalism and place himself within a recognizable, positive framework of American culture and history, which could appeal to voters previously disaffected from the Democrats. Even when not successful as a strategy to attract votes, Clinton's demonstrated position within mainstream Americana could still serve as inoculation against conservative charges of deviancy. Michigan autoworkers interviewed by the *New York Times*, for instance, saw neither a John Wayne nor a John Kennedy in the race, much to their unhappiness; enraged by Bush's attitude toward the recession, however, they predicted that they would split their votes between Clinton and Perot.[56] With Perot taking away votes from Bush (and Clinton getting strong support from black voters), Clinton won several states in the South, which had been a disaster area for Democrats in national races in the 1980s. Clinton's strategy of nostalgia may have enabled independent, middle-class voters to support Perot in large numbers instead of Bush. Perot voters may not have liked Clinton, but they did not see him as such a threat that they felt forced to vote for Bush to keep a wild child of the Sixties out of the White House.

CONCLUSION

By invoking Elvis Presley and John Kennedy as his longtime personal heroes, Clinton deflected Republican charges of political and cultural anti-Americanism and expressed his solidarity with fans of post-1954 American popular culture and the white working class. By reinflecting the Republican call for a return to the 1950s by claiming membership in the Fifties rock and roll generation, Clinton positioned himself in the American mainstream as no other recent Democratic presidential candidate had succeeded in doing. Clinton rewrote recent American history to highlight the achievements of the society through the early 1960s. In the face of continuing nostalgia for John Kennedy, conservatives in the 1980s had muted their criticisms of the New Frontier; the Clinton campaign took advantage of the continued glorification of the Kennedy years to make a strong historical claim to their legacy. This legacy included a revaluation of government efforts to deal with domestic social problems, an appeal to the nation's best instincts in resolving social and racial division, and a tough but sophisticated masculinity used to represent American interests abroad.

Articulations must be continually reinforced to maintain social effectivity. The decline of the linkages between Clinton, Elvis, and JFK within the Clinton administration's subsequent significatory practices was striking, and the absences created opportunities for administration opponents to reassert their own meanings of Clinton, Democrats, liberalism, and the nation's history. Newt Gingrich became particularly active in reinscribing Republican memories of the 1950s and 1960s as universalized social memory and as the basis for conservative social and economic policies. The discussion and debate about these decades reached a crescendo in the years after Clinton's election, as Republicans once more launched an ideological offensive based on public and national memory.

CHAPTER 7

Elvis Has Left the Building

THE RESURGENCE OF THE RIGHT

IN THE 1992 PRESIDENTIAL ELECTION Bill Clinton placed himself within a historical narrative that offered a political response to the conservative nostalgia of the Reagan era. He accomplished this particularly through his demonstrated fandom for figures from popular entertainment and politics, as signs of his cultural and social allegiances and political development. By invoking the legacies of Elvis Presley and John Kennedy, Clinton reconstructed arguments for Democratic programs to assist insecure middle- and working-class voters. Clinton seemed to share Reagan's view of a rosy American past, but located it in the time of the Kennedy administration. With his victory, many commentators made note that political power was passing to the Baby Boomer generation. A new era was starting that would move away from the conservatism of the Reagan presidency.

As president, however, Clinton was unable to continue to successfully articulate his powerful historical narrative and his own relation to popular culture, and thus provided his political opponents an opportunity to reassert their own vision of American history and its relation to contemporary society. Conservative nostalgia returned with a vengeance in the 1994 congressional elections, as Newt Gingrich, Rush Limbaugh, and other voices of the right led a new repudiation of liberalism. Despite conservatives' use of the prism of the past to explain the failings of America in the 1990s, the appeal of conservative nostalgia remained limited in the political sphere, even as its themes seemed pervasive in social discourse. Popular culture, meanwhile, continued to recycle styles and references from previous decades of American life.

THE CLINTON ADMINISTRATION

The Clinton administration opted for different strategies than those followed by the Clinton campaign in the attempt to win favor from the electorate. The administration largely abandoned its use of popular culture figures to illustrate a populist reconciliation of disparate social elements and values, linking middle- and working-class economic concerns to activist government intervention into the economy. In so doing, Clinton left American politics open to new efforts by Republicans to explain continuing economic and social dislocations by their own use of popular images of the past. The Republicans again invoked their vision of the 1950s to put themselves forward as defenders of the interests of middle-class voters.

The Early Days

After Clinton's victory in the election, the media continued to circulate his association with Elvis and JFK. Reporters debated whether Clinton would actually be able to bring about a new Camelot. One *Washington Post* writer proclaimed that, with Clinton's election, "we are on the brink of a renaissance of spirit that will make the '60s look like a dress rehearsal," a new era of frankness, emotional depth, and experimentation in popular culture.[1] He cited the reenergizing of the rock scene by Nirvana, the psychosexual explorations of Madonna, and the more realistic depictions of families in film and television (as epitomized by *Roseanne*, then the highest-rated series on television) as renewing American culture after the doldrums of Reaganism. Clinton would do his part by bringing new energy to Washington politics, facing up to the nation's problems, and finally enabling the country to recover from a society-wide alienation and depression induced by the assassination of John Kennedy.

Others struck a more cautionary note. Another piece in the *Post* warned of the dangers of high expectations brought on by Kennedy nostalgia—yet even that article concluded that Clinton was better prepared for the presidency than Kennedy had been in 1961.[2] A strong economic surge in the weeks after the election strengthened the sense of optimism among Clinton supporters. A Gallup poll declared that 57 percent of those polled thought that Clinton would "create a new spirit of idealism in the country."[3] In his public pronouncements, Clinton continued to refer to Kennedy frequently, and his inaugural address contained echoes of New Frontier rhetoric.[4] *Newsweek* opined that with Clinton's victory, the film of the boy from Arkansas shaking hands with President Kennedy "rises from mere advertising to the realm of prophetic history. For it documents JFK reaching across the years to a boy he did not know—and to whom the torch now passes in an emphatic statement of America's desire for change."[5] In the usual manner of the press in a post-election period, reporters manufactured a mandate for Clinton to rule; with this new president, the easiest *and* the historically most profound way to do so was by taking up the association of Clinton with his political role model. The new White House obliged; Hillary Clinton staged a television special in which she offered a small tour of the White House, as Jackie Kennedy famously had done in 1962. The new First Lady opened the program in "Jackie Kennedy's garden" and disclosed that her role models would be Jackie and Eleanor Roosevelt, balancing the roles of mother and social activist.[6]

Clinton's affinity for Elvis Presley continued to be discussed as well, particularly in relation to the generational changeover at the White House and its attendant differences in style. Newspapers referred to Clinton as "Elvis in the White House" and "The Man Who Would Be Elvis," and made much of his cultural roots.[7] *USA Today* listed his "formative influences" as "hamburger drive-ins and Elvis movies," constructing a prototypical adolescence of the late 1950s and early 1960s for the new president. He was a product of a "rock 'n' roll rebellion" that could now be considered "time-honored," legitimated by history and safely absorbed into mainstream American culture.[8] Indeed, his election was the apotheosis of rock's ascendancy, which prompted a few wistful regrets from music critics who saw rock's subversive power now diminished by its association with the most visible powers that be.[9]

Clinton's image continued to be treated playfully by the media, as he used cultural metaphors to appeal to varied constituencies. This was a president who jogged to McDonald's, thereby balancing yuppie exercise and working-class pleasure, discipline and trashiness, the markings of power and just-folks cultural taste. *Nightline* reported that compared with the Bush administration's parade of old white men, Clinton's team was young, hip, and culturally eclectic. Political humorist Calvin Trillin remarked that the Republicans had tended to wear blazers to work on Saturdays, but the new Democrats preferred jeans. He notes that Clinton's stylistic combinations were yielding a new cultural identity: "Ivy League yahoo."[10]

The historical narrative put forth through the Clinton campaign and validated by his election was illustrated by *In the Line of Fire*, a Clint Eastwood vehicle released in the summer of 1993.[11] Eastwood had been a Republican icon as law-and-order police officer Dirty Harry. Now, after Clinton's election, Eastwood plays a Secret Service officer who had idolized John Kennedy and still suffers from his memories of the president's death. The Secret Service's failure to protect Kennedy can be redeemed by Eastwood's capture of an embittered CIA assassin who is now threatening the current president. The film does not offer a prolonged characterization of its putative chief executive, but he can be assumed to be a Democrat by his warm reception at a convention of labor union officials. Eastwood's character can finally move beyond the trauma of November 1963, redeeming the promise of the Kennedy administration, by overcoming the malfeasance of government officials who have betrayed constitutional ideals for three decades. Personal and national trauma can be assuaged by a turn to the legacy of the New Frontier.

Film reviewers made note that Eastwood's image had become more complex in recent years; his macho toughness had added layers of sensitivity.[12] His character in *In the Line of Fire* even breaks into tears at the thought of his failure to prevent Kennedy's killing—before switching back to action mode to foil another assassination. Eastwood's new emotional openness corresponds to

11. Thirty years later, Clint Eastwood tears up at the thought of JFK's death in *In the Line of Fire*. Columbia.

Clinton's tendency to show emotional pain in public, particularly at the sight of others' suffering. The combination of strength and tears augurs a new model of Hollywood masculinity, after a decade of hypermasculine tough guys.[13]

Former Bush aide James Pinkerton, piqued by the sight of an Eastwood vehicle that could be useful to Democrats, took pains to respond to the film by asserting that "Clinton's no JFK, and this is no Camelot."[14] Pinkerton charged that Democrats had reversed the dynamic of the Kennedy administration: Kennedy had been activist in foreign policy but minimalist in using the government to solve social problems, whereas today's Democrats were noninterventionist internationally but in thrall to government bureaucracy at home.

Pinkerton need not have worried so greatly about Clinton's appropriation of Kennedy. The campaign-generated matrix of imagery and narrative that had offered a liberal challenge to conservative historiography did not remain active in the Clinton administration for very long. To a striking degree, Clinton and his chroniclers in the media dropped references to Elvis, JFK, the cultural politics of Fifties rock and roll, and the historical trajectory of the early 1960s when discussing the new administration. A number of factors contributed to this change, which ultimately allowed the Republican opposition to again seize the initiative in defining the past's relevance to contemporary politics. These factors included Clinton's choice of strategy for economic growth and the attendant implications for the definition of the government's role in class structure, the discussions of issues such as military acceptance of homosexuals, and the Paula Jones and Whitewater inquiries into Clinton's personal ethics. In his attempt to reconcile diverse strands of American social experience, the president failed to maintain a sense of coherence in his own image.[15]

The Government and the Economy

Clinton faced a choice between two economic strategies: emphasize the reduction of the federal budget deficit or increase government investment in education and training, infrastructure, and programs spurring technological and environmental innovation. His campaign had adopted the slogan "Putting People First" to denote an emphasis on human resource spending, so that American workers could compete in the world economy—an issue particularly addressed to middle- and working-class voters facing income stagnation and increased unemployment. (The recession of the early 1990s hit the middle class harder than any economic downturn since the Depression, and even middle-aged white males, usually the most economically protected segment of the population, saw their incomes fall significantly during the years before the election.)[16] After twelve years of antigovernment rhetoric from Republican administrations, the Clinton campaign put forward the argument that government had to play an active role in job creation, worker training, and technological progress. Government programs could be targeted to benefit the economically insecure lower- and middle-middle class.

Once in office, Clinton sided with advisers who emphasized the importance of reducing the federal deficit as a means of promoting private savings, lowering interest rates, and reassuring investors wary of a Democratic president.[17] Government economic activity thus was defined not as a solution to stagnation and international competition, but as a burden on private markets and an obstacle to growth. Rather than continuing the redefinition of government as an ally of workers, the administration concentrated on enacting policy that conformed to previous Republican rhetoric on the destructive nature of government as an overreaching threat to the private economy.

This move was instigated by officials with long-term ties to Washington politics or Wall Street, such as Treasury Secretary Lloyd Bentsen, National Economic Council director Robert Rubin (who later succeeded Bentsen as secretary of the treasury), and Office of Management and Budget director Leon Panetta (later White House chief of staff). It was opposed by Clinton's campaign advisers, who, with their eyes on the polls, wished to maintain a populist appeal that depended upon government spending targeted to middle- and working-class concerns, rather than on spending cuts and deficit reduction. They made the argument that most voters (particularly those who might vote Democratic) would support specific proactive efforts to promote their economic security rather than a generalized, seemingly remote effort to reduce the deficit.[18] Although Clinton did put forward a few suggestions on

programs for job creation and education, his overall budget plans and attendant rhetoric coincided with the concerns of the deficit hawks.

Given the administration's consequent message that excessive government
spending weakens the economy, many of Clinton's efforts at small increases in
specific programs were defeated in Congress by an alliance of Republicans and
conservative Democrats. As 1993 progressed, Clinton reduced his use of popular culture to reference his agenda; the Clinton White House increasingly was
focused on its troubles with Congress, and aides feared that placing Clinton in
the context of popular culture would make him appear unpresidential.[19] The
administration also stopped making significant efforts to argue that government
has a legitimate role to play in the economy. Voters were never recruited by the
administration into a consolidated bloc supportive of both domestic spending
and Clinton personally. The absence of Democratic discourse linking proactive
government efforts, American culture, and the perspectives of economically and
socially insecure segments of the population left the momentum generated by
Clinton's electoral victory vulnerable to rapid dissipation.

Clinton's Loss of Coherence

Several issues arose to dissipate the support Clinton had gathered during
the final months of the campaign and the interregnum. Charges of financial
and sexual misconduct enabled Clinton opponents to categorize him as a
sleazy politician, a characterization that many voters found easy to believe
after twenty years of scandalous disclosures regarding the political class. Voters'
view of Clinton as a typical member of the political elite worked against his
image as a harbinger of change and renewal. His image as a public official of
predictably dubious integrity worked against his identity as a fan, as a member of the national cultural audience who had somehow managed to take the
stage and move into the spotlight. The longer Clinton stayed in Washington,
with media attention fixed on his doings inside the Beltway, the more remote
he seemed to citizens distrustful of distinctly political signification. Clinton's
emphasis on congressional negotiations and complicated plans for deficit
reduction and health care reform placed him in a heavily political milieu and
displaced his use of popular culture tropes to playfully communicate his ideas
and values. In the hindsight of 1994, *Time* argued that Clinton had seemed to
understand working-class and middle-class anxieties during the 1992 campaign, but "once in office, seemed not so much a friend of the working class
as a captive of the economic and cultural elites."[20] The combination of Wall
Street economics and liberalism on volatile social issues distanced Clinton
from the swing voters of 1992; an astute cultural politics that might have made
up the distance was now lacking in the Clinton circle.

Clinton's image as an outsider coming to Washington to reform American
politics was also threatened by a growing perception of his weakness as a

leader. This perception was based on specific issues such as the controversy over acceptance of homosexuality in the armed forces and, ironically, on Clinton's penchant for sending mixed messages, which was transformed from a campaign asset into a presidential liability. His other-directedness, his desire to please, became increasingly criticized as unseemly and weak, as demonstrated by his frequent changes of political stance. No longer buttressed by his lifelong cultural and political allegiances, Clinton's persona became increasingly incoherent and suffered from the charges of inauthenticity that he had answered in 1992 with his links to Elvis and JFK.

Clinton's fall into incomprehensibility was related to the challenges politicians have faced for decades in maintaining images of strong, masculine selves. As argued by T. J. Jackson Lears, Warren Susman, and other social historians, early-twentieth-century America witnessed a shift from a culture of character and production to one of consumption and personality.[21] This shift was rooted in the increasing productive capacity of industrial capitalism, the growing urbanization of social space, and the encroaching bureaucratization of worklife, which combined to make social interaction more important than self-reliance in the determination of individual economic success. These changes reflected and reinforced a modern sense of the fragmentation of the self; individuals had to present multiple faces to the world to succeed socially, were increasingly economically interdependent, and had to master at least some of the specialized knowledges beginning to circulate in complex society. The other-directed personality had been associated traditionally with women, and their roles as wives and mothers. The introduction of other-directedness into prescriptions of male success effectively placed men into what had been feminized social roles.

Contemporary political candidates are the quintessential performative selves, seeking to be many things to many people, reconfiguring their identities according to specific social or political situations. Kathleen Hall Jamieson identifies political rhetoric in the twentieth century as increasingly self-disclosing, personalized, and emotional—what was deemed in classical rhetoric to be the "Effeminate" style, meant to connect to others.[22] This other-directed style is effective in communicating through mass media, which regularly features such personal disclosures in its entertainment genres and news-magazine shows. The extension of the culture of personality into the electoral sphere is illustrated by the importance of nontraditional sites of political discourse in the 1992 presidential election. Talk shows are prime purveyors of the Effeminate style, and Clinton excelled at disclosure of personal emotion when treating issues of early family trauma, marital infidelity, and the social fears and anxieties of the electorate.

Clinton's ability to convey emotion publicly can be compared to Ronald Reagan's vaunted skilled at communication via television, but their styles contained crucial differences. Reagan wove emotional cues into his presentation of historical and contemporary tableaux, but rarely discussed his personal life or private behavior. Reagan also was able to weave his emotionalism into a presentation of a coherent, whole self, solidified by his invocation of "traditional" values that looked back to a culture of production and character and by his militarist stance toward the Soviet Union.

Political figures have often attempted to convey images of strength that compensate for their fragmented public selves and dependence on others' approval; common strategies include the display of militarist attitudes or bellicosity, and calls for national unity and constraints on social diversity. The Cold War provided a strong rationale for such compensatory maneuvers, positing the need for national unity in facing the challenge of international communism (which was configured within Cold War attitudes as fearsomely unified). Reagan's anticommunism and strong identification with the social stability of the Fifties enabled him to counter the threat of fragmentation that political figures face as an occupational hazard. Thus, while Reagan's policies fluctuated at times, for both supporters and opponents his public persona retained a sense of consistency and coherence that often melded into an impression of strong leadership.

Clinton had no Cold War enemy to invoke to forge his public self; foreign policy was a noticeably muddled area for the new administration. Clinton also entered office by pledging to reconcile social diversity with a sense of Americanness, but could not easily subsume the former in the interest of the latter. His own communicative style was personalized but fragmented, and Hillary Rodham Clinton was a strong public figure in her own right. These factors contributed to a sense that Clinton was weak, without a strong sense of a coherently masculinist self. Only some voters seek such a persona; according to surveys, men place higher value on it than women, and Clinton's poll ratings were consistently lower among men than women.[23] Established interpreters of public opinion and governmental affairs, who are predominantly male, see a lack of such a sense of self as a severe liability, as do other political actors. These factors combined with Clinton's policy fluctuations and drawn-out decision-making processes to invite charges that he suffered from an absence of will beyond personal ambition, and displayed an irresponsible desire to please or appease everyone.[24]

The emergence of the acceptance of homosexuality in the armed forces as the first major issue in the new administration took on great significance in this context. Clinton seemed to be attacking a bulwark of American masculinity, creating a breach in one of the defining boundaries of an American masculinist self. His own record of service avoidance during the Vietnam War was already a matter of public controversy, and the goals and very raison d'être of American militarism were in crisis with the collapse of the Cold War (and had been only partially alleviated by the Gulf War victory). Clinton's attempt to secure space for sexual diversity in the military further closed off one of the main ways available to American presidents to create a strong, coherent public self. Despite his administration's initial continuation of high levels of military spending, Clinton was given little credence as a military leader; he was booed and heckled when he attended a public ceremony at the Vietnam Veterans Memorial in Washington.[25]

This unavailability to Clinton of effective militarist posturing made his failure to maintain a relation to other forms of American masculinity all the more damaging. The candidate's inculcation of Elvis and JFK during the campaign had served to mitigate his other-directed style and the revelation of draft dodging by placing him in a tradition of American male sexualized charisma, as performed by public figures. I may not be a soldier, Clinton was signifying, but I can be a rocker, and a president. Elvis and JFK were multifaceted but also individually distinctive; each was a stylistic innovator who conveyed a strong sense of self. Clinton had gained distinctiveness by combining the two in a way unseen before in American politics. The loss of symbolic connection to these figures by Clinton during his administration contributed to the loss of coherence in his public self. No alternative, positive persona emerged to take the place of his linkage to Elvis and JFK. Rather than the leader of a progressive Baby Boom ascension to power, Clinton appeared increasingly as an individual without the moorings of a set of personal ethics, strong sense of autonomous self, or loyalty to any particular social grouping. In the face of strong conservative attacks on both Clinton's character and government involvement in social programs, Clinton's incoherence as a political figure led to difficulties in rallying support for his social policy agenda, such as health care reform, and ultimately to the 1994 electoral debacle for the Democrats.

THE REPUBLICAN RESPONSE

Republicans such as Newt Gingrich and Rush Limbaugh responded to the Clinton electoral victory by insisting on the Reaganite narrative of recent history. The continuing economic and social crises of contemporary America had cast doubt on Republican claims of a return to pre-Sixties glory that had circulated during the Reagan administration. Republicans who subsequently rose to prominence offered the explanation that while most of the public had maintained or returned to pre-1960s values and practices, public policy had been hijacked by inheritors of the legacy of Sixties protesters and Great Society programs. Policies and attitudes initiated in the 1960s were the cause of the recurrent problems of poverty, crime, and general social breakdown. In putting forward this argument, Gingrich, Limbaugh, and other conservatives circulated their continuing redefinitions of the past as primary elements of their explanations of the present.

The 1950s and 1960s, Again, in Conservative Discourse

The 1990s saw the rise of new spokespersons for the cause of conservative nostalgia. Congressman Newt Gingrich, who had previously been identified with a forward-looking political message (he liked to talk about colonizing the moon), emerged as the dominant Republican on Capitol Hill and based strong attacks on Democrats by emphasizing the contrasts between the 1950s and the 1960s.[26] Radio talk show host Rush Limbaugh became a cultural hero for conservatives by attacking feminists, environmentalists, and other post-Sixties progressive activists.[27] William Kristol, who had served as Dan Quayle's chief of staff during the Bush administration, led a new generation of writers and political activists who continued the neoconservative attack on the New Class of liberal elites, based on the division in intellectual circles in the 1960s; being the son of Irving Kristol and Gertrude Himmelfarb, Kristol was the biological as well as the ideological progeny of the intellectuals who made up the neoconservative camp.[28]

Conservative depictions of the 1950s and 1960s during Clinton's terms in the White House followed the emphases laid down by the nostalgic writers and politicians of the early 1980s. The 1950s were celebrated for their purported social consensus, strong sense of family, and economic prosperity. They were seen as a more innocent time, before gendered antagonisms, government scandals, and foreign policy debacles made Americans come to expect personal and political strife as a constant in their lives. The conservative newsweekly *U.S. News and World Report* defined the era as "a time when the American political system worked, when prosperity was unprecedented, . . . when traditional values were unchallenged."[29] These values, according to Limbaugh, include "belief in God, monogamy, devotion to family, law and order, self-reliance, rugged individualism, commitment to excellence, and rewarding achievement."[30] This combination tempers a strident individualism inculcated by the capitalist economy with an obedience to legal and religious authorities and an unselfish commitment to family—the same combination trumpeted by social conservatives in the early 1980s.

In the telescoped chronology of the nostalgic conservatives, the 1960s derailed a social culture that, according to Newt Gingrich, had remained constant from the founding of the nation in the 1770s, a culture of character, production, and the work ethic.[31] Although the New Deal began the trend toward government interference in the economy, it was the Great Society programs and youth counterculture of the 1960s that imposed a set of alien and destructive values onto American society. During and after the 1994 elections that propelled him to the Speakership of the House of Representatives, Gingrich made clear his view of the divisions in American society based on the lingering impact of the Sixties. He described Democrats inspired by the legacy of the Sixties as "traitors" and the "enemy of normal Americans" (he then defined normality as the state of being middle class), and charged that the Democratic party itself was a manifestation of "total bizarreness, total weirdness."[32] In this scenario, more effectively articulated by Gingrich in 1994 and 1995 than by Bush in 1992, Clinton becomes the inheritor of the mantles not of Elvis and JFK, but of hippies and George McGovern. The 1960s are defined as a time of self-indulgence, social anarchy, and the destruction of family structures. The social movements of the time are collapsed by Gingrich into a "free-sex, free-speech, free-drugs" campaign antithetical to the values of middle-class America.[33] The counterculture resulted in riots, lewdness, and laziness at the time, and yields continued crime, poverty, and drug abuse in the present.

The only way to redeem the nation is to reject the Sixties legacy and return to the values of earlier times; the social extremism that the right is accused of promoting is actually an extension of the normality that enjoyed social approval during the 1950s. Gary Bauer, president of the social-conservative Family Research Council, proclaimed, "The religious right has no extreme agenda. There is not a single public-policy goal it endorses that was not understood as necessary for a healthy society when Eisenhower was president."[34] In this view the Eisenhower era is no longer characterized by the problems with which the 1950s had often been identified in the 1960s—McCarthyism and the Cold War, explicit racial segregation, a stifling homogenization of cultural products. Even conservatives had at times associated these problems with the previous era, but the disappearance of these issues in contemporary America enabled the nostalgic discourse to embrace the 1950s unhesitatingly.[35] With the Cold War over, public segregation illegal, and a panoply of cultural forms circulating in American society, the earlier decade could be taken up for its supposed strengths without evoking strong worries about its failures. The 1950s became a secure discursive base with which to legitimate social reaction, and the 1960s became a useful device to delegitimate public policy by association with that period's excesses, which conservatives related to social problems in the present.

Newt Gingrich blasted public housing and schooling as legacies of the 1960s, until reporters reminded him that both predated the Kennedy inauguration. He replied that housing and schools both turned bad in 1964 and 1965, that those years constituted a turning point for American society (as Clinton had tacitly asserted during the 1992 campaign).[36] "We have had," he later stated, "since Lyndon Johnson created the Great Society, a thirty-year experiment in destroying America. For thirty years, we have liberated prisoners, tolerated drug dealers, put up with violence, accepted brutality—and done it all in the name of some kind of bleeding-heart liberalism."[37] The Great Society spending programs are conflated here with issues of criminal justice, to associate social spending with increases in crime. Democratic advocates for the poor are thus positioned as threats to the physical security of the middle class, continuing the GOP association of liberal social planners with underclass criminals.

Many other conservatives saw the mid-1960s as crucial as well, the years in which government policy was divorced from (white, middle-class) public opinion in the creation of Great Society programs.[38] By identifying 1964 and 1965 in this way, conservatives could avoid programmatic criticism of President Kennedy and deflect fears that they wished to gut popular early-1960s programs such as Medicare. With this chronology, conservatives could also claim support for the early civil rights movement, rebuffing charges of racism by distinguishing laudatory struggles for equal rights from opportunistic, debilitating whining for affirmative action.

Conservatives focused on social, racial, and economic issues to trace the decline of American life since the triumph of Lyndon Johnson over Barry Goldwater in 1964. Early-1960s economic programs such as Medicare and the expansion of Social Security were attacked by Goldwater in the 1964 campaign, which contributed to his overwhelming defeat. Before the 1994 elections, conservatives limited their major economic attacks to post-1964 Great Society programs, such as the expansion of welfare and public housing, which were seen (inaccurately) as primarily benefiting racial minorities, and to government regulation of industry. Such regulation was configured as liberal bureaucratic hampering of productive industry, which paralleled conservative claims of liberal imposition of immorality onto what otherwise would be a productive body politic and social consensus.

This ideal consensus referred back to the 1950s, as the Goldwater attack on the basic tenets of New Deal and New Frontier programs had been replaced primarily not by other economic issues, but by what Mike Davis has termed "the defence of the sanctity of white suburban family life."[39] Social and racial issues became the focus, with a norm of suburban life as defined by its moment of social ascendancy in the 1950s and kept alive in media representations of the decade. The highly constricted representations of American life purveyed by film studios and television networks before the 1960s became ballast for a nostalgic suppression of the cultural diversity of the 1990s. Newt Gingrich asserted the eternal verities of pre-1964 America by pointing to old films and television series, seeking to invoke historical memory and social stability by placing them within the modern hearth of the white suburban family, the living room television console. He blamed the nation's social ills not only on liberal policies but on the capture of media institutions and attention by liberals since 1964. Thus echoing Nixon's Silent Majority strategy, Gingrich condemned the "free speech" of the Sixties as antithetical to the mores of average Americans, on a par with drug abuse and sexual license.

Social and Cultural Issues

Republicans in the 1980s and 1990s focused increasingly on the social aspects of the conflict, defined as occurring between liberal elites and Middle Americans. Twelve years of alliance between Republican presidents and corporate leaders had not eased economic dislocation or considerably lessened public support for government programs that assisted the middle class, so many conservatives preferred to emphasize the sense of social dislocation and moral chaos felt by many voters. Republican claims to national renewal under Reagan fell aside, as apparently sabotaged by liberals still holding power. Liberals could be defined as elites in the social sphere more easily than in economic areas, beyond their roles as government interventionists in what should be private economic mechanisms. Socially, liberals could be castigated as members of a cultural elite controlling universities, the press, liberal churches, foundations, schools, and show business.[40] Through their control of communications and the institutions of the public sphere, liberals were seen to have hijacked public morals from the middle-class Americans who ruled socially in the 1950s and who had never deviated from conservative values, despite the rise of the counterculture. Gingrich denounced the Clintons as "countercultural McGoverniks," members of the liberal elite who had brought New Left values into the Democratic party.[41] Now they had control of the White House, as well as the federal institutions of national memory.

Specifying 1964 as the moment of social breakdown and government incompetence also assists in linking these developments with the counterculture, 1964 being the year of the British Invasion in rock, with its eventual associations with drug use, hedonism, and rebellious social commentary. Avoiding George Bush's mistake, Clinton-era conservatives distinguished between the now-safe all-American rock of the 1950s from the subversive 1960s rock of hippies and leftists. Republican senator Phil Gramm claimed Elvis as his own musical hero, and William Bennett deflected charges of social reaction by mentioning his own participation in both the 1960s civil rights movement and a Fifties rock band.[42] Bennett bemoans the moral decline sketched in the change in music from the work of 1950s rocker Buddy Holly to current rock and rap bands. With the rise of a younger generation of Republican leaders, conservatives could assert their own connection to 1950s rock culture, working to minimize the distinctiveness of the Clinton-Elvis connection.

Democrats were depicted as combining underclass social pathology and elite ability to produce social meaning. The use of rap music by the advertising industry can be seen as emblematic of the combination—the bombardment of television sports programming, watched heavily by white middle- and working-class men, with advertisements using the aesthetics of black youth contributed to a conservative sense of cultural control held by raucous minorities abetted by Madison Avenue hucksters. In an economy increasingly based on information and services, the discrepancy between those who created physical goods and those who manipulated symbolic codes contributed to blue-collar nostalgia for the 1950s. The decade continued to loom in conservative ideology as the heyday of American industrial might, with its attendant stability and fixity of economic and social relations.

Conservative ideology was responding to the social and cultural gaps between producers of physical goods and those who worked either as, in Robert Reich's term, "symbolic analysts" or not at all. Reich, Clinton's secretary of labor, was a leading proponent of the new information age, and Clinton's cabinet was full of the East and West Coast lawyers, financiers, and professors identified by conservatives as members of the liberal cultural elite. The White House appeared as a locus of intellectualism and cosmopolitan values that had gained ascendancy in the media-saturated 1960s, rather than as a home for heartland Americana. Without Elvis and Cold War militarism as balancing elements, Clinton's residual articulation with Harvard-educated JFK worked to distance him from Middle America and his own southern background.

Some Republicans were less prone to discard all connections to the 1960s than Gingrich and Limbaugh. Following the empowerment line, William Bennett and black entrepreneurial advocate Robert Woodson argued that they were working in the color-blind tradition of the civil rights movement in their attacks on affirmative action and in their advocacy of reliance on private enterprise and individual morality to lift blacks out of poverty.[43] Fundamentalist Christians often portrayed themselves as members of an oppressed minority who were simply fighting for their rights, as African Americans had done. Christian Coalition director Ralph Reed repeatedly compared his movement to that for civil rights in his manifesto *Politically Incorrect* (with a foreword by Bennett).[44] Reed writes that religion has been shoved "to the back of the bus" in American politics, and that fundamentalists are depicted in the media as if they were "the new Amos and Andy."[45] Reed also stresses that the fundamentalist movement had acquiesced to racism in earlier times, and urges that social conservatives reach out to minorities who share their faith-based values. This strategy was followed by some groups combating gay and lesbian rights, who allied themselves with African Americans who opposed the application of civil rights laws to differences in sexual orientation.[46]

Shared ground between the Sixties left and Nineties right was also posited by some veterans of the left, with a different inflection. Todd Gitlin wrote that the right might attack the unbridled individualism of the Sixties, but seemed to have absorbed it in its more libertarian strain. Gitlin also accused the right of the same sort of Manichean, us versus them simplifications and revolutionary rhetoric that symbolized the left in the late 1960s for many. Whereas Sixties movements tried to balance the values of freedom and equality, and leavened their emphasis on nonconformity and self-realization with an appreciation for solidarity, the contemporary right was balancing its obsession with personal freedom only with appeals to social conformity. Gitlin saw capitalism as having abetted the libertarian themes of the Sixties, at the expense of the self-sacrificing solidarity that particularly marked the civil rights movement.[47]

Some Republicans seemed ready to lay siege to the 1960s in more radical ways than previously envisaged. GOP victories in 1994 brought to Washington a new cadre of congressional conservatives, marked by a strong antifederal bias and a belief in market mechanisms. Privatization of government services became more widely discussed, as some Republicans began to take aim at the two sacred cows of domestic spending, Social Security and Medicare, as well as proposing wholesale changes in the federal welfare system. Their initiatives sought to overturn those of the Kennedy administration, which had hitherto been relatively uncriticized, compared with the attacks on LBJ's Great Society programs.[48] Charles Murray, whose *Losing Ground* had provided ammunition against Great Society spending, now called for a rollback not to 1964, but to pre–New Frontier 1960: "If a wand were waved, and we had no Medicare or Medicaid or [Social Security, welfare, or civil rights laws], the thing you have to realize is that in most respects you're looking at the U.S. as it was in 1960. This is not the dark ages. The U.S. in 1960 wasn't some evil place. It *worked*."[49] Murray was wavering between the Republican and Libertarian parties, and many in the new class of conservatives in Washington had strong libertarian leanings. When the federal government actually shut down in the midst of a budget fight between Congress and the White House, negative public reaction indicated that most Americans were not quite ready to dispense with the federal government's activities, and Republicans moderated some of their legislation.

Still, the Republican offensive did have some effect on national policies. The conservatives' most striking victory was in the area of welfare reform, in which Clinton capitulated to a radical restructuring of welfare payments. The new system restricted the number of years recipients could receive federal payments, required efforts to find work, and removed guarantees that families with children in poverty would receive direct payments. The conservative attacks on the Great Society had finally overturned one of the most visible and controversial legacies of social ferment in the 1960s.[50]

While conservatives were able to make inroads in social policy, curtail government regulation of industry, and restructure tax policy to benefit upper-income Americans, their vaunted "Contract with America" remained largely unenforced. Conservatives were stymied by the combination of Clinton's veto power and sizable Democratic minorities, as well as by the defection of some of the more moderate Republicans on an issue-by-issue basis. Although enactment of much of their legislative agenda was frustrated, conservative rhetoric dominated public affairs reporting in the media. Indeed, their success in articulating their agenda, and the style in which they did so, resulted in an ultimate weakening of their popular appeal.

The New Politics of Voice

The Gingrich-led offensive ran into political trouble almost as soon as it began. Despite Republicans' attacks on liberals for controlling the media and dominating intellectual and cultural discourse, the right's leading spokespersons became members of the media elite as well. Many of the most vocal conservatives themselves had emerged from intellectual ranks before their capture of public office. Gingrich, Gramm, and House Majority Leader Richard Armey had all been college professors before going into politics.[51] They were crucially distinguished in their public personas from the liberal cultural elite, however, by their southern and Texan regional identities and by their championing of the business class. The conservatives' family backgrounds, previous professional marginality in academia, and geographic distance from Cambridge, New Haven, and Berkeley allowed them access to populist expression without the appearance of complete inauthenticity. Thus conservative reporter David Frum could state that "nobody could ever mistake Gramm for anything but a self-made man" on the basis of the senator's accent, dress, personal habits, and political philosophy, despite Gramm's having lived his entire life on public subsidy or in government jobs.[52]

Conservatives, however, ultimately faced difficulties spawned by their success in the public arena. It proved difficult to sustain populist resentment against liberal public voices when conservatives enjoyed high profiles resulting from the 1994 elections and their own penchant for talk. Gingrich complained on the day after the election that the mainstream media would not allow his message to be heard—a complaint that landed on the front page of the *New York Times*.[53] Gingrich's popularity ratings declined to catastrophic levels, as much because of public weariness with his rhetoric and incessant media presence as dissatisfaction with his positions on issues.

The public attention paid to the militia movement in the wake of the Oklahoma City bombing showed that even the most extreme conservatives enjoyed considerable access to the public sphere, that liberals were not the only manipulators of cultural codes. Now it was populist conservative men, not New Left college students and militant blacks, who charged the federal government with heinous crimes and vowed to use force if necessary to effect social change.[54] The violence of Gingrich's and Limbaugh's rhetoric now seemed matched by the deeds of the far right. The government shutdown spurred by congressional Republicans also attested to an ideological fanaticism and lack of maturity previously associated with the student left of the Sixties. Media attempts to create parallels between that left and the New

Right of the 1990s reinforced this placement of conservative ideologues at odds with a quieter, less politicized general populace.[55] When Newt Gingrich got compared in a Wichita, Kansas, newspaper to a young Jerry Rubin, conservatives clearly had lost their position as the beacons of populist reaction against the voiced class, and had become the epitome of those whose raucous capture of public attention distanced them from average Americans.[56] By contrast, Clinton's refusal to kowtow to Gingrich in 1995 enabled him to regain a measure of maturity and strength in his public image. The Baby Boomer president now assumed the role of steadfast parent facing down a group of political parvenus known for their rhetorical tantrums.

The 1996 Election and the Lewinsky Scandal

Republicans approaching the 1996 election held a position similar to that of Democrats in 1988—they could take aim at a troubled administration whose promises seemed to have run aground. Like the Democrats in 1988, the Republicans nominated a presidential candidate and ran a campaign incapable of establishing a compelling vision of American experience or accomplishing a change in White House regime. Their failure, however, did not win Bill Clinton a peaceful second term, as his presidency was engulfed in personal scandal that contained its own generational resonances.

Bob Dole challenged Clinton using the standard Republican themes of tax cuts and individual initiative, but Dole had successfully negotiated Senate legislation with Democrats over the years and seemed unwilling to sharpen his rhetoric to the new Republican standards. He presented his own personal history—as a small-town midwestern boy who had gone through the Depression, fought hard to recover from wounds suffered in World War II, and went on to adult success in his chosen field—as a prototypical American success story of his generation. In a media environment that now looked for cultural resonances from every presidential candidate, Dole seemed a creature of the 1940s, a hard-bitten, taciturn vet who put a premium on getting the job done. *New Yorker* reporter Michael Kelly wrote that "It is Elvis against Bogart, the Vietnam War boomers against the Good War generation, the man of many words against the few, the feeler of your pain against the tough guy who doesn't even feel his own."[57] Dole presented himself as the voice of hard-won wisdom in trying to connect his own stubborn plainness to the Republican narrative of national greatness, decline, and renewal (and, now, decline again). In reaching back to his war experiences, Dole was evoking a time before the lives of most Americans, and he lacked Reagan's gift (and speechwriters) for using historical pastiche and media references to assert timeless American truths. Although World War II had loomed large in national memory and historical understanding for generations, Dole faced difficulties in making the 1940s seem relevant to the 1990s, without recourse to the pleasurable myths of Reagan historiography.

At the Republican convention Dole stated, "Let me be the bridge to an America that only the unknowing call myth. Let me be the bridge to a time of tranquility, faith, and confidence in action. And to those who say it was never so, that America has not been better, I say, you're wrong, and I know, because I was there. And I have seen it. And I remember."[58] Dole's invocation of the reality principle in assessing the past could not have the impact of Reagan's mythologizing; after all, given his paralyzing and nearly fatal injuries in 1940s combat, who would really want Bob Dole's experiences of the time, or his memories?

Dole's invocation of the past played into Clinton's use of a generational construct that had lost little of its power in the four years since the Democrat's contest against Bush. If Dole insisted on being a bridge to the past, Clinton would gladly take the role of bridge to the future. That symbolic bridge became the central theme of Clinton's campaign, to explain his policies' value to the middle class facing economic globalization and rapid technological change. In his own convention address, Clinton stated that "the real choice is whether we will build a bridge to the future or a bridge to the past, about whether we believe our best days are still out there or our best days are behind us."[59] Clinton had lost the power afforded him by connection to Elvis and JFK, but the Republican fixation on the past provided him with an opportunity to position himself as a forward-looking Baby Boomer. By comparison to his generational counterpart Gingrich, Clinton appeared mature and finally ready to display leadership; by comparison with Dole, he still seemed fresh and culturally knowing. Doubts about Clinton continued to be held widely across ideological positions and partisan affiliations, but the Republican strategy of nostalgic discourse to justify conservative legislative and social agendas appeared exhausted.

A year after the 1996 election, revelations about Clinton's relationship with White House intern Monica Lewinsky unleashed a torrent of accusations and debate about Clinton's personal and political behavior. Amid the tumult, some Clinton opponents saw his actions as representative of the countercultural Baby Boomers' misguided quest for sexual liberation, their refusal of limits and resentment of middle-class propriety, and their belief that they could break rules with impunity. The fears that Boomers lacked the requisite self-control and maturity for capable national leadership consolidated themselves around the scandal.[60] Writing in William Kristol's *Weekly Standard*, David Frum located the last remaining core belief of Clinton's generation through the president's supporters' response to his travails. Having reconciled themselves to the impossibility of political revolution, the necessity of careerism, and the dangers of drugs, Clinton and his allies remain stubborn believers in the Sexual Revolution and are willing to condone any level of deceit in its pursuit.[61]

The scandal sparked a new round of conservative criticism against the Sixties, supplemented by new perspectives on the right. The American Enterprise Institute, a leading conservative think tank, placed Clinton on the cover of its house magazine in the guise of a late-1960s New Leftist, replete with peace sign, beard, Rolling Stones logo (anachronistically, as it was adopted by the band in the 1970s), and a "Free Huey Newton" button, under the banner "The '60s Return." Inside, Robert Bork states that Bill Clinton represented the "hedonistic" tendencies of the youth counterculture, while Hillary Rodham Clinton represented the "ideological" aspects. Both contributed to family dysfunction, though Bork identifies working women as primarily responsible and pressed for their return to the home.[62]

Other contributors to the issue accused the New Left of treason and procommunism, and identified "'60s ideas" as the causes of increases in crime, teenage pregnancy, educational decline, and damaged lives through drug use. The general tone was set by editor Karl Zinsmeister's recollection that, as a child, he saw the era as "a blur of protests, race riots, assassinations, hostile confrontations, announcements of social decay, military setbacks, drug deaths, violent concerts, takeovers, foreign bullying, impeachment hearings, and ghetto disturbances."[63] The issue, however, also included articles that praised the Sixties left for its emphasis on decentralization and anti-depersonalization, finally making connections between Sixties personal liberation and conservative individualism, although the writers blamed the left for devolving into a politics of victimhood and belief in government social programs. Michael Barone sees the New Left's hopes for nonconformity answered by contemporary capitalism, in which customization of commodities is the answer to social protest and the search for authentic life. For some social conservatives, however, the consumer culture's appeals to liberation are yet another troublesome legacy of the Sixties, not a conservative resolution of its tumult. William Bennett fondly recalls Fifties rock and roll and blames the Beatles and the Sixties for adults' surrender of positions of moral authority and guidance. Bennett now sees corporations mimicking this abdication of responsibility by feeding fantasies of unlimited personal freedom, parallel to Clinton's lack of control and recklessness in personal and political affairs.[64]

Some writers outside the conservative camp saw Clinton's actions not as classically Sixties behavior, but rather in keeping with the pre–Sexual Revolution hypocrisies of Fifties dating ethics and southern boys' attitudes toward the opposite sex.[65] The scandal, indeed, recombined Elvis and JFK in a new, unflattering way for Clinton; he could be seen as an over-sexed southern boy (in a state of perpetual adolescence) or as the inheritor of Kennedy's role as White House satyr. The Clinton who had identified himself with the young Elvis now seemed to be wallowing in the same sort of tawdry dissipation that marked the older Elvis, alternating between stonewalling against public

12. Clinton as a child of the late Sixties. Reprinted with permission of *The American Enterprise, a Magazine of Politics, Business and Culture,* www.TAEMAG.com.

curiosity about his personal peccadilloes and asking for the public's indulgence on the basis of previous good works. The effusive fakery of the late Elvis would not seem a promising touchstone for a president, and the Clinton camp continued to shy away from pop culture imagery.

To the frustration of Republicans, however, most of the public responded to the scandal in ways similar to the reaction to revelations of JFK's sexual

adventures; Clinton's popularity withstood the attacks, and the public ultimately turned against those who dwelled on his personal behavior. Gary
Bauer declared that "thirty years of relativism . . . [have] devalued our moral
currency," and William Bennett echoed the charge.[66] Indeed, some writers in
an issue of *Rolling Stone* designed to rally support for Clinton during the scandal specifically cited the right's attack on the Sixties as a reason to defend
Clinton, to forestall regression to earlier standards of behavior.[67] Public support for Clinton during his impeachment by congressional Republicans led
some social conservatives to conclude that their project had failed, that the
values of the Sixties counterculture had won over the majority of the nation
permanently. Paul Weyrich advised conservatives that they now could do little more than leave politics and retreat into havens of pre-Sixties values to protect themselves from the pervasive moral rot of contemporary America.[68]

Bill Clinton's political momentum had quickly dissipated in the opening
years of his administration. Republicans benefited from the Clinton persona's
loss of coherence, particularly in the 1994 congressional elections. With the
rise of Newt Gingrich, Rush Limbaugh, and other spinners of conservative
nostalgia, the narrative of decline that had been put forward by Republicans
in the 1980s reached new levels of dominance. Yet the Republicans were
unable to use their vision of the American past to consolidate their power, as
seen by their poor electoral performances in 1996 and 1998. Bill Clinton
withstood attempts to remove him from office, while Gingrich lost his hold
on the House of Representatives. Clinton had let his connections to the
Fifties and Sixties generally fall to the wayside; Republicans clung to their
nostalgic discourse even as it resulted in their political isolation.

In less direct fashion, conservative discourse resonated in a society buffeted by sexual scandal, continued family dysfunction, and new shocks such as
a spate of mass killings by grade-school students in small towns and suburbs.
Most Americans may not have thought a return to the strictures of social
behavior prescribed by nostalgic Republicans was realistic, but the conservative vision of what America had lost, and how it had been lost, had achieved
a new level of acceptance in social discourse. The social dissatisfactions and
controversies of the Clinton era, which remained despite a burgeoning national economy, gave new momentum to the idea that the country was paying
for its deviation from a previously clear path.

Old Themes in a New Century

In the 2000 presidential campaign, George W. Bush soft-pedaled nostalgic appeals during his candidacy, perhaps because of their strong associations
with Newt Gingrich and other discredited Republican officials. He did, however, seek to replicate his father's brand of Yalie populism in combination with
calls for strengthening families and social values, positioning his preference for
faith-based social programs against liberal, secular social planners. Populism

was an easier reach for the younger Bush than for his father, as George W. was more easily seen as a true Texan by voters, was clearly anti-intellectual, and had experienced failure and frustration in his earlier days. His turn to faith and family values in his forties deflected perceptions that his personal life in his postcollege years had not conformed to the strictures on behavior that anti-Sixties conservatives sought to institute as the norm in American society.

Bush had been influenced politically by many of the Republican Sixties critics, but he rarely put forward his program in specifically generational terms. Bush was attracted to the work of Myron Magnet and Marvin Olasky, whose books trace the consequences of liberal cultural values and welfare programs on the poor, as well as by David Horowitz's jeremiads against Sixties campus radicals.[69] Bush had entered Yale in 1964, just as Yale was changing its admission procedures to diversify beyond its traditional emphasis on East Coast, upper-class elites who dominated the college fraternity system. As Nicholas Lemann has noted, Bush may have entered Yale expecting to take a position in the central social elite of the school, and from there find easy entrance into the business class. During his years at Yale, however, the social and cultural tenor of the school changed, and his preppy, fraternity environment moved to the periphery of a politicized, intellectualized campus. Bush professed to having enjoyed his time at Yale, but a resentment of intellectual elites (many bound for government service) took root, especially as he foundered in his postcollege careers. Bush could use his resentment politically to castigate federal social policies as creations of arrogant elites, while softening the edge of his attacks by offering a positive alternative of religiosity and charity in the form of compassionate conservatism. Bush's essentially Victorian approach to poverty and social ills appeared to deflect charges of familiar Republican callousness for some voters.[70]

In addition to trying to demonstrate racial diversity at the Republican National Convention, GOP planners tried to shed the image of cultural obsolescence that had grown throughout the party. Finally working with a presidential candidate born after 1930, convention planners used a soundtrack of Motown hits to accompany convention action. They attempted a generational synthesis with the video projection of Kate Smith singing "God Bless America" from an early television production, thereby appealing to both (very) senior citizens who had been Smith fans and Boomers with a nostalgic remembrance of 1950s television. Emphasizing a new effort toward inclusiveness in the party, they even included the Beatles' "Come Together" to promote a more multivalent unity, to the presumed dismay of Elliott Abrams and William Bennett. By 2000, Baby Boomers made up the middle part of the electorate in terms of age, and the party also wanted to attract younger voters. For the first time, it featured contemporary, MTV-friendly rock bands performing from the podium.

Indeed, the 1950s would seem real and historically relevant to an ever-smaller portion of the electorate, and the GOP needed to update its treatment of historical eras to relate to younger voters. Tellingly, the first two songs played during prime-time coverage of the convention were Elton John's "Crocodile Rock" and the Stray Cats' "Rock This Town": songs of the Fifties revivals in the 1970s and 1980s. After failing to convince the American public to flee headlong back to the Fifties, the GOP seemed to indicate it was willing to compromise, with an embrace of the previous generation's nostalgia for the Fifties to replace the real thing. Bush's faith and family values campaign sought to demonstrate more flexibility and contemporaneity than a strictly restorationist project might show, and used the Fifties as a touchstone once removed.

Of course, the recent decade that the Republicans would have liked to use as a touchstone was the one dominated by Ronald Reagan, but they faced difficulties in doing so. The delegitimating scandals of the Reagan second term, the failure to fully resolve the Persian Gulf War, the (first) Bush recession, and the creeping debilitation of Reagan himself made the Reagan Eighties a problematic rhetorical trope. Most of all, the sustained economic boom during the Clinton presidency made explicit nostalgia for the Reagan Eighties largely inaccessible for Republicans as a rhetorical tool. If the nation had continued to suffer from economic recession after the Democrats had recaptured the White House, conservatives could have invoked the Reaganomic growth of the 1980s as a Golden Age and reinforced their claims to innovative economic stewardship. Instead, the Reagan boom paled in comparison to the Clinton boom in both longevity and the diffusion of its benefits to those below the upper-middle class. Republicans chose instead to invoke the social critiques launched by their own movement in the 1980s to respond to senses of social anxiety and dislocation that continued to manifest themselves in the nation, particularly with regard to such incidents as the mass shootings of students, by students, in Littleton, Colorado, and elsewhere. Once Bush took office, the increase in feelings of personal and social insecurity and militarism inspired by the September 11, 2001, attacks led to more calls by conservatives to return to pre-Sixties attitudes both domestically and abroad.

The Past in the Popular Culture of the 1990s

While Republicans intensified their talk about the past, popular culture continued to feature recyclings of previous styles. Film, television, and music seemed immersed in referentiality to previous eras, and now included the 1970s and 1980s as fodder for reappreciation. With the spread of cable television channels, the continuing popularity of video rentals and purchases, and the surge in compact disc sales, much of the recent cultural past of the nation was being newly marketed, on constant display and instantly accessible. When

William Faulkner wrote "The past is never dead. It's not even past," he was expressing the force of the past in structuring social relationships in the tradition-bound culture of the American South. In 1990s America, the past remained ever present in a new way: through the mediation of entertainment companies who profited from the ability of new technologies to re-present older cultural productions. Popular culture keeps voices and images from the past circulating in the society. Whereas Faulkner was writing of a history-soaked society with a central narrative of the War between the States, the cultural presentation of the past today is fragmented and only intermittently historical in any coherent way. Yet the recyclings and revivals within the culture continue to keep the past accessible for use in new and continuing political articulations.

As the cultural productions of more recent decades became defined as objects of nostalgia, the 1950s in particular lost some of their special resonance as the repository of the past. Most of the new revivals centered on work from the 1960s, 1970s, and even 1980s. With American culture steeped in representations of the past, some 1990s productions evinced a new self-consciousness in their treatments of the subject. A self-reflexive crash of past and present became a theme for popular entertainment in the Clinton era.

Shorthand, Synergy, and the Crash of Decades

Advertising continued to make use of shorthand definitions of historical eras in its effort to communicate meaning quickly and pithily. The Sixties was figured as a sign of authenticity and freedom, of which the 1990s seemed sorely in need. When Volkswagen reintroduced a modified Beetle, its ads proclaimed that those who sold their souls in the 1980s (presumably for Reagan-era riches) could retrieve them with the purchase of the new car, with its close associations to the youth culture of the 1960s. Another car company showed a couple of Sixties youth carousing down the highway in their van, then morphing into responsible 1990s adults in their new van with kids in tow, yet still able to enjoy the freedom and joy of the road.

With late and post-Boomers occupying key consumer demographics in the 1990s, nostalgic references to the 1970s and even the 1980s began to enjoy widespread distribution. "Classic rock" stations began playing music of the 1980s that they had ignored at first release in favor of standards from the 1960s and 1970s. Nick at Nite and TV Land, aiming to replicate viewing choices available to its viewers when they were children and teenagers, began to add late 1970s programs like *Charlie's Angels* to their schedules. Hollywood films such as *Jackie Brown* (1997), *The Ice Storm* (1997), *54* (1998), and *The Last Days of Disco* (1998) referenced or re-created the 1970s, often defining the decade as one of middle-class drift and hedonism. Only the cautionary *Boogie Nights* (1997) achieved significant popularity, however; with even celebratory takes

13. Volkswagen ad.

on the 1970s focusing on their superficiality and meaninglessness, cultural producers found it difficult to captivate audiences with new versions of Seventies life.[71] While escapism from the problems of the Sixties seemed to be a hallmark of the Seventies, boundaries between the two eras were often fluid or confused in press treatments of the Seventies revival, with Vietnam, Watergate, drug use, classic rock, and narcissistic attempts at self-realization constituting shared ground between them. One of the other hallmarks of the Seventies seemed to be its hazy eclecticism, presenting difficulties to those who tried to assign it a stable identity.[72]

    With the rapid consolidation of entertainment corporations in the 1990s, the opportunities for synergistic exploitation of old productions increased; such synergy fostered greater levels of public visibility for revivals and re-releases. For instance, Paramount re-released the film version of *Grease* in 1997; the re-release was accompanied by a month-long, intensive promotional campaign for the film on MTV and VH1, which had come to be owned by Paramount parent Viacom. *Grease* had been a popular film when released in 1979; in 1997 it was given the dimensions of an all-time classic, a major cultural event both then and now, by the arbiters of commercial youth culture at the music television networks. Such promotional campaigns for re-releases emerged with increasing frequency and asserted the importance of their products on the basis of their putative significance in the lives of fans at the time of their original release. Indeed, the return of *Grease* was as much a phenomenon of Seventies nostalgia as it was about the Fifties, its new success based on its conditions of original reception in the 1970s as much as on its Fifties content. In addition to the re-release of the film, new mixes of its songs scored well on the charts, a revival of the original play ran for years on Broadway, and productions such as *Grease on Ice* spun off from the original work.[73]

The music industry was particularly affected by re-releases. With the technological move to compact discs, music companies brought out thousands of old recordings from their vaults. CD reissues eventually flooded the market, leading to a downturn in the industry after several years of post-Nirvana financial success. In 1996 the long-awaited release of revamped Beatles records went to the top of the charts; the band became the fourth-biggest act in contemporary popular music album sales.[74] The Beatles' success was matched by George Lucas, whose re-release of the *Star Wars* trilogy was the biggest-selling film event of 1997.[75]

History, Entertainment, and the Uses of the Past

The most prominent new release after the election of Bill Clinton to make use of nostalgia was *Forrest Gump*, the hugely popular tour of American postwar experience.[76] The film revisited many of the best-known political figures and cultural phenomena of the 1950s, 1960s, and 1970s through the eyes of a mentally impaired paragon of goodness. By inserting him into newsreel footage of actual events, the film offers a postmodern, playful, but earnest mixing of fact and fiction. The film tries to avoid political controversy—as when the title character's final judgment about Vietnam, on the basis of his service there, is intentionally concealed from the audience. In a film that offers a range of political identifications, however, the New Left of the 1960s is given an exceedingly negative portrayal. The 1950s of the film are not completely benign—sexual harassment seems rampant, for instance, and segregation is alluded to—but the greatest calumny is reserved for those who tried to radically overthrow the old order. Leftist radicalism and immersion in the counterculture seemed to remain outside the limits of proper behavior for many people in post-Reagan America.[77]

After initially being lukewarm about the film, conservative reviewers rallied to it, asserting that it confirmed their views of the American past—the rightness of simple virtues, the destructiveness of the counterculture, the trauma of the Sixties that could be healed by renewed patriotism, family values, and private enterprise. Taking up the cause of the film, conservatives associated it with their family values campaign and the emphasis on old-fashioned virtue promulgated by William Bennett.[78]

In 1998 *Gump* star Tom Hanks revisited another historical era in *Saving Private Ryan*, part of a wave of reappreciation of the American experience in World War II.[79] After periodic celebrations of wartime events, particularly the fortieth and fiftieth anniversaries of D-Day, World War II nostalgia reached a high point in 1998 with the release of Steven Spielberg's film and the publication of NBC news anchor Tom Brokaw's *The Greatest Generation*.[80] Brokaw asserts the previous generation's greatness in facing the sacrifices of the Depression and World War II, contributing to economic growth in the post-war era, fighting the Cold War, and, in some cases, supporting the causes of racial justice and gender equality. His tribute to the unselfishness, common sense, and family values of his parents' generation contains an implicit rebuke to contemporary society and challenges the Baby Boomers' sense of their own generational distinctiveness as the engine of broad social progress. Brokaw and Spielberg position themselves as payers of filial debts, sons whose own middle-aged status has led them to reconsider their parents' lives with gratitude.

The fealty continued with the Hanks and Speilberg production *Band of Brothers*, an HBO miniseries depicting the struggles of a company of para-troopers in the European theater of operations.[81] As with *Saving Private Ryan*, the series was inspired by the work of historian Stephen Ambrose, whose work imbued GIs with the appealing combination of unassuming, unpreten-tious bravado and a grand historical mission. The interest in World War II had several sources—Americans' personal interest in the exploits of a generation now slipping away, a continuing fascination with the Holocaust, and as a way to ameliorate public uncertainty regarding America's role in a world of global economics and multiple sites of small-scale conflicts.[82] World War II offered a sense of American autonomy, clear-cut allies and enemies, and crucial yet finite goals.

Spike Lee's biopic of Malcolm X took a more critical look at the 1940s, connecting the racism of pre–civil rights America to the black nationalist movement of the 1960s. Television revisited the civil rights movement once again with *Any Day Now*, which premiered to critical praise on Lifetime in 1998. The series follows the friendship of two southern women, one black and one white, alternating between childhood scenes in the 1960s and scenes of adulthood in the present day. Series creator Nancy Miller conceived the show as a cross between *The Wonder Years* and *Mississippi Burning*, placing a focus on family relations within a context of social change and the working out of race relations. *Any Day Now* asserted the relevance of the history of American race relations to the contemporary daily life of both races. The series, J. Lynn Fuller states, suggested that "contemporary liberalism has always existed—indoors, among women and girls," in keeping with a general turn toward women-centered melodrama in civil rights productions in the 1990s.[83]

Other cable networks also offered stories on recent American history, usually focused on famous political figures. The 1980s had seen a wave of broadcast biopics on the Kennedys and LBJ. In the late 1990s historical biopics provided niche cablecasters the chance to build reputations for quality programming that could attract the most desired audience demographics. By focusing on the 1950s and 1960s, programmers could appeal to Baby Boomers who had reached their peak in purchasing power. By highlighting the civil rights movement in a number of individual productions, cablecasters could also bring in African-American audiences, who had finally become prized commodities after years of being underserved by the cable industry, without networks' committing themselves to continuing series at greater cost. The opportunity to do short-term work with social and political themes could also attract industry talent who might otherwise pass up work on cable channels. The result was the reexamination of political actors, movements, and crises from generally progressive perspectives across the cable schedule.

HBO's *Boycott* looked at the Montgomery bus boycott that gave Martin Luther King, Jr., his first exposure as a national leader. The film highlighted simple but brave steps taken by the protest movement to counter white intransigence. Exhibiting a number of stylistic flourishes that moved it away from the usual realist mode of television treatment of history, *Boycott* ended with a time-traveling motif to point to the continued relevance of the movement, as King walked from a 1950s Montgomery bus stop to a contemporary urban street to take his message to hip-hop youth.[84]

Other telefilms looked at key politicians of the 1960s. In *George Wallace*, noted film director John Frankenheimer depicted George Wallace's racial demogoguery in the 1960s and consequent search for redemption, without heroicizing his main character. Frankenheimer, who was an associate of Robert Kennedy's in the 1960s, also looked at Lyndon Johnson's slide into the Vietnam War in *Path to War*, emphasizing the ignorance and stubbornness of American decision makers in escalating the conflict and the damage the war did to Johnson's progressive domestic agenda. Robert Kennedy was the subject of the hagiographic *RFK*, which served as a distillation of liberal hopes and retrospective mourning for the symbol of the road not taken (or taken away) in 1968. Kennedy speechwriter Richard Goodwin was a consultant to the production, and *RFK* ends with a recitation of one of Kennedy's most famous speeches, which questioned the value of economic growth when unaccompanied by spiritual and humanistic progress. The speech offers a striking contrast to contemporary political rhetoric in its antimaterialistic tone and its separation of spiritual values from financial ones after two decades of conservative juxtaposition of these same elements.[85]

Larger production companies also revisited historical themes after a lull in the 1990s. Working from material by Robert Kennedy and New Frontier confidant Kenneth O'Donnell, the intelligence, toughness, and humanity of the Kennedys during the Cuban missile crisis were unsurprisingly featured in the film *Thirteen Days*. The Kennedys are counterposed in the film to a militaristic and short-sighted Washington establishment.[86] In 2002 CBS offered its own take on the Montgomery bus boycott in *The Rosa Parks Story*, directed

by Julie Dash, best known for the independent film *Daughters of the Dust.*[87] The
Parks film counters the contemporary tendency to center the struggle for civil
rights in the South completely around the figure of Martin Luther King, Jr.,
although it continues media focus on political celebrities, as Parks herself has
attained iconic status as a living monument to the movement. The early civil
rights movement and the New Frontier continue to be honored as parts of a
consensus national memory, even if those who work to culturally reenact
them have more pointed political agendas.

NBC tried for a broader sweep of history in the miniseries *The '60s*,
which suffered from its attempt to squeeze into its story seemingly every
noteworthy political, social, and cultural turn during the decade. The miniseries functioned less as drama than as a checklist of what had been passed
down as historically significant about the Sixties—rock and roll, civil rights,
Vietnam, the Sexual Revolution, and so on.[88] NBC's *American Dreams*, which
made the same inclusive effort, benefited from the more relaxed pace that a
weekly, continuing series can enjoy in presenting its narrative.[89] While referencing the same litany of significant developments as *The '60s*, *American
Dreams* offers a more nuanced look at the dynamics of social stress and change
and a greater depth in the portrayal of character and locale. Placing its characters in the fall of 1963 and hewing carefully to a chronology from thereon, the
series once more defines the Sixties as starting with John Kennedy's death and
the surge of youth culture predicated on rock and roll, except in a black community already caught up in the fight against white supremacy. The multigen-
erational narrative could appeal to Baby Boomers able to identify both with
the younger characters representing their own historical experiences and with
the parental characters who share the same adult responsibilities as current
viewers.

Produced by Dick Clark's production company, the series features *American Bandstand* as an important element, creating the sense of cultural specificity and vibrant youth culture that worked to *Happy Days'* benefit almost
thirty years earlier. *American Dreams*, however, evinces much greater self-
awareness as a chronicle of a historical epoch, in keeping with the rise of
explicit social conversation on the meanings of the Fifties and Sixties in recent
decades. If *American Dreams* stays on the air long enough, it may have to ven-
ture out of the first half of the 1960s, about which the series can purport to
represent a national, or at least generational consensus, and move into the late
1960s, for which no consensus has yet appeared.

Not all productions that contested conservative dichotomies did so with
serious looks at famous figures or heartfelt social dramas. The *Brady Bunch*
movies, for example, revived the *echt* suburban family of the late 1960s and
early 1970s, and placed them in contemporary Los Angeles.[90] The Brady family is clueless amid the troubling and threatening complexities of the 1990s, as

14. *The '60s* cataloged the familiar markings of a decade.

if the late 1960s from which they came were a time of innocence and simplicity. The Bradys seemed similarly clueless at the time of their original television series; the films enact a double movement of comparing the previous
era to the present, and comparing an old television representation of American suburbia to its darker reality, which can no longer remain hidden. The
films pay respect to the increased sophistication of their audiences—both
because the original youthful fans of the show are now adults, and because

audiences must be more sophisticated in the no-holds-barred media environment of the 1990s than in the apparently innocent 1960s and 1970s.

Another film takes the self-conscious juxtaposition of past and present into the realm of explicit social commentary. *Pleasantville* transports 1990s teenagers to a Fifties television world and inserts them into a *Father Knows Best*–type family comedy.[91] They soon rebel against the narrowness of experience that exists in the black-and-white milieu, and instigate an upheaval of its norms. A thoroughly domesticated housewife and mother discovers she is bored, emotionally stifled, and sexually repressed; she begins an affair with a soda shop owner who decides to follow his dream of becoming a painter. Others in the town also begin to rebel against the homogeneity of life in the Fifties sitcom world. The new social deviants are marked by taking on color, as the film becomes a metaphor for the challenge of the civil rights movement to Fifties America. Conversely, the civil rights movement becomes a metaphor for the entire range of changes the nation went through in moving away from a vision of itself as the staid and constricting Pleasantville.

The film is less a critique of the 1950s than an attack on the "Fifties," the contemporary notion that life had really been as simple and comforting as a television sitcom. "Everyone always evokes [the 1950s] nostalgically as the perfect era," director Gary Ross stated in an interview. "There was no strife; it was a kinder, gentler time. And all these bromides always evoked how America used to be so happy and well-adjusted and mighty and potent, and all those things. I thought it was a lie." Ross, who had previously served as a writer for both Dukakis and Clinton, continued, "What if I took this perfectly balanced world that has this kind of stasis to it, this world of our memory that never existed, and injected real life into it? . . . The whole thing started blowing up."[92] *Pleasantville* forces its characters to face the complexities and uncertainties of a world beyond the Fifties. The film disrupts the television dream world by introducing the elements of social change missing from the representations of Fifties America that have been posited as the model for a return to national greatness.

As the conservative discourse of nostalgia exhausts itself, the film challenges its audience to look not to the past, but at its representations. The film suggests that by understanding the system of inclusion and exclusion that marks conservative definitions of the past, its audience can emerge out of the infantilizing dreamworld of the Fifties and enter a less secure, more diverse, and more truthful world of adult choices. The nostalgic discourse in popular culture in the 1970s had evinced an understanding that the narrow, childhood-based conceptions of the 1950s it celebrated were inevitably to give way to the difficult freedoms and challenges of the 1960s. After twenty years of conservative nostalgia, *Pleasantville* argues for another movement beyond the Fifties, and into the present.

15. Two of today's teens (Tobey Maguire and Reese Witherspoon) cannot believe their eyes when transported into Fifties adolescence in *Pleasantville*. New Line.

CONCLUSION

Articulations and symbolic connections must be continually reinscribed to remain powerful. The decline of Clinton's linkage to Elvis and JFK in his administration's media practices created opportunities for administration opponents to reassert their own meanings of Clinton, Democrats, and the recent American past. Newt Gingrich, Rush Limbaugh, and other conservatives presented an American past based on media representations of white middle-class suburban norms, invoked as universalized public memory and used as a foundation for reactionary social and economic policies. In asserting the predominance of conservative truths in the development of the nation, Republicans presented themselves as spokespersons for a silenced American mainstream at odds with liberal cultural elites.

The conservative political offensive dominated public affairs discourse during Clinton's first term in office, as Republicans continued their campaign for patriarchal gender relations, cutbacks in government social spending, and cultural conservatism. The Republican right managed some significant victories, such as a major change in welfare policies. It was unable, however, to wrest the White House away from Bill Clinton by election or impeachment. The conservatives remained wedded to their narrative of national greatness, decline, and renewal, although the political efficacy of their strategy seemed to wane. In a nation that was experiencing a constant state of cultural revival and recycling, the specifically political use of nostalgia may have finally run its course. The definitions of family values, America's place in the world, and the role of the government in the economy, however, remain heavily contested areas of public debate, often inflected with the nostalgia discourses of the preceding three decades. Various groups continue to use their senses of the American past to claim the right to speak to the nation and articulate their visions of the future.

Conclusion

OVER THE LAST THIRTY YEARS the United States has experienced an ongoing discussion of its past, particularly of the meanings of the 1950s and 1960s. Both politically and culturally, various social groups have constructed narratives of national greatness, decline, and renewal. Through several presidential administrations, electoral cycles, and cultural revivals, the struggle to define the national experience has gone on. Political momentum has been gained by those who have been able to use the past to explain the present, and to legitimate their vision of the future.

The most obdurate attempt to justify policy initiatives by recourse to the past has been made by political conservatives. Their account of greatness and decline in the post–World War II era went basically unanswered by Washington Democrats and other political opponents during the Reagan and first Bush administrations. Instead, popular culture became the primary location for contesting the conservative critique of the Sixties. Film, television, and music provided critical responses to Reaganite interpretations of the past, and offered multivalent approaches to the political movements and cultural transformations that have come to represent the Sixties in public memory. By circulating interpretations of the 1960s that countered conservative discourse, popular culture kept positive senses of the era alive. In the 1992 presidential election, Bill Clinton finally provided a political response to conservative historiography, trading on the concepts of the past that popular culture had kept accessible. As president, however, Clinton failed to maintain a productive connection to popular culture and history and lapsed into symbolic incoherence.

The 1980s productions that centered on Vietnam, the civil rights struggle, and the contrasts between the Sixties and the Eighties functioned, often deliberately, as interventions in the social debate on directions in American history. More recent cultural trends have often blurred the boundaries between eras, as the popular culture industries mine older productions for their low-cost provision of familiar material. As older styles recirculate and political discourse dwells on the past, the use of the Fifties and Sixties as cultural shorthand to connote a range of social practices and political attitudes continues to grow.

204

Such easy and casual referencing buttresses the argument that the dichotomies represented by the Fifties and the Sixties are key to understanding the present moment.

Popular culture, social thought, and politics today share both a nostalgic tint and a means of transmission through mass media in many forms. The media that provide an onslaught of information about the world provoke a sense of dislocation and myriad challenges to stable social identities. Yet the same media provide a sense of stability in the act of cultural consumption itself. When the culture is immersed in representations of the past, it holds out the promise that such consumption can reconstitute a sense of historical coherence from the same realm that seems to disrupt it.

Politics intersects with media and culture in powerful ways, yet presents itself as having its own authority. Conservative political nostalgia asserts itself in a grounding of history, in a sense of the real, and in the recall of a less media-saturated world, when society and culture seem, in retrospect, to have been more stable. Conservative nostalgia promises the reconstitution of historical coherence through its grand narrative of American greatness, decline, and renewal, and its identification of the Sixties as the source of national problems. The instability of an ever-shifting cultural realm can be ameliorated by the solidity of history. Conservative discourse, however, reflects its own use of public memories that cannot be separated from media representations. Indeed, for much of a politically cynical public, popular culture may be considered a more trustworthy source of senses of the past—which makes appropriation of cultural themes that much more valuable for actors in the political realm.

Despite setbacks in the 1990s, conservatives continue to use a nostalgic narrative of recent American history as a foundation for their policies, and to blame the Sixties for most of the ills of the nation. The ubiquity of family values themes, and their connection to notions of the Fifties and the Sixties, demonstrate the success conservatives have enjoyed in determining the discursive terrain. The quest for a monopolization of national memory by conservative groups, however, has met with resistance both culturally and politically. As the decades of the 1950s and 1960s recede further into the past, their particularly powerful symbolic efficacy is likely to recede as well. In conservatives' continuing nostalgia for a time that most Americans do not personally remember, Republicans risk the charge of cultural and social obsolescence that Clinton successfully used against Bush in 1992. Conservatives continue to be in thrall to Ronald Reagan's successful use of nostalgia and suffer from their own nostalgia for the Reagan Eighties, when conservatism seemed on the cusp of establishing long-lasting political dominance. Just as the recurrent success of *Grease* can be said to be spurred by nostalgia for the Fifties nostalgia of the 1970s (as put forward by corporate marketing strategies), so Republican strategies signify a yearning to return to the days of Reaganism's look to the past. As popular culture increases the frequency of its recyclings, leading to a state of constant cultural revival, so the main thrust of contemporary conservatism has started to circle around itself, in a never-ending search for the better days behind it—for a time when conservative nostalgia worked in American politics.

NOTES

INTRODUCTION

1. Henceforth I will use the terms "1950s," "1960s," and so on to denote the actual years of these decades, while I use "the Fifties," "the Sixties," and so on to denote the agglomerations of cultural elements, political meanings, and other associations that have come to be attached to the temporal periods. It is a central contention of this work that various versions of these agglomerations compete with one another for discursive dominance, and are subject to change over time.

2. Greil Marcus, *Double Trouble: Bill Clinton and Elvis Presley in a Land of No Alternatives* (New York: Henry Holt and Company, 2000), 209. Marcus is no relation to this author.

3. Lawrence Grossberg, *Dancing in Spite of Myself: Essays on Popular Culture* (Durham, N.C.: Duke University Press, 1997), 234.

4. My understanding of these workings of American politics and culture has been informed by the theory of hegemony inspired by the work of Antonio Gramsci and elucidated by Ernesto Laclau and Chantal Mouffe, Stuart Hall, and other theorists. For the key points of the theory and the importance of definitional linkages, or artic- ulation, see Ernesto Laclau, *Politics and Ideology in Marxist Theory* (London: Verso, 1977); Ernesto Laclau and Chantal Mouffe, *Hegemony and Socialist Strategy* (London: Verso, 1985); Lawrence Grossberg, "On Postmodernism and Articulation: An Inter- view with Stuart Hall," in *Stuart Hall: Critical Dialogues in Cultural Studies*, ed. David Morley and Kuan-Hsing Chen (London: Routledge, 1996), 131–150; Jennifer Daryl Slack, "The Theory and Method of Articulation in Cultural Studies," in Morley and Chen, *Stuart Hall*, 112–130. For the importance of the heterogeneity of sources in diffusing powerful social meanings, see the discourse theory conceptualized in Michel Foucault, *The Archaeology of Knowledge*, trans. A. M. Sheridan Smith (New York: Pantheon, 1972). Although the present work emerges out of the insights of hegemony and discourse theory, I have tried to use the terminology specific to these theories sparingly, in order to make the work accessible to a wider readership.

5. My use of terms in the following schema draws on the work of a number of writ- ers on memory; there is no widespread agreement on definitional terms in the field of memory studies. The work of French sociologist Maurice Halbwachs is widely considered to provide the foundation for recent work in the field; see his *The Col- lective Memory* (New York: Harper Colophon, 1980).

6. Fredric Jameson, *Postmodernism: Or, the Cultural Logic of Late Capitalism* (Durham, N.C.: Duke University Press, 1991); David Harvey, *The Condition of Postmodernity* (Cambridge, Mass.: Blackwell, 1990).

7. Lynn Spigel and Henry Jenkins, "Same Bat Channel, Different Bat Times: Mass Culture and Popular Memory," in *The Many Lives of Batman: Critical Approaches to a Superhero and His Media*, ed. Roberta Pearson and William Uricchio (New York: Routledge, 1991), 117–148.

8. See Anne Norton, "The President as Sign," in Norton, *Republic of Signs: Liberal Theory and American Popular Culture* (Chicago: University of Chicago Press, 1993), 87–121.

9. Examples of writers in the United States who have attempted such projects regarding contemporary America include Lauren Berlant, *The Queen of America Goes to Washington City: Essays on Sex and Citizenship* (Durham, N.C.: Duke University Press, 1997), and John Fiske, in *Power Plays Power Works* (New York: Verso, 1993), and *Media Matters: Everyday Culture and Political Change* (Minneapolis: University of Minnesota Press, 1994).

CHAPTER 1   THE FIFTIES IN THE 1970S

1. For parallel developments in Britain, see Robert Hewison, *The Heritage Industry: Britain in a Climate of Decline* (London: Methuen, 1987), and Patrick Wright, "Heritage and Danger: The English Past in the Era of the Welfare State," in *Memory: History, Culture, and the Mind*, ed. Thomas Butler (Oxford: Basil Blackwell, 1989), 150–182.

2. Gerald Clarke, "The Meaning of Nostalgia," *Time*, 3 May 1971, 77.

3. See, for example, Jon Landau, "Little Richard," *Rolling Stone*, 9 November 1968, 18; Greil Marcus, "Roll Over, Chuck Berry," *Rolling Stone*, 14 June 1969, 15–17; and Peter Guralnick, "From Elvis in Memphis," *Rolling Stone*, 23 August 1969, 34–35. One article that did define the Fifties by way of a set of cultural markers was Michael Lydon, "Carl Perkins," *Rolling Stone*, 7 December 1968, 26. Lydon was among the most political of *Rolling Stone*'s writers at the time, yet even he asserts the timelessness of Perkins's music, thereby loosening its connection to its orginal milieu.

4. See, for example, David Dalton, "Elvis," *Rolling Stone*, 21 February 1970, 26–29.

5. Advertisement in *Rolling Stone*, 17 May 1969, 13.

6. Andrew H. Malcolm, "'Oldies' Are the New Sound as Radio Turns Nostalgic," *New York Times*, 17 July 1972, sec. 1; "Oldies Radio: A Natural for the 70's," *Broadcasting*, 12 March 1973, 63–65.

7. Jan Hodenfield, "Sha Na Na Na Yip Yip Mum Mum Get a Job," *Rolling Stone*, 18 October 1969, 30.

8. Michael Lydon, "Hail Hail Rock and Roll, Deliver Me from the Days of Old," *Ramparts*, December 1969, 47–56.

9. Richard Goldstein, "'A White Boy with Black Hips,'" *New York Times*, 10 August 1969, sec. D.

10. Richard Goldstein, "Sha Na Na, 'the Unreal Fifties,'" *Vogue*, November 1969, 126.

11. Fred Davis, *Yearning for Yesterday: A Sociology of Nostalgia* (New York: Free Press, 1979).

12. Ibid., 49, 104.

13. *ABC News*, 29 August 1969, Gregory Jackson, reporter.

14. Mike Jahn, "Rock Revival Show of '50's Fills Garden with 20,000 Fans," *New York Times*, 1 November 1970.

15. Mike Jahn, "'Rock Revival' Audience Cheers Bill Haley and 15-Year-Old Hit," *New York Times*, 20 October 1969.

16. Ellen Cohn, "Nostalgia Comes Early These Days," *TV Guide*, 18 September 1971, 20–23; Grace Lichtenstein, "Hey Kids, It's Howdy Doody Time Again," *New York Times*, 11 April 1971.

17. Commentator Jeff Greenfield, however, preferred to credit *Howdy Doody* with presaging the generational rebellion of the Sixties through its hostility to adult authority figures; Greenfield suggested that the show's anarchistic clown Clarabelle was the "first Yippie." Jeff Greenfield, "A Member of the First TV Generation Looks Back," *New York Times Magazine*, 4 July 1971, 8–11.

18. An account of immersion into Fifties styles is found in Pagan Kennedy, *Platforms: A*

Microwaved Cultural Chronicle of the 1970s (New York: St. Martin's Press, 1994), 5–9, which otherwise holds a painfully accurate correspondence to my own experience of the time.

19. For a view of Presley's impact on American culture and his fans, see Kevin Quain, ed., *The Elvis Reader* (New York: St. Martin's Press, 1992); for work that also emphasizes his continuing influence, see Greil Marcus, *Dead Elvis: A Chronicle of a Cultural Obsession* (New York: Doubleday, 1991), and Gilbert B. Rodman, *Elvis after Elvis: The Posthumous Career of a Living Legend* (New York: Routledge, 1996).

20. Sandra Ernst Moriarty and Anthony F. McGann, "Nostalgia and Consumer Sentiment," *Journalism Quarterly* 60, no. 1 (Spring 1983): 80–86.

21. *ABC News*, 27 August 1971, Dick Shoemaker, reporter.

22. *CBS Evening News*, 16 July 1974, Eric Sevareid, commentator.

23. Johnathan Rodgers, "Back to the '50's," *Newsweek*, 16 October 1972, 78–82; "The Nifty Fifties," *Life*, 16 June 1972, 38–46; Kathleen Fury, "Always Dandy, Always Fine, We're the Class of '59," *Redbook*, December 1972, 60; and Alix Kates Shulman, "The War in the Back Seat," *The Atlantic*, July 1972, 50–55. Shulman's article recounts her experiences as a teenager in the 1940s, but explicitly conflates them with the Fifties.

24. Richard Terdiman, *Present Past: Modernity and the Memory Crisis* (Ithaca, N.Y.: Cornell University Press, 1993), 22.

25. For other press reports in this vein, see also Andrew H. Malcolm, "Students Revive Good Old 1950's," *New York Times*, 17 May 1971; Paul P. Somers, Jr., "Ungrease: Confessions of a Goodie," *Harper's*, July 1974, 75–81; and Stefan Kanfer, "Back to the Unfabulous '50s," *Time*, 5 August 1974, 56–57.

26. Michael Schudson, *Watergate in American Memory* (New York: Basic Books, 1992), 127–141. Schudson studies media treatment of political celebrities, such as government figures involved in Watergate; treatment of celebrities from entertainment fields is even more likely to be absent notions of historical context.

27. For more on Monroe's image after her death, see S. Paige Baty, *American Monroe: The Making of a Body Politic* (Berkeley: University of California Press, 1995).

28. Davis, *Yearning for Yesterday*, 38, 112.

29. See, for example, Greenfield, "First TV Generation."

30. Rodgers, "Back to the '50's," 78.

31. John Nerone, "Professional History and Social Memory," *Communication* 11, no. 2 (1989): 89–104.

32. Colin L. Westerbeck, Jr., "The Screen: The American Dream," *Commonweal*, 5 October 1973, 12–13.

33. Rodgers, "Back to the '50's," 81.

34. *The Lords of Flatbush*, dir. Stephen F. Verona and Martin Davidson, Columbia, 1974.

35. Fury, "Class of '59," 114 (emphasis in original).

36. Maureen Orth, "All Shook Up," *Newsweek*, 29 August 1977, 46.

37. Barbara Ehrenreich, Elizabeth Hess, and Gloria Jacobs, "Beatlemania: Girls Just Want to Have Fun," in *The Adoring Audience: Fan Culture and Popular Media*, ed. Lisa Lewis (New York: Routledge, 1992), 84–106.

38. See the following articles from *Ebony*: "Civil Rights and the Warren Court," February 1970, 27–29; "There've Been Some Changes Made," August 1972, 168; and "Bus Boycott Anniversary," February 1976, 33–42.

39. See, from *Ebony*, James Meredith, "Black Leaders and the Wish to Die," May 1973, 154–155; Jesse Jackson, "Completing the Agenda of Dr. King," June 1974, 114–120; and "In Memory of 'Mamma King,'" September 1974, 145–146.

40. From *Ebony*, "Lyndon B. Johnson: He Still Tells It Like It Is," February 1973, 110–115; "Lyndon Baines Johnson 1908–1973," March 1973, 144–145; Charles L. Sanders, "LBJ and Civil Rights," March 1974, 154.

41. *American Graffiti*, dir. George Lucas, Universal, 1973.

42. Margaret Ronan, "Films," *Senior Scholastic*, 4 October 1973, 24.

43. Stephen Farber, "'Graffiti' Ranks With 'Bonnie and Clyde,'" *New York Times*, 5 August 1973, sec. II.

44. John Simon, "Films," *Esquire*, October 1973, 44.

45. Pauline Kael, "The Current Cinema: Un-People," *New Yorker*, 29 October 1973, 156.

46. In 1975, *Cooley High* presented an African-American version of teenage life in the past, depicting the adventures of four black teenagers in Chicago. The film is set in 1964, however, marking the 1960s as the site for nostalgic appreciation by black audiences. The civil rights movement is never addressed in the film and the bittersweet story is darker than that of *American Graffiti*; the main source of nostalgia in *Cooley High* is the omnipresence of classic mid-1960s Motown hits on its soundtrack. *Cooley High*, dir. Michael Schultz, American International, 1975.

   More American Graffiti revisited most of the main characters of the original film, and placed them in the midst of the turmoil of Vietnam and Berkeley in the late 1960s. The effort to move them figuratively from the Fifties to the most emblematic locations of the Sixties met with little commercial success, and the film is noteworthy mainly for its borrowing from older film and television styles—most strikingly and awkwardly, in shooting the Vietnam footage in pseudo-news style, akin to what audiences saw of the war on their television sets throughout the 1960s. *More American Graffiti*, dir. Bill L. Norton, Universal, 1979.

47. *M*A*S*H*, CBS, 1972–1983.

48. *Happy Days*, ABC, 1974–1984.

49. Cyclops, "It Wasn't All Ponytails," *New York Times*, 10 February 1974, sec. II.

50. Lynn Spigel, "From the Dark Ages to the Golden Age: Women's Memories and Television Reruns," *Screen* 36, no. 1 (Spring 1995): 16–33.

51. Jackie Stacey, "Hollywood Memories," *Screen* 35, no. 4 (Winter 1994): 317–335.

52. Derek Kompare, "Rerun Nation: American Television and the Regime of Repetition" (Ph.D. dissertation, University of Wisconsin–Madison, 1999).

53. Lynn Spigel and Henry Jenkins, "Same Bat Channel, Different Bat Times: Mass Culture and Popular Memory," in *The Many Lives of Batman: Critical Approaches to a Superhero and His Media*, ed. Roberta Pearson and William Uricchio (New York: Routledge, 1991), 117–148.

54. Terdiman, *Present Past*, 5.

55. *City of Angels*, NBC, 1976.

56. John J. O'Connor, "'Happy Days' and 'Chopper One' Prove Familiar Fare as A.B.C. Entries," *New York Times*, 17 January 1974.

57. Ibid.

58. Cleveland Amory, "Happy Days," *TV Guide*, 30 March 1974, 28.

59. Leslie Raddatz, "Dear Mickey Rooney, Wherever You Are," *TV Guide*, 15 June 1974, 26.

60. Janet Staiger, "What Good Old Days? The Meanings of 'Nostalgia' in the Reception of 'Happy Days' and 'Laverne and Shirley'" (paper presented at the Consoleing Passions annual conference, Madison, Wisconsin, 26 April 1996).

61. Cyclops, "Ponytails."

62. *Laverne and Shirley*, ABC, 1976–1983.

63. Burt Prelutsky, "It May Be Called 'Laverne & Shirley'. . . ," *TV Guide*, 22 May 1976, 24.

64. Advertisement in *New York Times*, 27 January 1976.

65. Aimee Lee Ball, "People on the Cover: Laverne and Shirley," *Redbook*, October 1976, 4, 11–12; Edwin Miller, "A Girl You Can't Resist," *Seventeen*, December 1976, 111, 130.

66. Prelutsky, "'Laverne & Shirley,'" 24.

67. Miller, "You Can't Resist," 111.

68. Arnold Hano, "This Dropout Has an M.A. from Yale," *TV Guide*, 10 January 1976, 20–22; John M. Wilson, "Can Henry Winkler Outgrow 'The Fonz'?" *New York Times*, 23 May 1976, sec. D.

69. Indeed, as the other young male leads left the show in its later years, the Fonz increasingly became counselor to the young women characters who rose in their place. After the Fifties revival had faded, he moved on the show from being the arbiter of masculinity to being the arbiter of femininity; his advice shifted from how to impress girls and entice their sexual interest to how to regulate boys' behavior and assert female desires in socially acceptable ways.

70. For countercultural takes on the Beats, see two obituaries for Jack Kerouac published by *Rolling Stone*, 29 November 1969: Eric Ehrmann and Stephen Davis, "There Is Really Nothing Inside," 34, and Lester Bangs, "Elegy for a Desolation Angel," 36. See also John Tytell, "The Beat Generation," *Commonweal*, 17 December 1971, 285–286. For a conservative refutation of the linkage between the Beats and the Sixties countercultural left, see John R. Coyne, Jr., "Coopting Kerouac," *National Review*, 5 November 1971, 1246–47.

71. The *Reader's Guide to Periodical Literature* records virtually no articles on Beats in the mainstream press in the early 1970s, and refers the interested reader to "Hippies"— until that social category loses its inscriptions as well.

72. For more on this view, see, see, inevitably, Pierre Bourdieu, *Distinction: A Social Critique of the Judgement of Taste*, trans. Richard Nice (Cambridge: Harvard University Press, 1984); for specific research on male working-class taste for rock music (in the British context), see Paul Willis, "The Golden Age," in *On Record: Rock, Pop, and the Written Word*, ed. Simon Frith and Andrew Goodwin (New York: Pantheon, 1990), 43–55.

73. For an analysis of the political economy of the 1970s and its effects on working-class positions, see Mike Davis, *Prisoners of the American Dream* (New York: Verso, 1986).

74. *Sha Na Na*, syndicated, 1977–1981.

75. Robert Palmer, "Chuck Berry, Carl Perkins Perform with Sha Na Na," *New York Times*, 4 February 1979, sec. I (the headline is misleading: the writer compares Sha Na Na unfavorably to its forerunners, who were decidedly not part of the show).

76. *Grease*, by Jim Jacobs and Warren Casey. Dir. Tim Moore. Premiered at the Eden Theater, New York City, 14 February 1972. Tom Buckley, "'Grease' Breaks a Record on Broadway," *New York Times*, 7 December 1979, sec. III.

77. *Grease*, dir. Randal Kleiser, Paramount, 1978.

78. *The Buddy Holly Story*, dir. Steve Rash, Columbia, 1978.

CHAPTER 2   THE CONSERVATIVE USES OF NOSTALGIA

1. Ronald Reagan, "The Morality Gap at Berkeley" (speech at San Francisco, California, 12 May 1966). Reprinted in Ronald Reagan, *The Creative Society: Some Comments on Problems Facing America* (New York: Devin-Adair Company, 1968), 125–127.

2. Ronald Reagan, "The Democratic Party Left *Us*," in Reagan, *The Creative Society*, 135–138; Lou Cannon, *Reagan* (New York: G. P. Putnam's Sons, 1982), 114, 148 (for Reagan's response as governor to student protests); Ronnie Dugger, *On Reagan: The Man and His Presidency* (New York: McGraw-Hill, 1983), 348 (for Reagan comments on Vietnam); and Marshall Frady, "California: The Rending of the Veil," *Harper's*, December 1969, 57–73 (for a contemporary account of Reagan's politics and appeal in the 1960s).

3. *The State of the Union: A Republican View*, 27 January 1980, Sen. Bill Brock, speaker.

4. Elizabeth Drew, *Portrait of an Election: The 1980 Presidential Campaign* (New York: Simon and Schuster, 1981); Cannon, *Reagan*. In a minor thread of the 1976 campaign, Carter had presented himself as a figure who could symbolically heal the social divisions of post-Sixties America, in his combination of rural southern heritage, born-again Christianity, and fandom for rock performers such as Bob Dylan and the Allman Brothers. Carter's deemphasis of issues during the campaign, in favor of avowals of personal values, also contributed to his conciliatory image. For a basic account of the 1976 campaign, see Jules Witcover, *Marathon: The Pursuit of the Presidency, 1972–1976* (New York: Viking, 1977); for Carter's attempts to evoke John Kennedy and pre-Vietnam America, see Paul R. Henggeler, *The Kennedy Persuasion: The Politics of Style since JFK* (Chicago: Ivan R. Dee, 1995), 86–88, 138–139.

5. Cannon, *Reagan*, 270.

6. Ibid., 271. For similar Reagan campaign statements, see Alexander Cockburn and James Ridgeway, "The World of Appearance: The Public Campaign," in *The Hidden Election: Politics and Economics in the 1980 Presidential Campaign*, ed. Thomas Ferguson and Joel Rogers (New York: Pantheon, 1981), 71–72.

7. Frances FitzGerald, "A Reporter at Large: A Disciplined, Charging Army," *New Yorker*, 18 May 1981, 53.

8. James Q. Wilson, "Reagan and the Republican Revival," *Commentary* 70, no. 4 (October 1980): 29.

9. In addition to banning organized school prayer, the Court had ordered school desegregation, weakened traditional segregationist restrictions on African-American voting rights with its "one man, one vote" rulings, made access to contraceptives a constitutional right, overturned obscenity restrictions, strengthened prisoner rights, upheld federal standards of due process over state and local practices, and (several years after Chief Justice Earl Warren had retired) made abortion legal nationally. For a litany of conservative complaints against the Warren Court era, see William A. Stanmeyer, "Judicial Supremacy," in *The New Right Papers*, ed. Robert Whitaker (New York: St. Martin's Press, 1982), 142–169.

10. For New Right pronouncements, see Jerry Falwell, *Listen, America!* (Garden City: Doubleday, 1980) and Connaught C. Marshner, *The New Traditional Woman* (Washington, D.C.: Free Congress Research & Education Foundation, 1982). For portraits of New Right leaders, see Susan Faludi, *Backlash: The Undeclared War against American Women* (New York: Doubleday, 1991) and FitzGerald, "Disciplined, Charging Army." For an insightful look at rank-and-file supporters, see Rebecca E. Klatch, *Women of the New Right* (Philadelphia: Temple University Press, 1987). For a recounting of New Right organizational activities, see Sara Diamond, *Roads to Dominion: Right-Wing Movements and Political Power in the United States* (New York: Guilford Press, 1995). For a wholesale, historically minded deconstruction of conservative claims for the family, see Stephanie Coontz, *The Way We Never Were: American Families and the Nostalgia Trap* (New York: Basic Books, 1992). For feminism's centrality to New Right criticisms of contemporary society, see Rosalind Pollack Petchesky, "Antiabortion, Antifeminism, and the Rise of the New Right," *Feminist Studies* 7, no. 2 (Summer 1981): 206–246. For an influential overview of the politics of cultural divisions at the time, see James Davison Hunter, *Culture Wars: The Struggle to Define America* (New York: Basic Books, 1991).

11. Falwell, *Listen, America!* 17.

12. Linda Kintz, "Clarity, Mothers, and the Mass-Mediated National Soul: A Defense of Ambiguity," in *Media, Culture, and the Religious Right*, ed. Linda Kintz and Julia Lesage (Minneapolis: University of Minnesota Press, 1998), 115–139.

13. Falwell, *Listen, America!* 15.

14. FitzGerald, "Disciplined, Charging Army," 110.

15. Allan C. Carlson, "Families, Sex, and the Liberal Agenda," *Public Interest* 58 (Winter 1980): 74. *Miss Winslow and Son* was a short-lived situation comedy about an unwed mother, aired by CBS in 1979.

16. Petchesky, "Rise of the New Right"; Zillah R. Eisenstein, *Feminism and Sexual Equality: Crisis in Liberal America* (New York: Monthly Review Press, 1984).

17. Klatch, *Women of the New Right*; Marshner, *New Traditional Woman.*

18. Marshner, *New Traditional Woman*, 3.

19. Klatch, *Women of the New Right*, 129.

20. Falwell, *Listen, America!* 197–198. Similar arguments in intellectualized form can be found in Allan Bloom, *The Closing of the American Mind* (New York: Simon and Schuster, 1987).

21. Richard G. Hutcheson, Jr., *God in the White House: How Religion Has Changed the Modern Presidency* (New York: Macmillan, 1988), 78–79, and Irene Diamond, "Introduction," in *Families, Politics, and Public Policy: A Feminist Dialogue on Women and the State*, ed. Irene Diamond (New York: Longman, 1983), 1–19.

22. Carlson, "The Liberal Agenda," 62–79.

23. FitzGerald, "Disciplined, Charging Army," 114.

24. Ibid.; Hutcheson, *God in the White House*, 161.

25. FitzGerald, "Disciplined, Charging Army," 114.

26. Falwell, *Listen, America!*; Matthew C. Moen, *The Christian Right and Congress* (Tuscaloosa: University of Alabama Press, 1989), 26. For other conservative complaints that use traditionalism to focus on federal racial policies, see Burton Yale Pines, *Back to Basics: The Traditionalist Movement That Is Sweeping Grass-Roots America* (New York: William Morrow and Company, 1982), and R. Emmett Tyrrell, Jr., "The Twenty Years' War of the So-Called Liberals," *American Spectator*, November 1979, 4–5, 42–44.

27. Faludi, *Backlash*, 283–290; Sidney Blumenthal, *The Rise of the Counter-Establishment: From Conservative Ideology to Political Power* (New York: Times Books, 1986), 203–209. Blumenthal went on to become a presidential aide during the second Clinton administration.

28. George Gilder, *Sexual Suicide* (New York: Quadrangle, 1973); George Gilder, *Naked Nomads: Unmarried Men in America* (New York: Quadrangle, 1974).

29. George Gilder, *Wealth and Poverty* (New York: Basic Books, 1981). The major media outlets offered largely positive reviews of the book. See Lewis Beman, "A Capitalist Manifesto from the New Right," *Business Week*, 29 December 1980, 18; Roger Starr, "A Guide to Capitalism," *New York Times*, 1 February 1981, Sunday Book Review; and Merrill Sheils, "What's Up Gilder's Sleeve," *Newsweek*, 16 February 1981, 64. For a colorful profile of Gilder, see Henry Allen, "George Gilder and the Capitalists' Creed," *Washington Post*, 18 February 1981, sec. B.

30. Blumenthal, *Rise of the Counter-Establishment*, 210.

31. Gilder, *Wealth and Poverty*, 68.

32. The first quote comes from *Sexual Suicide*, 5; the second comes from *Wealth and Poverty*, 68.

33. Jude Wanniski, *The Way the World Works: How Economies Fail—and Succeed* (New York: Basic Books, 1978); William E. Simon, *A Time for Truth* (New York: Reader's Digest Press/McGraw-Hill, 1978); Milton Friedman and Rose Friedman, *Freedom to Choose* (New York: Harcourt Brace Jovanovich, 1980); and Charles Murray, *Losing Ground: American Social Policy, 1950–1980* (New York: Basic Books, 1984). Wanniski was an editorial writer for the *Wall Street Journal*, Simon had been secretary of the treasury in the Ford administration, and Milton Friedman was a well-known economist at the University of Chicago. Murray's book inspired spirited debate about his statistical methods and general conclusions. For positive reviews, see Daniel B. Moskowitz, "Why Those at the Bottom Are Still Stuck There," *Business*

Week, 29 October 1984, 12; Lance Lamberton, "Losing Ground: American Social Policy 1950–1980," *National Review*, 14 December 1984, 44; Michael Barone, "The Battle over 'Losing Ground,'" *Washington Post*, 3 April 1985, sec. A. For criticisms of Murray, see Robert Kuttner, "Declaring War on the War on Poverty," *Washington Post*, 25 November 1984, Book World; Lawrence M. Mead, "Welfare: More Harm than Good?" *New York Times*, 16 December 1984, Sunday Book Review; Michael Harrington, "Crunched Numbers: Charles Murray's Stunted Statistics," *New Republic*, 28 January 1985, 7. Harrington was the author of *The Other America*, a book widely credited with inspiring the War on Poverty. For a more mixed view of Murray's work, see Herbert Stein, "A Poverty Paradox," *Fortune*, January 1985, 169; Stein had been head of the Council of Economic Advisers in the Nixon administration.

34. Tom Wicker, *One of Us: Richard Nixon and the American Dream* (New York: Random House, 1991), 551.

35. Reagan, *Creative Society*; Ronald Reagan, *An American Life* (New York: Simon and Schuster, 1990), 198. For a history of welfare policy and the changes debated during the New Deal, see Linda Gordon, *Pitied but Not Entitled: Single Mothers and the History of Welfare, 1890–1935* (New York: Free Press, 1994).

36. D. Lee Bawden and John L. Palmer, "Social Policy: Challenging the Welfare State," in *The Reagan Record: An Assessment of America's Changing Domestic Priorities*, ed. John L. Palmer and Isabel V. Sawhill (Cambridge, Mass.: Ballinger Publishing Company, 1984), 177–216; Nathan Glazer, "The Social Policy of the Reagan Administration: A Review," *Public Interest*, no. 75 (Spring 1984): 76–98.

37. Bawden and Palmer, "Social Policy."

38. Nicholas Lemann, "Fighting the Last War," *Atlantic*, February 1991, 28–33.

39. Simon, *Time for Truth*, 90; Friedman and Friedman, *Freedom to Choose*, 108.

40. Wanniski, *Way the World Works*, 212.

41. Irving Kristol, *Two Cheers for Capitalism* (New York: Basic Books, 1978), 236–237.

42. Adam Clymer, "President Says 'Big Spenders' Forced Ban on School Prayer," *New York Times*, 1 November 1982, sec. A.

43. Thomas Byrne Edsall and Mary D. Edsall, *Chain Reaction: The Impact of Race, Rights, and Taxes on American Politics* (New York: W. W. Norton and Company, 1991).

44. Ibid., 41.

45. Ibid.; a look at one northern white community's estrangement from Democratic liberalism can be found in Jonathan Rieder, *Canarsie: The Jews and Italians of Brooklyn against Liberalism* (Cambridge: Harvard University Press, 1985).

46. Peter Steinfels, *The Neoconservatives: The Men Who Are Changing America's Politics* (New York: Simon and Schuster, 1979), 25–32; Blumenthal, *Rise of the Counter-Establishment*, 122–154.

47. John Hellmann, *American Myth and the Legacy of Vietnam* (New York: Columbia University Press, 1986), 100.

48. Rowland Evans and Robert Novak, *The Reagan Revolution* (New York: E. P. Dutton, 1981), 2; Richard A. Viguerie, *The New Right: We're Ready to Lead* (Falls Church: Viguerie Company, 1981), 5, 109–110. For Reagan's pronouncements, before he was elected president, on liberal betrayal, see Dugger, *On Reagan*, 240, 348, 493–494, 514.

49. Norman Podhoretz, "The Culture of Appeasement," *Harper's*, October 1977, 25–32; Norman Podhoretz, *The Present Danger* (New York: Simon and Schuster, 1980); Norman Podhoretz, *Why We Were in Vietnam* (New York: Simon and Schuster, 1982).

50. Podhoretz, *Vietnam*, 172.

51. Podhoretz, "Culture of Appeasement."

52. Cannon, *Reagan*, 271; Falwell, *Listen, America!* 73. Podhoretz dismisses these claims, *Vietnam*, 178.

53. Peter Hannaford, *The Reagans: A Political Portrait* (New York: Coward-McCann, 1983), 51; after the Hanoi victory in 1975, Reagan said Congress had "blood on its hands." Dugger, *On Reagan*, 348.

54. Drew, *Portrait of an Election*, 103, 116.

55. Cockburn and Ridgeway, "World of Appearance," 71–72. Kevin Phillips compares the theme of betrayal through limits on military options in Vietnam to conservative sympathy with Gen. Douglas MacArthur's complaints during the Korean War that Harry Truman was not allowing him to win the war. Kevin P. Phillips, *Post-Conservative America: People, Politics, and Ideology in a Time of Crisis* (New York: Random House, 1982), 177. Truman had MacArthur replaced as commander of United Nations forces when the general's actions prompted China to join the war on North Korea's side. American policymakers during the Vietnam War refrained from full-scale invasion of North Vietnam for fear that China would once more commit its troops to battling American forces.

56. Paul D. Erickson, *Reagan Speaks: The Making of an American Myth* (New York: New York University Press, 1985), 55.

57. The rather chimerical nature of Reagan's popularity during his first months in office is usefully revealed in Michael Schudson, "Ronald Reagan Misremembered," in *Collective Remembering*, ed. David Middleton and Derek Edwards (London: Sage, 1990), 108–119.

58. George Gallup, "1980 Election One of the Most Unusual in Recent Political History," *Gallup Poll*, 7 December 1980, 2; Eisenstein, *Feminism and Sexual Equality*, 22; Bob Schieffer and Gary Paul Gates, *The Acting President* (New York: E. P. Dutton, 1989), 14.

59. Moen, *Christian Right and Congress*; William Greider, "The Education of David Stockman," *Atlantic*, December 1981, 27–54; Richard P. Nathan, "The Reagan Presidency in Domestic Affairs," in *The Reagan Presidency: An Early Assessment*, ed. Fred I. Greenstein (Baltimore: Johns Hopkins University Press, 1983), 48–81.

60. Steven V. Roberts, "New Conservative Coalition," *New York Times*, 7 January 1981, sec. A.

61. Martin Anderson, "The Objectives of the Reagan Administration's Social Welfare Policy," in *The Social Contract Revisited: Aims and Outcomes of President Reagan's Social Welfare Policy*, ed. D. Lee Bawden (Washington, D.C.: Urban Institute Press, 1984), 15–27.

62. Greider, "Education of David Stockman," 47–51; Nathan, "Reagan Presidency," 63.

63. Bawden and Palmer, "Social Policy"; Henry J. Aaron, "Comments," in Bawden, *Social Contract Revisited*, 241–244; Stuart E. Eizenstat, "Comments," in Bawden, *Social Contract Revisited*, 28–32.

64. Anderson, "Social Welfare Policy"; John L. Palmer and Isabel V. Sawhill, "Overview," in *The Reagan Record: An Assessment of America's Changing Domestic Priorities*, ed. John L. Palmer and Isabel V. Sawhill (Cambridge, Mass.: Ballinger Publishing Company, 1984), 16–18.

65. Palmer and Sawhill, "Overview," 16–18; Gillian Peele, *Revival and Reaction: The Right in Contemporary America* (Oxford: Oxford University Press, 1984), 158–160.

66. Greider, "Education of David Stockman," 40; John Kenneth White, *The New Politics of Old Values*, 2d ed. (Hanover, N.H.: University Press of New England, 1990), 58. For Reagan opposition to the Legal Services Corporation, see Edsall and Edsall, *Chain Reaction*, 169.

67. Glazer, "Reagan Administration," 83–85.

68. Aaron, "Comments," 242; Palmer and Sawhill, "Overview," 13; Laurence I. Barrett, *Gambling with History: Ronald Reagan in the White House* (Garden City, N.J.: Doubleday, 1983), 156–158.
69. Barrett, *Gambling with History*, 156–158.
70. Glazer, "Reagan Administration," 97. For the immediate consequences of these program cutbacks, see Harry Boyte, "Ronald Reagan and America's Neighborhoods: Undermining Community Initiative," in *What Reagan Is Doing to Us*, ed. Alan Gartner, Colin Greer, and Frank Riessman (New York: Harper & Row, 1982), 109–124.
71. Bawden and Palmer, "Social Policy," 201.
72. Glazer, "Reagan Administration," 97.
73. Aaron, "Comments," 242.
74. Nathan, "Reagan Presidency," 63.
75. Greider, "Education of David Stockman," 47–52.
76. Bawden and Palmer, "Social Policy," 208.
77. Augustus F. Hawkins, "Minorities and Unemployment," in Gartner, Greer, and Riessman, *What Reagan Is Doing to Us*, 134. Hawkins was a Democratic congressional representative. For judicial appointments, see Barrett, *Gambling with History*, 427.
78. Francis X. Clines and Bernard Weinraub, "Briefing," *New York Times*, 22 October 1981, sec. B; Irvin Molotsky, "Scholar Chosen as Humanities Chief," *New York Times*, 14 November 1981. For the continued appreciation of Bradford by segments of the right, see "Not in Memorium, but in Affirmation," a section of *Intercollegiate Review* 29, no. 2 (Spring 1994), in which Bradford's ardent fandom for the pro–Ku Klux Klan film *Birth of a Nation* is celebrated.
79. *The State of the Union: A Republican View.*
80. Strobe Talbott, *Deadly Gambits: The Reagan Administration and the Stalemate in Nuclear Arms Control* (New York: Alfred A. Knopf, 1984); Strobe Talbott, *The Master of the Game: Paul Nitze and the Nuclear Peace* (New York: Alfred A. Knopf, 1988). Talbott became a leading policymaker regarding U.S.-Russian relations in the Clinton administration.
81. Moen, *Christian Right and Congress*; Diamond, *Roads to Dominion*, 236; Nathan, "Reagan Presidency," 50–51.
82. Moen, *Christian Right and Congress*, 108; Faludi, *Backlash*, 235; Diamond, *Roads to Dominion*, 367.
83. Moen, *Christian Right and Congress*; Diamond, *Roads to Dominion*, 234.
84. Moen, *Christian Right and Congress*, 100.
85. Ibid., 28–29; Lou Cannon, *President Reagan: The Role of a Lifetime* (New York: Simon & Schuster, 1991), 521–523.
86. Schieffer and Gates, *Acting President*; Barrett, *Gambling with History*; Michael Deaver with Mickey Herskowitz, *Behind the Scenes* (New York: William Morrow and Company, 1987).
87. Deaver, *Behind the Scenes*; Cannon, *President Reagan*, 503–509.
88. Moen, *Christian Right and Congress*, 69.
89. Bawden and Palmer, "Welfare State," 204–207; for Reagan's defense of his administration's actions on civil rights, see Ronald Reagan, "Address to National Black Republican Council," speech presented at a meeting of the National Black Republican Council, Washington, D.C., 15 September 1982. Reprinted in Paul Boyer, ed., *Reagan as President: Contemporary Views of the Man, His Politics, and His Policies* (Chicago: Ivan R. Dee, 1990), 145–149.
90. On attacks on feminists and influence over educational materials, see Faludi, *Backlash*, 259–261. For conservative response to the AIDS crisis, see Randy Shilts, *And the Band Played On: Politics, People, and the AIDS Epidemic* (New York: St. Martin's

Press, 1987); Elinor Burkett, *The Gravest Show on Earth: America in the Age of AIDS* (Boston: Houghton Mifflin, 1995), 293–300; and Cannon, *President Reagan*, 813–819. Shilts blames slow federal response to the epidemic on bureaucratic inertia, opposition to new federal spending programs by the Office of Management and Budget, and reluctance to offer public support to the gay community by White House political staff. Such reluctance can be seen in part as evidence of New Right influence, as many figures on the right were vocal in their disdain for the gay liberation movement and opposed AIDS education and funding programs.

91. For an analysis of the antidrug campaign in the context of the conservative rhetoric of public and private spheres, see Susan Mackey-Kallis and Dan F. Hahn, "Questions of Public Will and Private Action: The Power of the Negative in the Reagans' 'Just Say No' Morality Campaign," *Communication Quarterly* 39, no. 1 (Winter 1991): 1–17.

CHAPTER 3   NOSTALGIA EMBODIED

1. See Andrew Kopkind, "The Age of Reaganism: A Man and a Movement," *The Nation*, 3 November 1984, cover–451.
2. For an early version of this, see Barry Farrell, "The Candidate from Disneyland: Ronald Duck for President," *Harper's*, February 1976, 9–14.
3. Roger Rosenblatt, with Laurence I. Barrett, "Man of the Year: Out of the Past, Fresh Choices for the Future: Invoking Old Values, Ronald Reagan Must Make Them Work for the '80s," *Time*, 5 January 1981, 10–23.
4. Rowland Evans and Robert Novak, *The Reagan Revolution* (New York: E. P. Dutton, 1981), xiii; Laurence I. Barrett, *Gambling with History: Ronald Reagan in the White House* (Garden City, N.J.: Doubleday, 1983), 48; Kevin Phillips, *Post-Conservative America: People, Politics, and Ideology in a Time of Crisis* (New York: Random House, 1982), 7–13.
5. Arthur P. Dudden, "Nostalgia and the American," *Journal of the History of Ideas* 22, no. 4 (October–December 1961): 527; Michael Kammen, *Mystic Chords of Memory: The Transformation of Tradition in American Culture* (New York: Alfred A. Knopf, 1991), 388. Dudden credits Frederick Lewis Allen in *Only Yesterday* for originally analyzing Coolidge's appeal.
6. Evans and Novak, *Reagan Revolution*, xiii.
7. Ibid., 2.
8. Ibid., xiii.
9. *ABC World News Tonight*, 21 March 1982, Mike von Freund, reporter.
10. Stephen E. Ambrose, "The Ike Age: The Revisionist View of Eisenhower," *New Republic*, 9 May 1981, 26–34; John P. Roche, "Eisenhower Redux," *New York Times*, 28 June 1981, Sunday Book Review. Books under review included Blanche Wiesen Cook, *The Declassified Eisenhower*, Robert A. Divine, *Eisenhower and the Cold War*, William Bragg Ewald Jr., *Eisenhower the President*, Robert H. Ferrell, ed., *The Eisenhower Diaries*, and Burton Kaufman, *Trade and Aid: Eisenhower's Foreign Economic Policy*.
11. *NBC Nightly News*, 30 October 1980, John Chancellor, reporter. The newly published books on Eisenhower made efforts, however, to portray Eisenhower as a more active leader as president than previously thought. See also Colin Campbell, "Scholars Meet to Laud Eisenhower as Leader," *New York Times*, 12 October 1981, sec. A.
12. Reagan defended Roosevelt even when attacking FDR's New Deal aides as protofascists and -communists. "Reagan Says Many New Dealers Wanted Fascism," *New York Times*, 23 December 1981, sec. A.
13. Elizabeth Drew, *Portrait of an Election: The 1980 Presidential Campaign* (New York: Simon & Schuster, 1981), 264; Jack W. Germond and Jules Witcover, *Wake Us When It's Over: Presidential Politics of 1984* (New York: Macmillan, 1985), 464–465.

14. Michael Wallace, "Ronald Reagan and the Politics of History," *Tikkun* 2, no. 1 (1987): 13–18, 127–131; Garry Wills, *Reagan's America: Innocents at Home* (Garden City, N.J.: Doubleday, 1987).

15. Wallace, "Politics of History"; Wills, *Reagan's America*. For other views of Reagan's use of Hollywood themes and imagery, see Jules Feiffer, "Movie America—or, The Past Recaptured," *The Nation*, 11–18 July 1981, 39–41, and Michael Paul Rogin, *"Ronald Reagan," The Movie, and Other Episodes in Political Demonology* (Berkeley: University of California Press, 1987), 1–43.

16. Lou Cannon, *Reagan* (New York: G. P. Putnam's Sons, 1982), 20.

17. Benjamin Barber, "Celluloid Vistas: What the President's Dreams Are Made Of," *Harper's*, July 1985, 74–75; Wills, *Reagan's America*, 380–381. Reagan's speech can be found in *Inaugural Addresses of the Presidents of the United States: From George Washington to George W. Bush* (Washington, D.C.: U.S. Government Printing Office, 2001).

18. Lauren Berlant, *The Anatomy of National Fantasy: Hawthorne, Utopia, and Everyday Life* (Chicago: University of Chicago Press, 1991), 4–5, 20–33.

19. J. Hoberman, *Vulgar Modernism* (Philadelphia: Temple University Press, 1991), 57.

20. Lou Cannon, *President Reagan: The Role of a Lifetime* (New York: Simon and Schuster, 1991), 24; Michael Deaver, Reagan's close aide and surrogate son for many years, also remarked on how Reagan's view of the world continued to be based on the 1950s. Michael K. Deaver with Mickey Herskowitz, *Behind the Scenes* (New York: William Morrow and Company, 1987), 101, 104.

21. Cannon, *President Reagan*, 88–90.

22. Cannon, *Reagan*, 99; Cannon, *President Reagan*, 89.

23. Reagan had campaign buttons depicting him in a cowboy hat; the *Time* "Man of the Year" story opened with a picture of Reagan on horseback and in western clothing. *Time*, 10.

24. Richard Schickel, "Duke Packs a Mean Paunch," *Life*, 4 August 1967, 8.

25. Ronald Reagan, "Unforgettable John Wayne," *Reader's Digest*, October 1979, 115–119. For more on Wayne's place in American culture, and Reagan's relation to Wayne and the settling of the West, see Richard Slotkin, *Gunfighter Nation: The Myth of the Frontier in Twentieth-Century America* (New York: Atheneum, 1992), 512–527, 644–654.

26. "Transcript of President's First News Conference on Foreign and Domestic Topics," *New York Times*, 30 January 1981, sec. A, for tough talk about the Soviet Union; *New York Times*, 23 December 1981, sec. A, for comments about communist front groups; and Ronnie Dugger, *On Reagan, the Man and His Presidency* (New York: McGraw-Hill, 1983), 240, 492–495, for Reagan's penchant over several decades for linking dissent in America to communist designs.

27. "The KGB's Spies in America," *Newsweek*, 23 November 1981, 50–61.

28. For examples, see Francis L. Loewenheim, "Reaganscribing History," *New York Times*, 23 March 1981, on Roosevelt's policies toward Germany; Charles Mohr, "Reagan Seems Confused on Vietnam's History," *New York Times*, 19 February 1982, sec. A.

29. Wallace, "Politics of History," 16, 130; Wills, *Reagan's America*, 386, 388.

30. Fred Davis, *Yearning for Yesterday: A Sociology of Nostalgia* (New York: Free Press, 1979); Barbie Zelizer, "Reading the Past against the Grain: The Shape of Memory Studies," *Critical Studies in Mass Communication* 12, no. 2 (June 1995): 214–239.

31. Frances FitzGerald, *America Revised: History Schoolbooks in the Twentieth Century* (Boston: Little, Brown, 1979), 10.

32. Stephanie Coontz, *The Way We Never Were: American Families and the Nostalgia Trap* (New York: Basic Books, 1992), 25–29; Elaine Tyler May, "Cold War–Warm Hearth: Politics and the Family in Postwar America," in *The Rise and Fall of the New*

Deal Order, 1930–1980, ed. Steve Fraser and Gary Gerstle (Princeton: Princeton University Press, 1989), 153–181.

33. May, "Cold War–Warm Hearth."

34. See chapter two for details of conservative claims regarding the government, families, and poverty.

35. Coontz, *Way We Never Were*, 76–77.

36. William Greider, "The Education of David Stockman," *Atlantic Monthly*, December 1981, 30.

37. See Jonathan Schell, *History in Sherman Park: An American Family and the Reagan-Mondale Election* (New York: Alfred A. Knopf, 1987), 124.

38. Sidney Blumenthal, "Reaganism and the Neokitsch Aesthetic," in *The Reagan Legacy*, ed. Sidney Blumenthal and Thomas Byrne Edsall (New York: Pantheon, 1988), 257.

39. Lewis Lapham, "The Precarious Eden," *Harper's*, March 1981, 14–16.

40. Reagan's last film, *The Killers*, was released in 1964, and, as is standard in Hollywood treatment of second-rate leading men once they hit fifty, he was finally cast as a heavy. His character even hit New Frontier sex symbol Angie Dickinson on screen. Reagan disliked the role and retired from the movies. *The Killers*, dir. Don Siegel, Universal, 1964.

41. Ronald Reagan, *The Creative Society* (New York: Devin-Adair, 1968), 38.

42. Ibid., 33.

43. Kurt Ritter, "Ronald Reagan's 1960s Southern Rhetoric: Courting Conservatives for the GOP," *Southern Communication Journal* 64, no. 4 (Summer 1999): 333–345.

44. Marshall Frady, "California: The Rending of the Veil," *Harper's*, December 1969, 57–73; Cannon, *Reagan*.

45. Ronald Reagan, "The Morality Gap at Berkeley," speech presented at San Francisco, California, 12 May 1966; reprinted in Reagan, *Creative Society*, 125.

46. Bob Schieffer and Gary Paul Gates, *The Acting President* (New York: E. P. Dutton, 1989), 33–45.

47. Cannon, *Reagan*, 148–152.

48. Drew, *Portrait of an Election*, 264, for the 1980 tactics; Germond and Witcover, *Wake Us When It's Over*, 537, for Reagan's 1960 views.

49. Germond and Witcover, *Wake Us When It's Over*, 468.

50. "Text of Reagan's Speech Accepting the Republicans' Nomination," *New York Times*, 18 July 1980, sec. A.

51. Arthur M. Schlesinger, Jr., ed., *Running for President: The Candidates and Their Images*, vol. 2 (New York: Simon & Schuster, 1994), 383.

52. Wills, *Reagan's America*, 370–388. Time Inc. weighed in on Reagan's theme by devoting issues of all seven of its magazines to a discussion of "American Renewal" shortly after his inauguration. See, for example, *Time*, 23 February 1981, 34–74.

53. Sheldon Wolin, *The Presence of the Past: Essays on the State and the Constitution* (Baltimore: Johns Hopkins University Press, 1989), 23–25.

54. See Eric Hobsbawm, "Introduction: Inventing Tradition," in *The Invention of Tradition*, ed. Eric Hobsbawm and Terence Ranger (Cambridge: Cambridge University Press, 1983), 1–14.

55. Cannon, *Reagan*, 99.

56. Wallace, "Politics of History"; Blumenthal, "Reaganism and the Neokitsch Aesthetic."

57. Paul D. Erickson, *Reagan Speaks: The Making of an American Myth* (New York: New York University Press, 1985), 62–67.

58. Greider, "Education of David Stockman"; supply-side economics is discussed in chapter two.

59. For one conservative attempt, see "Revolution," *Wall Street Journal*, 10 December 1980. The inadequacy of cultural and political conservatives' attempts at a rearticu-

lation of Lennon can be seen in their persistent misattribution of certain Beatles songs to Lennon's authorship—they invoked "Yesterday" and "Let It Be" in their claims of fandom, though both were written by Paul McCartney and disliked by Lennon.

60. Sidney Blumenthal, *The Rise of the Counter-Establishment: From Conservative Ideology to Political Power* (New York: Times Books, 1986), 161–162.

61. *ABC World News Tonight*, 22 August 1984, Richard Threlkeld, reporter.

62. Dinesh D'Souza, *Ronald Reagan: How an Ordinary Man Became an Extraordinary Leader* (New York: Free Press, 1997), 73.

63. George C. Edwards, "Comparing Chief Executives," *Public Opinion*, June/July 1985, 50.

64. Lawrence Grossberg, *Dancing in Spite of Myself* (Durham, N.J.: Duke University Press, 1997), 232–243.

65. Rebecca Klatch, *Women of the New Right* (Philadelphia: Temple University Press, 1987), 120–121; David Stockman attests that even he fell prey to the Sixties' attack on everything holy in his first semester as a Michigan State undergraduate: "My first professor was an atheist and socialist from Brooklyn, and within three months I think he destroyed everything I believed in, from God to the flag." Greider, "Education of David Stockman," 29.

66. May, "Cold War–Warm Hearth"; Coontz, *Way We Never Were*; George Lipsitz, *Time Passages: Collective Memory and American Popular Culture* (Minneapolis: University of Minnesota Press, 1990), 39–96; and Jackson Lears, "A Matter of Taste: Corporate Cultural Hegemony in a Mass-Consumption Society," in *Recasting America: Culture and Politics in the Age of Cold War*, ed. Lary May (Chicago: University of Chicago Press, 1989), 38–57.

67. An incisive and hilarious critique of civil defense efforts written at the height of their popularity, in which bomb shelters are referred to as the "canning" of the population, can be found in the "The Geopolitics of Hibernation," in *Situationist International Anthology*, ed. Ken Knabb (Berkeley: Bureau of Public Secrets, 1982), 76–82.

68. Michel Crozier, Samuel P. Huntington, and Joji Watanuki, *The Crisis of Democracy: Report on the Governability of Democracies to the Trilateral Commission* (New York: New York University Press, 1975); the book's political role is discussed in Russell L. Hanson, *The Democratic Imagination in America: Conversations with Our Past* (Princeton: Princeton University Press, 1985).

69. Susan Faludi, *Backlash: The Undeclared War against American Women* (New York: Doubleday, 1991), 230. It should be noted that the year 1954, invoked at the Heritage Foundation meeting, is perhaps best known politically as the year that the Supreme Court invalidated racial segregation in public education. Culturally, it is most identified as the year rock and roll emerged as an important force in white youth culture.

70. See the discussion of Jerry Falwell's political involvement in chapter two.

71. Ronald Reagan, *Abortion and the Conscience of the Nation* (Nashville: Thomas Nelson Publishers, 1984), 34.

72. Gerald Pomper, "The Presidential Election," in *The Election of 1980*, ed. Gerald Pomper (Chatham, N.J.: Chatham House, 1981), 72.

73. Ibid., 72; David Gergen, "Following the Leaders: How Ronald Reagan and Margaret Thatcher Have Changed Public Opinion," *Public Opinion*, June/July 1985, 55.

74. Scott Keeter, "Public Opinion in 1984," in *The Election of 1984*, ed. Gerald Pomper (Chatham, N.J.: Chatham House, 1985), 104.

75. For survey results from the late 1970s that show that the members of the " '60's generation" remained more liberal than their elders across a wide range of issues, see "Opinion Roundup: Gaping at the Generation Gap," *Public Opinion*, February/

March 1980, 38; for a study that showed liberals and leftists who were politically active in the 1960s generally retained their political viewpoints into the 1980s, see Gerald Marwell, Michael T. Aiken, and N. J. Demerath III, "The Persistence of Political Attitudes among 1960s Civil Rights Activists," *Public Opinion Quarterly* 51 (Fall 1987): 359–375.

76. Howard Schuman and Jacqueline Scott, "Generations and Collective Memories," *American Sociological Review* 54 (June 1989): 368–369.

77. See Klatch, *Women of the New Right*, for attitudes of conservative women on feminism; for voting totals, see Zillah R. Eisenstein, *Feminism and Sexual Equality: Crisis in Liberal America* (New York: Monthly Review Press, 1984), 22.

78. Harold Stanley, "The 1984 Presidential Election in the South: Race and Realignment," in *The 1984 Presidential Election in the South: Patterns of Southern Party Politics*, ed. Robert P. Steed, Laurence W. Moreland, and Tod A. Baker (New York: Praeger, 1986), 315.

79. Ben J. Wattenberg and Everett Ladd, "Moving Right Along? Campaign '84's Lessons for 1988: An Interview with Peter Hart and Richard Wirthlin," *Public Opinion*, December/January 1985, 61.

80. Reagan and other conservatives also opposed the creation of a national holiday to commemorate Martin Luther King, Jr. Congress passed legislation to create the holiday despite such opposition, and Reagan eventually signed it—but also hinted that King was a communist. Lena Williams, "Most of U.S. Will Honor Dr. King, But Some Still Dispute the Holiday," *New York Times*, 18 January 1987, sec. 1.

81. Herman Gray, *Watching Race: Television and the Struggle for "Blackness"* (Minneapolis: University of Minnesota Press, 1995), 14–34.

82. See Thomas Byrne Edsall and Mary D. Edsall, *Chain Reaction: The Impact of Race, Rights, and Taxes on American Politics* (New York: W. W. Norton, 1991).

83. Jonathan Rieder, *Canarsie: The Jews and Italians of Brooklyn against Liberalism* (Cambridge: Harvard University Press, 1985).

84. Charles Murray, *Losing Ground: American Social Policy, 1950–1980* (New York: Basic Books, 1984), 3–9.

85. Kathleen A. Frankovic, "Public Opinion Trends," in Pomper, *Election of 1980*, 97–118.

86. Schell, *History in Sherman Park*, 16–18, 76–77.

87. Robert Kuttner, *Revolt of the Haves: Tax Rebellions and Hard Times* (New York: Simon and Schuster, 1980).

88. Cannon, *Reagan*, 272.

89. Schuman and Scott, "Generations and Collective Memories"; Michael Mandelbaum and William Schneider, "The New Internationalisms: Public Opinion and American Foreign Policy," in *Eagle Entangled: U.S. Foreign Policy in a Complex World*, ed. Kenneth Oye, Donald Rothchild, and Robert J. Lieber (New York: Longman, 1979), 34–88.

90. Harry W. Haines, "'What Kind of War?': An Analysis of the Vietnam Veterans Memorial," *Critical Studies in Mass Communication* 3, no. 1 (March 1986): 1–20; Robin Wagner-Pacifici and Barry Schwartz, "The Vietnam Veterans Memorial: Commemorating a Difficult Past," *American Journal of Sociology* 97, no. 2 (September 1991): 376–420; Kristin Ann Hass, *Carried to the Wall: American Memory and the Vietnam Veterans Memorial* (Berkeley: University of California Press, 1998).

91. Tom Engelhardt, *The End of Victory Culture: Cold War America and the Disillusioning of a Generation* (New York: Basic Books, 1995), 274–280.

92. The POW-MIA myth is dissected in H. Bruce Franklin, *M.I.A., or Mythmaking in America* (Brooklyn: L. Hill Books, 1992).

93. During the later years of the war, many American soldiers were seen as just as much members of the drugs, sex, and rock and roll generation as stateside counterculturists.

NBC News reported that South Vietnamese authorities were complaining to American military officials about the decadent influence American troops were having on South Vietnamese youth, who had begun growing their hair long, taking drugs, and disrespecting their elders. *NBC Nightly News*, 19 November 1973, Dennis Troute, reporter.

94. Erickson, *Reagan Speaks*, 56–59.
95. Ibid., 55.
96. William L. Lunch and Peter W. Sperlich, "American Public Opinion and the War in Vietnam," *Western Political Quarterly* 32, no. 1 (March 1979): 21–44; Ole R. Holsti and James N. Rosenau, "Does Where You Stand Depend on When You Were Born? The Impact of Generation on Post-Vietnam Foreign Policy Beliefs," *Public Opinion Quarterly* 44, no. 1 (Spring 1980): 1–22.
97. Jane Mayer and Doyle McManus, *Landslide: The Unmaking of the President, 1984–1988* (Boston: Houghton Mifflin, 1988), 13.
98. Peggy Noonan, *What I Saw at the Revolution: A Political Life in the Reagan Era* (New York: Random House, 1990), 127.
99. Mark Hertsgaard, *On Bended Knee: The Press and the Reagan Presidency* (New York: Farrar, Straus and Giroux, 1988), 107.
100. Maureen Dowd, "Other Side of 'Gender Gap': Reagan Seen as Man's Man," *New York Times*, 17 September 1984, sec. A.
101. Wattenberg and Ladd, "Moving Right Along?" 10.
102. Susan G. Davis, "'Set Your Mood to Patriotic': History as Televised Special Event," *Radical History Review* 42 (1988): 122–143. For more on the dehistoricizing effects of such spectacles, see Michael Rogin, "'Make My Day!': Spectacle as Amnesia in Imperial Politics," *Representations* 20 (Winter 1990): 99–123.
103. Hertsgaard, *On Bended Knee*, 213.
104. J. Hoberman, "Stars & Hype Forever," *Village Voice*, 29 January 1985, 11–13, 38.
105. "Campaign '84: The Inside Story," *Newsweek*, November–December 1984, 88.
106. Attacking critical revisionists had long been a staple of Reagan rhetoric; see Erickson, *Reagan Speaks*, 64–65.
107. Gerald Pomper, "The Presidential Election," in Pomper, *Election of 1984*, 67.
108. Gergen, "Following the Leaders," 55.
109. Sidney Blumenthal, *Our Long National Daydream: A Political Pageant of the Reagan Era* (New York, Harper & Row, 1988), 118.
110. For more on the imagery of the administration and the campaign, see Blumenthal, *Our Long National Daydream*; Germond and Witcover, *Wake Us When It's Over*; William A. Henry III, *Visions of America: How We Saw the 1984 Election* (Boston: Atlantic Monthly Press, 1985); and, given the importance of visual imagery to Reagan's spectacles, perhaps most illuminatingly, Bill Moyers's *The Public Mind: Image and Reality in America*, Public Broadcasting System, 1989.
111. Blumenthal, *Rise of the Counter-Establishment*, 282; for more on Reagan's attempts to link himself with Kennedy, see Paul R. Henggeler, *The Kennedy Persuasion: The Politics of Style since JFK* (Chicago: Ivan R. Dee, 1995), 210–217. For Reagan's attempts to woo white southern Democrats in the 1960s, in the wake of Kennedy and Johnson desegregation efforts, see Dugger, *On Reagan*, and "The Democratic Party Left Us," in Reagan, *The Creative Society*, 135–138.
112. Frustrated by Reagan's claims to Democratic legacies, the Democratic National Committee and liberal historians joined forces to argue in a paid advertisement that Mondale, not Reagan, was the real Democrat. See the *New York Times*, 31 October 1984, sec. B for "Would FDR, Truman, and JFK Vote for Reagan?"
113. Blumenthal, *Our Long National Daydream*, 119.
114. For Democratic takes on Reagan's popularity, see Michael Schudson, "Ronald Reagan Misremembered," in *Collective Remembering*, ed. David Middleton and

Derek Edwards (London: Sage, 1990), 108–119. For Democratic congressional response to the Reaganomic package, see Greider, "Education of David Stockman."

115. Blumenthal, *Our Long National Daydream*, 36–37.

116. For more on the Hart candidacy, see Germond and Witcover, *Wake Us When It's Over*; Henggeler, *Kennedy Persuasion*, 194–206; and *Newsweek*, "Campaign '84."

117. See, for example, Theodore H. White, "The Shaping of the Presidency 1984," *Time*, 19 November 1984, 72.

118. For more on the Mondale campaign, see Germond and Witcover, *Wake Us When It's Over*, and *Newsweek*, "Campaign '84."

119. Edwards, "Comparing Chief Executives," 50; "Opinion Outlook: Trends Affecting Government Policy," *National Journal*, 28 January 1984, 190.

120. Schudson, "Ronald Reagan Misremembered"; Michael Warner sees Reagan's performance of popularity as making questions of the "reality" of his support irrelevant. Michael Warner, "The Mass Public and the Mass Subject," in *The Phantom Public Sphere*, ed. Bruce Robbins (Minneapolis: University of Minnesota Press, 1993), 234–256. Reagan repeatedly showed a smiling lack of concern about problems in his administration, providing no perceptual cues that might inspire concern or criticism in onlookers. During the early days of the Iran-Contra scandal, however, administration figures appeared in television news reports visibly concerned and agitated, thereby unwittingly alerting viewers that the scandal was serious and worthy of national attention.

121. Edwards, "Comparing Chief Executives," 51; Schudson, "Ronald Reagan Misremembered." The great exception, of course, occurred during Bill Clinton's second term, when administration policies enjoyed high levels of public support even as Clinton's personal approval ratings plunged in the wake of the Monica Lewinsky scandal.

CHAPTER 4 POPULAR CULTURE AND THE RESPONSE
TO CONSERVATIVE NOSTALGIA

1. Charles D. Elder and Roger W. Cobb, *The Political Use of Symbols* (New York: Longman, 1983); Doris Graber, *Processing the News* (New York: Longman, 1984); Norman R. Brown, Steven K. Shevell, and Lance J. Rips, "Public Memories and Their Personal Context," in *Autobiographical Memory*, ed. David C. Rubin (Cambridge: Cambridge University Press, 1986), 137–158; Jerome Bourdon, "Television and Political Memory," *Media, Culture and Society* 14, no. 4 (October 1992): 541–560; Robin Wagner-Pacifici, "Memories in the Making: The Shapes of Things That Went," *Qualitative Sociology* 19, no. 3 (1996): 301–321.

2. Brown, Shevell, and Rips, "Public Memories"; Lynn Spigel and Henry Jenkins, "Same Bat Channel, Different Bat Times: Mass Culture and Popular Memory," in *The Many Lives of Batman: Critical Approaches to a Superhero and His Media*, ed. Roberta Pearson and William Uricchio (New York: Routledge, 1991), 117–148.

3. Graber, *Processing the News*, 151.

4. Marianne Debouzy, "In Search of Working-Class Memory," *History and Anthropology* 2 (September 1985): 261–282; Michael Schudson, *Watergate in American Memory* (New York: Basic Books, 1992).

5. Graber, *Processing the News*, 92.

6. Barbie Zelizer, "Reading the Past against the Grain: The Shape of Memory Studies," *Critical Studies in Mass Communication* 12, no. 2 (June 1995): 214–239.

7. S. Paige Baty, *American Monroe: The Making of a Body Politic* (Berkeley: University of California Press, 1995), 34.

8. Graber, *Processing the News*.

9. Carol Brightman, *Sweet Chaos: The Grateful Dead's American Adventure* (New York: Clarkson Potter, 1998).

10. Fred Davis, *Yearning for Yesterday: A Sociology of Nostalgia* (New York: Free Press, 1979); Jackie Stacey, "Hollywood Memories," *Screen* 35, no. 4 (Winter 1994): 317–335.

11. Gerald Marwell, Michael T. Aiken and N. J. Demerath III, "The Persistence of Political Attitudes among 1960s Civil Rights Activists," *Public Opinion Quarterly* 51 (Fall 1987): 359–375.

12. Howard Schuman and Jacqueline Scott, "Generations and Collective Memories," *American Sociological Review* 54 (June 1989): 359–381; Howard Schuman and Cheryl Rieger, "Historical Analogies, Generational Effects, and Attitudes toward War," *American Sociological Review* 57 (June 1992): 315–326.

13. David James, "Rock and Roll in Representations of the Invasion of Vietnam," *Representations* 20 (Winter 1990): 78–98; Albert Auster and Leonard Quart, *How the War Was Remembered* (New York: Praeger, 1988).

14. *Coming Home*, dir. Hal Ashby, United Artists, 1978; *Who'll Stop the Rain*, dir. Karel Reisz, United Artists, 1978; *Apocalypse Now*, dir. Francis Ford Coppola, United Artists, 1979. United Artists had a reputation at the time for producing films with explicitly political subjects. For press reports of the films' politics, see David Gelman, "Vietnam Marches Home," *Newsweek*, 13 February 1978, 85–86; Lance Morrow, "Viet Nam Comes Home," *Time*, 23 April 1979, 22–28. David James, "Rock and Roll," specifically excludes *The Deer Hunter* from his list of critical films of the period; I think such exclusion misses the polysemic and ambivalent nature of the film's take on the war. Although many on the left criticized the film's depiction of North Vietnamese soldiers, the film's downbeat tone hardly lends itself to the simple jingoism that characterizes the film for James. See Robin Wood, "Two Films by Michael Cimino," in *Hollywood from Vietnam to Reagan* (New York: Columbia University Press, 1986), 270–317. *The Deer Hunter*, dir. Michael Cimino, Universal, 1978. For a comprehensive recounting of Vietnam-themed productions, see Jeremy M. Devine, *Vietnam at 24 Frames a Second* (Austin: University of Texas Press, 1999).

15. Robert Stone, *Dog Soldiers* (Boston: Houghton Mifflin, 1975); Tim O'Brien, *Going after Cacciato* (New York: Delacorte Press/Seymour Lawrence, 1978); Michael Herr, *Dispatches* (New York: Alfred A. Knopf, 1977).

16. *Friendly Fire*, dir. David Greene, ABC, 1979; *A Rumor of War*, dir. Richard T. Heffron, CBS, 1980.

17. *Uncommon Valor*, dir. Ted Kotcheff, Paramount, 1983; *Missing in Action*, dir. Joseph Zito, Cannon, 1984; *Missing in Action 2: The Beginning*, dir. Lance Hool, Cannon, 1985; *Rambo: First Blood Part II*, dir. George P. Cosmatos, Tri-Star, 1985.

18. *First Blood*, dir. Ted Kotcheff, Orion, 1982.

19. For an insightful analysis of styles of masculinity in Eighties heroes, see Susan Jeffords, *Hard Bodies: Hollywood Masculinity in the Reagan Era* (New Brunswick: Rutgers University Press, 1994). For a response that sees more contradictions in the portrayal of masculinity in Vietnam films, see Claudia Springer, "Rebellious Sons in Vietnam Combat Films: A Response," *Genre* 21 (Winter 1988): 517–522.

20. Richard Grenier, "Stallone on Patriotism and 'Rambo,'" *New York Times*, 6 June 1985, sec. C; for typically negative critical response to the film's politics and aesthetics, see Vincent Canby, "'Rambo' Delivers a Revenge Fantasy," *New York Times*, 26 May, 1985, sec. 2; Charles Champlin, "'Rambo's' Right-Wing Revisions," *Los Angeles Times*, 14 July 1985, Calendar (which inspired a spate of letters to the newspaper from *Rambo* defenders).

21. Tom Engelhardt, *The End of Victory Culture: Cold War America and the Disillusioning of a Generation* (New York: Basic Books, 1995), 278.

22. Eric Segal, "It's Called 'Rambomania' but Not Everyone's Cheering," *San Diego Union-Tribune*, 25 July 1985, sec. D (originally published in the *Baltimore Sun*, n.d.).

23. The two *Hot Shots* parodies surfaced within a few years, but public willingness to acknowledge *Rambo's* ridiculousness was occurring even among fans at the time of *Rambo's* release: after a *Tonight Show* crowd had applauded mention of *Rambo*, comedian Blake Clark won over the audience with an unsparing attack on the film's verisimilitude regarding military tactics and weaponry, based on his own experience as a GI in Vietnam.

24. Third-wave films include *Platoon*, dir. Oliver Stone, Orion, 1986; *Full Metal Jacket*, dir. Stanley Kubrick, Warner Bros., 1987; and in 1989, the height of the trend: *Born on the Fourth of July*, dir. Oliver Stone, Universal; *Casualties of War*, dir. Brian DePalma, Columbia; *Jacknife*, dir. David Jones, Cineplex Odeon; and *84 Charlie Mopic*, dir. Patrick S. Duncan, New Century/Vista. For individual analyses of many of these films, see the essays in *Inventing Vietnam: The War in Film and Television*, ed. Michael Anderegg (Philadelphia: Temple University Press, 1991).

25. Patricia Aufderheide, "Vietnam: Good Soldiers," in *Seeing through Movies*, ed. Mark Crispin Miller (New York: Pantheon, 1990), 81–111.

26. Aljean Harmetz, "Unwanted 'Platoon' Finds Success as U.S. Examines the Vietnam War," *New York Times*, 9 February 1987, sec. C. For accounts of veterans' positive but traumatized reactions, see Barry A. Toll, "Platoon: The Vietnam Combat Veterans' Revenge," *St. Petersburg Times*, 22 February 1987, sec. D; Janet Gardner, " 'Platoon' Raising Veterans' Anxieties," *New York Times* (New Jersey edition), 7 June 1987, sec. 11; George Eyre Masters, " 'Platoon' Looses Torrent of Tortured Memories for Vietnam Veteran," *Los Angeles Times*, 21 June 1987, Metro 2.

27. Charles Krauthammer, " 'Platoon' Chic," *Washington Post*, 20 February 1987, sec. A; Douglas A. Jeffrey, " 'Platoon' Is a Sinister, Mindless Abstraction from Reality," *San Diego Union-Tribune*, 24 February 1987, sec. B.

28. Herman Wong, "Viet Refugees Give 'Platoon' Good Reviews," *Los Angeles Times*, 25 January 1987, Calendar.

29. John Del Vecchio, *The 13th Valley* (New York: Bantam Books, 1982); Robert Lee Mason, *Chickenhawk* (New York: Viking, 1983); Stephen Wright, *Meditations in Green* (New York: Charles Scribner's Sons, 1983); Bobbie Ann Mason, *In Country* (New York: Harper & Row, 1985). *In Country* was also filmed, dir. Norman Jewison, Warner Bros., 1989. For a review of fiction on Vietnam, see Philip D. Beidler, *American Literature and the Experience of Vietnam* (Athens: University of Georgia Press, 1982).

30. *Good Morning, Vietnam*, dir. Barry Levinson, Touchstone, 1987.

31. *BAT 21*, dir. Peter Markle, Tri-Star, 1988.

32. "Vietnam Remembered," a series of reports on *CBS Evening News*, March 1985; *Honor, Duty, and the Vietnam War*, CBS, 25 April 1985; *Vietnam: Lessons of a Lost War*, NBC, 27 April 1985; and a *Nightline* return to Vietnam, ABC, 15 March 1989. See also *45/85*, ABC, 18 September 1985 for its section on the war.

33. *Vietnam: A Television History*, PBS, 1987–88.

34. *Tour of Duty*, CBS, 1987–1990. See Daniel Miller, "Primetime Television's Tour of Duty," in Anderegg, *Inventing Vietnam*, 166–189; Albert Auster, " 'Recollections of the Way Life Used to Be': *Tour of Duty, China Beach*, and the Memory of the Sixties," *Television Quarterly* 24 (1990): 61–69.

35. *China Beach*, ABC, 1988–1991. CBS's *60 Minutes* responded with "The Forgotten Veterans," a report on women who had served in the war, 26 February 1989.

36. Sasha Torres, "War and Remembrance: Televisual Narrative, National Memory, and *China Beach*," *Camera Obscura* 33–34 (1995): 147–165. See also Carolyn Reed Vartanian, "Women Next Door to War," in Anderegg, *Inventing Vietnam*, 190–203; Auster, " 'Recollections.' "

37. John Carlos Rowe, "From Documentary to Docudrama: Vietnam on Television in the 1980s," *Genre* 21 (Winter 1988): 451–477.

38. *Magnum, P.I.*, CBS, 1980–1988; *Simon & Simon*, CBS, 1981–1988; *The A-Team*, NBC, 1983–1987.

39. *Eyes on the Prize*, PBS, 1986. *Eyes on the Prize II* aired on PBS in 1990.

40. *Mississippi Burning*, dir. Alan Parker, Orion, 1988. *NBC Nightly News* revisited the site of the murders, 11 December 1988, to coincide with the film's release.

41. Peter S. Smith, "Fuming over 'Mississippi Burning,'" *Louisville Courier-Journal*, 10 February 1989, sec. A; Robert Marquand, "Feelings Smolder over 'Burning' Issue," *Christian Science Monitor*, 24 February 1989; Vincent Canby, "'Mississippi Burning': Generating Heat or Light?" *New York Times*, 8 January 1989, sec. 2. One viewer who vigorously defended the film in print was Willie Brown, the Speaker of the California State Assembly and among the most powerful African Americans in elected office at the time. "Mississippi Memories," *Los Angeles Times*, 19 February 1989, Calendar.

42. Richard Prince, "'Mississippi Burning' and Racism," *Louisville Courier-Journal*, 25 January 1989, sec. A.

43. *The Long Walk Home*, dir. Richard Pearce, New Visions, 1990.

44. *I'll Fly Away*, NBC, 1991–1993; *Any Day Now*, Lifetime, 1998–present.

45. See Thomas Doherty, "Witness to War: Oliver Stone, Ron Kovic, and *Born on the Fourth of July*," in Anderegg, *Inventing Vietnam*, 251–268; Robert Burgoyne, "National Identity, Gender Identity, and the Rescue Fantasy in *Born on the Fourth of July*," and "Modernism and the Narrative of Nation in *JFK*," both in Burgoyne, *Film Nation: Hollywood Looks at U.S. History* (Minneapolis: University of Minnesota Press, 1997), 57–87 and 88–103, respectively; William D. Romanowski, "Oliver Stone's *JFK*: Commercial Filmmaking, Cultural History, and Conflict," and James R. Keller, "Oliver Stone's *JFK* and the 'Circulation of Social Energy' and the 'The Textuality of History,'" both in *Journal of Popular Film and Television* 21, no. 2 (Summer 1993): 63–71 and 72–78, respectively; and the essays in "Oliver Stone as Cinematic Historian," a special section devoted to Stone's work, spread across four issues of *Film and History* 28, nos. 1–4 (1998).

46. *Return of the Secaucus 7*, dir. John Sayles, Cinecom, 1981.

47. *The Big Chill*, dir. Lawrence Kasdan, Columbia, 1983.

48. For positive responses, see Vincent Canby, "'The Big Chill,' Reunion of 60's Activists," *New York Times*, 23 September 1983, sec. C; Rita Kempley, "A Warm and Irresistible 'Big Chill,'" *Washington Post*, 30 September, 1983, Weekend. For a negative take, see Gary Arnold, "'60s Revisited: 'The Big Chill': Slick but Superficial," *Washington Post*, 30 September 1983, sec. E.

49. *thirtysomething*, ABC, 1987–1991. For positive reviews, see Howard Rosenberg, "New TV Generation Gets Older, Better at thirtysomething," *Los Angeles Times*, 29 September 1987, Calendar; Gigi Anders, "'thirtysomething'; Loving It; The Look, The Characters—C'est Moi!" *Washington Post*, 27 May 1990, sec. Y. Typical of negative write-ups was the first line of Ed Siegel's report that a character had contracted cancer on the show: "Well, at least now they have something to whine about." "Cancer Comes to 'thirtysomething,'" *Boston Globe*, 23 January 1990, Living. Jane Feuer looks at the show in "Yuppie Envy and Yuppie Guilt," *Seeing through the Eighties: Television and Reaganism* (Durham, N.C.: Duke University Press, 1995), 60–81.

50. For Ann Beattie, see her novel *Chilly Scenes of Winter* (Garden City, N.J.: Doubleday, 1976), and two short-story collections, *Distortions* (Garden City, N.J.: Doubleday, 1976) and *The Burning House* (New York: Random House, 1982). *Chilly Scenes of Winter* was made into a film that dropped the Sixties theme that pervaded the novel, though director Joan Micklin Silver's previous film *Between the Lines* detailed the

decline of a countercultural weekly as the Sixties receded. For Thomas Pynchon, see *Vineland* (Boston: Little, Brown, 1990).

51. *Family Ties*, NBC, 1982–1989.
52. Sidney Blumenthal, "Reaganism and the Neokitsch Aesthetic," in *The Reagan Legacy*, ed. Sidney Blumenthal and Thomas Byrne Edsall (New York: Pantheon, 1988), 275.
53. *Back to the Future*, dir. Robert Zemeckis, Universal, 1985.
54. *Dirty Dancing*, dir. Emile Ardolino, Vestron, 1987.
55. *The Wonder Years*, ABC, 1988–1993.
56. *Almost Grown*, CBS, 1988–89.
57. For a view at the time of the generational politics of pop nostalgia, see Stephen Holden, "Pop Nostalgia: A Counterrevolution," *Atlantic*, April 1985, 121–122.
58. Jerry Falwell, *Listen, America!* (New York: Doubleday, 1980), 196–199; Allan Bloom, *The Closing of the American Mind* (New York: Simon & Schuster, 1987), 78–79.
59. Brightman, *Sweet Chaos.*
60. For typical press reports, see Charles Leerhsen, "The Many Faces of Cher," *Newsweek*, 30 November 1987, 66; Cathleen McGuigan, "The Second Coming of Tina," *Newsweek*, 10 September 1984, 76; Blaise Simpson, "The Two Sides of Tina," *St. Petersburg Times*, 25 October 1989, sec. D.
61. Dave Marsh, *Glory Days: Bruce Springsteen in the 1980's* (New York: Pantheon, 1987).
62. Ibid.; David James, "The Vietnam War and American Music," *Social Text* 23 (Fall 1989): 123–144.
63. Leslie Savan, *The Sponsored Life: Ads, TV, and American Culture* (Philadelphia: Temple University Press, 1994), 109.
64. Ibid., 143–146.
65. Ibid., 198–200.
66. Ibid., 176–179.
67. Reports on the decline of long hair and rise of shorter styles on men include *NBC Nightly News*, 16 October 1982, David Hizinsky (?), reporter; *ABC World News Tonight*, 3 October 1982, Stephen Geer, reporter. For reports on drugs and the Sixties, see *ABC World News Tonight*, 8 November 1987, Jackie Judd, reporter (on marijuana and politicians); *NBC Nightly News*, 13 August 1986, Robert Elliott, reporter (on David Crosby and drugs). For anniversaries of Woodstock, see *CBS Evening News*, 5 August 1984, Renee Ferguson, reporter; *ABC World News Tonight*, 15 August 1984, Jack Smith, reporter; *Nightline*, ABC, 11 August 1989. For reports on yuppies rebuffing the values of the Sixties and embracing Reaganism, see *CBS Evening News*, 3 February 1985, Barry Peterson, reporter; *ABC World News Tonight*, 3 February 1985, Judd Rose, reporter.
68. *NBC Reports: Second Thoughts on Being Single*, 25 April 1984, Jack Reynolds, reporter.
69. *ABC World News Tonight*, 15 August 1984.
70. Schudson, *Watergate in American Memory.*
71. See Taylor Branch, "Uneasy Holiday," *New Republic*, 3 February 1986, 23–27.
72. Harry W. Haines, "'What Kind of War?' An Analysis of the Vietnam Veterans Memorial," *Critical Studies in Mass Communication* 3, no. 1 (March 1986): 1–20.
73. Derek Kompare, "Rerun Nation: American Television and the Regime of Repetition" (Ph.D. diss., University of Wisconsin–Madison, 1999).
74. Fredric Jameson, *Postmodernism, or, The Cultural Logic of Late Capitalism* (Durham, N.C.: Duke University Press, 1991); David Harvey, *The Condition of Postmodernity* (Cambridge, Mass.: Blackwell, 1990); Jean Baudrillard, *Simulacra and Simulation*, trans. Sheila Faria Glaser (Ann Arbor: University of Michigan Press, 1994).
75. Spigel, "Same Bat Channel."

CHAPTER 5 CONTESTS AND CONTESTATIONS

1. See chapter two for an extended analysis of early-1980s conservatism.
2. For details of Iran-Contra and its effect on the Reagan administration, see Theodore Draper, *A Very Thin Line: The Iran-Contra Affairs* (New York: Hill and Wang, 1991); Jane Mayer and Doyle McManus, *Landslide: The Unmaking of the President, 1984–1988* (Boston: Houghton Mifflin, 1988).
3. Even before the crash, the public was losing confidence in the Republicans' handling of the economy; see "Opinion Roundup," *Public Opinion*, November/December 1987, 24. For Wall Street scandals, see Connie Bruck, *The Predators' Ball: The Inside Story of Drexel Burnham and the Rise of the Junk Bond Raiders* (New York: Penguin Books, 1989); Michael Lewis, *Liar's Poker: Rising through the Wreckage on Wall Street* (New York: W. W. Norton, 1989).
4. For the televangelist scandals, see Arthur Frederick Ide, *Heaven's Hustler: The Rise and Fall of Jimmy Swaggart* (Dallas: Monument Press, 1988); Larry Martz with Ginny Carroll, *Ministry of Greed: The Inside Story of the Televangelists and Their Holy Wars* (New York: Weidenfeld & Nicholson, 1988).
5. For Leona Helmsley, see Richard Hammer, *The Helmsleys: The Rise and Fall of Harry and Leona* (New York: New American Library, 1990); for the Marcoses, see Raymond Bonner, *Waltzing with a Dictator: The Marcoses and the Making of American Policy* (New York: Times Books, 1987).
6. Andrew Kohut and Norman Ornstein, "Constructing a Winning Coalition," *Public Opinion*, November/December 1987, 41–44.
7. "Opinion Roundup: Societal Indicators," *Public Opinion*, November/December 1987, 38.
8. Bill Barol, "The Eighties Are Over," *Newsweek*, 4 January 1988, 40–48.
9. Much of the following discussion of Kennedy has been informed by Thomas Brown, *JFK: History of an Image* (Bloomington: Indiana University Press, 1988). See also Paul Henggeler, *The Kennedy Persuasion: The Politics of Style since JFK* (Chicago: Ivan R. Dee, 1995); Alan Brinkley, "The Posthumous Lives of John F. Kennedy," in Brinkley, *Liberalism and Its Discontents* (Cambridge: Harvard University Press, 1998), 210–221.
10. Brown, *JFK*, 8.
11. Barbie Zelizer, *Covering the Body: The Kennedy Assassination, the Media, and the Shaping of Collective Memory* (Chicago: University of Chicago Press, 1992).
12. Ibid., 105–111.
13. This was a favorite theme of the two most prominent of Kennedy's biographers from within the ranks of the New Frontier, Arthur Schlesinger, Jr., and Theodore Sorensen, each of whom went on to advise Robert Kennedy. See Arthur Schlesinger, Jr., "What the Thousand Days Wrought," *New Republic*, 21 November 1983, 20–30; Theodore Sorensen, "A Legacy of Inspiration," *Newsweek*, 28 November 1983, 72.
14. See David Halberstam, *The Unfinished Odyssey of Robert Kennedy* (New York: Random House, 1968); Jack Newfield, *Robert Kennedy: A Memoir* (New York: E. P. Dutton, 1969); Jules Witcover, *85 Days: The Last Campaign of Robert Kennedy* (New York: G. P. Putnam's Sons, 1969). For a skeptical analysis of RFK nostalgia, see Ronald Steel, *In Love with Night: The American Romance with Robert Kennedy* (New York: Simon & Schuster, 2000).
15. Major revisionist works regarding foreign policy include Noam Chomsky, *American Power and the New Mandarins* (New York: Alfred A. Knopf, 1969); Gabriel Kolko, *The Roots of American Foreign Policy: An Analysis of Power and Purpose* (Boston: Beacon Press, 1969); William Appleman Williams, *The Tragedy of American Diplomacy*, 2d rev. and enl. ed. (New York: Dell, 1972); and Walter LaFeber, *America, Russia, and*

the Cold War, 1945–1975 (New York: John Wiley and Sons, 1976). The Williams and LaFeber editions are updatings of volumes that predated the New Frontier; the original editions are generally credited with launching the Cold War revisionist movement.

16. Brown, *JFK*, 57–60.
17. Ibid., 72–78; for a view at the time, see Tom Wicker, "Kennedy without End, Amen," *Esquire*, June 1977, 65–69. S. Elizabeth Bird explores how JFK's personal life played as prime tabloid fodder, and finds treatment of his peccadilloes to be generally sympathetic; S. Elizabeth Bird, "The Kennedy Story in Folklore and Tabloids: Intertextuality in Political Communication," in *Politics in Familiar Contexts: Projecting Politics through Popular Media*, ed. Robert L. Savage and Dan Nimmo (Norwood, N.J.: Ablex, 1990), 247–268. John Hellman analyzes Kennedy's sexual appeal in "The Erotics of a Presidency," in his *The Kennedy Obsession: The American Myth of JFK* (New York: Columbia University Press, 1997), 113–143.
18. *New York Times* columnist (and former Nixon aide) William Safire was particularly vociferous in this argument. See Michael Schudson, *Watergate in American Memory: How We Remember, Forget, and Reconstruct the Past* (New York: Basic Books, 1992), 71–73.
19. Brown, *JFK*, 106.
20. Slavoj Žižek, "Identity and Its Vicissitudes: Hegel's 'Logic of Essence' as a Theory of Ideology," in *The Making of Political Identities*, ed. Ernesto Laclau (London: Verso, 1994), 77–78.
21. Lance Morrow, "J.F.K.: After Twenty Years, the Question: How Good a President?" *Time*, 14 November 1983, 67.
22. The 20 November 1983 edition of the *Post* featured the following articles on Kennedy in section F: David S. Broder, "What Was Passed On"; David Kaiser, "Did Oswald Act Alone? We Evaded the Truth Then, and Now It Can't Be Found"; Stanley Karnow, "No, He Wouldn't Have Spared Us Vietnam"; Joseph Kraft, "What Was Lost"; Nicholas Lemann, "Growing Up with the Kennedy Myth: Not Quite Camelot"; Mary McGrory, "You Had to Be There to Know the Pain"; George Will, "What His Party Has Come To."
23. The *New Republic*, known for its effort to separate the Democratic Party from leftist politics, devoted twenty-one pages to its cover section entitled "The Real John F. Kennedy: JFK plus 20," 21 November 1983, 10–31. *Newsweek* devoted thirty pages to "What JFK Meant to Us: Kennedy Remembered," 28 November 1983; *JFK* was a prime-time special, ABC, 11 November 1983; *Good Morning America* devoted an entire episode to Kennedy, ABC, 22 November 1983, as did the *Today Show*, NBC, 22 November 1983. See also Robert Scheer, "Ted Kennedy Cites Lasting Legacy of the New Frontier," *Los Angeles Times*, 21 November 1983.
24. ABC, *JFK*, 11 November 1983.
25. Harold Miller, "Why 'They' Killed Him," 66–67; Cissy Gagliano, "'People Just Went Crazy,'" 79; Marian Banks, "Then It Was All Downhill," 80; Margaret Boston, "Trying to Help All the Poor," 84; all in *Newsweek*, 28 November 1983.
26. Gloria Steinem, "The Day the Future Died," 66; Adam Walinsky (an aide to Robert Kennedy), "A Sense of Possibility," 91. Henry Fairlie repeats this refrain in "Citizen Kennedy: 'Let the Word Go Forth,'" *New Republic*, 3 February 1986, 14–17.
27. Michael Mandelbaum and William Schneider, "The New Internationalisms: Public Opinion and American Foreign Policy," in *Eagle Entangled: U. S. Foreign Policy in a Complex World*, ed. Kenneth Oye, Donald Fairchild, and Robert J. Lieber (New York: Longman, 1979), 86.
28. "Kennedy Has Become America's Favorite President," *Newsweek*, 28 November 1983, 64. Compare with a report from 1991: George Skelton, "Americans Rate Reagan as an Average President," *Los Angeles Times*, 4 November 1991, sec. A.

29. *Four Days in November*, CBS, 11 November, 1988; *CBS Evening News*, 14–18, 21–23 November 1988. See also *NBC Nightly News*, 21 November 1988; *JFK— That Day in November*, NBC, 22 November 1988. The A&E cable network re-ran NBC's coverage of the assassination and aftermath in its entirety.
30. *CBS Evening News*, 22 November 1988.
31. Ibid.
32. *CBS Evening News*, 23 November 1988, Bob McNamara, reporter.
33. *CBS Evening News*, 22 November 1988, Bruce Morton, reporter.
34. *NBC Nightly News*, 21 November 1988, Garrick Utley, reporter.
35. *CBS Evening News*, 22 November 1988.
36. *NBC Nightly News*, 21 November 1988.
37. The programs included *The Missiles of October*, ABC, 1974 (the Cuban missile crisis); *Jacqueline Bouvier Kennedy*, ABC, 1981; the truly hagiographic *Kennedy*, NBC, 1983; *Robert F. Kennedy and His Times*, NBC, 1985 (based on the book by family loyalist Arthur Schlesinger, Jr.); and two syndicated dramas more robust in tone than the network fare, *Blood Feud: The Kennedys vs. Hoffa*, Operation Prime Time, 1983, and *Hoover vs. the Kennedys: The Second Civil War*, Operation Prime Time, 1987. See Albert Auster, "All in the Family: The Kennedy Saga and Television," *Journal of Popular Film and Television* 19, no. 3 (Fall 1991): 128–137; Tom Carson, "The Kennedys," *American Film*, November 1988, 40–43. Although many of the programs were popular, Oliver Stone's feature film *JFK* attracted a great deal more public discussion than the television films.
38. See Tom Mathews, "Remembering Bobby," and Arthur J. Schlesinger, Jr., "What If RFK Had Lived?" both in *Newsweek*, 9 May 1988, 34–37 and 49, respectively; Roger Rosenblatt, "Remembering Bobby," *MacNeil/Lehrer NewsHour*, PBS, 3 June 1988; Anthony Lewis, "What Might Have Been," *New York Times*, 5 June 1988, sec. E; William Plummer, "RFKennedy: Bobby, As We Knew Him," *People*, 6 June 1988, 122–129; *Nightline*, ABC, 7 June 1988; Steve Daley, "Myth Still Stands behind the Man," *Chicago Tribune*, 9 June 1988, Tempo.
39. The conservative *National Review* tries to strip Robert Kennedy's image of the veneer of compassion and principle, to reinscribe the "ruthless" image that had plagued Kennedy from his earliest days of political fame. Thus the magazine's report concentrates on Kennedy's career up to the assassination of his brother, and has nothing to say of his later years as liberal tribune. John P. Roche, "The Bobby Kennedy Nobody Knows: Behind the Myth of Liberal Compassion: The Second Coming of R.F.K.," 22 July 1988, 32–35.
40. Lance Morrow, "1968: The Year That Shaped a Generation," *Time*, 11 January 1988, 26.
41. Todd Gitlin, *The Sixties: Years of Hope, Days of Rage* (New York: Bantam, 1987); Tom Hayden, *Reunion: A Memoir* (New York: Random House, 1988); James Miller, *"Democracy Is in the Streets": From Port Huron to the Siege of Chicago* (New York: Simon and Schuster, 1987); David J. Garrow, *Bearing the Cross: Martin Luther King, Jr., and the Southern Christian Leadership Conference* (New York: William Morrow and Company, 1986); Taylor Branch, *Parting the Waters: America in the King Years, 1954–63* (New York: Simon & Schuster, 1988). John Downton Hazlett examines the Sixties memoir as a genre in *My Generation: Collective Autobiography and Identity Politics* (Madison: University of Wisconsin Press, 1998). Branch continued his King project with *Pillar of Fire: America in the King Years, 1963–65* (New York: Simon and Schuster, 1998).
42. C. Wright Mills, *The Power Elite* (New York: Oxford University Press, 1956).
43. Feminist historian Alice Echols faults Gitlin and Hayden for failing to take the feminist argument to heart, by their failure to read back the entire history of the New Left in terms of gendered constructions and considerations. " 'We Gotta Get Out of

This Place': Notes toward a Remapping of the Sixties," *Socialist Review* 22, no. 2 (1992): 9–34. Echols published a history of the early feminist movement, *Daring to Be Bad: Radical Feminism in America, 1967–1975* (Minneapolis: University of Minnesota Press, 1989).

44. For reviews of Miller, see Hendrick Hertzberg, "Part of the Solution, Part of the Problem," *New York Times*, 21 June 1987, Sunday Book Review; Allen Matusow, "Linked Arms, Crossed Purposes," *Washington Post*, 5 July 1987, Book World; and David Lehman, "Radical Cheek," *Newsweek*, 13 July 1987, 64. For reviews of Gitlin, see Miller's own positive review, "Tears and Riots, Love and Regrets," *New York Times*, 8 November 1987, Sunday Book Review; Curtis Gans, "Looking Back at the Sixties," *Washington Post*, 20 December 1987, Book World. For reviews of Hayden, see David J. Garrow, "Tom Hayden, Born-Again Middle American," *Washington Post*, 22 May 1988, Book World; Taylor Branch, "If I Had a Hammer . . . ," *Washington Monthly*, May 1988, 51; Paul Berman, "At the Center of the 60's," *New York Times*, 12 June 1988, Sunday Book Review; and David Brooks, "The '60s, a Radical Remembers," *Wall Street Journal*, 17 June 1988. Of the two King biographers, Garrow praises Hayden's book, while Branch criticizes Hayden and the New Left for lacking the importance and maturity of the southern civil rights movement (Gans also makes this point in his review of Gitlin); the *Wall Street Journal* is unsurprisingly critical as well (Brooks later worked in the George W. Bush administration). For related takes on Hayden, most of them portraying him even-handedly or sympathetically as older, wiser, and moderately left-wing, see Charles Trueheart, "Tom Hayden and the Activist Road," *Washington Post*, 11 July 1988, sec. C; Frank Green, "Tom Hayden: Twenty Years Later," *San Diego Union-Tribune*, 18 July 1988, sec. C; Andrea Chambers, "For Ex-Firebrand Tom Hayden, Days of Rage Are Ones for the Book," *Time*, 8 August 1988, 111; *ABC World News Tonight*, "Tom Hayden—Person of the Week," 15 July 1988, Peter Jennings, reporter.

45. See James H. Jones, "A Man Seized by History," *Washington Post*, 14 November 1946, Book World, on Garrow; for reviews of Branch, see Eleanor Holmes Norton, "How the Dream Was Born," *New York Times*, 27 November 1988, Sunday Book Review; R. Z. Sheppard, "A Time for Heroes, Not Saints," *Time*, 28 November 1988, 95; Alvin P. Sanoff, "The Greening of a Martyr," *U.S. News & World Report*, 23 January 1989, 22; Jack Patterson, "How a Man with a Dream Woke Up America," *Business Week*, 26 December 1988, 22.

46. Garrow, *Bearing the Cross*, 625.

47. Sohnya Sayres et al., eds. *The 60s without Apology* (Minneapolis: University of Minnesota Press, 1984).

48. Barbara Tischler, ed. *Sights on the Sixties* (New Brunswick: Rutgers University Press, 1992). For a similar argument from a member of the SDS "Old Guard" who worked closely with Gitlin and Hayden, see Richard Flacks, "What Happened to the New Left?" *Socialist Review*, 1989, no. 1, 91–110. Flacks wrote his own history of the period, *Making History: The American Left and the American Mind* (New York: Columbia University Press, 1988). See also the generally positive appraisal in Maurice Isserman and Michael Kazin, "The Failure and Success of the New Radicalism," in *The Rise and Fall of the New Deal Order, 1930–1980*, ed. Steve Fraser and Gary Gerstle (Princeton: Princeton University Press, 1989), 212–242.

49. In Sayres, *The 60s without Apology*, see Ellen Willis, "Radical Feminism and Feminist Radicalism," 91–118. In Tischler, *Sights on the Sixties*, see Amy Swerdlow, "'Not My Son, Not Your Son, Not Their Sons': Mothers against the Draft for Vietnam," 163–175; Gerald Gill, "From Maternal Pacifism to Revolutionary Solidarity: African-American Women's Opposition to the Vietnam War," 177–195; and Gerald R. Giglio, "In the Belly of the Beast: Conscientious Objectors in the Military during the Vietnam War," 211–225.

50. For articles on the Right in *Ms.*, see Lisa Cronin Wohl, "Holding Our Own against a Conservative Tide," June 1981, 50–53, 86–89; Gloria Steinem, "How to Make War Not Love: A Right-Wing Lexicon," January 1982, 93–96; and Jane O'Reilly, "Watch on the Right: The Big-Time Players behind the Small-Town Image," January 1983, 37–38, 59–62. For a riposte against the family values campaign, see Steinem, "If Moral Decay Is the Question, Is a Feminist Ethic the Answer?" September 1987, 57–63. For the feminist movement's relation to the New Left, see Naomi Weisstein, "Chicago '60s: Ecstacy as Our Guide," September–October 1990, 65–67; for a history of the modern feminist movement, see "25 Years That Shook the World," December 1988, 50–58.

51. Peter Collier and David Horowitz, eds., *Second Thoughts: Former Radicals Look Back at the Sixties* (Lanham, Md.: Madison Books, 1989). The conference, which took place in 1987, inspired a scathing response by the Jewish left magazine *Tikkun*, many of whose contributors had been active in the New Left. See Michael Lerner, "The Legacy of the 1960s for the Politics of the 1990s," 44–48, 87–91; Todd Gitlin and Michael Kazin, "Two Thoughts Forward, One Thought Back: The Rise and Rapid Decline of the New Ex-Left," 49–52, 91–93; and Robert J. S. Ross, "Lennon and Lenin: The Politics of the New Left," 74–76 (a review of Gitlin's book), all in *Tikkun*, January/February 1988. See also an exchange of responses between Horowitz and Gitlin/Kazin in the Letters section of *Tikkun*, May/June 1988, 2–3.

52. Peter Collier and David Horowitz, *Destructive Generation: Second Thoughts about the Sixties* (New York: Summit Books, 1989); David Horowitz, *Radical Son: A Journey Through Our Times* (New York: Free Press, 1997).

53. See the chapters "Divided Loyalties," "McCarthy's Ghost," and "Radical Innocence, Radical Guilt" in Collier and Horowitz, *Destructive Generation*, for their vituperative criticism of left-wing support for Marxists abroad and their attacks on New Left veterans' attempts to rewrite the Sixties to hide their radicalism at the time.

54. Chambers, a repentant communist, gained fame in the 1940s for his accusation of pro-Soviet espionage against former State Department aide Alger Hiss. The case helped to cement Cold War attitudes among a large segment of the public.

55. Positive reviews for their work were confined largely to conservative publications, although prominent figures on the right were effusive in their praise. See Dinesh D'Souza, "Radical Reconsiderations and Recantations," *Wall Street Journal*, 29 March 1989; George Gilder, "The '60s: Look Back in Anger," *Washington Post*, 19 March 1989, Book World; Bruce Nussbaum, "This Is the Damning of the Age of Aquarius," *Business Week*, 3 April 1989, 16; Joseph Sobran, "Destructive Generation," *National Review*, 24 March 1989, 43; and Richard Gid Powers, "The Left He Left Behind," *New York Times*, 16 February 1997, Sunday Book Review. For critical reviews beyond the left-wing press, see Christopher Lehmann-Haupt, "Looking Back, Disillusioned, at the Radical 60's," *New York Times*, 1 June 1989, sec. C; Coleen M. O'Connor, "Ex-Radicals Haven't Wrapped Up '60s as Neatly as They Thought," *San Diego Union-Tribune*, 11 June 1989, sec. E; Jonathan Yardley, "Strife with Father," *Washington Post*, 9 February 1997, Book World. For Horowitz's later activities on the right, see Michael J. Ybarra, "A Rebel Reborn," *Los Angeles Times*, 28 February 1997, sec. E.

56. Rebecca Klatch, "The Counterculture, the New Left, and the New Right," in *Cultural Politics and Social Movements*, ed. Marcy Darnovsky, Barbara Epstein, and Richard Flacks (Philadelphia: Temple University Press, 1995), 74–89.

57. See chapter six for more on the Republican empowerment agenda.

58. Peter Steinfels, *The Neoconservatives: The Men Who Are Changing America's Politics* (New York: Simon & Schuster, 1979); Barbara Ehrenreich, *Fear of Falling: The Inner*

Life of the Middle Class (New York: HarperCollins, 1990), 144–195. For conservative formulations on the New Class, see Irving Kristol, *Two Cheers for Capitalism* (New York: Basic Books, 1978); Kristol, "The Adversary Culture of Intellectuals," in Kristol, *Reflections of a Neoconservative: Looking Back, Looking Ahead* (New York: Basic Books, 1983), 27–42; Norman Podhoretz, "The Adversary Culture and the New Class," 19–32, Robert Bartley, "Business and the New Class," 57–66, and Seymour Martin Lipset, "The New Class and the Professoriate," 67–87, all in *The New Class?* ed. B. Bruce-Biggs (New Brunswick: Transaction Books, 1979).

59. M. Stanton Evans, *The Liberal Establishment* (New York: Devin-Adair, 1965).
60. Kevin P. Phillips, *The Emerging Republican Majority* (New Rochelle, N.Y.: Arlington House, 1969).
61. Ibid., 83–85.
62. Steinfels, *Neoconservatives*; Sidney Blumenthal, *The Rise of the Counter-Establishment: From Conservative Ideology to Political Power* (New York: Times Books, 1986).
63. Kristol, *Two Cheers for Capitalism*, 177. See also Everett Carll Ladd, Jr., "Pursuing the New Class: Social Theory and Survey Data," in Bruce-Briggs, *The New Class?* 101–122, for comparisons of attitudes between intellectual and business elites.
64. Podhoretz particularly emphasizes the dovishness and anti-Americanism in foreign affairs of the New Class, which he sees as inherited from the New Left by way of the McGovern campaign and other trends in the 1970s. See his "The Culture of Appeasement," *Harper's*, October 1977, 25–32, and *The Present Danger* (New York: Simon and Schuster, 1980). Podhoretz's definition of highly educated, high-income liberals as suspiciously unpatriotic became a favorite theme of the right in the 1980s. According to polls in the 1960s and 1970s, however, the war in Vietnam enjoyed greater support from high-income earners and college-educated voters than from low-income earners and high-school graduates, until 1968; after 1968, high-income learners turned to more dovish positions, whereas middle-income voters lagged in opposing the war. More consistent with Podhoretz's thesis is the finding that voters with graduate educations were the most dovish during all phases of the war. William L. Lunch and Peter W. Sperlich, "American Public Opinion and the War in Vietnam," *Western Political Quarterly* 32, no. 1 (March 1979): 21–44.
65. Podhoretz, "Adversary Culture," 28.
66. Burton Yale Pines, *Back to Basics: The Traditionalist Movement That Is Sweeping Grass-Roots America* (New York: William Morrow and Company, 1982), 27.
67. Charles Murray, *Losing Ground: American Social Policy, 1950–1980* (New York: Basic Books, 1984), 42.
68. George Gilder, *Sexual Suicide* (New York: Quadrangle, 1973), 4.
69. Hilton Kramer, "Professor Howe's Prescriptions," *New Criterion*, April 1984, 1–5; Bartley, "Business and the New Class."
70. Richard Viguerie, *The Establishment vs. the People: Is a New Populist Revolt on the Way?* (Chicago: Regnery Gateway, 1983), 42–43; Samuel T. Francis, "Message from MARs: The Social Politics of the New Right," in *The New Right Papers*, ed. Robert W. Whitaker (New York: St. Martin's Press, 1982), 64–83.
71. Donald Warren, *The Radical Center: Middle Americans and the Politics of Alienation* (Notre Dame: University of Notre Dame Press, 1976), 21.
72. Pines, *Back to Basics*, 22.
73. For a history of populist themes in American politics, see Michael Kazin, *The Populist Persuasion* (New York: Basic Books, 1995).
74. Kevin P. Phillips, *Post-Conservative America: People, Politics, and Ideology in a Time of Crisis* (New York: Random House, 1982), 132.
75. Richard Viguerie, *The New Right: We're Ready to Lead* (Falls Church, Va.: Viguerie Company, 1981), 5; William Rusher, *The Making of the New Majority Party* (New York: Sheed and Ward, 1975), 27.

76. William Simon, *A Time for Truth* (New York: Reader's Digest Press, 1978), 90.

77. Viguerie, *Establishment vs. the People*, 2.

78. David Farber, "The Silent Majority and Talk about Revolution," in *The Sixties: From Memory to History*, ed. David Farber (Chapel Hill: University of North Carolina Press, 1994), 291–316.

79. Jonathan Rieder, "The Rise of the 'Silent Majority,' " in *The Rise and Fall of the New Deal Order, 1930–1980*, ed. Steve Fraser and Gary Gerstle (Princeton: Princeton University Press, 1989), 243–268; see also Rieder's examination of one "Middle American" neighborhood, *Canarsie: The Jews and Italians of Brooklyn against Liberalism* (Cambridge: Harvard University Press, 1985).

80. Farber, "Silent Majority," 299.

81. Jules Witcover, *White Knight: The Rise of Spiro Agnew* (New York: Random House, 1972), 305, 310.

82. Ibid., 310, 309.

83. The class background of the New Left remained a subject of controversy into the late 1980s. The association of New Left protests with pampered college students was established by the highly visible protests at Columbia University, the University of California at Berkeley, and other colleges and universities over the years. At the notorious "Chicago Eight" trial of protest organizers in 1969, the defendants included a college professor and alumni of Oberlin, Brandeis, and the University of Michigan (the last was Tom Hayden, although he was of modest economic background). Hayden, Gitlin, and others of the early SDS argue that the organization became more violent once its recruiting moved beyond the East Coast and elite research universities into more conservative communities in the Midwest and West, where activist students from less elite backgrounds felt more polarized and isolated. The tiny coterie of SDS members who ultimately joined the violence-oriented Weather Underground, however, included many from privileged backgrounds.

84. For extensive stories on the Silent Majority, see "The Troubled American: A Special Report on the White Majority" issue of *Newsweek*, 6 October 1969, 28–73; "Revolt of the Middle Class," *U.S. News & World Report*, 24 November 1969, 52–58; "Man and Woman of the Year: The Middle Americans," *Time*, 5 January 1970, 10–17. See also Robert Coles and Jon Erickson, *The Middle Americans: Proud and Uncertain* (Boston: Atlantic Monthly Press/Little, Brown and Company, 1971).

85. Ehrenreich, *Fear of Falling*, 197–243.

86. Rieder, " 'Silent Majority,' " 263.

87. See, for example, Norman Podhoretz, "The New American Majority," *Commentary*, January 1981, 19–28; Phillips, *Post-Conservative America*. Podhoretz is plainly celebratory in asserting the strength and durability of the Republican realignment; Phillips, who could be said to have prophesied it in 1969, is more circumspect about its long-term prospects.

88. Kazin, *Populist Persuasion*, 264.

89. Margaret Garrard Warner, "Bush Battles the 'Wimp Factor,' " *Newsweek*, 19 October 1987, 28–36.

90. See Peter Goldman and Tom Mathews, *The Quest for the Presidency, 1988* (New York: Simon & Schuster, 1989), 191; Elizabeth Drew, *Election Journal: The Political Events of 1987–1988* (New York: William Morrow and Company, 1989), 203, 263; J. Hoberman, *Vulgar Modernism* (Philadelphia: Temple University Press, 1991), 331–332. Ailes now directs operations for the Fox News Network.

91. Sidney Blumenthal, *Pledging Allegiance: The Last Campaign of the Cold War* (New York: HarperCollins, 1990), 53.

92. Ibid., 266.

93. Jack Germond and Jules Witcover, *Whose Broad Stripes and Bright Stars? The Trivial Pursuit of the Presidency, 1988* (New York: Warner Books, 1989).

94. Blumenthal, *Pledging Allegiance*, 295.

95. Drew, *Election Journal*, 204.

96. Blumenthal, *Pledging Allegiance*, 292.

97. Ibid., 252.

98. Germond and Witcover, *Whose Broad Stripes*, 158–159; *Campaign for President: The Managers Look at '88*, ed. David R. Runkel (Dover, Mass.: Auburn House, 1989), 111–115.

99. Blumenthal, *Pledging Allegiance*.

100. Joanne Morreale, "American Self Images and the Presidential Campaign Film, 1964–1992," in *Presidential Campaigns and American Self Images*, ed. Arthur H. Miller and Bruce E. Gronbeck (Boulder, Colo.: Westview Press, 1994), 29.

101. Allen Hunter, "The Role of Liberal Political Culture in the Construction of Middle America," *University of Miami Law Review* 42, no. 1 (September 1987): 104.

102. Maureen Dowd, "Bush Boasts of Turnaround from 'Easy Rider' Society," *New York Times*, 7 October 1988, sec. B.

103. Germond and Witcover, *Whose Broad Stripes*, 441.

104. Of course, when Quayle made the classic Baby Boomer (and 1980s Republican) move of connecting himself to John Kennedy in his nationally televised debate with Democratic vice-presidential candidate Lloyd Bentsen, the elderly Bentsen slapped him down rhetorically with Bentsen's claim of real-life knowledge of Kennedy in the 1950s and 1960s. Cartoonist Mark Alan Stamaty presciently noted young Republicans' attempts to stylistically evoke JFK, whose pre-Beatles visual image could now become a sign of wholesome charisma. In Stamaty's early-1980s series *Washingtoon*, conservative Republican congressman Bob Forehead is chair of the "JFK Look-Alike Caucus." Mark Alan Stamaty, *Washingtoon* (New York: Congdon and Weed, 1983); *More Washingtoons* (New York: Prentice Hall, 1986).

105. See, for example, Haynes Johnson, "Some Served; Some Resisted; Some . . . ," and Mary McGrory, "Sapping the GOP of Hope and Joy," both in the *Washington Post*, 19 August 1988, sec. A. Bush defended Quayle by asserting that Quayle was blameless because he had not protested the war. Germond and Witcover, *Whose Broad Stripes*, 461. Bush's son, George W. Bush, had also avoided the war by joining the National Guard; the younger Bush defended the actions of Quayle by saying, "The thing that's important is he didn't go to Canada." David Hoffman, "A Day of Damage Control," *Washington Post*, 19 August 1988, sec. A.

106. Bush made it explicit, saying, "I'm running against George McGovern." Blumenthal, *Pledging Allegiance*, 266.

107. 1984 Election Night coverage, CBS News, 6 November 1984, Bill Moyers, reporter.

108. David Kusnet, *Speaking American: How the Democrats Can Win in the Nineties* (New York: Thunder's Mouth Press, 1992). Kusnet went on to become a speechwriter for Bill Clinton in 1992, and was chief White House speechwriter in the early days of the Clinton administration.

109. William Schneider, "Tough Liberals Win, Weak Liberals Lose," *New Republic*, 5 December 1988, 11–15.

110. Paul Quirk, "The Election," in *The Elections of 1988*, ed. Michael Nelson (Washington, D.C.: CQ Press, 1989), 82.

CHAPTER 6 THE REINFLECTION OF THE PAST

1. See his conciliatory inauguration address: "Transcript of Bush's Inaugural Address: 'Nation Stands Ready to Push On,' *New York Times*, 21 January 1989, 10.

2. Evan Thomas, "'No Vietnam,'" *Newsweek*, 10 December 1990, 25.

3. See Douglas Kellner, *The Persian Gulf TV War* (Boulder, Colo.: Westview Press,

1992); Tom Engelhardt, *The End of Victory Culture: Cold War America and the Disillusioning of a Generation* (New York: Basic Books, 1995), 285–299; Marilyn B. Young, "This Is Not Vietnam/This Is Not a Pipe," *Middle East Report*, July–August 1991, 21–24.

4. Maureen Dowd, "War Introduces a Tougher Bush to Nation," *New York Times*, 2 March 1991, sec. 1.

5. Engelhardt, *End of Victory Culture*, 288.

6. Charles Kolb, *White House Daze: The Unmaking of Domestic Policy in the Bush Years* (New York: Free Press, 1994), 185–229; Michael Duffy and Dan Goodgame, *Marching in Place: The Status Quo Presidency of George Bush* (New York: Simon & Schuster, 1992). For a liberal critique of the precepts of conservative empowerment, see Nicholas Lemann, "Fighting the Last War," *Atlantic*, February 1991, 28–33.

7. Kolb, *White House Daze*, 192–193.

8. Kolb, *White House Daze*; Jason DeParle, "How Jack Kemp Lost the War on Poverty," *New York Times*, 28 February 1993, sec. 6; Joe Klein and Ann McDaniel, "What Went Wrong," *Newsweek*, 24 August 1992, 24. Kemp went on to found Empower America, a conservative policy and pressure group, with William Bennett and former congressman Vin Weber, after Bush's defeat. The group strayed from its antipoverty emphasis, however, and achieved renown mainly through Bennett's crusade against gangster rap music and sensationalistic talk shows on television. See Greg Braxton, "Bennett, Allies Open Fire on Daytime TV Talk Shows," *Los Angeles Times*, 27 October 1995, sec. A.

9. Duffy and Goodgame, *Marching in Place*, 100–102; "Bush's 'KKK' Campaign," *Newsweek*, 15 July 1991, 4. In addition, Dan Quayle began a highly publicized round of speeches addressing "family values," feminism, and urban unrest, encapsulating conservative anxieties about the underclass. Quayle used an attack on the white, middle-class television character Murphy Brown to deflect charges of racism in his criticism of single motherhood. See John Fiske, *Media Matters: Everyday Culture and Political Change* (Minneapolis: University of Minnesota Press, 1994), 21–74.

10. Duffy and Goodgame, *Marching in Place*, 101; Roberto Suro, "Duke Softens Past in Louisiana Race," *New York Times*, 24 September 1991, sec. A; Richard Cohen, "David Duke: At Home in the GOP," *Washington Post*, 22 October 1991, sec. A; Robin Toner, "Having Ridden Racial Issues, Parties Trying to Harness Them," *New York Times*, 27 October 1991, sec. 1; Ann Devoy, "Louisiana Runoff Puts Bush, GOP in Quandary," *Washington Post*, 30 October 1991, sec. A.

11. Bush copied this strategy from British prime minister John Major, who had recently won his own election after also following in the footsteps of a charismatic redefiner of his party's conservatism. See Sidney Blumenthal, "Letter from Washington: The Order of the Boot," *New Yorker*, 7 December 1992, 55–63.

12. For a general overview of the events of the 1992 election, see Jack Germond and Jules Witcover, *Mad as Hell: Revolt at the Ballot Box* (New York: Warner Books, 1993).

13. George Stephanopoulos, *All Too Human: A Political Education* (Boston: Little, Brown and Company, 1999), 82–83.

14. See, for example, James Gerstenzang, "Bush Ridicules Clinton over Marijuana Use," *Los Angeles Times*, 4 October 1992, sec. A.

15. Alessandra Stanley, "Marilyn Quayle Says the 1960's Had a Flip Side," *New York Times*, 20 August 1992, sec. A.

16. J. Hoberman, "American Myths: He Should Have Inhaled," *Artforum*, February 1993, 12.

17. David Kusnet, *Speaking American: How the Democrats Can Win in the Nineties* (New York: Thunder's Mouth Press, 1992).

18. My discussion of the meanings of Elvis has been significantly informed by two stud-

ies by Greil Marcus: "Elvis: Presliad," in *Mystery Train: Images of America in Rock 'n' Roll Music,* 3d ed. (New York: Penguin, 1990), 137–205; and *Dead Elvis: A Chronicle of a Cultural Obsession* (New York: Doubleday, 1991). For examinations of Clinton's use of Elvis in the campaign, see Gilbert B. Rodman, *Elvis after Elvis: The Posthumous Career of a Living Legend* (New York: Routledge, 1996), 89–92; George Plasketes, *Images of Elvis Presley in American Culture, 1977–1997: The Mystery Terrain* (New York: Harrington Park Press, 1997), 270–286; and Greil Marcus, *Double Trouble: Bill Clinton and Elvis Presley in a Land of No Alternatives* (New York: Henry Holt and Company, 2000); for an analysis written while the campaign was going on, see Greil Marcus, "The Elvis Strategy," *New York Times,* 27 October 1992, A:23. For a more extensive treatment of Clinton's use of Kennedy in the campaign, see Paul R. Henggeler, *The Kennedy Persuasion: The Politics of Style since JFK* (Chicago: Ivan Dee, 1995), 253–276.

19. *The Arsenio Hall Show,* syndicated (Paramount), 3 June 1992.
20. Marcus, "The Elvis Strategy."
21. Howard Kurtz, "The Woman Who Put Clinton on 'Arsenio,'" *Washington Post,* 10 August 1992, sec. B.
22. "Excerpts from Speech by Gore at Convention," *New York Times,* 17 July 1992, sec. A.
23. Leah Garchik, "What Goes On inside Clinton's 'Air Elvis,'" *San Francisco Chronicle,* 27 September, 1992, sec. E.
24. Kurtz, "Clinton on 'Arsenio.'"
25. Landon Y. Jones, "At Home with the Clinton Family: Road Warriors," *People Weekly,* 20 July 1992, 68–79.
26. Bill Greider et al., "Bill Clinton: The *Rolling Stone* Interview," *Rolling Stone,* 17 September 1992, 41.
27. Marcus, *Mystery Train,* 170.
28. Laura Kalpakian, "Spirit of Elvis," *USA Today,* 14 August 1992, sec. D.
29. Lester Bangs, "Where Were You When Elvis Died?" *Psychotic Reactions and Carburetor Dung,* ed. Greil Marcus (New York: Alfred A. Knopf, 1987), 216.
30. Marcus, "The Elvis Strategy."
31. "Transcript of Speech by Clinton Accepting Democratic Nomination," *New York Times,* 17 July 1992, sec. A.
32. Murray Edelman, "Language, Myths, and Rhetoric," *Society* 12, no. 5 (July/August 1975): 14.
33. Marcus, "The Elvis Strategy."
34. Kathleen Hall Jamieson, *Packaging the Presidency* (New York: Oxford University Press, 1984), 126.
35. Theodore H. White, *The Making of the President 1960* (New York: Atheneum House, 1961), 126.
36. Henggeler, *Kennedy Persuasion,* 261.
37. Robert B. Reich, *Locked in the Cabinet* (New York: Vintage, 1998), 3–4. Reich was one of the architects of the "Putting People First" economic package, and one of its chief proponents in Clinton's administration as secretary of labor. See also Clinton's recitation of the theme in his speech to the Democratic convention, *New York Times,* 17 July 1992, sec. A.
38. Greider, "*Rolling Stone* Interview," 42.
39. Bill Clinton, speech to the national convention of the American Legion, Chicago, Illinois, 25 August 1992.
40. Scott Shepard, "The Coming Battle of the Generations: '92 Race May Turn on Age Gap," *Atlanta Journal-Constitution,* 22 March 1992, sec. D; Michael Kelly, "A Contest of Two Generations, Molded by Two Different Wars," *New York Times,* 30 August 1992, sec. 1.

41. Henggeler, *Kennedy Persuasion*, 263.
42. B. Drummond Ayres, Jr., "The 1992 Campaign: Campaign Trail; Riddles for Bush and Rumors That Elvis Advises Clinton," *New York Times*, 22 October 1992, sec. A.
43. Sean Piccoli, "Elvis in Camelot," *Washington Times*, 21 October 1992, sec. E.
44. Marcus, *Double Trouble*, xx.
45. Hoberman, "He Should Have Inhaled," 12.
46. "Transcript of Bush Speech Accepting the Nomination for Another Four Years," *New York Times*, 21 August 1992, sec. A.
47. Marcus, "The Elvis Strategy."
48. Lloyd Grove, "The Clinton Tour's Rocky Road," *Washington Post*, 31 August 1992, sec. B.
49. Marjorie Pritchard, "On the Bus: Campaign Countdown," *Boston Globe*, 9 October 1992, 23.
50. Peggy Noonan, "The Speech: A Time to Get Serious," *Newsweek*, 24 August 1992, 30–31.
51. Elizabeth Drew, "Letter from Washington: Change," *New Yorker*, 16 November 1992, 67–75.
52. *The War Room*, dir. Chris Hegedus and D.A. Pennebaker, October Films, 1993.
53. Clinton's campaign also trumpeted his support from Silicon Valley magnates and other high-technology business executives, positioning him as the leader of a new digital economy. When the Bush campaign countered by running an ad attempting a multilayered, contemporary style, it featured letters appearing across the screen as if coming from a word processor, to connote Bush's own proximity to technologies of the future. The color of the letters, however, was the infamously garish green of early 1980s computer screens, which had been displaced by more soothing colors several years before the 1992 election. In his own campaign significations, Bush seemed out of date.
54. *New York Times*, 21 August 1992, sec. A.
55. For analysis of polling and election results, see Kathleen A. Frankovic, "Public Opinion in the 1992 Campaign" and Gerald M. Pomper, "The Presidential Election," both in *The Election of 1992*, ed. Gerald M. Pomper (Chatham, N.J.: Chatham House, 1993), 110–131 and 132–156, respectively.
56. Sara Rimer, "Hard Times Change Many Minds," *New York Times*, 2 October 1992, sec. D.

CHAPTER 7 ELVIS HAS LEFT THE BUILDING

1. Hal Hinson, "And the Winner Is . . . Us; The New Cultural Revolution Started Long before the Campaign," *Washington Post*, 1 November 1992, sec. G.
2. Michael R. Beschloss, "Camelot (Not): JFK's Misunderstood Legacy: Kennedy Influenced the Kid from Hope—but Not How You Think," *Washington Post*, 15 November 1992, sec. C.
3. "The Transition," *Gallup Poll Monthly* 328, January 1993, 23.
4. David E. Procter and Kurt Ritter, "Inaugurating the Clinton Presidency: Regenerative Rhetoric and the American Community," in *The Clinton Presidency: Images, Issues, and Communication Strategies*, ed. Robert E. Denton, Jr., and Rachel L. Holloway (Westport, Conn.: Praeger, 1996), 1–16. Clinton's "regenerative" tone, similar to JFK's energizing tones after the end of the Eisenhower administration, also contained parallels to the Republican narrative of greatness, decline, and renewal.
5. Howard Fineman, "The Torch Passes," *Newsweek*, November/December 1992, 4. See also Erik Lacitis, "Clinton Stirs Generations That Still Want to Dream and Feel the Charisma," *Seattle Times*, 4 November 1992, sec. A, for an account of the youngest voters' association of Clinton with Kennedy.

6. *Hillary: America's First Lady*, NBC, 10 June 1993.
7. Patrick Mott, "The Economy Has Spoken: The Newest Design Trend Is Value," *Los Angeles Times*, 2 January 1993, sec. N; Anthony Violanti, "Killer Bluesman: Guitarist Jim Thackery and the Drivers Play in Classic Chicago Style," *Buffalo News*, 22 January 1993, Gusto.
8. Jerry Dean, "Down Home in Clinton's Arkansas," *USA Today*, 24 January 1993.
9. Jack Garner, "Good Golly Miss Molly: Rock Finally Comes of Age," *Gannett News Service*, 20 January 1993, Lexis/Nexis; Peter Eisler, "Roll Over, Rock 'n' Roll," *Gannett News Service*, 22 January 1993, Lexis/Nexis.
10. *Nightline*, ABC, 16 November 1992.
11. *In the Line of Fire*, dir. Wolfgang Petersen, Columbia, 1993.
12. Caryn James, "Clint Eastwood Cozies Up to the 1990's," *New York Times*, 11 July 1993, sec. 2; Martha Sherrill, "Clint Eastwood: The Last Action Hero," *Washington Post*, 11 July 1993, sec. G; Paul Freeman, "'In the Line of Fire' Eastwood Unforgiven as Secret Serviceman," *San Francisco Chronicle*, 4 July, 1993, Datebook. In the *Washington Post* article, Eastwood reveals he has modified his Republicanism enough to have voted for Perot in 1992.
13. See also Susan Jeffords, *Hard Bodies: Hollywood Masculinity in the Reagan Era* (New Brunswick: Rutgers University Press, 1994) for changes in masculine personae after Reagan left office.
14. James P. Pinkerton, "Democrats Can't Go Back; Clinton's No JFK, and This Is No Camelot," *Star Tribune* (Minneapolis), 3 August 1993, sec. A.
15. See Rita K. Whillock, "The Compromising Clinton: Images of Failure, a Record of Success," in Denton and Holloway, *Clinton Presidency*, 123–138, for an account of Clinton's worsening media image in this period. See also J. Hoberman, *The Magic Hour: Film at Fin de Siècle* (Philadelphia: Temple University Press, 2003), 181–216. One indication of the president's failure was the steadfast nostalgia for the Kennedys that continued to be expressed in the media. See Michael Barone, "The Lost World of JFK: The America He Left Behind," *U.S. News and World Report*, 15 November 1993, 38–44 (followed by a story on the Clinton administration entitled "Drifting at Sea"); Tom Mathews, "The Lessons of Bobby," *Newsweek*, 31 May 1993, 26–28; Evan Thomas, "RFK's Last Campaign," *Newsweek*, 8 June 1998, 46–54. The traumas of the past seemed to remain stubbornly unredeemable by Clinton.
16. Samuel Popkin, "Voting and Campaigning in 1992," paper presented at the University of Wisconsin–Madison, 6 May 1994.
17. Bob Woodward, *The Agenda: Inside the Clinton White House* (New York: Pocket Books, 1994); Elizabeth Drew, *On the Edge* (New York: Simon & Schuster, 1994); Robert B. Reich, *Locked in the Cabinet* (New York: Vintage, 1998); George Stephanopolous, *All Too Human: A Political Education* (Boston: Little, Brown, 1999).
18. Woodward, *The Agenda*.
19. Greil Marcus, *Double Trouble: Bill Clinton and Elvis Presley in a Land of No Alternatives* (New York: Henry Holt and Company, 2000), 176.
20. John F. Stacks, "The Election: Stampede," *Time*, 21 November 1994, 48.
21. T. J. Jackson Lears, *No Place of Grace* (Chicago: University of Chicago Press, 1981); T. J. Jackson Lears, "From Salvation to Self-Realization: Advertising and the Therapeutic Roots of the Consumer Culture, 1880–1930," in *The Culture of Consumption*, ed. Richard Wrightman Fox and T. J. Jackson Lears (New York: Pantheon, 1983), 1–38; Warren Susman, "'Personality' and the Making of Twentieth-Century Culture," in Susman, *Culture as History* (New York: Pantheon, 1984), 271–285.
22. Kathleen Hall Jamieson, *Eloquence in an Electronic Age* (New York: Oxford University Press, 1988).

23. Thomas B. Edsall, "The Battle of the Sexes Gets Political," *Washington Post*, 27 August 1995, National Weekly Edition.

24. David Maraniss, *First in His Class: A Biography of Bill Clinton* (New York: Simon and Schuster, 1995); Woodward, *The Agenda*; Reich, *Locked in the Cabinet*.

25. Clinton speech at the Vietnam Veterans Memorial, Washington, D.C., 3 May 1993.

26. See Connie Bruck, "The Politics of Perception," *New Yorker*, 9 October 1995, 50–77, for Gingrich's strategies before becoming Speaker; see Elizabeth Drew, *Showdown: The Struggle between the Gingrich Congress and the Clinton White House* (New York: Simon & Schuster, 1996), for Beltway maneuvering in the wake of the 1994 elections.

27. Rush Limbaugh, *The Way Things Ought to Be* (New York: Pocket Books, 1992) and *See, I Told You So* (New York: Pocket Books, 1993), were both best-sellers.

28. See William Kristol, "A Conservative Looks at Liberalism," in *Backward and Upward: The New Conservative Writing*, ed. David Brooks (New York: Vintage, 1996), 286–294.

29. Kenneth T. Walsh and Jennifer Seter, "Run Silents, Run Hard," *U.S. News and World Report*, 17 April 1995, 25–26.

30. Limbaugh, *See, I Told You So*, 275.

31. Maureen Dowd, "The 1994 Elections: Leaders," *New York Times*, 10 November 1994, sec. A.

32. Mark Hosenball with Vern E. Smith, "How 'Normal' Is Newt?" *Newsweek*, 7 November 1994, 34; Dowd, "The 1994 Elections: Leaders."

33. Tom Morganthau, "Decade Shock," *Newsweek*, 5 September 1988, 14.

34. Gary Bauer, "Letter," *Wall Street Journal*, 27 June 1994, sec. A.

35. Joseph Epstein, "My 1950s: How the Decade Really Was," *Commentary*, September 1993, 37–43.

36. Newt Gingrich, "Daily Press Conference by House Speaker Newt Gingrich (R-GA)," *Federal News Service*, 7 March 1995, Lexis/Nexis.

37. Hendrick Hertzberg, "Stoned Again," *New Yorker*, 8 January 1996, 4.

38. John Podhoretz, "After the Knockout," *Washington Times*, 10 November 1994, sec. A; "George Will Talks about the Future of Politics," *Charlie Rose Show*, PBS, 17 November 1994.

39. Mike Davis, *Prisoners of the American Dream* (New York: Verso, 1986), 170.

40. Richard Bernstein, *Dictatorship of Virtue: Multiculturalism and the Battle for America's Future* (New York: Alfred Knopf, 1994), 230. For the complaint that Sixties-styled leftists had taken over American universities, see Roger Kimball, *Tenured Radicals: How Politics Has Corrupted Our Higher Education* (New York: Harper & Row, 1990); for a leftist complaint that working in academia has prevented the left from more activism, see Russell Jacoby, *The Last Intellectuals: American Culture in the Age of Academe* (New York: Basic Books, 1987), and a response, Paul Berman, "Intellectuals after the Revolution: What's Happened since the Sixties?" *Dissent*, Winter 1989, 86–93.

41. Stacks, "Stampede!" 48.

42. Walsh and Seter, "Run Silents, Run Hard," 32; Nina J. Easton, "Merchants of Virtue," *Los Angeles Times*, 21 August 1994, Magazine.

43. Robert Woodson and William J. Bennett, "The Conservative Virtues of Dr. Martin Luther King," *Heritage Lectures* 481 (1994).

44. Ralph Reed, *Politically Incorrect: The Emerging Faith Factor in American Politics* (Dallas: Word Publishing, 1994).

45. Ibid., vii.

46. Ioannis Mookas, "Faultlines: Homophobic Innovation in *Gay Rights/Special Rights*," in *Media, Culture, and the Religious Right*, ed. Linda Kintz and Julia Lesage (Minneapolis: University of Minnesota Press, 1998), 345–361.

47. Todd Gitlin, "Straight from the Sixties: What Conservatives Owe the Decade They Hate," *American Prospect*, May–June 1996, 54–59.

48. Drew, *Showdown*; Stephanopolous, *All Too Human*.

49. Malcolm Gladwell, "The Vital Center," *New Yorker*, 18 November 1996, 39 (italics in original). *The Vital Center* was Arthur Schlesinger, Jr.'s manifesto of postwar, anticommunist liberalism, published in 1949, that presciently fashioned most of the elements of John Kennedy's appeal in 1960. The book goes unmentioned in this report on conservative Libertarian attitudes.

50. Stephanopolous, *All Too Human*; David T. Ellwood, "When Bad Things Happen to Good Policies," *American Prospect*, May–June, 1996, 22–30; Christopher Jencks, "The Hidden Paradox of Welfare Reform," *American Prospect*, May–June 1997, 33–42.

51. For an analysis of a telecourse on American society that Gingrich continued to teach while in Congress, see David Samuels, "Tinkers, Dreamers, and Madmen: The New History According to Newt," *Lingua Franca*, January/February 1995, 32–39.

52. David Frum, "Righter than Newt," *The Atlantic*, March 1995, 82; for Gramm's history of being on the public payroll, see Stephanie Coontz, *The Way We Never Were* (New York: Basic Books, 1992), 69.

53. Dowd, "The 1994 Elections: Leaders."

54. See, for example, Keith Schneider, "Fearing a Conspiracy, Some Heed a Call to Arms," *New York Times*, 14 November 1994, sec. A; Philip Weiss, "Outcasts Digging In for The Apocalypse," *Time*, 1 May 1995, 48–49; Tom Morganthau, "The 'Patriots': The View from the Far Right," *Newsweek*, 1 May 1995, 36–39; Jill Smolowe, "Enemies of the State," *Time*, 8 May 1995, 58–69.

55. Peter Applebome, "An Unlikely Legacy of the 1960's: The Violent Right," *New York Times*, 7 May 1995, sec. A.

56. David Awbrey, "Radical Gingrich?" *Wichita Eagle*, n.d., reprinted in *Atlanta Journal-Constitution*, 15 December 1994, sec. A.

57. Michael Kelly, "Letter from Washington: Accentuate the Negative," *New Yorker*, 1 April 1996, 46.

58. "Dole's Speech Accepting the G.O.P. Nomination for President," *New York Times*, 16 August 1996, sec. A.

59. "Clinton's Speech Accepting the Democratic Nomination for President," *New York Times*, 30 August 1996, sec. A.

60. Peter Collier, "From the Sixties to the Nineties," *Weekly Standard*, 16 February 1998, 23–26.

61. David Frum, "A Generation on Trial," *Weekly Standard*, 16 February 1998, 19–23. For more on the cultural politics of the scandal, see Eli Zaretsky, "The Culture Wars of the 1960s and the Assault on the Presidency," in *Our Monica, Ourselves: The Clinton Affair and the National Interest*, ed. Lauren Berlant and Lisa Duggan (New York: New York University Press, 2001), 9–33.

62. Scott Walter, "'Live' with TAE: Robert Bork and P. J. O'Rourke," *American Enterprise* 8, no. 3 (May/June 1997): 23–27.

63. Karl Zinsmeister, "Days of Confusion," *American Enterprise* 8, no. 3 (May/June 1997): 7.

64. For accusations against Sixties values, see "Indicators," 18–19; James Webb, "Sleeping with the Enemy," 46–49; Dave Geisler, "A Ruined Life," 50–51; Karl Zinsmeister and Douglas Lasken, "The '60s Rule in Public School"; and Joseph Epstein and John Leo, "Radicals' Refuge," 68–69. For reappreciations of Sixties liberatory impulses, see Dana Rohrabacher, "Us Young Americans for Freedom," 37–38 (Rohrabacher was a Republican congressional representative); Lynn Scarlett, "Power to the Politics," 42–44; Michael Barone, "Stumbling toward a Littler America," 44–45; and Bill

Kauffman, "Barry Goldwater: New Leftist?" 80. For Bennett's piece, see William Bennett, "Did '60s Rock Rot?" 72. All in *American Enterprise* 8, no. 3 (May/June 1997).

65. Adam Gopnick, "American Studies," *New Yorker*, 28 September 1998, 40. See also Jack Hitt, "Isn't It Romantic?" *Harper's*, November 1998, 17–20, for a reading of Clinton's actions as typical for a southern white man of his generation.

66. Ceci Connolly and Thomas B. Edsall, "Puzzling the Political Pros," *Washington Post Weekly Edition*, 16 February 1998.

67. See, in particular, the responses of Jimmy Buffett and Patti Smith, in "The Clinton Conversation," *Rolling Stone*, 12 November 1998, 68–90.

68. Weyrich posted his comments as an open letter to conservatives on his Free Congress Foundation website, *www.freecongress.org*, 16 February 1999.

69. See Myron Magnet, *The Dream and the Nightmare: The Sixties' Legacy to the Underclass* (New York: William Morrow and Company, 1993); and Marvin N. Olasky, *The Tragedy of American Compassion* (Wheaton, Ill.: Crossway Books, 1992).

70. For Bush's experience at Yale and its subsequent impact on his thinking, see Nicholas Lemann, "The Redemption," *New Yorker*, 31 January 2000, 48–63; and Hanna Rosin, "The Seeds of a Life's Philosophy," *Washington Post* Weekly Edition, 28 August 2000.

71. *Boogie Nights*, dir. Paul Thomas Anderson, New Line Cinema, 1997.

72. For post-Boomer influences on retro culture, see Kristi Turnquist, "Boomer Culture Shift Redefines Nostalgia," *Ann Arbor News*, 16 November 2000, sec. D; for explorations of the Seventies, see Tom Long, "The '70s: The Era That Won't Die," *Detroit News*, 26 December 2000, sec. E, and "The Best 1975–85," issue of *Swing Generation* (magazine devoted to the post-Boomer cohort), May 1998.

73. Albert Kim, "Hopelessly Devoted to Grease," *Entertainment Weekly*, 20 December 1996, 38–45.

74. "The Year in Music: Pop," *Billboard*, 28 December 1996, YE-26.

75. "Top 250 of 1997," *Variety*, 24 January 1998, Film 17. The satirical weekly *The Onion* responded to these accelerating trends in music and film with a headline announcing that the "U.S. Dept. of Retro Warns: 'We May Be Running Out of Past,'" 5 November 1997, 1.

76. *Forrest Gump*, dir. Robert Zemeckis, Paramount, 1994.

77. Robert Burgoyne, "Prosthetic Memory/National Memory: *Forrest Gump*," in *Film Nation: Hollywood Looks at U.S. History* (Minneapolis: University of Minnesota Press, 1997), 104–119.

78. See Jennifer Hyland Wang, "'A Struggle of Contending Stories': Race, Gender, and Political Memory in *Forrest Gump*," *Cinema Journal* 39, no. 3 (Spring 2000): 92–115.

79. *Saving Private Ryan*, dir. Steven Spielberg, DreamWorks SKG and Paramount, 1998. For media reaction, see *Newsweek*'s series of articles on the film in the 13 July 1998 issue: Jon Meacham, "Caught in the Line of Fire," 48–55; David Ansen, "Celluloid Soldiers," 52–53; Stephen E. Ambrose, "The Kids Who Changed the World," 59. See also Thomas Doherty, "Saving Private Ryan," *Cineaste* 24, no. 1 (1998): 68–71.

80. Tom Brokaw, *The Greatest Generation* (New York: Random House, 1998). See also its sequel, Tom Brokaw, *The Greatest Generation Speaks: Letters and Reflections* (New York: Random House, 1999). For a British perspective on D-Day nostalgia, see Jean Pickering, "Remembering D-Day: A Case History in Nostalgia," in *Narratives of Nostalgia, Gender, and Nationalism*, ed. Jean Pickering and Suzanne Kehde (New York: New York University Press, 1997), 182–210.

81. *Band of Brothers*, dir. David Frankel et al., HBO, 2001.

82. For *Saving Private Ryan*'s nostalgic power, see Marouf Hasian, Jr., "Nostalgic Longings, Memories of the 'Good War,' and Cinematic Representations in *Saving Private Ryan*," *Critical Studies in Media Communication* 18, no. 3 (September 2001): 338–

358. For a thesis on its relationship to the Holocaust, see Peter Ehrenhaus, "Why We Fought: Holocaust Memory in Spielberg's *Saving Private Ryan*," *Critical Studies in Media Communication* 18, no. 3 (September 2001): 321–337.

83. *Malcolm X*, dir. Spike Lee, Warner Bros., 1992. J. Lynn Fuller, "Reading Television, Watching History: Reception of *Any Day Now* as Historical Text," paper presented at the annual meeting of the Society for Cinema Studies, Chicago, Illinois, 11 March 2000.

84. *Boycott*, dir. Clark Johnson, Home Box Office, 2001.

85. *George Wallace*, dir. John Frankenheimer, TNT, 1997; *Path to War*, dir. John Frankenheimer, HBO, 2002; *RFK*, dir. Robert Dornhelm, fX, 2002.

86. *Thirteen Days*, dir. Roger Donaldson, New Line, 2000.

87. *The Rosa Parks Story*, dir. Julie Dash, CBS, 2002.

88. *The '60s*, dir. Mark Piznarski, NBC, 1999.

89. *American Dreams*, NBC, 2002–present.

90. *The Brady Bunch Movie*, dir. Betty Thomas, Paramount, 1995; *A Very Brady Sequel*, dir. Arlene Sanford, Paramount, 1996. Another film that made explicit use of the comedic contrasts between the Sixties and the present day was *Flashback*, which features Sixties icon Dennis Hopper as a yippie prankster who has been a fugitive for twenty years. He is caught and transported to prison by FBI agent Kiefer Sutherland, a symbol of the Reagan Youth of the 1980s. During the journey, Hopper gets Sutherland (real-life son, of course, of Donald Sutherland, another figure of hip Sixties subversion) to reveal that he was born in a left-wing commune to hippie parents. The two generations' values meet, as Sutherland finally loses his emotional repression and reconnects with his unconventional past, and Hopper turns his newly regained political celebrity into a financial windfall. The film evinces considerable nostalgia for the ideals of the countercultural commune even as it acknowledges the participants' failure to sustain them. Hopper himself had perhaps the biggest comeback of any Sixties figure who had lapsed into near-total obscurity, reforging a commercially and critically successful acting career in the late 1980s—and becoming a Republican in the process. *Flashback*, dir. Franco Amurri, Paramount, 1990.

91. *Pleasantville*, dir. Gary Ross, New Line, 1998.

92. Joshua Klein, "Inside Pleasantville," *The Onion*, 22 October 1998, 22.

INDEX

About the Author

Daniel Marcus teaches media arts and studies in the Department of Communication at Wayne State University in Detroit. As a member of the Paper Tiger Television collective, he edited *ROAR! The Paper Tiger Guide to Media Activism*.

CPSIA information can be obtained
at www.ICGtesting.com
Printed in the USA
LVHW091919081219
639838LV00001B/6/P